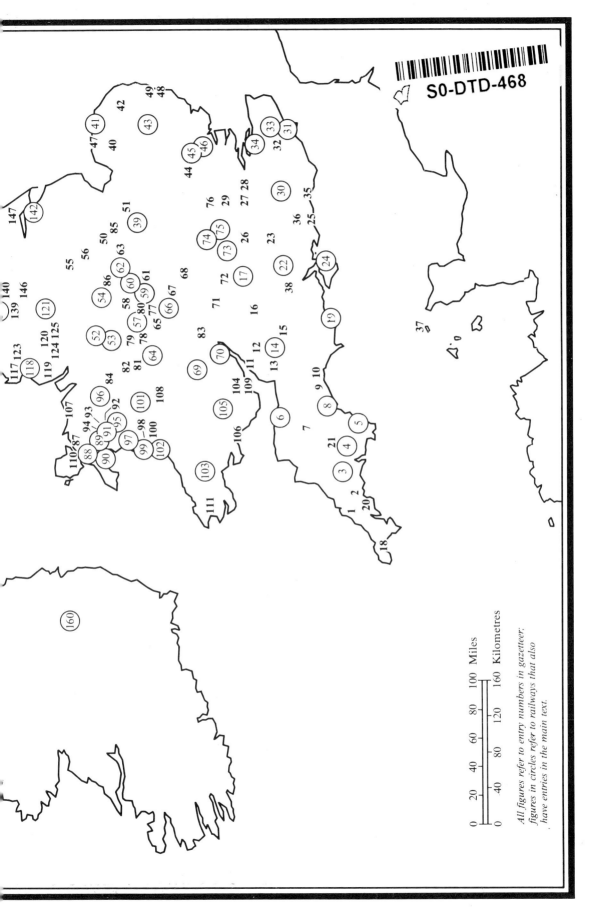

SO-DTD-468

All figures refer to entry numbers in gazetteer;
figures in circles refer to railways that also
have entries in the main text.

| 0 | 20 | 40 | 60 | 80 | 100 Miles |

| 0 | 40 | 80 | 120 | 160 Kilometres |

A GUIDE TO
THE STEAM RAILWAYS
OF GREAT BRITAIN

To Roddy — Happy Birthday
7·6·89

Some further memorabilia
with love
from
Mum & Dad

A GUIDE TO THE
STEAM RAILWAYS
OF GREAT BRITAIN

EDITED BY

The Reverend W. Awdry

AND

Chris Cook

REVISED BY

Roger Crombleholme

PELHAM BOOKS

London

First published in Great Britain by
Pelham Books Ltd
44 Bedford Square
London WC1B 3DU
1979
Second impression 1980
Revised edition 1984

ISBN 0 7207 1417 6

Printed in Great Britain by
Jarrold & Sons Ltd, Norwich

FRONTISPIECE: Class 5MT No. 45212, built in 1935 for the L.M.S.,
leaves Mytholmes Tunnel on the Keighley and Worth Valley Railway

CONTENTS

GUIDE

THE SOUTH-WEST

by Reg Palk

LONDON AND THE HOME COUNTIES

by Bertram Vigor

EAST ANGLIA

by Revd. Eric Buck

THE MIDLANDS

by Edgar Jones

WALES

by John Ransom

LANCASHIRE AND THE NORTH-WEST

by Edgar Jones

YORKSHIRE AND THE NORTH-EAST

SCOTLAND

by John Hume

IRELAND

GAZETTEER

by Roger Crombleholme

INDEX

FOREWORD

BY DAVID WILCOCK
Editor, *Steam World* magazine

Twenty years ago, anyone publishing *A Guide to the Steam Railways of Great Britain* would have produced not a volume such as this but a pamphlet with perhaps less than a dozen railways listed in it. The sheer number of railways covered in this revised edition is itself a commentary on the quite phenomenal acceleration of interest which has taken place in the railway preservation sphere in the past two decades.

It was perhaps only to be expected, though, that the country which gave birth to railways would never take the excesses of Beeching lying down, and there can scarcely be a single closed railway anywhere in the country which has not at least been considered for re-opening by an enthusiast group at some stage.

Already more than 150 miles of main and branch line track have been successfully reopened to steam; perhaps as much again on the narrow and miniature gauges, and still now, in 1983, it goes on. Hardly a month passes without fresh proposals being announced for the re-opening of this or that section of line.

In a *Steam World* survey earlier this year, it was projected that if expansion continues at its present rate, by 1993 there will be 87 principal standard-gauge railway schemes in operation alone. Now, for the first time, the movement (under the aegis of the Association of Railway Preservation Societies) is seriously questioning whether the market can support preserved railways at such an intense level. That problem, of course, is for the movement itself to solve.

For those just discovering the steam railways of Great Britain, there has never been a bigger choice of where to go – or a better time to get involved. Most people (except perhaps those living in the more distant parts of Scotland) are within an hour's journey to a steam line. And that is something we ought not to take for granted: if you lived in, say, Canada, your nearest steam railway could be 2,000 miles away!

PREFACE

The second edition of this book has been considerably enlarged and updated. It had to be – the world of steam railway preservation is moving forward and growing at such a pace that nearly forty new railways have come into being or become worthy of attention since the first edition was printed. Additionally, the chapters concerning the well-established lines needed to be brought up to date to cover the extension of services and the acquisition of new locomotives and rolling stock.

The book retains the same style and approach as its predecessor, dividing the country regionally with chapters covering each of the main steam attractions, whilst the much-expanded gazetteer gives details of many additional sites and explains how to reach them.

Each railway has its own individual character and this has been reflected in the different styles adopted by the descriptive chapters. For herein lies the charm of Britain's steam railways – their individuality, their idiosyncracies, even their waywardness, weave a lasting magic which I hope this book will help you discover for yourself.

ROGER CROMBLEHOLME

EDITORS' NOTE

Some wheel arrangements are named; ones in this book include 4-4-2, Atlantic; 2-6-0, Mogul; 2-6-2, Prairie, and 4-6-2, Pacific. Power classes consist of a digit denoting the power of the engine (the higher, the more powerful) and letters denoting Passenger (P), Freight (F) or Mixed Traffic (MT). T (as in 0-6-0T) means 'tank'; PT, pannier tank; ST, saddle tank; WT, well tank (the tank slung between the sides of the frame); VB, vertical-boilered; TG, tank with geared drive.

KEY TO MAPS

———————— steam railway line

+ + + + + + + steam railway line, narrow gauge

British Rail line

· ▬ ▬ ▬ ▬ · track-bed

built-up area

River Dwyryd
river

Llyn
water feature

road
A4085

PENRHYN
station on steam line, or site

York
other place names

A496
Harlech
destination of route

scale bar, representing one mile

ACKNOWLEDGEMENTS

Editors and publisher would like to thank all those officers of railway preservation societies and other organisations who have helped in providing information and photographs for the first and second editions of this book. The publisher would like to thank R.C. Riley, Roger Crombleholme, Patrick Russell and particularly Andrew Roberts for their suggestions concerning sources for pictures.

Original chapters were contributed by Reg Palk (The South-West), Bertram Vigor (London and the Home Counties), the Rev. Eric Buck (East Anglia), Edgar Jones (The Midlands), John Ransom (Wales), Edgar Jones (Lancashire and the North-West) and John Hume (Scotland).

The maps are by David Charles.

THE SOUTH~WEST

Dart Valley Railway

The line and its history

A railway to Ashburton – then a thriving town – was first proposed in 1845. The junction with the main line was to have been at Newton Abbot. Brunel, engineer for the project, quoted a sum of £103,500 for a single broad-gauge line, and the company backing the project, allowing for Brunel's optimism, aimed at an authorized capital for the project of £130,000. But the scheme came to nothing. A less ambitious proposal was floated in 1864 and an Act authorizing the line from Buckfastleigh to Totnes was passed by Parliament in the same year, and an extension to Ashburton received Parliamentary approval a year later. Financial troubles caused delay, and the line was not opened till the spring of 1872, though possibly part of the line was working before this. By this

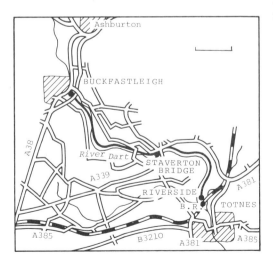

time, however, Ashburton's once thriving woollen industry had dwindled, though wool traffic to and from Buckfastleigh was still considerable.

The line was owned by an independent company (The Buckfastleigh, Totnes and South Devon Railway), but it was worked by the South Devon Railway till it was absorbed by the Great Western Railway. Like other lines west of Exeter, it was converted from broad gauge to standard in the spring of 1892.

The growth of motor transport within the area, between the Wars, gave local people the option of travelling direct to Newton Abbot, instead of taking the circuitous rail route via Totnes. The railway journey was made tedious by long delays at Totnes, where the signalmen had to play a frantic 'game of chess' with the branch train from Ashburton, to ensure that it caused the least possible delay to main-line trains when running over the main line and into Totnes station. Besides being tedious, it often meant that branch passengers missed their main-line connections.

Had the promoters of the original railway been successful, and built the railway from Ashburton to Newton Abbot, the surrender of traffic from the branch railway to the roads would possibly have taken longer, but in the event, it was probably made inevitable because the G.W.R. seemed either unable or unwilling to provide a convenient timetable for the branch trains. The end came slowly; passenger traffic was withdrawn in November 1958; freight traffic lingered on until September 1962.

Preservation

All was not lost however. In September 1962 an item in the *Western Morning News* mentioned that a group of businessmen was planning to

re-open the Dart Valley Railway. Eleven years before this, a small band of pioneer railway enthusiasts, led by the late Tom Rolt, had successfully formed the world's first railway preservation scheme and saved the Talyllyn Narrow-Gauge Railway in mid Wales. It is not surprising that two members of this pioneer group which had saved the Talyllyn (Patrick Whitehouse and Patrick Garland) were also prominent among the group of businessmen involved in the attempt to re-open the Dart Valley line. Being situated in a popular tourist area, and running as it does part way along the banks of the River Dart, the line had great possibilities as a tourist attraction. However, the gremlins which had been active when the railway was first proposed were obviously still in residence along the River Dart when the first attempts were made to preserve the line. Although the possible preservation of the line had been proposed as early as 1962, it was not until spring 1969 that the Light Railway Order was finally granted, and the official opening was performed by Dr Richard Beeching, now Lord Beeching, in May 1969. Dr Beeching had closed it in 1962. In 1969 he said he had great pleasure in declaring it open again!

In 1962, when the Dart Valley Railway preservation project got under way, it was the first preservation scheme to abandon the normal system of appeals to the general public for funds for the line. Instead, as the promoters believed that operation of the line would be a commercially viable proposition, they decided to raise funds from normal commercial sources and formed a Company, The Dart Valley Light Railway Company. Its purpose was both to acquire the line from British Railways, and to purchase locomotives, rolling stock and other equipment needed for operating the line.

By the time the railway was officially opened to the public in spring 1969, the Company board comprised 9 Directors and a Company Secretary, and at that time employed 13 permanent paid staff (11 full-time and 2 part-time). Although the permanent staff formed the back-bone of the

G.W.R. Collett 0-4-2 tank No. 1420 awaits departure from Buckfastleigh. Alongside is Hawksworth 0-6-0 pannier tank No. 1638. (R. Bastin)

working team which had brought steam trains back to the Dart Valley, a working force of volunteers had nevertheless been responsible for, amongst other things, a considerable amount of permanent-way work and undergrowth clearance along the line. In autumn 1966, these volunteer workers formed an official organization known as the Dart Valley Railway Association. In addition to the usual privileges which go with membership of these organizations (free travel on the line and a journal) the Association have their own clubroom, in the shape of ex-Great-Western Super Saloon Coach No. 9111, 'King George', which normally resides at Buckfastleigh. During the decade or so of the Association's existence, it has been responsible for many specialist projects, such as the replacement of signals (all signals had been removed before acquisition of the line from B.R.) and the refurbishing of stations.

The Dart Valley Railway can perhaps be described as the more rural of the two railways operated by Dart Valley Light Railway Ltd. In contrast with its sister railway, the Torbay and Dartmouth Railway, it has never carried express traffic. Since its first opening in 1872 it has been a branch line pure and simple.

Access
Buckfastleigh is the operating centre of the line and visitors are well advised to start their journeys from there. Ample car parking is provided – there are refreshment facilities and a well stocked shop. The present station approach road passes under the new dual carriageway of the A38 trunk road and joins a section of the old A38 road which now connects the town of Buckfastleigh with the roundabout at the junction with the dual carriageway A38 road.

A journey down the line
Our chocolate-and-cream train at the platform will most likely be drawn by one of the small ex-Great-Western pannier or side tank engines, which were a common sight on Great Western branches in former days. There is usually an observation car on the train: it was once used on the Devon Belle. Passengers can travel in it by paying a small supplement to the guard.

The journey to Totnes starts rather unspectacularly, as the first place of note to be seen on the left is the local sewage works! After this, the line traverses a bridge over the river and the full charm of the scenery, with the Dart as its focal point, becomes apparent. From here on river and railway follow nearly the same course down to Totnes. The only intermediate station on the present line is at Staverton Bridge. This is a charming and typical Great Western branch station with a level crossing and ground-level signal box at its platform end. It is interesting to note that before the D.V.R. took over the line, this signal box had been bought by a local rector for use as a garden shed. Thanks to his co-operation, the building was restored to the railway in exchange for a new garden shed; it is now once more in its original position.

A new run-round loop has been installed beyond the platform at the Buckfastleigh end of the station by the Dart Valley company. Places worth investigation here are Staverton Bridge, one of Devon's oldest road bridges, the Staverton Mill building, and the local hostelry dating from the thirteenth century, once used by the monks of Buckfast Abbey as a rest home.

Leaving Staverton Bridge behind, we proceed down the valley towards Totnes. Our train cannot take the former branch-line route into the British Rail station at Totnes as this would involve travelling along the British Rail main line which crosses over the River Dart on a bridge before entering the station. Our train therefore comes to a halt just before the junction with British Rail at Totnes Riverside station. A grant from the Manpower Services Commission has financed the employment of building-trade workers, who have constructed a station platform, fencing, drainage, etc.

The specialist railway work, such as alterations to the track-work, signalling, station lighting, etc. has been carried out by volunteers.

Our engine now runs round the train, and the crew make preparations for the return journey, which involves harder locomotive work because the line climbs steadily up to Buckfastleigh.

Arriving back at Buckfastleigh the visitor will note that the present line now ends in buffer stops just beyond the Buckfastleigh signal cabin; the remainder of the line to

Ashburton was sacrificed to the new dual carriageway of the A38 trunk road which cut the line just beyond this point. In the early years of the preserved railway, the spacious goods shed at Ashburton was turned into the main workshop for the D.V.R., and the D.V.R.'s push-pull trains made periodic visits to this station, with its distinctive Brunel over-roof. Unfortunately the track at this end of the line has now completely disappeared. The handsome Brunel over-roof terminus building still survives however, and has been converted into a garage and service station. Now an assortment of Land Rovers and Range Rovers await their turn for servicing, where for many years past the branch-line train would stand, its diminutive tank locomotive simmering quietly, waiting for the run down to Totnes. Across the road can be seen the former Railway Hotel, now aptly named The Silent Whistle.

Stock

Before we leave the site at Buckfastleigh, it would be well worth while to inspect the locomotives and rolling stock stored here. If we leave the platform through the small booking hall and turn right, following the rough road-way (which leads past the shop, the refreshment room, the maintenance workshop – once the goods shed – and behind the signal cabin), we can bear right again and, without crossing the running tracks, look over the locomotives and other vehicles which are stored either in the open, or under the partial cover of an open-sided shed.

Amongst the usual residents during the working season are the little blue 0-4-0 saddle tank locomotives built by Peckett & Sons Ltd of Bristol, one of which formerly shunted wagons at Exeter gas works. The other Peckett locomotive is the larger of the two, and is a more recent arrival, having come to the D.V.R. from Leicester in the summer of 1976.

Another small locomotive usually to be found here is No. 1369, a 0-6-0 pannier tank. She is an outside-cylinder locomotive, specially designed for work in places where the curves were too sharp for the larger inside-cylinder pannier tank engines. Only six of this type were built, all in 1934 to replace worn-out saddle tank locomotives. One interesting haunt of these loco-motives was the tortuous line from the main-line station at Weymouth, along the public roads, to the harbour. For duty there, the locomotives were fitted with steam train-heating pipes and warning bells, as the working involved the hauling of the Channel Island Boat Express through the crowded streets of the town. Another use was at the wagon works at Swindon where the loco would perform shunt-ing duties and would have one of the one-time familiar shunter's trucks attached for this duty. (One of these trucks, No. 41873, is to be found on the line.)

Five slightly larger Swindon-built tank loco-motives form the backbone of the locomotive fleet on the Dart Valley. It is most likely that you will find one of them at the head of the train if you travel on the line. Perhaps the most interesting of these are the two 0-4-2 side tank locomotives Nos. 1420 and 1450; this type of locomotive was a familiar sight on many of the quiet branch lines in the 30s and 40s and was also useful on local services on main lines.

Although at first appearance these two engines appear to be much older than tiny No. 1369, which was built in 1934, it is interesting to note that No. 1420 was built the year before No. 1369 and No. 1450 the year after! Engines of this class were in fact criticized when they originally appeared for their old-fashioned design; this appearance is however deceptive, as they had many advanced design features built into them when they were constructed. The two engines of the class which survive on the Dart Valley line now carry the names *Bulliver* and *Ashburton* on their tank sides, as well as their former Great Western number-plate.

Three of the once numerous inside-cylinder 0-6-0 pannier tank locomotives complete the group. Two of these, Nos. 6430 and 6435, were built at Swindon in 1937, and were primarily designed for working 'push-pull' trains.

The remaining engine, No. 1638, is the most modern of the five engines; although built to a Great Western design introduced by the late Mr F. W. Hawksworth (the last Chief Mechanical Engineer of the Great Western Railway), not one of these engines saw service with the Great Western. The first engine of the class appeared

over a year after the nationalization of Britain's railways. No. 1638 was built at Swindon in 1951.

Before we leave locomotives, mention should be made of two much larger locomotives in residence at Buckfastleigh, both of which have been rescued from Woodham's scrapyard at Barry in South Wales, and are being gradually renovated by small groups of enthusiasts. The first of these engines arrived early in 1973, and is a British Railways Standard 2-6-4 tank locomotive No. 80064 (built at Brighton Works in 1951). The other came from Barry during the summer of 1976, an ex-Great-Western-Railway 4-6-0 mixed traffic tender locomotive, No. 4920 *Dumbleton Hall*. The engines of the Hall class were well liked by enginemen, and were the maids of all work on the Great Western main lines; whilst they were regularly to be found on vacuum-fitted fast freight trains, and the lighter passenger trains, they were quite capable of standing in for the four-cylinder Castles on much more arduous duties when the need arose, in spite of the fact that they were only two-cylindered engines.

From time to time locomotives, and indeed rolling stock, are exchanged between the Dart Valley and Torbay and Dartmouth lines, so trains from Buckfastleigh may well be hauled by the G.W.R. small Prairie tanks 4555 or 4588. Accordingly it is expected that once *Dumbleton Hall* and No. 80064 are restored to working order, they will be employed between Paignton and Kingswear.

Moving on to coaching stock, we find an interesting selection of historic vehicles. The former G.W.R. Super Saloon takes pride of place – No. 9111, 'King George', is used by the Dart Valley Railway Association as a clubroom. These vehicles are just as luxurious as Pullman cars; although built by the G.W.R., the panel-ling, furnishing and fitting were carried out by a specialist firm. Another of the 'elite' vehicles on the line is the former Pullman Observation Car No. 13, one of two vehicles which were rebuilt just after World War II into observation cars for use on the Southern Railway's Devon Belle Pullman train. This vehicle is now regularly used on Dart Valley trains, and enables passengers to get an excellent view of the Dart Valley during the journey. Other rolling stock in regular use on the line are corridor coaches constructed by British Railways in the 1950s; although painted in 'chocolate-and-cream' livery, they are distinguished from the genuine Great Western coaches by the letters 'D.V.R.' on each side of the coaches instead of 'G.W.R.' insignia.

Also in regular use are the two former G.W.R. excursion coaches, built in 1937 for anticipated traffic which never fully materialized because of World War II. These vehicles can be recognized by the ornate plate-glass panels, bearing the G.W.R. monogram, which sub-divide the interior of each coach.

In early B.R. days, a number of push-pull coaches were constructed to a Hawksworth design, and they follow Great Western practice closely. The vehicles were built to replace a number of similar but aging 'trailers', as the old railwaymen called them. They have a control cab at one end, and when running with a specially adapted engine, the train can work not only the normal way, with the driver and fireman on the engine at the front of the train pulling the coach behind it, but also in the opposite direction, with the coach at the front being pushed by the engine. In this latter situation the driver sits in the control cab at the front of the coach and controls the train from there; the fireman looks after the engine at the rear. For his controls in the control cab of the trailer, the driver has a vacuum-brake control, a steam regulator handle (connected by a linkage under the coach to the regulator in the engine cab), and a large gong fitted on the end of the coach, worked by a foot treadle, which he uses to give warning of the train's approach.

Trains using these trailers were extensively used on branch lines, and for light suburban traffic, as the need to change the engine from one end of the train to the other at each end of the journey was eliminated. A train with two trailer coaches (a coach at each end and the engine in the middle) was not an uncommon sight, and was known as a 'sandwich'. The maximum size of train permitted to use this sytem was four trailer coaches (two coaches at each end and an engine in the middle); this was referred to as a 'double sandwich'.

The Dart Valley Railway originally purchased five trailer coaches, which did sterling service in the early years of the preserved line; the sight of a typical Great Western double sandwich was not uncommon. With the increase in traffic, the provision of loops, and the current thinking on safety regarding trailer-train working, trains are now again worked in the traditional manner with the engine at the front of the train. But one or other of these trailers can be seen running from time to time.

Crossing the River Dart is G.W.R. tank 0-4-2 No. 1420. The Devon Belle observation car is leading the train. (Patrick Russell)

Torbay and Dartmouth Railway

The line and its history

The present railway from Paignton to Kingswear follows an extremely picturesque route, and owes its existence to a compromise solution to the problem of providing rail access to Dartmouth.

The early proposals of the South Devon Railway to serve the area would have linked Exeter to Plymouth by a roundabout route through Dartmouth. Had the scheme been carried through, it is unlikely that the Torbay line would ever have been constructed. However, Isambard Kingdom Brunel, the S.D.R.'s engineer, insisted on taking the shortest practicable route, and left Dartmouth without its promised railway.

Brunel's Exeter–Plymouth main line was built to the broad gauge, and completed in the late 1840s. A branch to Torquay opened in the same period. An extension to Brixham was mooted at this time, but never materialized. Instead, a small independent company was formed, calling itself the Dartmouth and Torbay Railway Company. After much difficulty, they managed to reach Paignton in 1859, and by 1861 had got as far as Churston (then known as Brixham Road). By this time, their finances were precarious, because of the very high cost of the viaducts at Broadsands and Hookhills and the soil stabilization works at Goodrington, where the line crossed boggy land. Dartmouth, only four miles beyond Churston, never got its railway. The Company had planned to bridge the River Dart near Greenway, but local landowners strongly objected; finally, a compromise scheme was adopted which brought the line down to the east bank of the River Dart, to Kingswear, in 1864. A station was built at Dartmouth, permanently separated from the railway by the River Dart, and a ferry service was provided from the railhead at Kingswear. The railway had bypassed Brixham, so in the same year as the Kingswear branch was completed, yet another Railway Company was formed: the Torbay and Brixham. The

Company's line, which was slightly over two miles long, linked Brixham to the Torbay line (joining it at Brixham Road), and was completed late in 1867. With the opening of the line, Brixham Road station was renamed 'Churston' by which name it has been known up to the present day, in spite of the fact that the Brixham branch was closed in 1963. It is interesting to note that the Torbay and Brixham Railway retained its independent status until 1883 (seven years after the South Devon had been absorbed by the Great Western).

Apart from the conversion from the broad gauge to standard gauge in 1892, the line remained virtually unchanged until the 1920s, when considerable improvements were made to enable even the largest of the Great Western locomotives (the King class 4-6-0s) to use it. The improvements were made necessary by a great increase in holiday traffic, which enabled the line to earn good revenue throughout the 1930s. Although the line was capable of accepting King class locomotives, they were rarely seen, for Castles and Halls handled most of the through workings from the main line. The most famous through train was the Torbay Express from

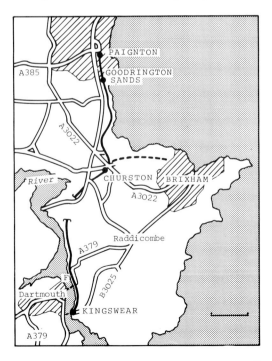

Paddington. Most of the local traffic was the preserve of the small Prairie (2-6-2) tanks of the 41XX and 45XX classes. Two locomotives of this type have been preserved and are regularly used on the line at present. Until the early 1960s, the Brixham branch was worked by the small 0-4-2 tank locomotives like *Bulliver* and *Ashburton*, which now operate on the Dart Valley Railway from Totnes to Buckfastleigh.

Preservation

In common with other lines, the Torbay line never regained its tourist traffic after World War II. Brixham traffic declined, and that branch was closed in 1963. Through services to Kingswear ceased in 1971, and British Rail applied to close the line from Paignton. Consent was given early in 1972, but the Dart Valley Railway Company applied to purchase the line with a view to running it as a tourist railway. Accordingly, Devon County Council agreed to pay a subsidy which enabled British Rail to continue its operating responsibilities whilst the Dart Valley Light Railway Ltd completed their negotiations with British Rail for the purchase. These were successful and the Dart Valley company took over the running of the Torbay line in autumn 1972, after considerable track alterations had been made at Paignton so as to provide an independent line running out of Paignton, alongside the B.R. track, as far as Goodrington; British Rail carriage sidings are there, and B.R. need independent access.

Since 1972 much work had been done on the line, both on a paid and volunteer basis. Churston station is a good example of volunteer work. Fencing repairs, painting and general tidying up has all been done by people willing to give their time free of charge for the sake of seeing the line return to life. By necessity, however, some jobs on the line must be left to professional staff; for instance, since the Torbay Steam Railway's trains are under the control of the B.R. signalman working Paignton South box for a short distance west of Paignton station, it is important that the railway's train crews must be fully qualified to British Rail standards. This naturally bars an amateur, however skilled.

The line can be described as the more spectacular of the two preserved lines operated

by the Dart Valley company.

Access

Paignton is possibly the most convenient point for most visitors to join the train. A multi-storey car park is within easy walking distance of the station. As the Torbay line station is immediately alongside that of British Rail, it is also the convenient starting point for people who arrive by British Rail.

The Torbay Steam Railway station entrance is tucked away on the west side of the British Rail line, and opens on to the Torbay Road.

As part of the re-organization necessary to operate the Torbay line as an independent railway, a new station has been constructed. The new and well-lit building provides booking and catering facilities and a spacious shop where railway and souvenir items are available. This building also houses the Paignton Model Railway, which is well worth a visit. The overall size of the model railway layout is 48 feet by 12 feet, and it is an excellent representation of the Great Western West Country main line during the 1930s, with typical trains in operation. The main station is a very impressive model of that at Westbury.

Returning once again to the full-size railway, a look around the station will reveal that this is the operating centre of the line and that provision is made here not only for servicing locomotives, but for maintenance and repair work as well.

A journey down the line

Our train will be of chocolate-and-cream coaches, hauled by a steam locomotive in full G.W.R. livery. On leaving, we pass Paignton South signal box, over a gated level crossing, and then run alongside the British Rail carriage sidings before halting at Goodrington Sands station. As the train pulls away again, we get, on the left of the line, a sight of the open sands of Tor Bay and the sea beyond; our locomotive will now be working hard as it climbs up to Broadsands Viaduct and inland to the line's highest point at Churston. Passing under a stone railway bridge, our locomotive eases and comes to rest at Churston. Much restoration work has been put in at Churston station to rescue it from

the derelict state in which it was inherited from B.R. and transform it back to its former smart appearance as a quiet country junction and passing-place. The bay platform for the former Brixham branch still remains between the road bridge and the main station building.

After Churston station, the line runs inland, down to Greenway tunnel, beyond which it passes through woodland, and then over Maypool viaduct. The River Dart can now be glimp-

High above the treetops on the lofty Maypool viaduct, 2-6-2T No. 4588 heads for Paignton with a Torbay and Dartmouth line train. (Tim Stephens)

sed through the trees on the right of the line. After passing a small ship-building yard, the river opens out; we can here see the Dart Marina. The next station, Britannia Crossing, is a small halt used by those who wish to use the

9

up-river ferry across the river. The Dartmouth Naval College can be seen on the hill-side on the other side of the river, as the train finally pulls into Kingswear. The locomotive now runs round the train in readiness for the return to Paignton. There is a landing stage just beyond the end of the railway station platform. Here passengers may board the ferry to Dartmouth. This ferry, formerly railway-owned, is now operated by the local authority. It is often severely congested and prospective passengers are warned to allow a spare half-hour or so when travelling across from Dartmouth to make their connection with the Torbay Railway trains at Kingswear.

Stock

The Torbay line is usually worked by the larger steam locomotives belonging to the Dart Valley company; the two former Great Western small Prairie 2-6-2 tank locomotives (Nos. 4555 and 4588) together with the powerful 52XX class mineral tank No. 5239 are the mainstay of the service. No. 4555 was the last locomotive to work the Dart Valley line from Totnes to Ashburton under British Railways, and she returned to the Dart Valley line in autumn 1965. The other Prairie (No. 4588) can be distinguished easily from her counterpart because her water tanks slope down in front. The tank tops on the other locomotive (No. 4555) are straight.

No. 4555 was saved by purchase direct from British Rail, but No. 4588 was sold to Messrs. Woodhams, scrap merchants of Barry; she remained there for some eight years before the Dart Valley Railway rescued her.

No. 5239 also came from Barry scrapyard, having spent ten years there following withdrawal in 1963. The salt-laden air had corroded

OPPOSITE: *No. 7828* Lydham Manor *stirs the echoes from the surrounding countryside as it gets to grips with a heavy train on the Torbay and Dartmouth Railway. (*Patrick Russell*)*
BELOW: *A G.W.R. pannier tank hauls a train into Kingswear at the end of its run from Paignton. The Royal Naval College, Dartmouth, dominates the hill in the background. (*Patrick Russell*)*

A holiday scene reminiscent of the Great Western in the 1930s. A train from Paignton arrives at Kingswear for Dartmouth.

her platework, but these big 2–8–0 tanks are astoundingly robust and, following an intensive five-year restoration programme at Newton Abbot, she entered service on the Torbay line in July 1978.

The only named locomotive used regularly on the Torbay line is the 4-6-0 tender locomotive No. 7828, *Lydham Manor*. After four years in Barry scrapyard, she was rescued, with enthusiastic help from the Dart Valley Association, and can now be seen, fully restored to her former Great Western livery, working the heaviest of the seasonal summer traffic.

When the Dart Valley company took over the Torbay line, more passenger coaches were needed to cope with summer tourist traffic on this line. As a result, the then-small fleet of readily available former British Rail Mark I

coaches was quickly expanded to meet the needs of the Torbay traffic. These vehicles, although painted in chocolate-and-cream livery are distinguished from their Great-Western-built counterparts by the letters 'D.V.R.' on their sides, instead of the usual Great Western insignia. A typical peak-season train on the Torbay line will be made up almost entirely of these vehicles, with the addition of one of the Hawksworth auto-coaches on the Kingswear end of the train. The line also handles through-excursion trains from British Rail. The track was relaid into the bay platform at Kingswear during 1976, to enable B.R. excursion stock to be stabled there whilst regular timetable services carry on unhindered.

The latest addition to the carriage fleet are three non-gangwayed second class coaches which worked until the end of 1977 on King's Cross outer suburban services. They were repainted in D.V.R. chocolate and cream during 1978.

The West Somerset Railway

The line and its history

Brunel's broad-gauge Bristol–Exeter main line reached Taunton in 1842. The next railway proposal for the area was for a small mineral line to link iron workings high in the Brendon Hills with the little sea port of Watchet. This was the West Somerset Mineral Railway, and its last three-quarter-mile run up into the Brendons was laid on a massive 1-in-4 incline. Work started in 1856, and the first section was opened, from Watchet to Roadwater, the follow-ing year. The incline, which was worked by a stationary steam engine hauling wagons up and down by means of a long cable, was first brought into use in 1858. The lengthy extension on the upper section, to Gupworthy, was eventually completed in 1864. The railway, unlike most in the area, was laid to standard 4 ft 8½ in. gauge. The choice of this gauge for this line brought about a minor 'war of the gauges' in the Watchet area, when another company, the West Somerset Railway (with Brunel as en-gineer), constructed a broad-gauge branch which left the main line at Norton Fitzwarren and terminated at Watchet. This broad-gauge line, with an extension to the East Pier at Watchet, was opened in spring 1862. The

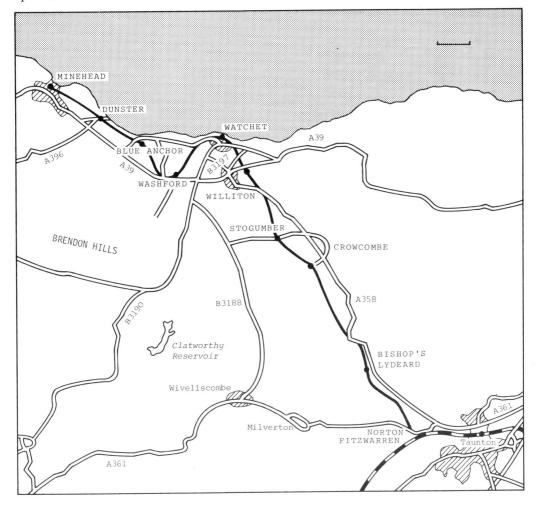

The last Minehead-Williton train of the day turns inland from Watchet on the West Somerset Railway, headed by Bagnall 0–6–0ST Victor, which was built in 1951. (Patrick Russell)

broad-gauge promoters had tried without success to obtain running powers over the narrow-gauge Mineral Railway track-bed by converting the track to mixed gauge. As the two companies would not co-operate, the little port of Watchet had two piers and two completely separate railways, the narrow-gauge line using the West Pier, and the broad-gauge the East Pier. The broad-gauge line was extended from Watchet to Minehead in 1874, under the auspices of the Minehead Railway Company. The broad-gauge West Somerset line and the extension (the Minehead Railway) were both worked by the Bristol and Exeter Railway until all were absorbed by the Great Western.

The narrow-gauge mineral line closed in 1898, but renewed interest in iron ore led to its re-opening in 1907. Its revival proved to be short-lived, however, and the line was again closed in 1910. The track was left, however, and two years later an Australian inventor used a

section to demonstrate his system of automatic train control. During World War I the rails were commandeered for scrap; the operating company was finally wound up in the mid 1920s.

The broad-gauge West Somerset line from Taunton to Minehead was converted to standard gauge in 1882. It was taken over in due course by the Great Western Railway, and apart from the 1930s when some improvements were carried out on the line by the G.W.R. under the auspices of a Government unemployment relief scheme, time passed uneventfully on the line until 1948 when the branch became part of British Railways.

The opening of Butlin's Holiday Camp at Minehead in 1962 brought a welcome injection of traffic, but B.R. issued a closure notice for passenger services to apply from 6 January 1969. Objections and an enquiry delayed the closure until 4 January 1971. The last two trains to run on the line were two Specials organized by the Great Western Society Ltd and Minehead Round Table. These ran on 2 January 1971 (the last actual day of service).

Tank engines have always worked the line. The once-numerous 0-6-0 pannier tanks were well in evidence latterly, together with the small Prairie (2-6-2) side tank locomotives. Large Prairies of the 41XX and 61XX classes were also used. Although introduced by Churchward as early as 1903, these swift and powerful tank locomotives were still being built at Swindon in the 1940s (some, in fact, were built after nationalization). Tender locomotives were used from time to time; double-framed 4-4-0s of the Bulldog class sometimes found their way to Minehead, as well as Collett's 0-6-0s of the 2251 class.

Towards the end of British Rail operation, the line was reduced as an economy measure, to single track throughout, apart from the section between Norton Fitzwarren and Bishops Lydeard, and the short length from Dunster to the Minehead terminus. Another economy was the introduction of conductor-guards in October 1968.

Preservation

Shortly after the closure a new organization was formed, calling itself the West Somerset Railway Company. The object of the new Company was to purchase and re-open the line, and negotiations with B.R. were begun. Two years later, the Somerset County Council became involved, and agreed to buy the line and lease it to the West Somerset Railway Company.

Formal agreement was finally reached between B.R. and the County Council in the summer of 1973, but due to objections the granting of a Light Railway Order to enable the line to be re-opened was delayed. In fact the Order was eventually made, late in 1974, by the Department of the Environment, to British Rail. All that remained to complete the formalities to enable the line to open was the granting of a 'Light Railway Transfer Order' to the Company. By autumn 1975 approval had been given to the granting of the transfer order, and the scene was set for the line to open early in 1976.

The official re-opening of the first stage of the revived railway took place on 28 March 1976, when after a short ceremony on Minehead platform, witnessed by a large crowd of onlookers, Lord Montagu of Beaulieu, resplendent in a top hat, waved the green flag to give the 'right away' to the first of the new Company's

trains to carry fare-paying passengers. The train comprised ex-British-Rail Mark I coaches still in B.R. blue-and-grey livery, drawn by the Bagnall 0-6-0 saddle tank locomotive *Victor*, gaily bedecked in bunting. The train left Minehead station to an accompaniment of music from the Watchet British Legion Band, and a volley of exploding detonators.

The new service, which initially ran from Minehead through Dunster and terminated at Blue Anchor (a journey of just over 3 miles), continued to operate through the summer of 1976. The railway was fortunate in receiving a grant of £49,000 from the Manpower Services Commission which covered the cost of employing 45 men for a period of 6 months. This additional labour made a not inconsiderable contribution to refurbishing along the line, and the Company was able to re-open a further stretch of line, from Blue Anchor to Williton, at the start of the Late Summer Holiday of 1976, on Saturday 28 August. In spite of a rather wild start to the day, with waves breaking over the Minehead promenade within fifty yards or so of the station platforms, the storms held off until well after the 'first train to Williton' had completed its return trip. For the second time that year, the bunting appeared at Minehead station and a further touch of ceremony was added by an elderly town crier, in scarlet uniform and white gaiters and black tricorn hat, ringing his handbell and inviting prospective travellers to: 'Take a trip on the Steam Train of the West Somerset Railway running from Minehead to Blue Anchor, Watchet Harbour and Williton.' *Victor* then drew out of the platform with the train of former B.R. coaches (by now repainted in the company's maroon-and-cream livery).

In successive seasons, services have been extended further and further along the line, until trains now run through to Bishops Lydeard. This makes the West Somerset Railway the longest privately owned passenger railway in the British Isles. Problems still surround the re-entry of West Somerset trains into Taunton B.R. station, but in the meantime the section of line down to the junction at Norton Fitzwarren will be brought up to a standard where it can be used by B.R. through excursion trains.

Access

The most convenient point for the present-day visitor to join the train is Minehead, as the summer steam service operates from this end of the line as far as Williton. Minehead station is conveniently situated next to the promenade, and a small but handy car park is provided in the station forecourt. The stone-built station buildings, although modernized by the G.W.R. in the early 1930s, still retain a strong Victorian appearance. The facilities here include the booking office, a light-refreshments room, and a souvenir shop. For those visitors requiring a cooked meal, a large café is on the sea-front near the station. Between this café and Butlin's Camp is a fascinating model village complete with church, shops, airport and – of course – a working 3½ in. gauge model railway. Also to be found on the same site is a passenger-carrying miniature railway which has an American steam-outline but diesel-powered locomotive as its motive power. At the half-way point of its circuit the miniature railway train passes alongside the West Somerset line. There is also an attractive miniature golf course.

A journey down the line

For the full-size railway, we obtain our tickets from the tiny ticket window in the Victorian booking hall, and pass through on to the station platform. The Victorian era is still with us, in the form of a beautifully preserved drinking fountain of ornate design set in the station wall. Our train will probably consist of ex-British-Rail coaches in the maroon-and-cream livery of the W.S.R.; our locomotive may be an ex-Great-Western tank loco, or perhaps one of the two Bagnall-built 0-6-0 tank locomotives once used at Austin's Longbridge factory.

As the train pulls out of the platform we pass the miniature railway on our left and beyond this again on our left is the massive Butlin's complex which has spread itself along the coastline between the promenade and the railway. Soon we are in open country passing over marshlands on a straight stretch of line laid with double tracks. The first stop on the journey is Dunster; by then the track is reduced to single line. The handsome stone-built goods shed stands marooned, its track removed, but still

sports a loading gauge. Dunster village is about ten minutes' walk from the station. For visitors with a taste for historic buildings, Dunster has much to offer, with its exquisite Yarn Market forming the focal point in a picturesque Somerset street scene. Also worth mention is Dunster Castle, built in 1070 on the site of a Saxon fortress and now the property of the National Trust. The Castle is open to visitors only on certain weekdays; prospective visitors are advised to check before making the journey.

As the train pulls away from Dunster, we pass over Dunster beach crossing (level crossing gates here have been replaced by modern warning bells and flashing lights). The countryside is still very flat: the line sweeps gradually around the back of Blue Anchor Bay, over the old gated level crossing (still controlled from a traditional signal box) and into Blue Anchor station. The station has two platforms and a passing loop, and was of course the temporary terminus during 1976. The holiday caravans and adjacent beach help to give the place a strong seaside atmosphere.

Leaving Blue Anchor, the train enters a shallow cutting; the line curves sharply away from the coast, and enters low farmland, with the Brendon Hills in the background to the right. The line then enters a deep cutting, and beyond this runs alongside the busy A39 road to enter Washford station. The track here is again single-line, with the addition of one short siding. The twelfth-century Cleeve Abbey is within easy reach.

After Washford, the line curves back towards the coast, and we are soon passing the picturesque village of Old Cleeve on the left and the B.B.C. transmitter on the right. After a cutting, the line runs through open country for a short distance. The scene then suddenly changes, and we pass the busy Wansborough Paper Mills, then under a road bridge and into Watchet station. The train pulls out of Watchet past a busy dock area which will be crowded with goods ranging from timber to new tractors. Beyond the docks, the line climbs and curves sharply to the right and passes a beach with an assortment of holiday caravans and a few chalets. From here the line runs inland, to Williton, Stogumber, Crowcombe and Bishops

Lydeard, the terminus of operations. We shall have travelled twenty miles since leaving Minehead – the longest single journey it's possible to book on a British preserved railway.

How the line is run

The organization behind a fully operational private railway is quite complex, and it is worth discussing it in some detail. The new West Somerset Railway Company was incorporated on 5 May 1971. The Board comprises 7 Directors and a Company Secretary. The Company went public in spring 1976; the £65,000 share capital (in 10p shares) was quickly over-subscribed.

In addition to the present West Somerset Railway Company, whose object was the reopening and is the running of the line, two other allied organizations have been created to complement the work of the Company.

The West Somerset Railway Association was formed in 1971 to provide volunteer support, chiefly in the restoration, operating and main-

tenance of stock, permanent way and buildings. The Association has its headquarters at Bishops Lydeard, and when renovated, the station buildings there will become the Association's office and information centre. Engineering and repair facilities will be in the nearby goods shed.

The Stock Fund is an organization closely related to the Association. Its purpose is to act as a holding company, acquiring locomotives and stock with Association funds, and then leasing them to the Railway Company. The most significant item acquired so far is the ex-G.W.R. 0-6-0 pannier tank locomotive No. 6412, which was formerly owned by the Dart Valley Railway.

Stock

Apart from the 0-6-0 pannier tank, Stock Fund acquisitions include some ex-British-Rail Mark I coaches, a steam crane, and two ex-G.W.R. 2-6-2 tank locos known in Great Western Circles as small 'Prairies'. These locomotives (obtained from the Barry scrapyards), Nos. 4561 and 5542, still require a considerable amount of restoration work to bring them into running order. No. 5542 has been completely dismantled at Bishops Lydeard as the first stage in a complete

G.W.R. 0-6-0 pannier tank No. 6412 masquerades as the Flockton Flyer *for the TV series filmed on the West Somerset Railway. (*Paul Barber*)*

*The Diesel and Electric Group's Hymek locomotive No. D7017 is sometimes called upon to haul trains on the West Somerset Railway. (*Stephen Edge*)*

rebuild. A colossal amount of work is needed to make good the ravages of the elements during the fourteen long years the engine lay in the scrapyard at Barry, but the basic condition of the locomotive is sound. In fact it was withdrawn from service on the Western Region in 1961 only twelve months after receiving a major overhaul at Caerphilly works.

Whilst on the subject of locomotives mention should be made that the two Bagnall 0-6-0 saddle tank engines, *Victor* and *Vulcan*, are both on loan from an Association member. *Victor* was in excellent working order at the commencement of steam working in spring 1976 and, as previously mentioned, hauled the two opening trains.

Turning now to diesel power, two twin-car Park Royal diesel multiple unit trains were acquired from British Rail, both sets having been purchased from the Taunton–Minehead commuter service. One set was in service in May 1976 on the Minehead–Blue Anchor run; it was also running on the Minehead–Williton run on

the day of the Williton opening in August 1976.

Other rolling stock includes an assortment of goods vehicles and a six-wheel parcels van. Three ex-Great-Western toplight camping coaches have been saved from the breakers and help contribute to the Great Western atmosphere. The railway also acts as host to the locomotives and rolling stock in the care of the Somerset and Dorset Railway Trust. The Trust has established its headquarters at Washford station where it operates a small museum devoted to the history of the former S. & D.J.R. Pride of its collection of rolling stock is the Somerset and Dorset 2-8-0 heavy freight locomotive No. 88, which is yet another former resident of Barry scrapyard and now undergoing a thorough restoration in Washford goods yard. A major boost to the available diesel power on the railway has been provided by the Diesel and Electric Group. They have been responsible for the preservation of the 'Hymek' main line diesel-hydraulic locomotive No. D7017 and a pair of class 14 0-6-0 diesel-hydraulic freight locomotives obtained from industrial service. The Hymek has been restored to its original two-tone green livery and has put in much reliable service on the line.

The Bicton Woodland Railway

The line and its history

Bicton Gardens and the adjoining Bicton House, (originally referred to as 'The Manor Bukinton') came into existence in early mediaeval times, when King Henry I granted the estate to John Janitor in recognition for his services to the crown in maintaining the Castle Gate and gaol at Exeter Castle.

By distinct contrast, the Bicton Woodland Railway has a very short history, the line being first mooted around 1961. On the death of the then Lord Clinton in 1957, the title passed to his great grandson, the present owner of Bicton Gardens. In 1957 Bicton House (and the Home Farm which adjoins it) were sold to the Devon County Council to be used as an Agricultural Institute, leaving the present gardens and wood still in the estate ownership.

In 1961 the present owner decided to open the gardens to the public, but the Bicton House had been sold four years earlier; it was felt that if the public were to be attracted to the gardens in reasonable numbers, at least one further attraction should be added, to make up for the loss in tourist attraction caused by the non-availability of the House for public viewing.

It was decided in the autumn of 1961 that a miniature passenger-carrying railway (similar to the Romney, Hythe and Dymchurch in Kent) would meet the requirement, and enquiry to a London company who supplied narrow-gauge railway equipment to civil engineering contractors produced results. The firm knew of an 18 in. gauge steam locomotive lying in a Northamptonshire yard, which they thought might suit.

This locomotive had, until shortly before, worked on the Woolwich Arsenal Railway. The locomotive was inspected late in November 1961; it appeared quite suitable, and it was decided to purchase her, subject to her passing

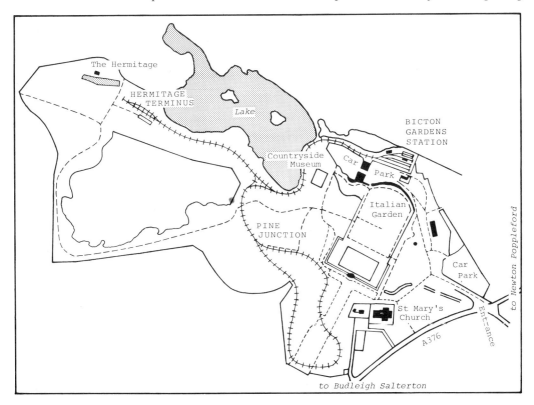

the necessary tests. The boiler was found to be in remarkably good condition, being probably less than five years old. A Bedfordshire firm put the locomotive into working order, and attention was now turned to building the track. After a detailed survey, the track components were purchased – except for the sleepers. These were cut at the estate's own sawmills, from timber grown on the estate. In order to save time and expense in cutting rails, the track joints were staggered.

By early April 1962, the little steam locomotive was ready for acceptance trials. Work done on her included the replacement of the 'spark-arrester' chimney necessary for her former duties at the Royal Arsenal with one of a more conventional pattern. She was tested in steam whilst still in Northamptonshire, and after acceptance was transported to Bicton immediately. She was unloaded onto two lengths of channel iron. Actual track-laying started early in May 1962 in Bicton Gardens station. By the middle of the month enough track was laid to justify placing the steam locomotive on the track. A length of temporary track was laid from the engine to the railhead and, with the aid of a winch-equipped Land Rover, the railing operation was quickly accomplished. A few days later the locomotive was steamed for the first time at Bicton and, after the curing of a few minor problems, she proved an excellent aid to the laying of the permanent way. The one major unsolved problem still outstanding in spring 1962 was that of providing the line with suitable rolling stock. Seven goods vehicles were purchased from the Royal Arsenal in spring 1962; six covered bogie wagons (previously used for transporting explosives), and an open bogie goods truck. But since the trucks had been used for explosives, the Arsenal regulations decreed that the timber bodies of the six covered vehicles must be burned before the vehicles were sold. This meant that six body-less wagon frames and one open wagon arrived at Bicton in June 1962. The open wagon proved valuable for permanent-way construction. It is retained on the line in its original form.

A covered coach from a 24 in. gauge Air Ministry line in Staffordshire was acquired the following month and was re-gauged to 18 in.

Unfortunately, the chassis was unreliable, and so the body was soon transferred to an ex-Arsenal underframe. Further passenger vehicles were built on the ex-Arsenal frames by the estate staff.

Bicton's 'main line' was completed in August 1962 when the ends of the two tracks from Pine Junction were joined on the down line. (The point is almost directly in line with the obelisk when viewed from the centre of the Italian gardens.) A small ceremony was held, Lord Clinton driving in the last spike to close the circuit. Although a 'golden spike' was not available, a small commemorative plate was affixed to the adjoining sleeper to record the event.

A finishing touch was soon added when some ex-London-and-South-Western-Railway lattice-type signal posts were acquired from British Rail. These were shortened to fit into their new setting, but retain the full-size signal arms.

Early the following year, a small siding was constructed at Pine Junction to house a buffet car. The buffet car, in which teas were served during high season, comprised a body built by the estate staff on one of the ex-Woolwich-Arsenal underframes.

1963 also saw the acquisition of the railway's first diesel locomotive. This small engine, weighing a mere 3 tons, had worked in a War Department storage depot in Leicestershire during World War II.

Early in 1966, a further diesel locomotive was acquired. This locomotive is powerful enough to handle the heaviest trains on the line. She is a relatively modern machine and, like Bicton's steam loco, had been retired from service in Woolwich Arsenal.

In order to provide much-needed additional siding accommodation at Bicton Gardens station, it was decided to lift the buffet car siding at Pine Junction and transfer the point and trackwork to the Gardens station. At this time the buffet car was converted into a passenger coach (bringing the total passenger-carrying vehicles to six, three open and three covered coaches), all of which are on ex-Woolwich underframes.

The increase in traffic during the early

summer of 1966 emphasized the need for yet another passenger vehicle, and when the surplus ex-Air-Ministry underframe and bogies had been successfully modified and fitted with an estate-built open body, the new vehicle entered service in July 1966.

At Bicton Gardens station, the original locomotive shed (built for two locomotives in 1962) was extended to accommodate a third in 1966, and an island platform was added at the station in the same year. This was to make working with two trains possible at busy times.

After this chain of developments in 1966, the 'dreaded competition' from alternative transport arrived – in the shape of two small and ancient open-sided buses, which transported their passengers from the main car park, across the railway crossing, and along the roadway around the outskirts of the estate to the delightful little nineteenth-century summer retreat known as the Hermitage. It is pleasing to record however that the iron road fought back, and in spring 1976 Lady Clinton planted a tree to commemorate the opening of the third-of-a-mile extension to the railway, which leaves the main line at a junction between the lake and the roadway crossing, and terminates a short walk away from the Hermitage. With the bringing into use of this short branch line, the vintage bus service has been discontinued.

Access

The visitor can reach Bicton Gardens via the A376 road between Newton Poppleford and Budleigh Salterton. The entrance to the gardens is slightly to the north of St Mary's Church. Ample parking is provided for cars and coaches, and the car park adjoins the railway. For visitors coming by bus, the Devon General operates, during the summer months, a half-hourly service passing the gates.

Entering the Bicton Gardens station area, the character of the line soon becomes apparent. The station area is extremely tidy, and the combination of this and the spotless royal blue locomotives with their bright red underframes tends to remind the more railway-oriented visitor of the standard-gauge Longmoor Military Railway in its later days.

When only one train is operating, it may alternate between trips on the main line and trips on the branch to the Hermitage; it is as well to make sure which route the train is taking before you board.

The main line

Leaving the terminus, our train passes the main car park on the left. Beyond this, the line curves sharply to the left, following the shore of the lake (now on the right). In the distance beyond the lake is Bicton House; on the left down the embankment can be seen the Countryside Museum. Taking the left-hand route at the junction (the original route), we enter woodland, and are soon passing over the level crossing previously used by the vintage bus service to the Hermitage. The line still curves to the left. As we enter Pine Junction, we take the left-hand line, which winds around through woodland until we suddenly enter a clearing and are confronted with the beautiful Italian gardens, the Temple forming a background to the scene. At this point we pass over the sleeper where the last spike was driven in to complete the main line. The line then goes back into woodland, and curves sharply around in a semi-circle, out in the clearing again briefly, and then climbs up to enter Pine Junction again. From there, the return journey is made over the same route, back to Bicton Gardens.

Other attractions

Before we take our second railway trip, on the branch line to the Hermitage, we will take a look around the various non-railway attractions which Bicton has to offer. These include a well-stocked souvenir shop, and a garden shop stocking numerous varieties of plants. The shops adjoin Bicton Gardens station, and from here the Italian and American gardens are within easy reach. Ice cream, cold drinks, etc. are available from a small kiosk adjoining the Palm House, and for those who require a meal, afternoon teas are served in the rather stately atmosphere of the Temple which overlooks the Italian Gardens. For those with an interest in farming, engineering or early transport, a visit to the Countryside Museum near the main car parks is worthwhile. The rather plain appearance of the outside of the building skilfully hides the mass of contrasting colour which

The Bicton Woodland Railway combines all the delights of a steam narrow gauge line with the lush vegetation of Bicton Gardens through which it runs. Avonside 0-4-0 tank Woolwich *usually provides the motive power.*

greets the visitor on entering. The most prominent display in the main hall is a comprehensive collection of farm tractors, stationary engines, and farm machinery; at the back of the hall is a collection of steam-powered items including a large stationary engine, a traction engine, and a 1926 steam roller. In the side hall, there is a display of horse-drawn carts and wagons; the pride of this collection is a massive

miller's wagon of the 1860s. There are many other smaller displays in the Museum.

The Hermitage branch line
The train for the branch line to the Hermitage, as before, leaves the terminus past the car park and travels alongside the lake to the junction. Here, however, the train takes the right-hand route, and still keeping within a short distance of the lakeside, climbs to enter a shallow cutting; after passing through another much deeper cutting the train is some twenty feet or so above the lake. Just beyond the end of the lake, it enters the terminus which is a very simple affair with a run-round loop and a single platform.

The East Somerset Railway

The line and its history

The original East Somerset Railway opened with great celebration on 9 November 1858 when 'a prodigious multitude awaited the arrival of the first train, with a band of music when *Homer* arrived decked with flowers from stem to stern'. *Homer*, a 4-4-0 saddle tank, was driven by R. J. Ward, the company's engineer. The broad gauge single-track line stretched from Witham to Shepton Mallet and had been laid out by Isambard Kingdom Brunel himself. In 1862, an extension of the line was opened from Shepton Mallet to Wells, where connection was subsequently made with the Bristol and Exeter's Cheddar Valley branch. The line was not a flourishing concern and only the preference shareholders ever got a small dividend; the ordinary shareholders got nothing.

By 1872 the East Somerset directors were trying to sell their railway to the mighty Great Western, but Paddington was not impressed with the prospects for this penurious rural line and only offered half the sum the E.S.R. was looking for. Negotiations thus fell through, but two years later the Great Western announced its intention of converting its main line through Witham to Weymouth to standard gauge and invited the East Somerset to find a sum of over £7,000 to convert their line to match. The E.S.R. was, of course, in no position to come up with such a large sum of money and reopened talks with the G.W.R. on selling their line lock, stock and barrel. This time the price agreed was £67,442, a drop of 20 per cent on the previous figure that negotiations had broken down over. It was a buyers' market. The East Somerset directors approved the offer – they had little choice – and the E.S.R. passed to the Great Western in December 1874.

Once its gauge had been converted, the line settled down into a tranquil and largely uneventful existence with four or five trains a day pursuing their unhurried course between Witham and Wells. Inevitably, the end came as a result of the Beeching purges in the 1960s, the passenger service being withdrawn on 9 September 1963. By 1969 the track west of Dulcote siding (Shepton Mallet) had been lifted, but development of the Merehead stone quarry east of Cranmore brought renewed activity to the easternmost portion of the line.

Restoration

It was in August 1971 that David Shepherd discovered Cranmore. He had been searching the South of England for a site to house his two

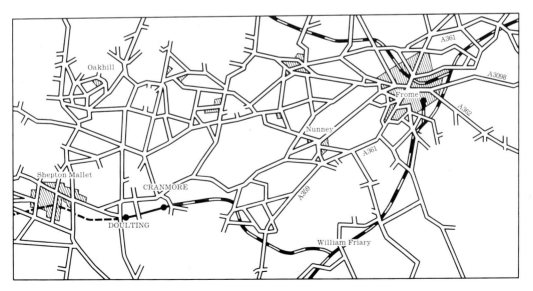

large ex-B.R. steam locomotives, *Black Prince* and *The Green Knight*. After looking at no less than thirty-one sites in eighteen months, the search seemed a hopeless one as, in turn, each decaying country station and disused line festering with old mattresses and rusting cars was discarded, and bureaucracy quietly but firmly was telling him to go away.

Cranmore in 1971 presented a scene of neglect and abandonment. Weeds grew waist-high amid the rusty sidings and the only building on site was an old tin shed which collapsed in a gale the night before the building of David's new locomotive depot was due to start. This, then, was the headquarters of the new East Somerset Railway.

The new shed set the standard of appearance that the new line sought to achieve throughout. The design follows closely the traditions established by the great Victorian railway builders, down to the finest detail. The magnificent brick building, which took nine months to complete and which must be one of the finest of its type in the country, is 130 feet long with two roads and an inspection pit, and a 4000-square-foot, fully equipped workshop adjoining. All but the heaviest locomotive repairs can be made here.

Meanwhile the true character of a country branch line station was restored to Cranmore. A new station house was erected next to the original station building and uniting the two is the traditional platform canopy from Ash Vale station in Surrey. New fencing and station nameboards were put up to complete the scene, together with period lighting, seats and railway posters. The station signal box, once derelict, has now been smartly restored; though until it is once more able to be used to control the points and signals at Cranmore, it has become an art gallery for prints of David Shepherd paintings.

Stock

The majority of the railway's stock made a triumphant arrival at Cranmore on 18 November 1973, marshalled into two trains arriving thirty minutes apart behind David's two locomotives. *Black Prince* is a B.R. class 9F heavy freight locomotive No. 92203, bought for preservation straight out of revenue-earning service at Birkenhead shed. No. 75029, now named

The Green Knight, also was still at work for B.R. when purchased by David in 1967. This is a Riddles Standard class 4MT 4-6-0 and is now painted in lined Brunswick green livery. Most of the work on the East Somerset Railway nowadays is performed by the smaller steam locomotives in the care of the Lord Fisher Locomotive Group. These include L.M.S. 'Jinty' 0-6-0T No. 47493, obtained from Barry scrapyard and painstakingly restored to working order, and 'Austerity' saddle tank No. 68005. Passenger trains are also entrusted to former South Eastern and Chatham Railway P class 0-6-0T No. 323 *Bluebell* which is on loan from the Bluebell Railway in Sussex in exchange for the SR Schools class 4-4-0 express locomotive *Stowe*, a former inmate of Cranmore shed.

More Southern atmosphere is lent by the presence of one of William Stroudley's E1 class tank engines, No. 32110, formerly known as *Burgundy*. This old veteran has a fascinating history, having been sold out of service by the Southern Railway in 1927 to the Cannock and Rugeley Colliery Co. in Staffordshire, where it became No. 9 *Cannock Wood*. It was withdrawn from service in 1963 and preserved on the Chasewater Light Railway, but purely as a static exhibit. A group of E.S.R. members bought the engine in 1978 with the long-term intention of restoring it to steaming condition once more, though this will be a long and expensive process.

There is a number of coaches, all built under British Rail. They include a B.S.O. bogie carriage No. 9241 (1955), an L.N.E.R.-designed second-class sleeper, No. 1767 (1951), and one L.M.S. first-class saloon coach, No. 3322, built in 1929 and now rebuilt as an audio-visual display coach. There is also an experimental all-fibreglass coach No. 1000, the first and last of its kind, as well as a variety of goods rolling stock from different companies.

Services

Passenger trains from Cranmore head westwards as far as Merryfield Lane, Doulting, a distance of $\frac{3}{4}$ mile. Eventually it is hoped to push the railhead forward to Shepton Mallet which will double the length of run available. Services operate every Sunday, Bank Holiday and other advertised days from April to the end of October.

The Great Western Society, Didcot

Although railway enthusiasts tend to think in terms of famous lines, trains or stations, one of the most important centres for the restoration and preservation of steam locomotives has no direct connection with any of these. It is an old maintenance depot at Didcot Junction. Didcot, with its medium-sized station, yards and tri-angular configuration of tracks, has developed under the auspices of the Great Western Society to become one of the most successful steam enterprises in the country. While the Society lacks a long stretch of line to run its trains at speed, they have succeeded in amassing a wide variety of Great Western locomotives, coaches, rolling stock and memorabilia. In addition, they have gathered together a magni-ficent range of repair facilities, including cranes, lifting gear, and machine tools. The depot also features the numerous sheds, a coaling stage, water tower and (more recently) a turntable. The site is easily approached from the British Rail station to which it is linked by an underground passage under the main line running to Bristol and Paddington.

Historically, the junction owes its importance to the desire to link the Welsh Borders with the main line constructed by Brunel between London and the South-West. The important market centres of Worcester and Hereford, and the growing industrial might of Birmingham, called out for a rail link with Paddington. The obvious place from which to make the extension was Didcot. The line was constructed, running north to take in the outskirts of Oxford, and then Banbury, where it split, going to Worces-tershire, and also continuing north into the Black Country. The connection to Oxford proved a particularly popular one. The engine storage and maintenance yard is at the point where this line joined the main line to the West.

The origin of the Great Western Society lies with the 48XX Class Preservation Society founded in 1961. Its aim then, was modest enough: to preserve this engine with its auto-coach (see under Dart Valley Railway

for further details of auto-coach working). With small numbers, the task was a difficult one, and it was not until 1964 that the Society was able to purchase the now well-known tank engine, No. 1466. In the following year the Society, which had meantime changed its name to the present form, set up a fund to preserve a larger locomotive. In 1966, No. 6998, *Burton Agnes Hall*, was acquired. Regional branches were opened in areas once served by the old Great Western, and the scope and scale of the Society's operations was expanded. Shortly afterwards the Bristol Group were responsible for the purchase of *Cookham Manor*, another 4-6-0 loco. In 1967 the Society moved in to Didcot, when British Rail decided that the depot was no longer of value, the transition to diesel being almost complete. Since this important acquisition – until then the Society had con-tented themselves with short runs on the branch line from Cholsey to Wallingford – the pro-gramme of preservation, restoration and main line running has prospered. The depot now features an impressive display of engines and rolling stock.

Among the finely restored engines of distinc-tion at Didcot is No. 5900, *Hinderton Hall*, one of the more recently preserved locomotives. Designed by Collett, the Hall class was a general purpose two-cylinder engine. It was used for mixed passenger and goods trains working over

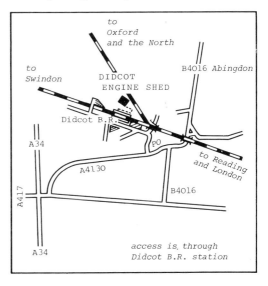

longish distances; Halls were the maids of all work on the Great Western. *Hinderton Hall* was built in 1930, and has now been thoroughly overhauled, turned out in Swindon green livery. The other 4-6-0 engines which have been completed are *Burton Agnes Hall* and *Cookham Manor*. The former is a 'modified Hall'. More recent than 5900, built in 1949, this engine was the product of the revisionary work of Hawksworth, the Chief Mechanical Engineer who had succeeded Collett. *Burton Agnes Hall* (No. 6998) was purchased on the completion of her service with British Rail, and was said to be the last Great Western loco to haul a passenger train on B.R. Fully restored, No. 6998 is now painted in post-war Great Western livery. The engine is easily distinguished from the other 4-6-0s at Didcot by its tender, which has straight sides, as distinct from the more stylish flanged tenders of the pre-war period. *Burton Agnes Hall* has been used for many of the recent steam runs made by the Society on B.R. lines.

No. 7808, *Cookham Manor*, was built in 1938. The Manor class is the smallest of this 4-6-0 class. The small driving wheels were in-

Its exhaust standing out crisply against the winter sky, No. 1363 at Didcot. (Frank Dumbleton)

corporated largely to provide a loco to work on the Cambrian Coast line. They were however, powerful engines, with high pressure boilers.

At Didcot are two of the best-known Collett design, No. 5029, *Nunney Castle*, and No. 5051, *Drysllwyn Castle*. These were two of the famous engines used to haul the major express trains running to the holiday resorts of Devon and Cornwall and to South Wales. The last of these two was renamed *Earl Bathurst* after the Second World War because certain peers had objected to their titles being used on then antiquated locomotives. The names were switched by the G.W.R. in order to keep their custom.

No. 5051 was withdrawn by B.R. in 1963 and sold for scrap to Woodham Brothers of Barry, where it languished until purchased for preservation and moved to Didcot in February 1970. A ten-year restoration programme was completed in time to allow the engine to represent the Great Western Society at the 'Rocket 150' parade at Rainhill in 1980. No. 5029, meanwhile, must wait its turn for a thorough overhaul.

Great Western heavy freight power is well represented by 2-8-0 No. 3822 and 2-8-2T No. 7202, both erstwhile inhabitants of Barry scrapyard, which are long-term restoration projects.

In addition to these bigger locos, the Great Western Society has a number of suburban and goods engines from various periods of the Company's history. Apart from No. 1466, their first acquisition, there is No. 6697, one of the classic 0-6-2 tank engine designs. Produced for work in South Wales, they were ideal for hauling short-distance goods and passenger trains. Larger, but of similar appearance, is No. 6106, a suburban tank designed to work out of Paddington with commuter trains to Reading. This engine, built in 1931, is a 2-6-2, and may be distinguished by the words 'Great Western' painted in yellow and red on the sides of the water tanks, and by the outside cylinders. Also well remembered on the Great Western are the pannier tank engines which were used for shunting duties and light trains. The Society has two of these at present under restoration, Nos. 3650 and 3738. They were part of one of the most numerous classes of engines on the system, numbering some eight hundred.

No. 7808 Cookham Manor *and No. 6998* Burton Agnes Hall *leave Ledbury tunnel. (*Alan Wilkinson*)*

One of the oldest engines preserved at Didcot is the Churchward-designed No. 5322, a 2-6-0 tender engine. This loco, built in 1917, actually saw service in France during World War I and subsequently worked over almost the entire G.W.R. system. It was withdrawn from Pontypool Road in 1964 and rescued from Barry scrapyard five years later. It was the first Society engine from Barry to be steamed.

*0-4-2T No. 1466 runs a demonstration push-pull working with the auto-trailer. (*John Gardner*)*

ABOVE: *B.R.'s last steam locomotive* Evening Star *during a Travelling Post Office demonstration at Didcot. (*Frank Dumbleton*)*

BELOW: *G.W.R. 2-6-0 No. 5322 comes face to face with No. 5051* Drysllwyn Castle *as the latter is displayed on Didcot's turntable. (*Tom Heavyside*)*

Perhaps the most ambitious project yet to be undertaken by the G.W.S. is the planned rebuilding of the 'Hall' class 4-6-0 No. 4942 *Maindy Hall* into a 'Saint' class express locomotive. This will be a reversal of the process carried out in 1925 when C.B. Collett rebuilt No. 2925 *Saint Martin* with six-foot driving wheels to form the prototype of his 259-strong 'Hall' class. Needless to say, this will be a very expensive and time-consuming project as new driving wheels will have to be cast and many detail alterations made to the locomotive's frames and boiler mountings.

Didcot is also the home of a fascinating collection of smaller locomotives. Of course, by far the most interesting is *Shannon*, the sole surviving engine from the Wantage Tramway in Berkshire. She was built in 1858 for Captain Peel, son of the prime minister, who had his own private railway and who named her after a ship he had commanded in the Royal Navy.

Shannon worked originally on the Sandy and Potton Railway in Bedfordshire before becoming absorbed into L. & N.W.R. stock. After many years of faithful service at Wantage, the Great Western bought her for £100 in 1946 and, after an overhaul and repaint at Swindon, set her up on a plinth at Wantage Road station. After the station had been closed she was placed in the care of the G.W.S. at Didcot and had her moment of glory in 1975 at the ripe old age of 118 years, when she ran under her own steam in the Shildon Cavalcade to commemorate the 150th Anniversary of the Stockton and Darlington Railway.

No Great Western depot would be complete without a vision of the famous chocolate-and-cream coaches. Didcot offers the visitor a wide choice of these liveried designs. Coach designs vary much more than people imagine. Carriages are classified into suburban, excursion, buffet, ocean saloon, and auto-carriage, not to mention the variations produced on these. The Society has tried to build up a picture of how carriages changed and differed. There are carriages (requiring extensive restoration) from the Victorian era, and one 'Dreadnought' coach, 70 feet long, from the first decade of the twentieth century. The Society has two of the famous ocean saloons, 'Queen Mary' and 'Princess Elizabeth'; these were exceptionally luxurious, and more expensive to travel in than first class. Of later design is No. 9002; its class is unusual in that each bogie has six rather than four wheels. These too were beautifully fitted carriages. This particular coach was designed with a lounge, conference room and kitchen.

The Society also has a number of freight vehicles, including the distinctive 'Royal Daylight' petrol tanker, a milk-churn van, a cattle wagon, coal wagons and a curious weed-killer truck. There are also a few vans used by permanent way staff in their work of maintaining the line.

At Didcot it is possible to obtain a comprehensive picture of most facets of the operation of the Great Western Railway.

A galaxy of Great Western steam power parades at a Didcot Steam Day. (Great Western Society)

Forest Railroad Park

John Southern, the creator of the Forest Railroad, makes the modest claim that it is simply the result of a boyhood hobby that got out of hand. But the impact that this line makes on the visitor is considerable and vastly greater than John Southern's claim or its modest $7\frac{1}{4}$ in. gauge would suggest.

The rail*way*, for such it was then, first opened its gates to the public on 23 May 1970 after three years had been spent bulldozing and constructing a tortuous and exacting $\frac{1}{2}$-mile track round a four-acre site that was part of the Southerns' pig farm. The sole motive power was provided by an L.M.S. 'Coronation' class pacific, *Duchess of Sutherland*, which ultimately recorded more than 1500 miles without a single breakdown. The original intention had been to create a forest setting with a severely graded line running through it, and so, although not intended, it became apparent quite early on that the scenery was in many ways more typical of America than of Britain. When the first American outline locomotive, Denver and Rio Grande 2-8-2 *General Palmer*, arrived the picture was complete. This, coupled with the need for larger and more powerful engines to cope efficiently

with the increasing numbers of visitors attracted to the line, persuaded the Southerns that this was the direction in which the future of their venture lay. So the Forest Railway became the Forest Railroad Park.

Whilst some visitors may be disappointed that there is not a British locomotive in sight, it is John Southern's view that steam is what matters – and surely no one can deny that the Americans produced the mightiest and most powerful steam locomotives in the world. To prove the point, 1974 saw the arrival of a veritable giant of a locomotive, a Union Pacific 800 class 4-8-4 *Queen of Wyoming*.

The next few years slipped by successfully yet undramatically, with more and more children of all ages arriving to see and ride on the trains, reflecting the growing interest in railways generally and in steam in particular, albeit in miniature. Soon, the idea began to form of creating a new extension to the railroad, which had already been lengthened to a full one-mile circuit, by adding a Wyoming landscape through which the UP 4-8-4 could be viewed in a miniaturized version of its natural environment.

American giants in miniature. The Forest Railroad's steam superpower includes two Union Pacific 4-8-4s. No. 8 is the Hudswell Clarke 2-6-2 David Curwen (Forest Railroad Park)

And then, of course, there would be the excuse to operate the world's supreme steam locomotive both in size and power, the Union Pacific 'Big Boy'. . . .

Late in 1976 the plans were finalized. There would be two separate – and scenically very different – routes: the existing Rio Grande line snaking its way through the Colorado forests, and in stark contrast, the wild, barren and desolate Wyoming scene through which the 'Big Boy' could battle its way. Nearly another three years of construction saw the project through to completion. Over 600 tons of rock, dragged in from Bodmin Moor, had been laboriously hoisted into position high on the man-made Sherman Hill; lakes and waterfalls were made, bridges built, platforms cleared and a mile of track laid and ballasted.

The inaugural day for the new route, 7 April 1979, dawned bright and clear, the sun shining on Sherman Hill and on 'Big Boy' – 4-8-8-4 No. 4008 *William Jeffers* – as it steamed to the top, hauling a train with 88 passengers. Since then, the Forest Railroad has gone on from strength to strength, adding a further UP 4-8-4 *Queen of Nebraska*, a Rio Grande 2-8-2 *Otto Mears* and a Union Pacific 'Centennial' class diesel to cope with ever-increasing traffic.

Overall, it is the most arduous and spectacular $7\frac{1}{4}$ in gauge railway in the country. It has severe gradients (up to 1 in 25), high embankments, deep cuttings and five tunnels ranging from 60 to 85 feet in length. The track layout is in the form of continuous, intertwined ovals and up to four trains can use each circuit at once. Operation is protected by automatic, four-aspect colour-light signalling installed by B.R. signal engineers and follows North American practice.

In concept and fact, the Forest Railroad is a spectacular railway entertainment for its visitors – plenty of moving trains to watch and ride, complete with all the atmosphere conjured up by steam, hot oil and chime whistles. Visitors with an appreciation for wildlife and painting should on no account miss visiting the Thorburn Museum and Gallery, commemorating Britain's greatest wildlife artist, Archibald Thorburn. Opening times are the same as for the Railroad.

Swanage Railway

The branch line to Swanage was not opened until 1885; the late arrival of a rail connection to the resort being mainly due to the opposition of local inhabitants who did not want a noisy, smoky railway thrust under their noses. The campaign to bring the railway to Swanage was spearheaded by Mr George Burt who worked tirelessly to sway local support behind him. Doubtless, he intended to figure prominently in the increased prosperity which the line's supporters argued would come to the little resort in the wake of the railway.

The Swanage Railway Act of 1881 received the Royal Assent on 18 July of that year and George Burt was naturally elected Chairman of the new company. To appease the objectors in Wareham, the intended junction with the L.S.W.R., the Swanage line was arranged to leave the main line at Worgret, a point one mile westward. The Swanage company ran their line for their first year of operation after which responsibility for its running and maintenance passed to the L.S.W.R. As allowed for in the Act, the South Western later purchased the line outright.

Thereafter, the Swanage branch settled down to the calm and unhurried existence of the country railway, its peaceful atmosphere only disturbed at weekends by the influx of trains carrying holiday visitors. By the early years of this century the holiday traffic was expanding so rapidly that opinions were expressed that the line would have to be doubled to cope with all the extra trains. This would have been relatively easy as the line had been built with double track in mind for much of its length. However, this work was never carried out, and the Swanage branch remained an attractive outpost of first the L.S.W.R., then the Southern Railway and finally the Southern Region of British Railways until its ultimate demise in 1972.

Throughout its length, the branch ran through the delightful countryside of south Dorset and The Purbeck Hills, dominated at its mid-point by the striking ancient ruins of Corfe Castle. Its stations were attractively built in local stone and the line, with its terminus, must have inspired many a railway modeller. Steam was the principal motive power right up to July 1967 when it was finally abolished throughout the Southern Region. Thereafter services were diesel-worked until the branch closed to all traffic south of Furzebrook sidings on 5 January 1972.

Immediately the branch closed attempts were made to reopen it, with a view to reinstating a local amenity service. But in the climate of the early 1970s, the problems were too great to overcome, particularly as the proposed service would have had to run over B.R. tracks between Worgret Junction and Wareham. However, a second attempt to save the line a few years later met with greater success and laid the foundations of today's operations at Swanage. By 1976 all the track had been lifted south of Furzebrook sidings and the new preservation body had to start from a completely bare trackbed. But even after the preservationists had gained a toe-hold in Swanage station yard, there was still a very real possibility that the handsome terminus station building might be bulldozed by the local authority to make way for a car park. Lengthy negotiations ensued with Swanage Town Council and Dorset County Council, but the matter was settled when a Referendum of townspeople produced an 83 per cent majority in favour of the Railway Society being allowed to use the station and part of the yard.

Meanwhile, the County Council had been considering the use of the trackbed at Corfe Castle to provide a route for a by-pass road. Yet they were prepared to make the land occupied by the route of the former railway available to the Society on the condition that in the long term they reinstated a local amenity service over the entirety of the line between Swanage and Wareham. This of course raised the problem of operation over B.R. track from Worgret Junction. As a further complication, traffic over the remaining two miles of the branch to the oil terminal at Furzebrook began increasing steadily after 1977.

Despite these difficulties, potential and real, the Swanage Railway Society soldiered on and in August 1979 were able to offer short train rides up and down a few hundred yards of reinstated track in Swanage goods yard using a Fowler diesel shunter and a restored S.R. Bulleid coach. The following summer steam rides became possible with the oil-fired Barclay 0-4-0ST *Richard Trevithick* providing the motive power. Thirty thousand passengers were carried over a quarter-mile of track and the County Council were sufficiently impressed that they granted permission for the line to be extended to Herston, a mile up the line from Swanage.

Although operations were confined to only a fraction of the former railway site at Swanage, the Society has succeeded in restoring an air of prosperity and optimism to the little terminus. Fresh green and cream paint, S.R. hanging signs and the bustle of platform activity recreate the atmosphere of summer holidays in the sixties spent happily exploring Southern branch lines.

The shuttle service out to Herston is still in the hands of industrial saddle tanks, but in the station yard undergoing restoration is a pair of B.R. Standard 4MT class tanks, Nos. 80078 and 80104 and a Great Western 0-6-2T No. 6695. The Standard tanks will form most appropriate motive power for the Society's trains as this class of engine was the mainstay of the Swanage branch services before dieselization. Both these engines together with a number of carriages and wagons are owned by the Southern Steam Trust.

As funds and negotiations permit, the Swanage Railway Society will be pushing its railhead forward towards Corfe Castle and, in this connection, visitors are encouraged to sign the petition to persuade Dorset County Council to allow the railway its old route to Corfe rather than use it for a road.

LONDON
AND THE HOME COUNTIES

Bluebell Railway

The Bluebell Railway has the distinction of having been the first standard-gauge railway to re-open after closure by British Railways (though the Middleton Railway in Leeds was the first preserved standard-gauge line of all); the official re-opening ceremony was conducted on Sunday 7 August 1960.

The line and its history
The track, which is single and approximately five miles long, links Sheffield Park station at the southernmost end with Horsted Keynes station to the north after a climb of some two hundred feet. It was formerly a part of the old Lewes and East Grinstead railway, proposed in 1876 and opened on 1 August 1883. Like so many rural systems, the project was never a money spinner, passing as it did through countryside which was devoted mainly to agriculture, sparsely populated, and with most villages rather remote from the stations bearing their names. Furthermore, the train services appeared to be geared to milk and mineral traffic rather than the needs of passengers, who experienced long waits whilst loading was in progress. The stations really came to life in the days of social functions at nearby stately homes, of which Sheffield Park probably attracted the largest contingents. Among Lord Sheffield's visitors were the Australian touring cricketers, whose first match in this country was always played on the pitch at the Park. (Cricket lovers may connect this with the Sheffield Shield, awarded in inter-state competition in Australia, for which Lord Sheffield donated the trophy.) A period of great activity at the stations came during World War I when much of the countryside came under control of the War Office for troop training. The unmechanized army threw a heavy load onto the railways.

Trains on the Bluebell line continued to jog along into the early years of nationalization. An amazing assortment of locomotives contributed to the scene, from 'Terriers' to Brighton Atlantics (4-4-2s) and Moguls (2-6-0s), some of Bulleid's West Country and Battle of Britain classes, and even ex-S.E. & C.R. and ex-L. & S.W.R. engines. All these were then joined by

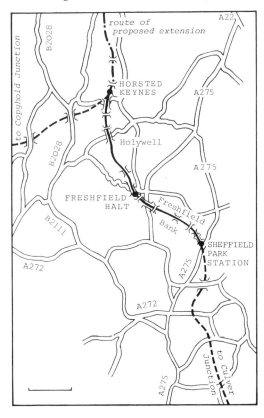

Rousing memories of hop-pickers' specials in the Weald of Kent, S.E. & C.R. 'C' class goods engine No. 592 attacks Freshfield Bank with a heavy train. (David Wigley)

engines of British Railways design, including one of the early diesels, Bo-Bo No. 10800. All this was too good to last. Following two enquiries, British Railways closed the line from East Grinstead through Horsted Keynes to Culver Junction (where it converged with the Tunbridge Wells to Lewes line), from 28 May 1955.

However, an astute local lady, Miss Bessemer, pointed out that under a clause in its original Act, the line could not legally be closed in this way; British Railways were obliged to re-introduce a minimum service. They made the timetable as inconvenient as possible, with four trains each way daily from Monday to Saturday. This commenced in August 1956; the programme fell within the scope of an eight-hour shift for train crews. Once B.R. had adjusted

their legal position they withdrew this pathetic train service, on 16 March 1958. British Railways did however retain the electrified route from Haywards Heath through Ardingly to Horsted Keynes, this being expedient from a traffic rather than revenue point of view.

Preservation

In 1959, three young students called a meeting of interested people, to discuss the possibility of operating the line on a private basis. As a result the authorities at Waterloo were approached. Eventually it became possible to lease the section of line between Sheffield Park station and a point south of Horsted Keynes station (without access to the latter), and a price was quoted for eventual purchase. A second meeting held at Haywards Heath resulted in the founding of The Bluebell Railway Preservation Society on 14 June 1959. The founders could hardly have visualized that in little over a decade the annual passenger journeys over the preserved line would be in the order of a quarter of a million!

Temporarily reverting to its B.R. identity as No. 9017, the Dukedog recreates a scene on the Cambrian lines of the 1950s. The engine was specially posed with a typical short freight train just outside Sheffield Park station. (Peter Zabek)

At first British Railways refused to allow Bluebell trains into Horsted Keynes station; the Society had to build Bluebell Halt, clear of the junction but within easy walking distance. There was no run-round loop, so trains had to be run with an engine at each end. After a while British Railways relented somewhat, and allowed Bluebell trains to use one platform at Horsted Keynes; they rather negated this concession by insisting that a British Railways pilotman should join or leave the Bluebell engine at the halt and inevitably this tiresome service was not provided free of charge. A bitter blow followed in 1963 when the Haywards Heath–Horsted Keynes branch was closed. Lifting of the tracks isolated the preserved line. All future deliveries of locomotives and rolling stock had perforce to rely upon road haulage, over somewhat winding routes. Thanks to the one-hundred-per-cent co-operation of the Sussex Police, many giant loads over the years have been safely delivered without undue dislocation of road traffic – indeed, most motorists appear to be intrigued rather than antagonized.

Access
The station at Sheffield Park has been restored to its former L.B. & S.C.R. colour scheme, and houses, in addition to administrative offices, a very interesting museum, and a solidly built bookshop offering a wide variety of Bluebell and other railway interest publications. Refreshments are available near the same platform. The headquarters of the Locomotive Department are at Sheffield Park and here may be seen those locomotives not actually in steam, some undergoing repair and some restoration.

At the northern end of the line Horsted Keynes station is unusually spacious, with five platforms. The predominant atmosphere here is

Freshfield Bank, a gradient of 1 in 75, always provides fine smoke. Here G.W.R. 4-4-0 Earl of Berkeley *heads a four-coach train from Sheffield Park to Horsted Keynes. (John Vaughan)*

one of Southern Railway days, with decor in accordance with that company's colour scheme. Again refreshments are available from the original refreshment room on the island platform (2 and 3), but the premises like those at Sheffield Park are now unlicensed. As one approaches Horsted Keynes by train, the large carriage shed is passed on the east side of the track; this is the headquarters of the Carriage and Wagon Department. Adjoining the station is a large picnic area in a delightfully rural setting with the station facilities conveniently to hand.

A round trip on the railway can be made in just under three-quarters of an hour, but this leaves little time for inspecting the many attractive exhibits after the first leg of the journey. You do not, however, have to return immediately, for the choice of train is your own.

For those wishing to visit the railway in their own cars, Sheffield Park station lies just off the A275 East Grinstead to Lewes road, approximately midway between those towns.

Horsted Keynes station, situated in the middle of nowhere and over a mile from the village of that name, is approached by secondary roads, the most direct of which is that from West Hoathly to Horsted Keynes, thence along a road running westwards at Great Oddynes turning. There is also another approach, this time from the west, using a turning off the B2028 Turners Hill–Lindfield road at a point south of Ardingly and which includes, shortly before reaching the station, an extremely restricted bridge over which Bluebell trains pass. Should you have need to ask the way, the correct pronunciation of Keynes is 'Canes', whilst Ardingly is locally 'Arding-lie'.

The Bluebell Railway's twenty-plus years in the preservation business show through in the solid and well-founded appearance of all facets of the line. Quite apart from the two imposing

L. & S.W.R. 4-4-2 No. 488, built in 1885, was designed for suburban passenger work but ended its British Rail days on the tortuous Lyme Regis branch in 1960. (Brian Stephenson)

stations, the railway boasts well-maintained permanent way in good condition and a vast amount of rolling stock to run on it. Superb new workshops at Sheffield Park complement the adjacent locomotive shed – a modern concrete-framed structure which has been clothed in traditional brickwork with arched windows so that it resembles the original L.B.S.C.R. shed at Tunbridge Wells. There could be no more fitting building in which to house the magnificent collection of nearly thirty steam locomotives, most of them originating from the Southern Railway or one of its constituent railways. Each year well over a quarter of a million passengers travel in Bluebell trains, evidence enough of the continuing and still-growing popularity of the country's first standard-gauge passenger-carrying preserved railway.

Having achieved so much in splendid isolation from the national railway system, it is small wonder that the Bluebell Railway of the 1980s feels the pressing need to expand its frontiers. The railway in its present form has long outgrown the restrictions of its five-mile route. Apart from the desirability of re-establishing a main-line connection with B.R., the railway needs to reach out through a new landscape to fully justify its massive investment in facilities and rolling stock and, not least, to reach a new public.

The long-term development plan involves the reinstatement of the 6$\frac{1}{4}$-mile connection northward from Horsted Keynes to East Grinstead, where it will link up with Southern Region's route from London via East Croydon and Oxted. This would include the Imberhorne Viaduct at East Grinstead and the 730-yard-long West Hoathly tunnel. There are, however, many problems to be overcome, such as the sale by British Railways of some of the original route to nearby landowners, and the filling-in of a cutting towards East Grinstead. Much diplomacy

TOP: *0-6-0 tank No. 27, built in 1909 and now painted in full S.E. & C.R. passenger livery, hauls the 1700 from Sheffield Park to Horsted Keynes on a March afternoon.* (David Idle)

INSET: *Footplate view from L.B. & S.C.R. No. 55 Stepney as it climbs towards Horsted Keynes. Built in 1875, one of the famous Stroudley 'Terriers' (A1X class), Stepney was the first engine to arrive on the Bluebell, in 1960, having been withdrawn from Eastleigh B.R. shed in May of that year.* (R. C. Riley)

and patience will have to be exercised if the scheme is to be brought to fruition. At the time of writing a public enquiry is awaited to hear the Bluebell's appeal for planning permission to operate trains into East Grinstead over the proposed route.

Stock

As befits one of Britain's preservation pioneers, the Bluebell's collection of historic locomotives, carriages and wagons is quite superb and must be one of the principal reasons for visiting the line. For a once-sleepy rural byway, home of small tank engines on lightweight trains, it may seem strange that the railway is now host to thirteen tender locomotives including a mighty 9F 2-10-0! Yet all are logical choices, given the availability of suitable classes to preserve in the dying years of B.R. mainline steam. No fewer than eight engines have been rescued from Barry scrapyard in the last few years and of those only one is a tank engine – appropriately enough the Brighton-built 4MT 2-6-4T No. 80100. This class had strong links with the Bluebell line in B.R. days, and indeed the last train to run from East Grinstead to Lewes was

Maunsell-designed class U 2-6-0 No. 1618 bursts under Ketches Bridge. (David Idle)

hauled by the very last of the class, No. 80154.

Eighty years previously, Brighton works was busy turning out another class of tank engine also designed for suburban and country passenger duties: William Stroudley's famous 'Terriers'. Two of these are to be found on the Bluebell Railway, No. 55 *Stepney* and No. 72 *Fenchurch*, the former freshly restored, after a long overhaul, to the gorgeously ornate yellow livery of the L.B.S.C.R. under Stroudley. *Fen-church* first took to the rails in 1872 and fittingly represented the Bluebell Railway 103 years later at the Shildon 'Rail 150' parade. The 'Terrier' concept was copied on the S.E. & C.R. over thirty years later in 1909. The result was the P class – rather undersized for extensive use on branch-line passenger trains but just the thing for early Bluebell services. There are three: Nos. 27, 323 and 1178. Of these three, No. 323 *Bluebell* was on loan to the East Somerset Railway at the time of writing (early 1983).

A group of medium-sized tank engines from the railways of south-east England makes up

7

ABOVE: *Wainwright C class No. 592, built in 1901, heads one of the goods trains which the Bluebell Railway runs each month for photography and authenticity. (*David Idle*)*

BELOW: *West Country class 21C123,* Blackmoor Vale, *here leaving Sheffield Park, was built in 1946 to Bulleid's design and joined the Bluebell in 1971 after withdrawal from B.R. Southern Region in 1967. (*G. W. Morrison*)*

one of the most fascinating parts of the Bluebell collection. From the L.B.S.C.R. comes *Birch Grove*, an E4 class 0-6-2T of 1898; from the rival L.S.W.R. comes Adams Radial Tank No. 488 of 1885; and there is the S.E. & C.R. 'H' class 0-4-4T of 1905 and the North London Railway 0-6-0T No. 2650 of 1880 vintage. Two former inhabitants of Southampton Docks are L.S.W.R. B4 class 0-4-0T No. 96 *Normandy* and the American-designed 0-6-0T No. 30064 which was brought to England for use in World War II and afterwards bought by the Southern Railway.

The Maunsell era of the Southern is well represented by two of his U-class 'Moguls', a Q-class 0-6-0 goods engine, an S15 mixed traffic 4-6-0 No. 847 and the superb 'Schools' class 4-4-0 No. 928 *Stowe*. Oliver Bulleid's unorthodox designs are present in the shape of Q1-class 0-6-0 No. 33001 and Light Pacific's *Blackmoor Vale* and *Sir Archibald Sinclair*. Finally, the B.R. era is represented by the Riddles Standard engines of class 4MT (4-6-0 and 2-6-4T), 5MT 4-6-0 *Camelot* and 9F 2-10-0 No. 92240.

Making an interesting contrast with these modern S.R. and B.R. engines is the much more traditionally designed G.W.R. 'Dukedog' 4-4-0

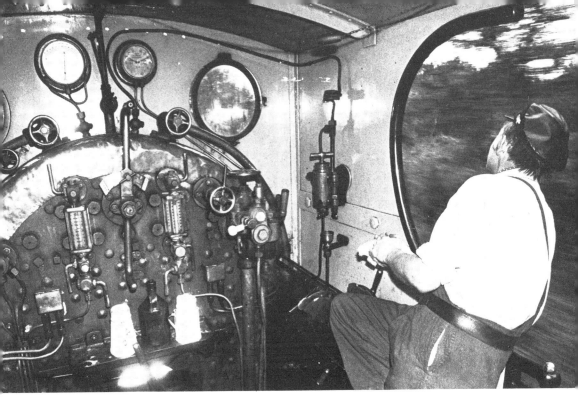

ABOVE: *With their billycans of tea brewing above the firehole door, the crew of No. 592 keep a sharp lookout on the approach to Horsted Keynes.* (Mike Esau)

BELOW: *Recreating the magic of a steam railway by night. Headlamps pierce the gloom as Bulleid Q1 No. 33001 prepares to take the last train of the day out of Sheffield Park.* (David Wilcock)

Earl of Berkeley. Last of all, and far from least, comes *Baxter*, the diminutive Fletcher Jennings 0-4-0T of 1877 vintage that celebrated the Bluebell line's centenary, and the engine's own 105th birthday, by returning to steam in impeccable order, garlanded in paper flowers, hanging baskets and garden gnomes and wearing a Royal Train coat of arms!

Passenger rolling stock, too, covers a long period of development. Pre-grouping railways are well represented, yet one may travel if one wishes in British-Railways-built compartment coaches. The 'in-between' period of the Southern Railway is represented by the products of Maunsell and Bulleid. (The latter, in the writer's opinion, are the acme of comfort and layout.) Three further vehicles are worthy of special mention, these being the old L.B. & S.C.R. Directors' saloon, carried on six-wheel bogies; a rather similar vehicle originating from the old Great Northern Railway; and a London and North Western observation car once used on the scenic lines of North Wales.

They call her the 'Iron Duck' – but Yankee dock tank No. 30064 is one of the most useful locomotives on the Bluebell line. Here is the 'Duck' in full flight with a five-coach train. (Steve Owen)

The first-named vehicles are used only on special occasions when their limited seating capacity is not a drawback. The observation car however, is used frequently, passengers in it being charged a small supplementary fare. It has a useful seating capacity of seventy-two. Other passenger vehicles will be seen, reserved for departmental use. Curiously, it was until 1974 possible to make the Bluebell trip seated in bogie coach No. 3339 from the Caledonian Railway, but this vehicle has now returned to Scotland. This was not, however, the only Caledonian product to visit Sussex: on 15 September 1963 the famous 'Caley Single' No. 123 came to the Bluebell on a special train from Victoria. In her blue livery, with whitewashed coal, she was a wonderful sight; she attracted large crowds throughout the day.

10

A journey down the line

The Bluebell traveller will see rural England at its best as the train threads its way through farmland interspersed with woods and copses displaying masses of bluebells, primroses and other wild flowers. Wild life of all varieties can be seen, especially from the first train of the day in the summer. The noise of the approaching train sends birds of many species into the air.

Shortly after leaving Sheffield Park station, you may see a white post on the east of the track, inscribed 'Greenwich Meridian': the Bluebell must be the only preserved line to serve two hemispheres. Next is the bridge spanning the River Ouse; little more than a brook in summer, it rises to turbulent levels after autumn rains. In the 1830s, the river was the scene of great activity when some eleven million Dutch-made bricks were ferried up-river from Newhaven to the thirty-seven-arch viaduct a few miles upstream from Sheffield Park on the Brighton main line. Little remains of this giant task — disused locks here and there, a building named 'Wharf Cottage' by the A275 near Sheffield Bridge, and an inn named 'The Sloop' overlooking the once-navigable river.

The area around

The surrounding countryside has much to offer in the way of stately homes, gardens, and other attractions open to the public during the summer. Of these the most convenient are the National Trust gardens at Sheffield Park (the mansion is privately owned) and Wings Haven Bird Sanctuary and Hospital (where birds are restored to health after accident or illness). In the grounds of Beech Hurst Park on the A272 road at Haywards Heath, the Sussex Miniature Locomotive Society operates, on summer weekends and Bank Holidays from 2 to 5.30 p.m., a service of trains on tracks of $3\frac{1}{2}$ in. and 5 in. gauge, over a circuit of half a mile. Trains carry passengers and are hauled by a wide variety of steam locomotives modelled on their main-line counterparts, plus some of 'freelance' design. Rather further afield, at Hove, is the Brighton and Hove Engineerium, housed in the old Goldstone Pumping station. There is an admission fee here, but among the many exhibits is an extremely rare working beam engine.

Romney, Hythe and Dymchurch Light Railway

The line and its history

The Kent Coast is justifiably popular among holiday makers, one much-favoured area being that in the south-east of the County. Here one finds a railway of world-wide repute known as the Romney, Hythe and Dymchurch Light Railway. It is in no sense a preserved line, having provided local people and holiday makers with a summer service since its opening in 1927 (although closed to the public during World War II). The main terminus is at Hythe, from which, travelling in a westerly direction, trains run alongside the Royal Military Canal (a defence relic from the Napoleonic Wars). The line then traverses a portion of Romney Marsh, before arriving at Dymchurch, a place famous for its association with Russell Thorndyke's novels about Dr Syn. St Mary's Bay follows, after which one arrives at the busy station of New Romney, headquarters of the line and $8\frac{1}{4}$ miles from the starting point. The railway, following the wide sweep of St Mary's Bay, continues through more holiday centres, now running southwards, and arrives at Dungeness ($13\frac{3}{4}$ miles) with its great shingle banks and lighthouses. Dungeness, however, is not a true terminus, for before reaching the station the railway divides and describes a giant loop round which trains run in a clockwise direction. The station is approximately in the centre of the loop, and affords an intriguing sight of the approaching and departing trains.

One might think the line just a coastal route which has escaped the axe, but it is laid to a gauge of fifteen inches (approximately one quarter of the standard gauge), and in the summer, it carries passengers by the thousand.

In the early nineteen-twenties, two racing drivers were making headlines – Captain J. E. P. Howey, and Count Zbrowski, by birth a Pole. Both men were steam enthusiasts as well as racing drivers, and this combination led to a close friendship. Together they planned a 15 in. gauge railway, to use steam as motive power, and situated in a locality with commercial

11

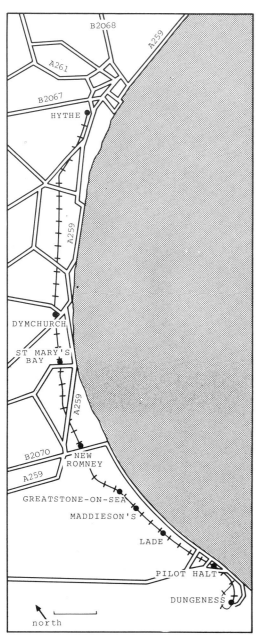

possibilities. Unfortunately, before their plans matured the Count was killed in a car crash at Monza. Although Captain Howey was thus left to pursue the scheme on his own, he did continue, and the Romney, Hythe and Dymchurch Light Railway was built. The first section of the railway was opened in June 1927,

from Hythe to New Romney; the extension to Dungeness followed in two stages in 1928–9. The Southern Railway supported the new line, for it provided a link between two of their ailing branches, that from Sandling Junction to Hythe and that from Appledore to Dungeness and New Romney. Unfortunately the coming of the family car blunted any possible increase in passengers on these branches; both have been closed.

Stock
Captain Howey appointed for his Engineer the late Mr Henry Greenly, who had vast experience in miniature railway design. For motive power, Greenly designed Pacific-type engines which were Gresley's fine A1 class scaled down, in the case of rail gauge to approximately quarter-scale, and, since there were no loading-gauge problems, to one-third full-size for the superstructures. This enabled him to use large boilers, and he blended the two scales so cleverly that there is no difference whatever to the average observer. Ten steam locomotives were built between 1925 and 1931, eight of which were of the 4-6-2 wheel arrangement and the remainder 4-8-2s. Until 1927, all the locomotives were built by Davey Paxman of Colchester: they supplied six Pacifics and the two 4-8-2s. The two further Pacifics were delivered in 1931 from the Yorkshire Engine Co. Ltd, both being based on Canadian Pacific practice, in striking contrast to the Gresley-outline Pacifics and original 4-8-2s. These original engines have now been supplemented by another Greenly-designed Pacific, but this time built in Germany by Krupps of Essen in 1937. No. 11 *Black Prince* was built for use in an exhibition park in Düsseldorf and later worked at Munich and Cologne before being overhauled in preparation for entering service in an amusement park beside the Rhine. It was in fact never used there and, together with its sister locomotives *Rosenkavalier* and *Männertreu* (now at Bressingham), was bought for use in England.

In early days the locomotives and trains were equipped with the Westinghouse automatic air brake, but the detailed precision required for maintenance in such a small scale prompted the substitution of the automatic vacuum brake,

It could be a transcontinental departure setting out to cross the Rocky Mountains, but in fact it's the miniature Canadian outline Pacific No. 10 Doctor Syn departing from New Romney with a 15-inch gauge express. (Tom Heavyside)

which is now standard on the railway. Passenger rolling stock comprised four- and eight-wheel coaches, and wagons were put into service too, in anticipation of a certain amount of goods traffic.

The official opening took place on Saturday 16 July 1927, but almost a year before this, whilst the line was still under construction, a member of the Royal Family showed interest in what was going on. In those days a children's holiday centre at Jesson was sponsored by the then Duke of York (later King George VI). It was known as the Duke of York's Camp. His Royal Highness expressed a wish to travel on one of the engines and was granted a footplate ride,

accompanied by Captain Howey and Nigel (later Sir Nigel) Gresley; the journey began at a bridge, since named 'Duke of York's Bridge'.

After the official opening, the railway provided an all-the-year-round service. The winter service however, was not a success, for local residents, aware of conditions when the winds blew across the Channel direct from a frozen Continent, wisely remained indoors. But trains in the holiday season were packed, as the area began to develop. The line prospered until the outbreak of World War II. With the fall of France in 1940, the R.H. & D.R. found itself in a prohibited area, and for the remainder of the War its trains became part of the War effort; an armoured train was built and run. The railway's greatest achievement came before the Allied landings in Normandy in 1944. It had been decided to supply the invasion forces with petrol from England by means of an undersea pipe line, safe from enemy action. The feed

13

source of 'PLUTO' (Pipe Line Under The Ocean) was at Lade, between New Romney and Dungeness. The R.H. & D.R. was used to convey the piping and all necessary equipment to the site, after its transfer from the Southern Railway. As can well be imagined, the rolling stock and track took a terrible pounding. After the War, two years were needed to restore the line to running order. This restoration was very costly and Captain Howey decided to reinstate only a single line towards Dungeness from New Romney, instead of the original double track. The re-opening was performed by the two world-famous comedians Stan Laurel and Oliver Hardy.

Captain Howey died in 1963 and his life-long interest passed into the control of others; nevertheless the line carries on as ever, its trains still hauled by those magnificently designed and built locomotives dating from the late 1920s.

The area around

Whilst in the area, do not miss a marshland tour by car. Here is an expanse of pasturage where sheep may safely graze and small villages cluster around giant parish churches. In the graveyard at St Mary-in-the-Marsh is buried E. Nesbit, authoress of *The Railway Children* (filmed first nearly 20 years ago by the B.B.C. on the S.R. Horsham–Guildford branch, and latterly for the large screen on the preserved Keighley and Worth Valley Railway).

A marshland church worthy of note is St Augustine's at Brookland, on the main A259 road. Its unique feature is that it has a spire resembling three candle extinguishers one above the other, standing not on the traditional tower, but at ground level by the church. The writer has heard that after all material had been delivered, it was realized that the marshy foundations would not bear the weight of both tower and spire.

Just inland, at the Dungeness end of the line, is the little town of Lydd, from which was derived the name of the explosive Lyddite. The parish church of All Saints, devastated by bombing in 1940 and rebuilt 1951–8, deserves a visit; it is quite breathtaking and it fully justifies its reputation as 'The Cathedral of the Marsh'.

The Kent and East Sussex Railway

The line and its history

The Kent and East Sussex Railway owes its origin to the late Colonel H. F. Stephens, a pioneer of light railway projects in this country, and dates from 1900. It was then known as the Rother Valley Light Railway. It linked Robertsbridge, on the main South Eastern and Chatham Railway London–Hastings line, with the market town of Tenterden – or at least within one-and-a-half miles of the latter! As its name implies, the railway traversed the valley of the River Rother (sometimes referred to as the Eastern Rother in order to avoid confusion with the Western Rother at the opposite end of Sussex), and its length was some twelve miles. Often called 'The Farmers' Line' it ran through open country devoted almost entirely to agriculture, with the accent on fruit and hops. The railway was extended in 1902, first to Tenterden Town after

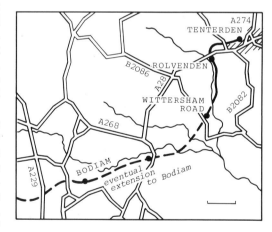

Two of the Kent and East Sussex Railway's locomotives leave Tenterden Town with the midday departure to Wittersham Road. Piloting the train is No. 10 Sutton, *one of the famous Terrier class engines built to the design of William Stroudley at the Brighton works of the L.B. & S.C.R. in 1876. The train locomotive is No. 23, a Hunslet Austerity saddletank built in 1952 and named* Holman F. Stephens *after the engineer who built the K. & E.S.R. (B. Stephenson)*

G.W.R. diesel railcar No. 20, built in 1940, was used by the K. & E.S.R. to provide an off-peak economical shoppers' service until replaced by the more modern AC Cars railbus. (Brian Stephenson)

a stiff climb out of the valley, and then in 1904–5, through Biddenden, to Headcorn, a station on the S.E. & C.R.'s main London–Dover route. The total length of the railway was now twenty-one-and-a-half miles, and plans were made for further extensions.

Lack of capital, however, and very heavy engineering problems, prevented these being put in hand and Colonel Stephens contented himself with the Robertsbridge to Headcorn line, renaming it the Kent and East Sussex Light Railway; the original Tenterden station was renamed Rolvenden. The boundary between the two counties occurs where the railway crosses the River Rother just to the east of Northiam station.

A remarkable collection of locomotives was acquired to run the line. These included some outside-cylinder tank engines; 'Terrier' 0-6-0

tank engines from the L.B. & S.C.R.; a couple of 0-6-0 tender engines of the Ilfracombe goods class of the L. & S.W.R.; and, last but not least, a sturdy 0-8-0 tank engine weighing no less than $43\frac{1}{2}$ tons. This unique engine, named *Hecate*, saw but little service. Much too heavy for the lightly laid track, she was acquired by the Southern Railway in 1932, being utilized for stock marshalling at Clapham Junction, a duty for which she was well suited.

Passenger rolling stock, too, was very varied, including bogie, six-wheeled and four-wheeled coaches from various pre-grouping companies, mainly the L. & S.W.R. Among the four-wheeled examples was the royal saloon built for the South Western Railway in 1848. With the increase in road competition three different versions of rail car were tried – one steam-driven and two with internal combustion engines, but they achieved little success. A miscellaneous collection of goods wagons completed the picture.

The K. & E.S.R. escaped grouping in 1923 and preserved its identity right up to national-ization, apart from a period during World War

This L.B. & S.C.R. Terrier (Stroudley A1 class) was built in 1876. In the tradition of the L.B. & S.C.R., it was named to match the locality in which it worked and so, built as Whitechapel, *it became* Fishbourne *when moved to the Isle of Wight in 1930, and was nameless from 1937 when used for shunting duties. In 1963 it was sold to Sutton Borough Council and named* Sutton. *Here it crosses the A28 towards Wittersham Road, piloting the Norwegian No. 19 which is running tender-first. (*Brian Stephenson*)*

II when it was requisitioned. At that time the Southern Railway loaned several locomotives to keep trains moving. Upon nationalization, the line was merged into the Southern Region, but its passenger services were withdrawn in 1954. Goods traffic continued on the Robertsbridge–Tenterden section until complete closure in 1961. For the last few years the goods traffic was operated by a 0-6-0 Drewry diesel locomotive, which on occasion hauled special passenger trains. It is interesting to note that during this period a steam engine was kept in reserve at St Leonards nearby.

Preservation

Immediately after closure, enthusiasts proposed plans for operating the line as a tourist attraction, using volunteer labour. They persevered in the face of endless obstruction from B.R. and the Ministry of Transport. A severe set-back occurred when the then Minister of Transport refused sanction to re-open the section between Robertsbridge and Bodiam because of its main-road level crossings. This reduced the line to the Tenterden–Bodiam length, some ten miles, and isolated it from all B.R. contact. The pre-servationists pressed on however. They reclaimed station buildings, track, bridges and signalling equipment, ready for the day when the bark of 'Terrier' tanks would again echo over the countryside. This work could be done only at weekends, for all the volunteer staff were otherwise occupied during the week. Reward for their efforts came in 1974, when the line from Tenterden to Rolvenden was passed for traffic; and passengers could be carried for the first time since 1954. All this had been done by volunteer labour as had been intended, but in 1976 the K. & E.S. was able to take advantage

of the Government's Job Creation programme. The scheme worked well and within months rather than years, the line has been extended to Wittersham Road. It is not yet over the border into Sussex, but there is a five-mile run from Tenterden. The next phase of restoration will take the railway over the county boundary into East Sussex, and the Railway's title will be fully justified.

Stock

Over the years there has been a steady influx of locomotives and rolling stock, and its wide variety would surely have made Colonel Stephens sigh with envy. Appropriately, the locomotive stock includes two ex-L.B. & S.C.R. 'Terrier' tanks. One has quite a history, for it is the one which Colonel Stephens bought to work his original Rother Valley line in 1901. It was then No. 3 on the Company's books, and named *Bodiam*. Built at Brighton Works in 1872, it carried the name *Poplar* until it came to the Rother Valley. Apart from some prolonged

ABOVE: Sutton *celebrates its centenary in fine style, hauling a special train which includes G.W.R. railcar No. 20, out of Tenterden Town station and down the 1 in 50 bank to Rolvenden. This is the steepest gradient on the railway and it brings many a locomotive to a standstill to blow up more steam!* (Brian Stephenson)

OPPOSITE ABOVE: *Class A1X Terrier 0-6-0T No. 3* Bodiam *climbs Tenterden bank with the 14.59 train from New Mill Bridge to Tenterden Town. This engine was built to the design of William Stroudley at Brighton in 1872 and was purchased by the K. & E.S.R. in 1901.* (B. Stephenson)

OPPOSITE BELOW: *A sight to delight Colonel Stephens. Norwegian Mogul No. 19 heads a smartly painted set of ex-Southern Region Maunsell coaches in K. & E.S.R. colours through the Kentish countryside. The railway has now acquired a rake of B.R. Mark I corridor coaches to maintain most of its regular services.* (Patrick Russell)

Norwegian 2-6-0 No. 19 rounds Orpin's curve outside Tenterden. Built in 1919, it provides the motive power for many of the Kent and East Sussex Railway's scheduled services. (Brian Stephenson)

periods of inactivity, it performed its daily tasks right up to nationalization, when B.R. robbed it of its name and renumbered it 32670, thus restoring it to its original slot in the 'Terrier' list. Upon the withdrawal of the Tenterden passenger service in 1954, B.R. transferred it to Hampshire, where it worked the Hayling Island branch until the closure of that in 1963. It was then purchased privately. The new owner placed it on permanent loan to the K. & E.S.R.; it now proudly bears again its number '3' and of course its name, *Bodiam*. *Bodiam*'s shed mates include the other 'Terrier', No. 10, *Sutton* and an

S.E. & C.R. P class 0-6-0 tank, which bears the name *Pride of Sussex* (bestowed on it by its previous owners, who traded in that county).

Fittingly for a Colonel Stephens line, a covey of Manning Wardle 0-6-0STs has been collected at Rolvenden, the line's locomotive headquarters; for who could imagine one of his light railways without a classic Leeds saddle tank? *Arthur*, *Rhyl* and *Dolobran* await their turn to haul trains up the bank to Tenterden, whilst *Charwelton*, fresh from overhaul in the autumn of 1982, is now back in service.

Thanks to a programme of bridge renewal, the K. & E.S.R. as a preserved line is able to accommodate larger motive power than was ever possible in Stephen's day. (Even the elephantine *Hecate* could be used here if she still existed today.) Consequently, the line has become home for a squad of British War Department 'Austerity' 0-6-0STs as well as a pair of USA class 0-6-0Ts *Wainwright* and *Maunsell*. And there is the Norwegian 2-6-0 No. 19, an engine which would surely have delighted the Colonel as being close in spirit to the lightweight 'Ilfracombe Goods' tender engines *Rother* and *Juno* that for so many years had their domain amongst the weeds and nettles at Rolvenden.

As an occasional treat for railway connoisseurs, the K. & E.S.R. sometimes steams *Marcia*. She is a tiny Peckett 0-4-0T and far too small for proper passenger work, although just the thing for barging through the undergrowth at the Bodiam end of the line with a single former District Railway four-wheel coach in tow.

Passenger rolling stock is equally varied, with Pullman cars, Maunsell coaches, ex-S.E. & C.R. 'birdcages', an L. & S.W.R. bogie coach and a unique four-wheel brake-end coach of London and North Western Railway origin. More recently, British Railways MK I main-line saloon coaches have been introduced and make up the majority of passenger workings. But, mindful of the Stephens heritage, the K. & E.S.R. is busy rescuing old four-wheel coach bodies of the 1880s from their slumbers as henhouses and lineside huts and intends refitting them to make up a vintage light railway train. Then we shall never forget the way it once was at Tenterden.

The goods stock side has not been neglected and much renovation work has been done. Apart from a Shell tank wagon, all vehicles are painted in K. & E.S.R. livery, unifying a heterogeneous collection that includes such gems as a S.E. & C.R. six-wheeled goods brake van and an L.B.S.C.R. ventilated van.

In order to become a successful tourist attraction, as today's Kent and East Sussex Railway surely has, the old sleepy atmosphere of the Stephens days has, perforce, disappeared. Instead, the line presents a brisk, workmanlike appearance, handling its traffic efficiently in smartly painted rolling stock. However, waiting for a train at Rolvenden or Wittersham Road, standing on a short platform alongside the little cream-painted wooden station building, you still feel a little of the old atmosphere from those far-off days. Who knows, it might just be old *Juno* or *Hesperus* that comes puffing round the curve, or even the Ford back-to-back railcars?

Access and the area around

How does one get to the K. & E.S.R.; what other attractions are there in the area? Access is by road, with Tenterden and Rolvenden served by the A28 between Hastings and Ashford. This in turn is intersected at Northiam (which the railway has yet to reach) by the A268 Rye–Flimwell road, the latter diverging at Flimwell from the A21 London–Hastings road. From Maidstone and the Medway towns, use the A274 to Biddenden, turning eastwards there and finally converging with the A28 north of Tenterden. And if you have been to, or wish to go on to the Romney, Hythe and Dymchurch Railway, your road is the B2080 Tenterden–New Romney. Furthermore, a visit to the K. & E.S.R. will bring you to a historic corner of England. Bodiam Castle is an almost perfect example of a moated stronghold, dating back to 1386. Battle Abbey near Hastings is a little further afield. Other places of interest within easy reach are the Hastings Old Town (with its Castle), St Clement's Caves, and Winchelsea, and Rye, which will both well repay a visit. As you drive around you will notice features peculiar to this part of the Kent/Sussex borders, such as a wealth of weather-boarded houses, and those buildings with a cone-shaped tiled roof surmounted by a white rotating cowl. These are oast houses, once used for drying hops by a method now almost, if not quite, obsolete. The solidly built oast houses have survived.

When in Tenterden you should on no account miss visiting the excellent little Colonel Stephens museum near the station. Here are displayed many memorabilia of the man and his railways, including the vast selection of ornamental free passes granted to him for travel over nearly all Britain's pre-grouping railways.

21

The Mid-Hants 'Watercress' Railway

The line and its history

The Mid-Hants 'Watercress' line operated between Winchester and Alton for nearly 108 years before it was closed by British Railways in 1973. Why 'Watercress'? The line runs through part of the Itchen valley, a river whose water favours the growth of excellent cress.

The railway was built by a private company, as the Alton, Alresford and Winchester Railway. Generally speaking it followed an east–west course. It left the main London–Southampton line at Winchester Junction, some two miles north of Winchester station, and after a 17-mile run, made an end-on junction at Alton with the L. & S.W.R. branch at that place. The countryside is undulating, entailing stiff gradients in

*On loan to the Mid-Hants Railway from the National collection is London and South Western Railway T9 class 4-4-0 No. 120. As running on the 'Watercress Line', it has been repainted in early British Rail black livery. (*John Gardner*)*

places, especially between Medstead and Alton. The route was often referred to as 'Over the Alps'. The L. & S.W.R. bought out the private company in 1884, and used the line as an alternative route to Southampton in addition to their existing service via Basingstoke and Worting Junction. However, when the Southern Railway electrified the Woking–Farnham–Alton line in 1937, through services were withdrawn and a purely local service between Southampton Terminus and Alton, via Eastleigh and Winchester, took their place. The line became a preserve for the ex-L. & S.W.R. 0-4-4 tanks, class M7, usually with two, sometimes with three coaches. The two-coach trains were for the most part pull-and-push units; this simplified movements at Alton, now the terminus for a half-hourly electric train service. When diesel-electric multiple units ('Hampshire units') took over from steam in November 1957, a more frequent even-interval service – still between Southampton Terminus and Alton – was introduced, and passenger traffic increased in consequence. Steam traction did not entirely disappear, for the line provided a useful alternative route when the main London to Southampton was

ABOVE: *A magnificent restoration job was carried out on Bulleid West Country class Pacific* Bodmin *to return it to first-class steaming order on the Mid-Hants Railway. It is the first of the rebuilt members of this famous class to be returned to working condition and has served as an inspiration to other preservation groups who are restoring* Bodmin's *sister engines.* (Patrick Russell)

RIGHT: *Fittingly for a class that was the mainstay of Southern Region secondary services, the Mid-Hants Railway, too, makes great use of its Maunsell 2-6-0s. Here U class No. 31806 draws a train into Alresford station. The smaller-wheeled N class engine No. 31874 is also in service on the line whilst No. 31625 waits its turn for restoration.* (Mid-Hants Railway)

obstructed by derailments or engineering work, (the latter particularly at weekends). Owing to the heavy gradients, many of these diverted trains required double heading and an hour or so spent by the Watercress line could prove very rewarding to the engine spotter.

British Railways' proposal to close it in 1968 met with severe opposition both from rail users and Rural District Councils. At length, after three or more public enquiries, the Ministry of Transport confirmed their previous closure decision. The line ceased operating in February 1973.

Preservation

An effort to continue train services resulted in the formation of two companies, The Winchester and Alton Railway Ltd, and the Mid-Hants Railway Preservation Society Ltd, of which the former, in 1975, endeavoured to raise the necessary funds by a public share issue amounting to over £600,000. The result, after the forty statutory days, was most discouraging; the hoped-for through train service had to be curtailed into the section of line between Alresford and Alton, towards which the necessary capital was assured. By this time British Rail had lifted the track between Alton and Ropley, but had been persuaded not to lift that between Ropley and Alresford, a distance of $2\frac{3}{4}$ miles.

It was this truncated portion of the line that was reopened by the Preservation Society on 30 April 1977 and since then the railway has become one of the fastest growing lines in the country. A concerted effort has been made to recreate on the Mid-Hants Railway the atmosphere of the Southern Region of B.R. as it was in the late 1950s and early 1960s. The restoration of stations and rolling stock is being carried out to fit in with this period. Inevitably, with a line coming into existence ten years after the end of Southern mainline steam, the collection of locomotives and stock amassed to date by the Society contains no items of great antiquity, being for the most part made up of S.R. Maunsell Moguls and post-war Bulleid Pacifics hauling rakes of B.R. MK I coaches. This, however, is quite representative of the Southern Region in the period chosen – and no one can deny twinges of nostalgia at the sight of a gleaming Bulleid Pacific setting out at the head of a long train of green coaches.

So rapid has been the growth of the Mid-Hants rolling stock collection that the railway has a pressing need to expand and lengthen its running line – if only to provide more storage space! A provident move was the early purchase of the entire trackbed right back from Ropley to Alton and the start of the 1980s saw a determined programme of expansion put into effect. Prefabricated track panels were assembled at Alresford and during the 1981–2 seasons the railhead pushed dramatically northeastwards to reach Medstead and Four Marks station. Gangs of volunteers used simple but effective automated methods such as a powered track-laying gantry running on 10-foot gauge

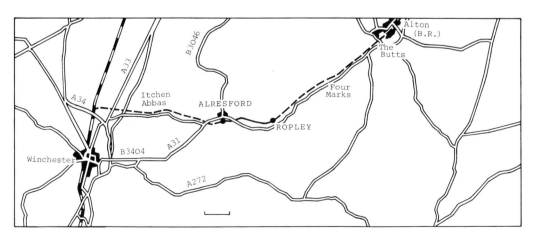

Tablet exchange at Alresford on the Mid-Hants Railway. The S.R. N class No. 31874 was built largely of parts made at Woolwich Arsenal as part of a scheme to relieve post-World War I unemployment. It was actually assembled, as a mixed-traffic loco, at Ashford. (Brian Fisher)

temporary rails which straddled the old formation. Such was the efficiency of this operation that demand for fresh track panels often exceeded the available supply! Around 200 yards of track were laid each weekend until the 3-mile extension was complete at a cost of around £250,000. In May 1983 trains began running to Medstead.

Stock

Pride of place goes to the four Bulleid Pacifics, all of which have been rescued from Woodham Bros scrapyard at Barry in South Wales. 'West Country' class locos *Bodmin* and *Swanage* were joined by 'Battle of Britain' class *Tangmere* and 'Merchant Navy' No. 35018 *British India Line*. So far only *Bodmin* has returned to service – the only preserved example of a rebuilt Bulleid light Pacific to do so. The three Maunsell Moguls – the Southern's 'maids of all work' – also came from Barry and to date two of these, N class No. 31874 and U class No. 31806, have been restored. The latter is a particularly interesting loco as it started life as an express 2-6-4T No. A806 *River Torridge* in 1926, but was converted to a tender loco only two years later after an engine of the same class had been involved in the Sevenoaks crash.

The oldest engines on the line are the two L.S.W.R. S15 class 4-6-0s Nos. 30499 and 30506, both built in 1920. They too have been saved from Barry scrapyard, this time by the Urie S15 Locomotive Preservation Group. Sister engine No. 30825 has also been bought to act as a reservoir of spare parts to maintain the Urie engines in working order. Two L.M.S. locos, a

3F 'Jinty' tank No. 47324 and a 4F 0-6-0 tender loco No. 44123, have also come from Barry, though it will be some time before either is returned to steam. Finally, there is a B.R. Standard 4MT Mogul No. 76017 undergoing restoration.

In the spring of 1982 the railway received on loan from the National Railway Museum the grand old L.S.W.R. T9 class 4-4-0 No. 120 – and how fitting to see one of Dugall Drummond's famous 'Greyhounds' back on its native line.

Coaching stock for the most part consists of B.R. MK I corridor vehicles, although wherever possible the railway has made efforts to purchase genuine Southern Railway Maunsell or Bulleid coaches. To date eight of these are on the line.

The area around

Only eight miles away is the cathedral city of Winchester, once capital of Wessex. The present Cathedral dates back to Norman days and superseded a much earlier Saxon building. The city too has much of interest to offer. There is now only one railway station, that on the old L. & S. W. R. London–Southampton main line, although until recent years the Didcot, Newbury and Southampton Railway served the town at an entirely separate station eventually named Winchester Chesil. From 1957 onwards, for a few years, a celebrated engine was seen on this line: the G.W.R.'s *City of Truro* was brought out of retirement, and overhauled for use on enthusiasts' specials. In between times she did light duties on the G.W.R. line to Southampton. But her re-activated life lasted only a few years – she is now in Swindon Museum.

Should you prefer wild animals to cathedral cities, there is, on the Winchester–Portsmouth A333 road, at Colden Common, about half way between Winchester and Bishops Waltham, the Marwell Zoological Park. The surrounding countryside has rolling hills, attractive villages and small towns, and the Meon Valley (through which a railway once ran from Alton to Fareham but now, alas, is no more). The economy axe has fallen very heavily upon railways of Hampshire, and its eastern neighbour Sussex; but thanks to preservationists, all is not lost.

The Isle of Wight Steam Railway

The line and its history

The Isle of Wight was formerly covered with a fairly comprehensive railway network. The centre of the system was Newport, and from the west the Freshwater, Yarmouth and Newport Railway ran almost directly to the island's capital. Running almost due north–south, splitting the Isle in half, was the Isle of Wight Central Railway. There were two connecting branches from this line to another north–south railway in the east. This was the Isle of Wight Railway, still in operation, although in a reduced form. It ran from Ryde Pier Head, south to Ventnor. It is rather sad that an island which was once so rich in steam railways is now reduced to a short electric line and one preserved steam society. The Isle of Wight Steam Locomotive Society operates a restricted section of track north from Haven Street Station, towards Wooton. This is part of the former Isle of Wight Central Railway, the northernmost link between the Cowes–Ventnor line and the east coast line. It ran from Newport to Smallbrook Junction and today is derelict except for the restored section.

Unfortunately the island's railways proved to be unpopular amongst the local inhabitants. They were really designed for holidaymakers, and their prices and facilities were attuned to their requirements. Fares were high in the winter season when there were no trippers to fill the trains, and there were few third-class carriages. Until 1914 trains were composed of first- and second-class stock only. As soon as the motor car started to steal away passengers in the post-war period, the railways began to suffer. The Isle of Wight was among the steam railways to suffer closures. Some had argued that the island had an over-generous supply of lines anyway. In 1952 the Merstone–Ventnor section was shut down. Then in the following September, the Freshwater-Newport line was closed, the only line in the west. The Newport–Sandown branch managed to survive until February 1956. There was a storm of protest over this spate of closures and the

No. 32640 at Brighton shed on 15 September 1963. A few weeks' later this locomotive was sold to Butlins at Pwllheli. In 1973 it returned to the Isle of Wight as W11 Newport. (Derek Smith)

Transport Commission was forced to pledge that five years' notice would be given in future if any more closures were being considered. This promise was repudiated in 1964. It was argued that the publication of the Beeching Report effectively annulled the earlier agreement. Ryde–Cowes passenger trains (including the Haven Street section) ceased to run from 21 February 1966, Shanklin–Ventnor closed in the following April, and freight services ended in the May. The only remaining line, Ryde Pier to Shanklin, was temporarily closed for electrification, and re-opened in March 1967 using ex-London Transport tube stock.

Stock
For forty years or so, L. & S.W.R. 0-4-4 tank No. 24, *Calbourne* (class 02), served the Island's railways. She was one of the first purchases when the moves to preserve something of the I.O.W.'s unique railway heritage were made. Overhauled in 1976–7, she headed all the passenger trains run in the 1977 season. Before that, the mainstay of the 'tourist' service was a Hawthorn Leslie 0-4-0 saddle tank, No. 37,

27

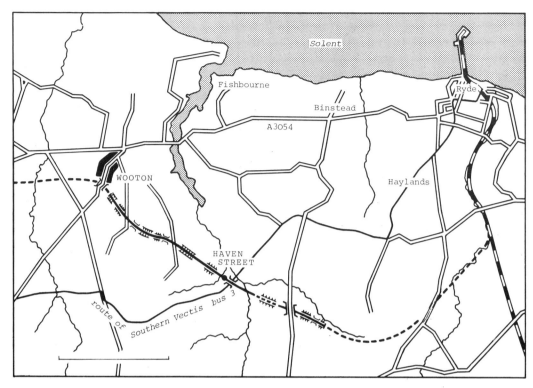

Invincible, originally built for the Woolwich Arsenal during World War I. She had to be fitted with Westinghouse brake equipment to make her suitable for passenger work. She has outside cylinders, and is in a mid-green livery, lined in yellow and black.

Recently restored is a 'Terrier', an A1X class 0-6-0, No. 11, *Newport*. Originally L.B. & S.C.R. No. 40, *Brighton*, she was sold to the I.W.C.R. in 1902. Withdrawn from B.R. in 1963, she returned to the I.O.W. Steam Railway in 1973 after a time at a Butlin's camp, and is now restored to I.W.C. livery: white-and-red-lined black, with 'I.W.C.' in gold.

A second 'Terrier' returned to the Isle of Wight in 1979. This engine has an even more varied career than No. 11, having been built as L.B.S.C.R. No. 46 in 1876, then sold to the neighbouring L.S.W.R. to become their No. 734 in 1903. Sold again ten years later, the engine made its first crossing to the island and became Freshwater, Yarmouth and Newport Railway No. 2. Under the Southern Railway she acquired the name *Freshwater*, was renumbered W8 and

worked the IOW branch lines until nationalization. British Railways returned her to the mainland in 1949 and as No. 32646 she worked on the Hayling Island branch. In 1964 the engine was sold once more, this time to the Sadler Railcoach Company for experimental work on the L.S.W.R. Meon Valley line, but two years later she was sold yet again to Brickwoods Breweries to become a 'pub sign' on Hayling Island. Here she regained her L.B. & S.C.R. yellow livery and her original name, *Newington*. Now she is again W8 *Freshwater* and, in smart Southern green paintwork, hauls holiday-makers through the peaceful Isle of Wight countryside. Quite a history for such a diminutive engine!

The 'Terriers' were designed by William Stroudley for use on the L.B. & S.C.R., and introduced in 1872. Though relatively small and simple, they were exceptionally powerful for their size, with a tractive effort of 10,695 lb. They were used for light shunting and short passenger trains. Those which operated on the Southern were named after the districts they

28

At the Isle of Wight Railway headquarters at Haven Street, L. & S.W.R. 0-4-4 Calbourne *takes on fuel. (*R. Macdonald*)*

served. (*Stepney* and *Fenchurch* are now on the Bluebell line; *Bodiam* and *Sutton* on the Kent and East Sussex.)

There are several appropriate carriages, of L.B. & S.C.R., L.C.D.R., S.E. & C.R. or I.W.R. origin. The three in regular use for the passenger service are non-corridor compartments, and fit in perfectly with the general atmosphere. They have been repainted in Southern green and had yellow '3's painted on the carriage doors. Inside, they still have the moquette-covered benches and small framed advertisements and maps. Leather straps with perforations are used to open the windows, and there are running boards to assist entry. When sitting in one of these behind a 'Terrier' chugging through the pleasant countryside it is easy to imagine that one is back fifty or so years.

A journey down the line

Though the journey from Haven Street to Wooton is not particularly long, it is certainly picturesque. Haven Street station was rebuilt by the Southern Railway in 1926, a passing place on the Ryde–Newport line. Leaving this station, the line passes between fields bordered with trees and thick hedges. The fields give way to woods, and the line passes through a thickly wooded cutting, ending at Wooton Station Road bridge. The train has to stop here, some two miles from Haven Street. The original Wooton Station, on the other side of the bridge, was closed, and the buildings demolished, in 1953. Although it was hoped to re-open on the original site, an extensive land slip has made that impossible. A completely new Wooton Station is therefore being built, designed with care to I.O.W. railway traditions.

New sidings and inspection pits are being built at Haven Street, and a small shed and workshop is planned. At first, when the train reached Wooton, it had to back to Haven Street. Run-round facilities at Wooton are now complete, however.

Haven Street Station has a small museum nearby, which has a collection of station signs, signals, rail chairs, timetables, tickets, badges and photographs. The station, an island platform, has a water tower intact, and the original semaphore signals have survived.

Access

Southern Vectis bus 3, from Newport, stops outside Haven Street station. On steam days, tickets including a ride on the Railway are available from many S.R. stations, as 'Away-days'. Operation is on Sundays and Bank Holidays from May to September, with some mid-week trains in peak season.

The area around

Newport, the island's commercial capital, is not far from Haven Street, situated on the River Medina.

Carisbrooke was of course the island's former capital. It was both a market and administrative centre. As a result the Isle's major castle was built here. The main buildings are set on a plateau 150 feet above sea level. The turrets and walls date from the Norman to the Jacobean period demonstrating a continuing pre-occupation with military security. The keep is Norman. The Well House is a restored sixteenth-century building, though the deep well was actually sunk in 1150. Water is still raised today in buckets wound up by donkeys. There is a fine museum depicting varied aspects of the island's history.

Slightly to the north and east of the railway is the village of Binstead. Here is Quarr Abbey, originally built by Cistercian monks in 1132. The monks were then forced out and it later became a defensive blockhouse, and then a farm. The ruins may now be compared with the new abbey maintained by the Benedictines who live half a mile distant. There is also a shell museum in the village.

The Sittingbourne and Kemsley Light Railway

The line and its history

Not all preserved steam railways in England are operated over former British Rail lines with standard-gauge locomotives. Many industrial concerns which required their raw materials brought some distance from depot or dock laid down their own railway system. Often these were of standard-gauge using small 0-6-0 tank engines to haul short trains to and from the works. Where the scale of the enterprise did not require such powerful engines, narrow-gauge railways were constructed. This was the case with the Sittingbourne paper mill. In 1906 a 2 ft 6 in. gauge railway was laid between the mill and a wharf at Milton Creek. The mill belonged to Edward Lloyd and Co. It was an expanding company and it was soon realized that the existing dock facilities were inadequate. Accordingly it was decided to build a dock on the River Swale which could accommodate ocean-going ships. Work started in 1913 but was interrupted the following year by the outbreak of World War I. The new dock was not completed until 1919. After the War the demand for newsprint rose steadily, so it was decided to construct a new and larger paper mill at Kemsley, half way along the line between Sittingbourne and Ridham. This was opened in 1924. A number of new locomotives were purchased to cope with the increased traffic using the railway. Fresh rolling stock was also acquired and extensive sidings laid down to accommodate the expansion in business. The railway continued to operate twenty-four hours a day throughout World War II. Never were the mills closed down because of any failure to get supplies through to the works. In 1948 Edward Lloyd was taken over by the large Bowater Group to form an additional part of their papermaking complex. More engines were purchased and the line well maintained. The most noticeable acquisition in post-war years was the new Bagnall articulated 0-4-4-0 tank engine named *Monarch*. The line was working at its peak in the late 1950s, when there were no economic argument, but felt that part of the line should be preserved in recognition of its valuable service and interesting history. Consequently the firm contacted the Locomotive Club of Great Britain in 1969. They handed over the section of the line, a mile or so long, between Kemsley Down and Sittingbourne stations. They also donated three 0-4-2 saddle tanks, *Leader, Premier* and *Mellor*, and three 0-6-2 tank engines named *Alpha, Triumph* and *Superb*.

A journey down the line

The journey itself is quite varied. Starting at Sittingbourne the line moves north to cross Milton Creek. The surroundings here are not particularly attractive. The tracks are carried by a quarter-mile viaduct through an area of light industry and much debris. Milton Creek itself is not a clear stretch of water, but has been polluted by effluent from the paper mill.

The scenery improves once the Creek has been crossed. Marshy fields give way to a small orchard and Milton Regis church is visible. There are refreshments at both stations, as well as souvenir shops. A grassed picnic area has been established at Kemsley, together with swings for children. Parties are welcomed, though advance warning is preferred. Sittingbourne station can be reached from the British Rail town station in Milton Road. There are regular trains to here from Charing Cross, Waterloo, London Bridge and Victoria.

Stock

There is a wide variety of rolling stock preserved on the railway. At first the line was worked by teams of horses, but it was decided to change to steam, and three 0-4-2 saddle tanks were purchased, from Kerr-Stuart. These were manufactured in 1905 and introduced on the line three years later. Two of these have been preserved. They are No. 886, named *Premier*, and No. 926 *Leader*. These locomotives sufficed until 1920 when the first 0-6-2, *Superior*, was purchased, another Kerr-Stuart engine. Five more 0-6-2Ts followed between 1922 and 1940, four brand new and manufactured by Bagnall, and one second-hand Manning Wardle built in 1915. Three of the Bagnalls, *Alpha, Triumph* and *Superb*, have been retained at Sittingbourne,

A Sittingbourne and Kemsley Railway train threads its way between the pipelines in an industrial setting on the former Bowaters Paper Mills line. (Brian Stephenson)

less than 13 locomotives at work on the railway. The line was not only used to carry pulp and newsprint, but also to carry workmen to the mills, and so performed a passenger as well as a freight function.

In 1965 Bowaters called in a time-and-motion study group to assess the railway's efficiency. By this time railways generally were being closed down and steam engines were being withdrawn. Public opinion was against the line. The study concluded that the firm would be better off closing the line and employing a fleet of lorries. Bowater's reluctantly accepted this

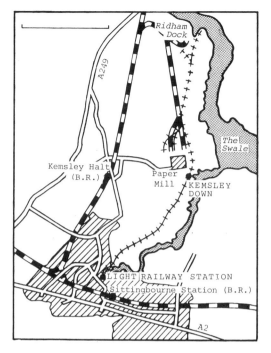

whilst the remaining engine, *Conqueror*, together with the Manning Wardle, *Chevalier*, now work on the Whipsnade and Umfolozi narrow gauge line. All the engines have outside frames, and special spark-arresting chimneys, a vital requirement in a paper mill. The 0-6-2 tank engines have prominent sand boxes fitted on top of their boilers, which, with their wide-topped chimneys, give them a pleasantly 'British Colonial' outline. A further Bagnall engine is present – the 2-4-0 Fireless engine *Unique*, which of course has no need of a spark-arresting chimney for it has no fire and takes its steam secondhand from the paper mill's own supply.

In addition, the Light Railway Company has acquired a number of types of narrow-gauge locomotives from elsewhere. There is a Hunslet diesel inherited from Bowaters. In October 1972 this loco was named *Victor* by the actor Richard Hearne. There is a Ruston and Hornsby diesel, No. 434403, which has been named *Edward Lloyd* after the first owner of the railway. It was built in 1961 and formerly worked on the Whipsnade Zoo Railway from whom it was purchased in 1972. On static display are three small standard-gauge engines. The earliest is a

Peckett 0-4-0 saddle tank, No. 614, *Bear*, built in 1896. Larger is the Hawthorn Leslie 0-4-0ST *Swanscombe No. 4*, which dates from 1928, whilst the third is yet another Fireless, this time built by Andrew Barclay of Kilmarnock in 1925.

There is a variety of passenger coaches on the line. They include five former workmen's vehicles (one for staff use), an open coach constructed by the railway in 1971, and two open standees for use at peak periods. A semi-open coach with a welded tubular steel framework has also been built by the Company for passengers. Four interesting passenger coaches from the nearby Chattenden and Upnor Light Railway were obtained thirdhand from the Welshpool and Llanfair Light Railway, having been used to inaugurate passenger services on that line in 1963. The C. & U.L.R. was an Admiralty-operated 2 ft 6 in.-gauge line in North Kent which is now closed. Apart from these coaches, one of its engines survives – this is *Chevalier*, now at Whipsnade. Residual from the railway's freight days are the fifty wagons, mostly fitted with bogies. There is a variety of tippers, hoppers, coal and rubbish boxes, wooden- and steel-bodied flats. Some are in general use, while a selection have been restored in their original condition for permanent display.

There is a regular, timetabled service on Saturdays and Sundays from the end of March to mid-October, and extra trains on Easter and Summer Bank Holidays. The journey itself takes about fifteen minutes and there are trains about every half-hour. Full details appear in the British Rail timetable.

The area around
Unfortunately Sittingbourne is not a town with a rich history. The British Rail station on the former London Chatham and Dover Railway is possibly one of the most interesting features of the town. The buildings were erected as early as 1858 and in common with the company's other prestigious stations, the roofs were designed with elegant, delicately curved brackets supported by iron columns. It is a fairly simple brick structure which appears to have been enlarged in the 1870s. The line continued on eastwards either to Dover or Margate and was a popular holiday route for Londoners.

EAST ANGLIA

The Bressingham Steam Museum and Gardens

Alan Bloom is a name known and respected not only in the world of preserved steam but also in the world of hardy plants.

At Bressingham, a small village on the boundary between Norfolk and Suffolk, by the River Waveney, is the embodiment of his vision of a living steam museum. Bressingham Hall offered him scope for both his farming and a horticultural nursery, and space to indulge his passion for steam. Since his purchase of the Hall in 1946, he has established what is now certainly a mecca for those fired by the same passion.

The small beginning was 'Bertha', a traction-engine made by the famous Burrell's of Thetford. From that start, a Steam Museum has grown which is unique not only in having steam engines of all kinds, but also in its setting, within beautiful gardens, a busy farm and a thriving and interesting nursery.

Traction engines and steam wagons continued to arrive at Bressingham throughout the 50s, many in a state of abject deterioration through neglect, but all, in due course, to be lovingly and accurately restored. Steam-engine rallies were arranged there from 1963 on, and in this short space of time the collection of traction engines, steam-rollers, steam-wagons and portable engines was stretching the resources of the owner in time and cash to the limit. All had been purchased from Alan Bloom's own pocket. There are now fourteen engines that once used the roads, and the like of which played a vital part in East Anglian agriculture. Very recently a new exhibition hall has been built for them and

there they may be enjoyed in their bright paint and shining brass-work.

The first visitors to Bressingham came to see the gardens which Mr and Mrs Bloom laid out on an acre of meadow in front of the Hall. To satisfy their love of plants, they allowed plants to grow naturally: island beds were carved out in the extensive lawns, and in them beautiful and often exotically rare plants displayed themselves.

It was in 1958 that, after a few special openings at the request of charitable organizations and for horticultural societies, the gardens were first opened to the public.

A visitor to the gardens in 1961, peering under the 'tilt' which sheltered 'Bertha' from the elements, asked if she could not be brought to life again. This probably really triggered off the chain of happenings which was to make the Bloom collection of steam engines in variety freely available for an enthusiastic public.

Bressingham Hall is now the nerve-centre of 480 acres of land and the estate is an entity. The intertwining of its various activities must be recorded. The farm, the nursery, the gardens, the Steam Museum, and the practical railways are all there on the same site. Each limb has its own particular function and its own unique attraction but all belong to the same body – hence the more than passing references to farm and nursery.

The arrival of railways

Steam railways now enter the scene. Rail locomotion, now the largest and most compellingly interesting part of the whole enterprise at Bressingham, began in a small way. A $9\frac{1}{2}$ in. gauge locomotive, freely modelled on the L.M.S. 4-6-2 Princess class, and built specially for passenger hauling, was purchased in 1964,

1

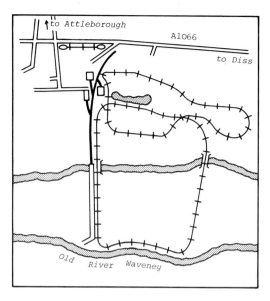

along with five hundred yards of track and some bogie trucks for passengers. Purists will look with a tinge of regret, perhaps, on its under-size wheels, but it is their reduced dimensions which provide a hauling capacity beyond what its size would suggest. In 1965 was born the 'Garden Railway', a 750-yard length of track on the northern boundary of the garden frontage, with turning loops at each end. Here it was discovered that visitors were eager to pay for their ride and this little railway was soon to have the appearance of a mini-commuter line as children, pressed by equally enthusiastic parents, surged forward to savour the thrill of steam propulsion.

The startling success of the Garden Railway encouraged further expansion. The more distant nursery fields (a riot of colour in the summer) and parts of the farm should not be completely out of bounds to visitors (although in a busy commercial enterprise they could not be allowed unlimited access). Alan Bloom's capacity to transform a hard necessity into a pleasant virtue is seen in his conclusion that a railway through the nursery fields, where winter access, because of the nature of the soil, was always hazardous, would serve business needs as well as provide an additional attraction

BELOW: *The famous L.M.S. express 4-6-0 No. 6100* Royal Scot *has found a secure home at Bressingham. As preserved, the locomotive is in its rebuilt form, with taper boiler and double chimney.*

ABOVE: *Combining the best of French and American locomotive engineering practice, the S.N.C.F. 141R class was among Europe's most celebrated classes. No. 141R73 was built by Lima in 1945 and now steams in retirement at Bressingham.* (Phil Wood)

for the visitors who were, after 1965, to make Bressingham a place of pilgrimage.

A journey to North Wales by Alan Bloom and his helper Roger Garnham was the prelude to the first two-foot-gauge railway through the nurseries. At the Penrhyn Slate Quarries, near the North Wales coast, steam had succumbed to diesel traction. Much of the steam equipment had already been sold but two engines, despite their sorry condition, looked capable of restoration at Bressingham. They, together with some track, a few slate-carrying trucks, and some venerable 'toast-rack' coaches provided for the slate workers, ended up at Bressingham. One of the locomotives still bore a name *George Sholto*; the other was not only nameless but also faceless, no more than a rust-ravaged chassis, but fortunately still equipped with its intriguing Walschaerts valve-gear, which holds many people spellbound with its graceful movement.

In 1966 the 'Nursery Line' of half a mile was at work. It ran along the northern edge of a two-acre lake, before doubling back alongside plunge beds where six hundred thousand pot-grown plants and alpines were laid out. It operated from a station very near the entrance to the actual gardens, and became an immediate attraction. Extensions to the line had to be made, and it now provides a ride of over two miles, passing the large Museum building and the end of the lake down to the fen fields. Turning east, with woods and ditches on one side, it reaches a sandy area pleasantly dotted with oaks and birches, before turning westwards again and, having passed several fields of colourful flowers and myriads of pot plants, completes the circuit. The open 'toast-rack'

Männertreu, one of Bressingham's miniature Krupp Pacifics, heads a train on the Waveney Valley line. (James Caldwell)

coaches, while a bit primitive in appearance, are authentic for the gauge, and not only give passengers a clear view of the terrain, but also give them a closer appreciation of the feel and atmosphere of a locomotive at work. The writer has been invited by Mr Bloom to be at the regulator of a locomotive on this line and can vouch for the real thrill of the foot-plate. Four locomotives now share the work there and include *Bronllwyd*, the once-sorry chassis at Penrhyn; *Gwynedd*, also once at Penrhyn and built by the well-known Hunslet Engineering Company of Leeds; and *Eigiau* and *Brunhilde*, both of German origin. The Nursery Line is still as popular as ever and further interest is excited by the discovery, to the surprise of many passengers, that their driver is not only the driver, but also the founder of the whole enterprise. In his overalls, wielding his shovel, he undoubtedly gathers a whole store of visitors' reactions to Bressingham.

Just one narrow-gauge line traversing the farm land soon revealed its inadequacy to meet the demand for rides. So in the winter of 1968–9, another line was laid. The 'Woodland Line' took visitors due south from the station behind the museum, through an attractive avenue of mature trees down into the Waveney valley itself, and over the Bressingham Drain (a relief channel for the inadequate river). The work entailed in pioneering this route through swampy woods, involving bridge-building, drain-digging and track-laying, was daunting, done as it was in winter; it was completed, however, in time to enable the first trip over this line to be made on 17 May 1969. The southern part of this line took passengers on to higher ground where rhododendrons flourished in the spring, among the boxwood and the overhanging oaks and pines.

Four narrow-gauge railways were in operation between 1970 and 1972, the last one making use of the lake a short distance from the Museum. Till 1955 the lake was a small pond, but diggings with tractor-scoop then and later, to provide soil for the raising up of hollows in the adjoining fields and giving body to the soil, had increased it to an area of two acres. Water lilies and other aquatic plants soon established themselves, and with other flora colonizing the edges it had scenic qualities ripe for exploitation. In 1970 a $10\frac{1}{4}$ in. gauge track made a half-mile circuit round the lake, but the 'Lakeside' never became a going concern, due largely to the constraints imposed by the sharp curves. So this railway ceased operation in 1972.

To cope with the ever-growing traffic, a railway of at least 15 in. gauge was needed. At about this time, two locomotives of this gauge in Germany were for sale. A dash to Cologne resulted in the arrival, just before Christmas 1972, of two very attractive 4-6-2 locomotives, and 19 well-appointed coaches. Built by the famous Krupps of Essen in 1937, for use in an exhibition park at Düsseldorf, they were then destined for a similar park by the Rhine at Cologne. But they were never used there, and Cologne's loss of *Rosenkavalier* and *Männertreu* became Bressingham's gain. In building the new 15 in. gauge railway, it soon became clear that a much more attractive line could be made by using only one side of the lake. To do so, however, would involve duplicating the existing Woodland Line. By the opening of the 1973 season, more than a mile of new track had been laid, crossing the Nursery Line on the level, and Bressingham Drain by a new bridge. The Woodland Line has now become the 'Waveney Line', $2\frac{1}{4}$ miles long and following much of the former line's course. While one two-foot-gauge line has had to go, Mr Bloom does not rule out that there may be another one in the future.

Alan Bloom on the footplate of Bronllwyd, *one of the engines rescued from the Penrhyn Slate Quarries which now provide the motive power on the 2 ft gauge Nursery Line. (Alan Bloom)*

Standard-gauge locomotives

The standard-gauge railway locomotive section was the last to be established. It must be said that the standard-gauge engines there dwarf all other exhibits in majesty and beauty.

The over-hasty replacement of steam by diesel traction on British Railways presented enthusiasts with the opportunity of saving for preservation some of the glorious relics of the Age of Steam from the breaker's and cutter's torch. It was open to anyone to acquire a withdrawn locomotive if he could meet the scrap price (measured in thousands of pounds)

together with the transport costs (which might well be more than the locomotive). Railway engines which had thrilled him were still fixed images in the vision of Alan Bloom and the more the vision was pondered the more insistent became its realization.

In 1968, the first standard-gauge locomotive, *William Francis*, the last of its kind in Great Britain, arrived. This locomotive was built on an articulated chassis with four cylinders powering two sets of driving wheels, and was redundant to the Coal Board. Another steam enthusiast, Mr J. R. Price, with the co-operation of the Association of Railway Preservation Societies, purchased it and had it removed from Baddesley Colliery to Bressingham. Its condition was poor, after a long period of neglect. The challenge of restoring it to its original form was a massive one, but the 1970 season saw it running along a track some two hundred yards long.

1951 had been a notable year on the Eastern

No. 70013 Oliver Cromwell *crossing Saddleworth Viaduct with an enthusiasts' special train in 1967. This famous locomotive can now be seen in steam on Bressingham's short standard gauge line.* (J. A. Bodfish)

Region of British Railways. The first B.R.-designed engines, Britannias, were assigned there. Something of a minor revolution in British locomotive design, they were, in 1952, on the line between Ipswich and Norwich which had never been the scene of very high speeds, responsible for the third fastest run in Great Britain. In 1961, Alan Bloom was accorded the privilege of a foot-plate ride from Diss to London on No. 70034, *Thomas Hardy*, of that class. Was this the seed of a later growth at Bressingham?

Under the Transport Act of 1968, certain steam locomotives were to be scheduled for preservation. The capacity of York and Clapham Museums would be insufficient for them – Clapham was due to close in any case. Of the Britannia class, the first of them, No. 70000, *Britannia*, was understandably the one marked for preservation. Steam haulage on British Rail was to cease by the end of 1968, and another of the class No. 70013, *Oliver Cromwell*, recently overhauled at Crewe, was to be used on 'specials' until the final rites of sale for scrap.

But *Oliver Cromwell* was finally allocated to the Bressingham Museum. In the autumn of 1968, by rail from Carlisle to Diss and thence by low-loader on road, it returned to within ear-shot of

Reflected in the waters of the river that gives the line its name, the 15 in. gauge Pacific Rosenkavalier *steams sedately along on the Waveney Valley Line.*

the sounds of its former great exploits. Meanwhile a museum building covering 12,500 square feet had been erected, a pre-condition of B.R. allocating engines to Bressingham.

In another building some twelve miles away at Attleborough, another episode in the saga of railway preservation had begun. In the old goods shed there, known to only a handful of people all sworn to secrecy, stood *Thundersley*, a 4-4-2 tank engine which had earned its keep on the London, Tilbury and Southend Railway. It was scheduled for preservation. The secret storage was necessary because railway relics, and especially any removable parts of locomotives, like name-plates, whistles and brass or copper accessories, had by then become big business, and 'asset-stripping' was growing apace. The Hellifield shed in West Yorkshire, its previous storage place, was insecure, and a move for *Thundersley* from there had become urgent. The museum building at Bressingham was not yet ready to take it. The Norfolk Railway Society found that the Attleborough goods shed could be made available. With a signalman on duty in the box opposite, its safety there seemed assured. Moreover, members of the Society, under the skilled direction and enthusiasm of Mr David (Bill) Harvey, ex-Shedmaster at Norwich, would undertake her restoration. In March 1968, the resplendent *Thundersley* emerged from her hiding-place to move to Bressingham, the first B.R. locomotive there on permanent loan (*Oliver Cromwell* was first in steam there on 22 September 1968).

The Steam Museum was now firmly established. British Rail, satisfied and pleased with the facilities, were to make other locomotives available and another was soon to join the three then there. Fittingly enough a 2-6-4 tank engine built by the L.M.S. in 1934 to replace the *Thundersley* class was allocated to Bressingham. Two industrial locomotives 'Beckton No. 25' and 'Beckton No. 1', had spent their life in London's gas-making town Beckton, on the Essex side of the Thames.

Butlin's Holiday Camps' proprietors had not been slow to appreciate the magnetic pull of a steam locomotive. Two of the most famous engines on the Midland Region (born in the L.M.S. era) had been allocated to holiday camps:

the first was No. 6100, *Royal Scot*, built in 1927 by one of the most famous locomotive-building concerns in the country, the North British Locomotive Company of Glasgow, to inaugurate the big-engine policy of the former L.M.S. In the salt-laden air of Skegness, she had deteriorated sadly. In 1971 this historic locomotive came into care at Bressingham, where she was restored at terrific cost and steamed. The second was the last pre-1939 development in locomotive engineering, the *Duchess of Sutherland*, built in 1938; a massive locomotive of 4-6-2 wheel arrangement, she had hauled the express trains on the West Coast route to Scotland in the late thirties, among them the Coronation Scot; she was one of the most powerful class of that time. In 1971 as well, the *Duchess* was hauled 'dead' from Ayr to Diss, to be followed by one of the widely-loved 'Brighton Terrier' 0-6-0 tank engines, *Martello*, and a former stable-mate of *Royal Scot* at Skegness, a 0-4-0 which had seen service at Southampton docks.

More engines were to follow: *Solomon*, a small shunting engine, was removed from a plinth at Dagenham, where it had served at Messrs Samuel Williams Wharf Ltd; and *Millfield*, a crane-engine from Sunderland (another presentation by Mr J. M. Price). Another ex-Great-Eastern engine was to come home, when the last steam locomotive to be stationed in East Anglia, a 0-6-0 of the powerful J17 class, one of the national collection, arrived to stand alongside the larger passenger engines.

With thirteen standard-gauge engines in his charge at Bressingham, Alan Bloom might well have been pardoned for declaring his hands to be full. They were indeed, but in 1975 two 'foreigners' were to find happy exile on Norfolk soil. Both these engines can only be described as gigantic, and, in external appearance, they are strangers to the British railway scene. Because they were conspicuously fine examples of later developments outside Britain, and in danger of being lost to posterity, they were purchased by Mr Bloom.

One is a German locomotive, an example of one of the most famous and numerous classes to run anywhere in the world – the *Kriegsloks* or Deutsche Reichsbahn class 52. Over nine thousand of these rugged two-cylinder 2-10-0s were built

Built in Sweden for service in Norway, this attractive little 2-6-0 now carries the name King Haakon VII *in commemoration of having hauled the train that carried the Norwegian monarch into exile during World War II.*

to follow Hitler's armies all over Europe and by the end of World War II there was hardly a European railway that did not have some of them among its stock. No. 5856 was built in 1944 and sent for service in occupied Norway. It was absorbed into N.S.B. stock at the end of hostilities and overhauled in 1953 before being stored away in a tunnel to be remembered some twenty years later. It well illustrates German thoroughness and attention to detail.

The second is one of thirteen hundred built under the Marshall Plan to aid war-torn Europe: French railways had been devastated in the war, and the Lima works in Ohio combined elements of French and American practice to produce these heavy, 156-ton, successful locomotives. Known as S.N.C.F. class 141R and nicknamed 'Les Braves Americaines', they lasted until the very end of French steam in the early 1970s. They are remembered with affection by enthusiasts as being Europe's loudest steam locomotives: once you have heard the sound of a 141R at full regulator on a heavy train, you will never forget it! Both these locomotives are in running order.

The length of standard-gauge track is now over five hundred yards and passengers have been able to ride for that distance on a locomotive.

Long efforts to establish the Steam Museum as a charitable trust came to fruition in 1973 and Alan Bloom is very happy that it will continue to give pleasure and provide interest for future generations.

Other attractions
Bressingham provides much for the lovers of

9

A familiar sight throughout nearly every railway system in Europe after World War II were the Kriegslok 2-10-0s of Deutsche Reichsbahn class 52. Now living on in peacetime is Peer Gynt, *imported from Norway in 1975. (*Phil Wood*)*

steam. It offers more.

There are the steam roundabouts retrieved from Scotland in 1967; 'Flora's Gallopers', powered by the authentic engine, works overtime in the summer months.

In the new exhibition hall, a host of interesting relics, ranging from guards' lamps to a steam-driven fire-fighting pump of 1890 (used locally by the Norwich firm of Jeremiah Colman), catch the eye. Plans are in hand to extend this hall to accommodate further exhibits and provide an internal gallery and a shop selling railway souvenirs and books.

There are the gardens, several refreshment points and a tea room, no restrictions on those wishing to picnic, and numerous vantage points for the photographer.

Enormous costs are incurred in maintaining the Steam Museum; the restoration of *Duchess of Sutherland* cost £17,000; one steaming of a large engine on an open day costs £80. A permanent staff of eight and a part-time one of two are needed. But admission charges are very reasonable.

The North Norfolk Railway

It is fortunate that of the 183¼ miles of the former Midland and Great Northern Joint Railway, the three miles that now see passenger trains running again are without doubt the most scenically attractive of the whole system. The three miles are to be found on the North Norfolk coast, in a designated 'Area of Outstanding Natural Beauty'. They link the attractive seaside town of Sheringham with Weybourne: the village is some two miles west of Sheringham, but the station lies at the foot of a ridge about one mile inland. Weybourne Station is planned to be a terminus only temporarily, as the North Norfolk Railway Company, which operates the line, hopes to extend the line, by about a mile, over the beautiful Kelling Heath.

The closure; the beginnings of the Preservation Society
In early 1959, the axe was laid to the very trunk of the vast M. & G.N.J.R. system; passenger traffic over most of the long west–east axis from Little Bytham in Lincolnshire to Great Yarmouth on the east Norfolk coast was withdrawn. The railway enthusiasts of the late fifties resolved that the railway should not be allowed to become extinct. The M. & G.N.J.R. was an odd intruder into Great Eastern territory but it inspired a great respect and affection among those who lived near it or used it for cross-country journeys, to visit Norfolk and Suffolk seaside resorts, to go to Norwich, or perhaps journey to school in its distinctive yellowish-brown coaches. 28 February 1959 saw withdrawal of passenger services over all but about twenty miles; some eighty miles of the system were to be closed completely.

The last train on the day of closure left Yarmouth South Town at 10.48 p.m. for Melton Constable, the nerve-centre of the system which once had its own locomotive-building works. A band of loyal enthusiasts travelled on it; also, they left on the station typed notices: 'Save the M. & G.N. Join the Preservation Society'. These typed messages were to start something. Ideas exchanged on the train changed a concept into a reality – a Preservation Society to re-open part of the line in Norfolk.

Among those present at the birth of the Society were David Rees of Ilford, Founder of the Society, and Bernard Amies of Worstead. Bernard Amies, from his farm-house home, had watched the distinctive mustard-yellow M. & G.N. locomotives climbing (with protest) the Honing bank. When steam trains stopped, he was determined to 'get the puffers running again somewhere'. He has remained faithful to this ambition for over twenty eventful years.

Over-optimistic plans
The first Newsletter of the Society, issued in April 1960, suggested grandiose plans for re-opening the Aylsham (North)–Yarmouth Beach, and Melton Constable–Norwich (City) sections, and even sections to the west of the system, including King's Lynn–Fakenham, Sutton Bridge–Bourne, and Peterborough–Sutton Bridge; in all, the suggested routes totalled 119 miles. None of these was really viable. Parts of the line between Aylsham and Yarmouth were to become re-aligned roads, and the Beach Station at Yarmouth was to become a terminal for buses instead of trains. No local authority support would be forthcoming for this plan.

The Melton Constable–Norwich (City) line had a lot in its favour. The countryside round Melton Constable is attractive, and the small town, built, like a small-scale Crewe or Swindon, as a railway town, was the hub of the system of radiating lines. Moreover, as the M. & G.N. works, it had sheds and other facilities for sorting and maintaining locomotives and rolling stock. But it was fortunate that the difficulties in the way of this plan were too formidable to overcome: hindsight was to show that accessibility and outstanding scenic or other special interests are essential to the success of a preserved railway.

The first stock
In 1961 the society began locomotive preservation: it planned to buy two locomotives. One was the last remaining B12, a 4-6-0 class of express engine which had done yeoman service on the G.E.R. system for over forty years; No. 61572 was soon to be withdrawn. The other was No. 65469, a J15 class 0-6-0 tender engine.

11

British Rail quoted prices of £1500 for the B12 and £850 for the J15. An appeal fund was promptly launched.

Track projects

It was proposed to set up the 'Central Norfolk Railway Company' with a share capital of £17,000, the sum estimated as being the minimum required to relay track and operate a railway for just over two miles southwards from Melton Constable to Hindolveston. While this was conceived as the fore-runner of a more extensive project, with long-range sights still set on Norwich City station, the operation of this short stretch would surely convince British Railways that M. & G.N.R.P.S. members could run a railway. For the reason that they were not yet operating a railway British Rail made it a condition that the name of the company should be changed to Central Norfolk Enterprises Ltd. A short time, however, was to show that insufficient capital would be attracted to this venture. But at least by 1964 the Society took possession of two locomotives from B.R., Nos. 61572 and 65462, the second being a substitute J15, replacing No. 65469, which had been found to have a badly cracked frame.

Further negotiations with British Rail were fruitless: the Society could gain no option on a length of line. Its fortunes were now at their nadir. 'M. & G.N.' had always been jokingly supposed to stand for 'Muddle and Get Nowhere'. This seemed to be true of the Preservation Society.

Five years, in railway preservation, is a long time. Not only does it become more difficult and costly to acquire the material of railway operations as time goes on, but hope continually deferred is in danger of dying. It was not till 1964 that further developments produced realistic proposals. The last passenger train was run between Melton Constable and Sheringham. This section was most attractive, especially at the northern extremity between Holt and Sheringham, where the line ran over heathlands, between the hills carved by the ice ages, to the attractive holiday town (which owed its development as a resort to the coming of the Midland and Great Northern in 1887).

Acquiring the eleven-mile length now became the aim. But B.R. valued it at £85,000, and early in 1965 a scrap-dealer started lifting the track. B.R. was persuaded, however, to leave the three miles between Weybourne and Sheringham *in situ*, and to give the re-openers a chance to raise a much lower amount. In August 1965, Central Norfolk Enterprises, aided by loans, paid £17,000 for the track.

The railway is established

Now that the railway had a physical base, with a station headquarters at Weybourne, the project, six years in the waiting, had reached the jumping-off point. The enthusiasts now set to work. Weybourne Station became full of life at weekends and members scoured the countryside for all kinds of railway equipment. Two modern diesel-engined railbuses were purchased, with a view to future stand-by use; members of the locomotive department were busy on the two steam locomotives, then housed at sheds at March in Cambridgeshire; a M. &

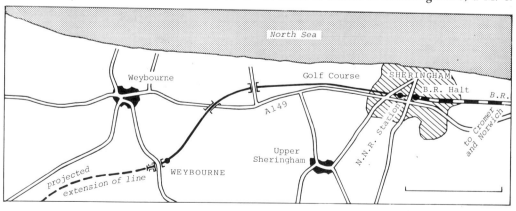

Colwyn, carriages and cows' parsley! An idyllic summer scene on the N.N.R. (Brian Fisher)

G.N.R. gangers' trolley, buffer-stops and an ex-G.E.R. bogie coach were bought, the coach a joint purchase by the home Society, the G.E.R. Group, and the London Railway Preservation Society. These were followed by a 'quad' set (four coaches articulated on five bogies instead of eight) designed by Gresley.

In January 1967, the old M. & G.N. station at Sheringham was abandoned by British Rail, and a new halt built to the east of the level crossing. The Society accepted terms for a lease on the old station until it should be sold; the disused station then became the headquarters. In June, the two steam locomotives, two diesel railbuses, the G.E.R. coach and the 'quad' set arrived at Sheringham to the accompaniment of much television and press publicity.

Equipment of all kinds continued to arrive at Sheringham; No. 65462 (the J15) was steamed at Easter 1968 for testing purposes, and Mr Geoffrey Sircom loaned a splendid L. & N.W.R. Directors' saloon. A third locomotive, an industrial 0-6-0 saddle tank (made by Peckett's of Bristol, it had worked with the National Coal Board) joined the two G.E.R. engines. A Colman's Mustard goods van, another Directors' saloon (Lancashire and Yorkshire Railway) and an open second-class B.R. coach arrived on the scene.

The preserved section is part of the former Eastern and Midlands Railway from Melton Constable to Cromer Beach. This line was authorized by Parliament in 1880 and opened to Holt in October 1884, being extended to Cromer by a further Act in June 1887. The E. & M. was subsequently taken over by the Midland and Great Northern Joint Company on 1 July 1893. In 1923 it became part of the L.N.E.R.

The first railway to Cromer had been projected by the East Norfolk with assistance from the Great Eastern, the extension from North Walsham, more or less due south of Cromer, being completed in March 1877. It fell under complete G.E.R. control in 1881. The purpose of the E. & M. branch to Cromer was to provide a direct link to this popular holiday resort from the North and Midlands, a link which was not reliant on the Great Eastern. In contrast with most other British regions, East Anglia was virtually controlled by one monopolistic railway, the G.E.R. However, most of its lines radiated from

London with connecting branches in between. There was room, therefore, for a railway to be constructed on an east–west axis across the northern quarter of the region. The branch from Melton Constable to Cromer was simply a further extension of the Midland and Great Northern's rival route from the Midlands, that via Spalding, in the Fens, to South Lynn, Fakenham, North Walsham and Yarmouth. There was also a branch from Melton Constable south-east to Norwich City.

The venerable J15 class 0-6-0 sporting G.E.R. wartime grey livery, runs along the clifftops on its way to Weybourne on the North Norfolk Railway. (Geoff King)

ABOVE: *L.N.E.R. class B12 No. 61572 is the only preserved example of that classic British locomotive type, the inside-cylinder 4-6-0.*

RIGHT: *Capturing the atmosphere of East Anglian branchline travel in bygone days, the J15 class No. 564 trundles on towards Weybourne on the North Norfolk Railway. (D. Tuck)*

Continued growth

1969 was the year that saw the beginning of assured success: Sir John Betjeman accepted the Presidency of the Society and the North Norfolk Railway Company Ltd was set up to raise money by offering shares, and to negotiate for a Light Railway Order to enable the running of trains for the public.

The Company prospectus showed the need for a share capital of £11,000 at once, and for one whose stated prospects were of never paying a dividend, the response was astonishing. £14,000 was raised in the statutory forty days.

To bring the railway up to the operating and safety standards needed for a Light Railway Order meant unremitting hard work and a steady inflow of cash. Both were now forthcoming as never before. Membership of the M. & G.N. Society leapt ahead, as only members were able to have steam rides on open days.

The more settled period attracted more locomotives, largely saddle tanks, and more rolling stock was bought, partly from the proceeds of the sale of books and souvenirs, and the profits from rail tours. More and more exhibits arrived for the museum; the station at

A contrast in ancient and modern motive power at Sheringham. Hunslet saddletank Ring Haw *waits to depart with the afternoon train to Weybourne. The two British Rail diesel railbuses are used to meet off-peak travel needs. (Paul Barber)*

Sheringham was re-painted in M. & G.N. tan-and-stone; a shop was set up in the station; part of the L. & N.W.R. Directors' Saloon became a refreshment room.

A run-round loop was provided at Weybourne, sidings laid, and the re-erection of the Norwich (City) engine-shed begun; at Sheringham, more roads were laid, a water tank erected, an inspection-pit dug, and locomotives, wagons and coaches repaired and re-painted. Temporary track from B.R.'s halt, across Station Road into Sheringham station, was laid overnight to enable two Southern Region Pullman cars of the famous Brighton Belle to come on

loan from Ind Coope, to be restored at their new home at Sheringham.

A rigorous and approved series of training courses for drivers, firemen, guards and others started and the rapid progress the railway was now making culminated in the granting of a Light Railway Order to British Rail in 1973. This was transferred to the North Norfolk Railway in April 1976. Thereafter a service for the public was inaugurated.

The restoration of passenger services between Sheringham and Weybourne was followed by the recommissioning of the J15, initially in G.E.R. grey livery as No. 564 and later in a temporary coat of L.N.E.R. black as No. 7564. Enthusiasts eagerly await the day when she once more assumes her original Great Eastern royal blue livery. In the meantime, the sight of this veteran pounding the gradients to Weybourne at the head of a short train of compartment stock is pure nostalgia for those who recall East Anglian railway byways in the 1930s.

What to see, and a journey down the line
Visitors should start at Sheringham station, where they will find the museum, and a shop offering a wide range of railway and holiday books, cards and souvenirs. Where railway directors once sipped their brandy, visitors may now sip their tea and relax comfortably. At one end of the platform is a grassed area with small tables and sunshades, a favourite spot for watching trains leave for Weybourne.

From Sheringham, the line rises on a fairly severe gradient. Beyond the summit lies a succession of glorious views for two miles or more. Leaving behind the western outskirts of the town, the golf course comes into view on the right. Then a V-shaped depression on the course reveals a triangle of sea. To the left, the land rises to rounded and wooded hills. As the line turns away from the sea, the view is over a typical Norfolk agricultural landscape of fields and meadows. Weybourne Station is the present end of the line, but the prospects of the line climbing another mile or so to the highest point of Kelling Heath are encouraging. The area round Weybourne Station is pleasant undulating country and the station itself offers refreshments and books.

The Nene Valley Railway

The Reverend Richard Paten, also a Chartered Engineer, was a curate in the cathedral city of Peterborough in the late sixties. When, in 1968, he purchased for preservation a British Railways class 5 mixed-traffic locomotive, No. 73050, he could have had no idea that it was to lead to a five-and-a-half-mile steam railway running through a large pleasure park.

No. 73050, then nameless, came straight out of service from Patricroft Shed to Peterborough. The original idea was that it should be preserved on a plinth outside the Technical College there, as a reminder of the city's railway and engineering heritage. But so good was its condition that Mr Paten and four or five fellow enthusiasts decided to undertake what little restoration was needed – mainly painting – to preserve it as a working exhibit. A local engineering firm, Baker Perkins, offered a siding where the work could be done.

Now in possession of a fine locomotive that could run under its own steam, Mr Paten – and his colleagues, now growing in number – felt strongly that the loco must be more than a static display. The sympathetic manager of the British

Sugar Corporation factory at Peterborough welcomed the engine to their sidings, where it was soon steamed and giving footplate rides. It was to provide more than pleasure at the factory, for when a boiler there was out of commission, No. 73050 deputized as a stationary boiler most successfully. The owner was invited to leave it there. The Peterborough Locomotive Society had been born.

In 1971 a second locomotive came into the hands of the Society, a little 0-6-0 saddle tank engine *Jack's Green*. It had worked in the nearby Nassington iron-ore quarries, whence it travelled under its own steam.

With the dispersal of locomotives from the Clapham Museum pending, the Society, with the support of local authorities, conceived the idea of having a railway museum at the old Peterborough East Station, with a working steam section on the former L. & N.W.R. line then *in situ* as far as Oundle. While the scheme was not acceptable to the government, it did raise the possibility of a steam centre at Peterborough. About this time, the Peterborough Development Corporation was planning Nene Park, a pleasure area some five miles in length and straddling the River Nene from Orton westwards to Castor. Could the old L. & N.W.R. metals through the area be the basis of a

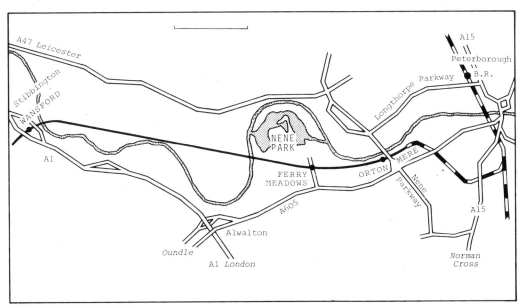

B.R. Standard 5MT 4-6-0 No. 73050 has been named City of Peterborough. *The locomotive is on the turntable at Wansford. (*Laurie Manns)

pleasure railway through the park? A feasibility study was undertaken by the Society and it was concluded that it could be done.

In 1972 the plan was presented to the Development Corporation, just as B.R. were preparing to abandon the line. The Corporation looked favourably on another amenity in their proposed pleasure park, and in 1973 purchased the single track from Longueville Junction to Yarwell Junction, paying £66,000 for some six miles of track, which was then leased to what had now become the Peterborough Railway Society Limited, a registered charity.

Meanwhile, locomotives continued to arrive. The firm of Derek Crouch offered another 0-6-0 saddle tank, formerly used on the Wissington Light Railway in south-west Norfolk, which served a beet sugar factory. Named *Derek Crouch*, it is now with the Society on permanent loan. In 1973 arrived two more 0-6-0 engines (one of which was later to be named *Thomas* by the Reverend W. Awdry), and a coach was purchased from the profits of open days and

from members' gifts and subscriptions. This was to provide rides behind No. 73050, now aptly named *City of Peterborough* (its nominal owner-ship had now passed to the City Council, who in turn leased it to the Society on a 99-year lease).

Wansford became the operating centre for the Society in 1974, and locomotives and stock were transferred there. The station there offered great possibilities, with space for additional sidings, an engine shed and car parking. Unfortunately, the station building, built of local stone and architecturally of enough interest to be 'listed', is in private hands. Across the road from the station is Wansford signal box, the largest preserved fully-equipped box in the country.

The Society ran its first steam trains under B.R. supervision with the approval of the Railway Inspectorate, until, at the end of 1974, B.R. were happy to allow the Society to run its trains unsupervised. The first trains ran for about one mile, westwards through the 616-yard Wansford Tunnel, to Yarwell. The tunnel has some interesting features, among them being the incorporation in the eastern portal of some two-foot-square granite sleeper blocks from the early days of railways.

Now that the Society had earned the full

ABOVE: *'Thomas the Tank Engine' puts on a happy face at Wansford whilst marshalling a rake of former S.R. electric stock during one of the N.V.R.'s celebrated 'Eurosteam' days.* (R.N. Mann)

BELOW: *The stirring sight of a Nord 4-cylinder compound accelerating through the English countryside. This classic French locomotive is finished in an attractive chocolate-brown livery.* (R. N. Mann)

ABOVE: *Danish class F 0-6-0 No. 656 stands in platform 3 at Wansford with a Nene Valley permanent way train which includes a Smith Rodley 5-ton steam crane of 1934. (John Titlow)*

OPPOSITE: *The N.V.R. runs a commercial freight service for an insulation company, moving stock from Stirling to a depot in the former station yard at Wansford. The Swedish oil-burning engine, 2-6-4 No. 1928 (built in 1953) pulls the through-train on the last leg. (Nene Valley Railway)*

confidence of British Rail, the Development Corporation and the local authorities, and was firmly established at Wansford, its suitability as a home for preserved locomotives was noticed by other owners. A great advantage of Wansford is its easy physical connection with B.R. metals, and other locomotives, mainly small industrial types, continued to arrive. In 1973, Suffolk farmer Richard Hurlock asked the Society if a home could be found there for a Swedish tank locomotive, a 2-6-4, No. 1928: the difficulty here was the dimensions of the locomotive, which is too large for the British loading gauge. A survey of the line revealed that little work would be needed to accommodate larger continental engines, and the idea of being able to operate continental trains offered new attractions; the Railway Inspectorate was approached for advice on the matter. The Society decided to adopt the Berne loading gauge along the Nene Valley Railway, although running over-size stock does present problems, like setting platform faces further back for clearance, which means an unacceptable gap between platform and footboards on British stock, and involves fitting wider boards. Signals too have to be set back, and the six-foot way between the tracks has to be widened by some two feet.

In 1975 Richard Hurlock offered two more continental locomotives on permanent loan: one came from Danish Railways, 0-6-0 No. 656; the other was another Swedish loco, 2-6-2 tank engine No. 1178, built in 1914. The closure of Ashford Steam Centre in Kent meant that a magnificent French locomotive would be homeless. This was a Nord engine (Northern Railway of France), one of the 3500 class of 4-6-0s which set new standards of locomotive performance in Europe between the wars. No. 3628, now at Wansford, is in impeccable condition; whilst its appearance may be unusual to British eyes, with many of the mechanisms, pipes and apparatus exposed, it is perhaps exposure of its works which makes it all the more interesting. Built in 1911, it had 54 years in main-line service and is the only working example of its class left. Among the famous trains it headed is the Rome

Express. It belongs to the Nord Locomotive Preservation Group, who can now see it hauling continental coaching stock along the Nene Valley Railway. It has been used in filming the B.B.C. series 'Secret Army'.

The Nene Valley Railway has now considerably strengthened its collection of continental locomotives and rolling stock by importing one of the handsome Swedish B class 4-6-0s, No. 1797. This has been much in demand for filming purposes since its arrival at Wansford and has consequently retained its protective bituminous coating to provide an engine in authentic 'dirty' working appearance. Another impressive Scandinavian arrival is Danish S class express suburban tank No. 740 whose appearance is dominated by a pair of enormous smoke deflectors – to British eyes an unusual feature on a tank engine. Two German tank engines, a 64 class 2-6-2T and an 80 class 0-6-0T now bring a Teutonic air to proceedings. Both were imported into this country towards the end of steam working on the Deutsche Bundesbahn and were originally housed on the Severn Valley Railway and at Steamtown, Carnforth respectively. Two more locomotives from the continent are anticipated – an Italian 740 class 2-8-0 and one of the famous Prussian P8 4-6-0s, this one an example now running in Romania.

But to redress the balance, and to ensure a prominent British component in the Nene Valley Railway's international brigade, it is the appearance of *Britannia* at the head of a train that lends a special atmosphere at departure time. The prototype B.R. Pacific of 1951 was the first of the 999 Riddles Standard designs to emerge after nationalization. She was a milestone in British locomotive practice, since she was the first two-cylinder Pacific built for use in this country. Had it not been for the introduction of diesels, it is very likely that several hundred 'Britannias' would have been built, for use in all parts of the country. As it was, only 55 engines of the class were constructed and they suffered the fate of other steam locos, being sent to the scrapheap in the prime of their lives after only about 15 years' service. *Britannia* was set aside after withdrawal for official preservation, but was replaced at the

last minute by *Oliver Cromwell*. Thus it was left to a group of amateur enthusiasts to save this historic engine for posterity. Now, restored to full working order, she has a special majesty; the exclusiveness of a celebrity.

Southern Railway Battle of Britain class No. 34081 92 Squadron has also been saved from the rust of Barry scrapyard and is fast approaching its return to steaming condition.

The Southern Electric Group owns six third-rail electric multiple coaches, and asked if these could be moved from Ashford to Wansford. These vehicles are air-braked, whereas all British preserved steam locomotives are vacuum-braked. At Wansford there were air-braked continental locomotives needing air-braked stock. The arrival of the ex-Southern vehicles meant that trains could now be made up behind the continental locomotives. The six coaches are in the old Southern olive green.

The S.R. electric coaches now take their turn on passenger duties with a rake of Danish steel-bodied post-war saloon vehicles in maroon livery. These are very appropriately complemented by a Wagon-Lits dining car No. 2975 in full C.I.W.L. royal blue and gold colours.

Peter Brotherhoods of Peterborough undertook the mechanical overhaul of *Jack's Green*, and the apprentices at Baker Perkins overhauled, as part of their training, a petrol-driven Wickham trolley. A small four-wheeled diesel locomotive bought from British Oil and Cake Mills in 1972 was rebuilt by Perkins Engines, and they installed one of their own engines. Named *Frank* after one of the Perkins family, it carries a plaque naming five other firms associated in restoring it.

Other firms have helped the project in their own special way. A.R.C. have provided blocks for platform building; Dowmac, concrete sleepers; Ready-Mix, concrete. An interest-free

OPPOSITE: *Don't be misled by the locomotive numbers – the Nene Valley Railway has not yet imported any East German stock! The two Swedish locomotives are in disguise for their starring role in the James Bond film 'Octopussy'.* (John Rudd)

British Hudswell Clarke industrial 0-6-0T Thomas *makes a night-time sortie with German Prairie tank No. 64.305.* (John Titlow)

loan from the Peterborough City Council enabled the Society to buy an old cattle-market building which is being turned into a serviceable engine shed at Wansford. The Northamptonshire County Council have made a gift of Barnwell Station Office, and Ross Foods are assisting in its restoration. It is to serve as a sales centre at the station. A water tower is being built, and Perkins Engines have found the site of the engine shed a very useful testbed for their diesel engines. The Manpower Services Commission sees the railway as a viable enterprise, and made a grant available in 1976 enabling the Society to employ thirteen men.

Preserved railways are pleasure railways, but already the Nene Valley Railway has served commercial interests. A boat-building firm, Seasteel, based at Nassington Quarries, has provided freight traffic, and one of the engines has been the motive power for the track-lifting trains between Peterborough and Yarwell.

Steam trains operate on weekends and Bank Holidays between Wansford and Orton Mere. Family tickets for train rides are issued. On steam days, refreshments, souvenirs and books are available. On other days, the station at Wansford is open to visitors, who are welcome to look around and photograph the rolling stock. The Nene Park itself offers photographers numerous lineside vantage points.

The Park around

The future of the Nene Valley Railway is indissolubly linked with that of the Nene Park. This is the result of the Development Corporation's insistence on assuring an expanding population of a wide range of leisure facilities. The Park runs for some five miles either side of the Nene, between Orton in the east and Castor in the west. It is bounded by the A47 road to the north and the A605 to the south. The railway cuts a straight line through this attractive stretch of pastoral countryside, crossing the river twice. There are 500 acres of grassland, woodland and lakes with facilities for sailing, fishing, riding and golf. Miles of footpaths, horse routes and cycleways connect the various facilities and at Ferry Meadows, not far from the Nene Valley Railway's station serving that area of the park, is a fine half-mile $10\frac{1}{4}$ in. gauge steam railway offering rides alongside the lake.

24

The Stour Valley Railway

Preservation

The Stour Valley Railway began as a preservation society on 24 December 1968, when a number of enthusiasts decided that a part of the great Great Eastern Railway must be preserved. The first objective, somewhat ambitious in hindsight, was to save a part, or even the whole, of the line from Sudbury to Shelford on the main Cambridge–Liverpool Street line. Passenger services had been withdrawn beyond Sudbury. The part finally selected was between Sudbury and Long Melford, just over three miles, but British Rail sold the track before sufficient funds could be attracted to the scheme to enable the Society to purchase it.

A sound financial base is a *sine qua non* of railway preservation, so in February 1970 a private company, the Branch Line Preservation Society, was formed. Its intentions were specific: to raise funds and negotiate with British Rail to purchase a part of the Stour Valley Branch. As the Marks Tey–Sudbury branch was, unhappily, a candidate for closure, the company felt that funds might be more readily attracted to a project which would save a stretch of line presently being worked, so that not only track-bed but also track could be acquired.

On the Stour Valley branch, stations had been reduced to unstaffed halts. Chappel and Wakes Colne, perched on the northern slope of the Colne Valley, and with a spacious goods yard, goods shed and signal box, would serve well as headquarters for the Society and home for locomotives and rolling stock. The need for some three to five miles of track was still in the forefront of the Society's plans and two stretches of line of that length were kept in view: northwards from Chappel to Bures and southwards from Chappel to Marks Tey.

In December 1970, the Society moved to Chappel and Wakes Colne station. The station building, signal box and goods shed bore the customary marks of neglect and the stealthy visits of vandals. The goods yard was a scene of depressing and daunting dereliction. Part of it had become a convenient dumping ground for ash from Colchester locomotive yard and weeds and bushes had colonized it. All the track had been lifted, and lay piled up in heaps ready for removal by scrap merchants. Among the debris in the yard was found the broken remains of the lever frame from the signal box, now no more than a shell. Prompt action by two members some time earlier had saved the track. The contractors and British Rail co-operated in giving the Company time in which to purchase the waiting piles of track. Gifts and loans came in quickly to make this possible.

The hard work of re-laying track and points then began. More track was brought in, too: a private siding from Margaretting near Chelmsford, and the Acton sidings of Cerebos Salt, given to the Society by the Company. In about three months, a third of a mile of track had been re-laid in the goods yard.

Initial stock

The railway first provided rides for members on 13 March 1971, the train being drawn by a 0-6-0 saddle tank *Gunby* of the War Department

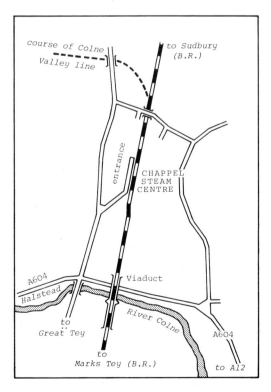

The Stour Valley Railway operates at present only within the former yard of Chappel and Wakes Colne B.R. station, the site being known as the Chappel Steam Centre. The 'main' line is only a quarter of a mile or so, and, accepting this limitation, the Centre concentrates on details of railway operation, permanent way, etc. Visitors have unusually free access to everything within the site, and Chappel can provide opportunities to see details which cannot be closely studied on more 'conventional' preserved railways. An example is the lever frame in this picture of No. 54, a 0-6-0 saddletank built in 1941, shunting. On the right is the B.R. Sudbury–Marks Tey line. (Geoff King)

Austerity class. She had come from an iron-ore quarry to Chappel about a month previously. Another 0-6-0 saddle tank, *Jupiter*, had arrived three days after *Gunby*.

The next year saw the arrival of three more locomotives, first, a small 0-6-0 saddle tank *Belvoir* (now finely restored), then a side tank, No. 7597, which had been bought by the '7597 Fund' (later to become the Railway Vehicle Preservations Group). In September 1972, the

Essex Locomotive Society provided Chappel and Wakes Colne with an ex-Southern Railway 4-6-0 S15 class, No. 841, which had been a very adaptable work-horse at the head of passenger and express goods trains. After a long and expensive programme of restoration which involved the fabrication of many new parts, in recognition of the great help accorded by the local brewery, Greene King, this fine locomotive was named *Greene King*. Its restoration was carried out to such a high standard that she was selected to be one of the engines appearing in the Cavalcade of Steam at Shildon on 31 August 1975, when the 150th anniversary of steam railways in Britain was celebrated. *Greene King* subsequently moved to the Nene Valley Railway and from there to the North Yorkshire Moors line. Three more locomotives in 1973 brought the total at Chappel to eight.

In the next year, the first locomotive to be owned by the Society arrived. This was No. 80151, a 2-6-4 tank of B.R. design. It was rescued just in time from the graveyard of locomotives at Barry. Like No. 841, she has had some essential parts removed and rust has eaten

Robert Stephensons and Hawthorns saddletank No. 54 has been named Pen Green *in honour of the locomotive headquarters of the Stewarts and Lloyds ironstone railway at Corby, where it once used to work. (*Geoff King*)*

into her steel plate, but she is capable of being restored to full working condition. There is also the last Great Eastern loco to be built at Stratford Works, 0-6-2 tank, No. 999.

Other equipment

There is great temptation to concentrate on the locomotives in a railway preservation enterprise. But the running of locomotives needs not only track and points, but signalling equipment, coaches for passengers, and many other far-from-glamorous but nevertheless essential items. A new signal box has been erected at the northern limit of the Society's track and fitted with equipment from as far afield as East Lincolnshire. Signals, points and crossing gates are fully interlocking to conform to normal railway practice. Engine movements are under the discipline of the staff-and-token system, which means that no driver may move his engine unless the signalman has handed him the necessary staff or token. The signal box by the B.R. tracks, which became redundant with the de-staffing of the station, has also been reinstated as a working box, and it is hoped that this may be moved on to the land leased by the Society. The frame, found in several pieces in the goods yard, has been repaired and replaced. The goods shed is now a well-equipped workshop. In March 1981, the Society reinstated the station footbridge at Chappel using the span from Sudbury, to give direct public access to the preservation site without the need to cross the B.R. line at rail level.

Rolling stock

A very interesting collection of rolling stock has been assembled at the station. A veritable railway antique is a six-wheel coach, No. 373, of the old Manchester, Sheffield and Lincolnshire Railway, built in 1899. Another six-wheeler, even older, was built in 1890 by the Great Eastern Railway. Numbered 550, it is owned by the Great Eastern Railway Group and is due to

ABOVE: *An 80-ton crane lifts the footbridge main span into position at the Stour Valley Railway Centre, Chappel, Essex on Sunday 8 March 1981.* (G. T. Abraham)

BELOW: Jupiter, *a 0-6-0 saddletank built in 1950, collects the staff (the token of the right to pass over a line) from the Chappel North box.* (Geoff King)

be restored to its 1915 state. Of more ancient lineage still is a four-wheeled first-class coach of the Great Eastern which was built in 1877 at a cost of £281. Restoration is proceeding on this vehicle.

Other vehicles of interest are a four-wheel Grafton Steam Crane, on loan from the Felixstowe Dock and Railway Co. Ltd, which is of

great use for lifting sleepers, track, and saddle tanks from locomotives, and one (E765W) of two wagons only of a special kind built at Stratford Works in 1951, on six wheels, used for transporting horses (between the two horse compartments is one for the groom). There is a strong Great Eastern element in the rolling stock.

What to see on a visit

While a longer trip behind a steam locomotive must await the acquisition of more track (consequent perhaps on the possible closure by B.R. of the Mark's Tey–Sudbury branch, or, in the event of that line remaining open, on re-establishment on a new site) there is very much there to draw the visitor. Entry to the railway is through the Booking Office which now serves also as a well-stocked shop with a fine display of books, cards and other railway souvenirs. The station building is very attractive architecturally, quite different from the usual Great Eastern station, constructed in brick of unusual shades and with unique decorative touches on the exterior. Refreshment facilities are available, most appropriately, in B.R. Prototype Bar Car No. E1883 which is parked close to the goods shed.

In an attempt to prevent the ultimate closure of the Sudbury branch, the Society has opened negotiations with British Rail with a view to boosting traffic and providing a tourist attraction by running steam-hauled trains over the entire branch on Sundays. If successful, this line-sharing proposal would be unique in railway preservation in Great Britain, though it is a well-tried feature of steam railway operation on the continent.

Access to the Stour Valley Railway is easy. Just off the A604 at Chappel a B.R. sign points the way to the station.

Less than a quarter mile from the station is the imposing Chappel viaduct spanning the Colne Valley. It is a listed structure. It was the longest viaduct on the Great Eastern Railway, 1,066 ft long, 75 ft high at the maximum, and supported on 32 graceful arches. Those visiting the railway should also see this great monument to railway civil engineering of the last century.

The Colne Valley Railway

This preservation venture has but a short history. Early in 1972, Dick Hymas purchased a 0-6-0 saddle tank No. 190, an Austerity class built for the War Department. Gordon Warren, another local enthusiast, joined Hymas at the head of a small group and then decided to try to re-open about one mile of the railway to provide a home for 190 and other engines. A private company, the Colne Valley Railway Co. Ltd, was formed to launch the scheme. There was so much local interest, that a supporting body for the general public was soon in being – the Colne Valley Railway Preservation Society.

Long negotiations with British Rail came to a conclusion when the Company purchased a one-mile length of track-bed at Castle Hedingham, close to the A604 road and the River Colne. Late in 1973, they gained access to the area, from which the track had been lifted ten years previously. Three months clearing the track-bed caused workers to wonder if a nature reserve might have been a more suitable project!

Just enough track – about 60 ft – was laid, including an inspection pit, to take one locomotive comfortably. In September 1973, No. 190 was transferred to the place prepared for her.

No buildings, not even a platelayer's hut, stood on the mile of track-bed. A search began

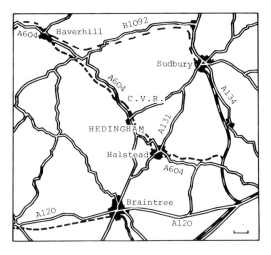

29

for authentic Cólne Valley Railway buildings. Fortunately, three of the original station buildings remained, and one, at Castle and Sible Hedingham, had been recently sold to Rippers Ltd. The station was more or less structurally sound and solidly built. On being approached and learning of the intentions for the station, Messrs Rippers generously gave it to the Society. Members set to work on reducing the building to its component parts and in six weeks they were moved the two miles. The station was re-built to look exactly as it had at Castle Hedingham. A two-hundred-foot platform was built around it, and on the opposite side a similar platform, which accommodates another station building containing offices, a shop, a cafe, and the museum.

So track-laying proceeded, yard-by-yard on £5 sleepers, slowly but steadily towards Yeldham.

With more track laid there was room for more locomotives; W.D. No. 190 was joined by others, all industrials, some in group ownership.

ABOVE: *The atmosphere of the country railway. At Castle Hedingham station a G.E.R. footbridge frames an Austerity saddletank and a Norwegian coach.* (Colne Valley Railway)

OPPOSITE ABOVE: *Looking down on the reconstructed Castle Hedingham station showing what has been achieved.* (Colne Valley Railway)

OPPOSITE BELOW: *Construction of the Colne Valley Railway on the track-bed of the old line. Work began in 1975, ten years after the track had been lifted. Castle Hedingham station was moved two miles and the beginnings of the new platform are on the left.* (Colne Valley Railway)

Among them is a beautifully restored Avonside 0-4-0 saddle-tank locomotive named *Barrington*, expertly painted and lined out in L.M.S. maroon, owned by the Avonside Steam Preservation Group.

Essex County Council offered the Society the old crossing-keeper's ground-frame hut at

Castle Hedingham station, rebuilt exactly as it was before being moved. (J. C. E. Carleton)

White Colne; this too was dismantled, taken to the new railway, and reconstructed as it was before. An engine shed became a priority, and the Great Yeldham goods shed was acquired.

The foundations of a re-born stretch of the Colne Valley and Halstead railway are truly laid.

Over the one mile it is a close replica of the original. The five engines, and the rolling-stock (including a B.R. second-class saloon, an ex-L.M.S. brake van and a signal-post wagon dating back to 1911) can be seen from the A604 road between Great Yeldham and Castle Heding-ham. A spacious lay-by provides both a stopping place and easy access to the railway. Pictures may be taken anywhere along the line.

THE MIDLANDS

The Severn Valley Railway

The line and its history

The Severn Valley Railway formerly ran from Shrewsbury in Shropshire to Hartlebury in Worcestershire. The route selected by the original promoters included historic towns such as Ironbridge, Bewdley and Stourport. A railway linking Worcester with Shrewsbury was proposed by the Oxford, Worcester and Wolverhampton Railway in the 1850s, and the railway obtained its Act in August 1853. Work began in 1858, and apart from earth slips caused by heavy rain in the summer of 1860 there were no great engineering difficulties. The line was completed in the autumn of 1861, but the opening was delayed in view of previous earthslips, to allow the trackbed to consolidate. The line was finally opened with great rejoicing in January 1862. By 1863, the Severn Valley, though then absorbed by the new West Midland Railway, was operating as part of the G.W.R., but its formal amalgamation was not until 1872.

The Severn Valley Railway remained part of the G.W.R. till nationalization. During World War II, it was of great importance as a supply route for air bases at Bridgnorth and Hartlebury, but it was never part of any main route, and with few towns of any size near, it was not an economic line in post-War conditions. In 1962, following the Beeching report, the line was scheduled for closure.

After the passing of the 1962 Transport Act, the passenger service ended on 7 September 1963, and freight traffic ceased on 30 November.

*Great Western 'small Prairie' tank No. 4566 captured at speed on the Severn Valley Railway as the driver hurries home. (*Mike Wood*)*

ABOVE: *No. 7819* Hinton Manor *is seen leaving Northwood with a train for Bewdley on 28 December 1977. No. 7819, built in 1939, was withdrawn from Shrewsbury in 1965 and languished at Barry scrapyard in increasingly derelict condition until 1973. Renovation took several years and* Hinton Manor *began service on the Severn Valley in 1977. (*Bob Green*)*

LEFT: *Stanier 8F heavy goods engine No. 8233 prepares to leave Bridgnorth shed. This much-travelled locomotive saw service in Iran and Egypt before B.R. bought it prior to preservation.*

RIGHT: *0-6-0 pannier tank No. 5764 crosses Victoria Bridge over the River Severn on the frosty morning of 4 December 1976. It is heading a train of Great Western coaches between Bewdley and Arley on the Severn Valley Railway. (*David Williams*)*

South of Alveley, the line remained open for local coal traffic, but the track north of Buildwas was lifted in 1965, and later as far south as Bridgnorth.

Preservation

In February 1966 the Severn Valley Railway Society, formed the previous year to preserve the line for steam traction, purchased the line between Bridgnorth and Hampton Loade for £25,000; this line was re-opened in the summer of 1970. This was but a small section of the original line, and money was raised to extend the scheme southwards to join the ex-G.W.R. main line from Worcester to Birmingham. Once the line had been purchased from B.R., volunteers set about improving the line and restoring the station buildings. There is now a regular, timetabled service from Bridgnorth, south to Eardington, Hampton Loade, Highley, Arley, Northwood and Bewdley, a total of $12\frac{1}{2}$ miles. Another 3 miles will be added to this when the section of line to Kidderminster is opened shortly.

Stock

Fittingly for a former G.W.R. line, the Severn

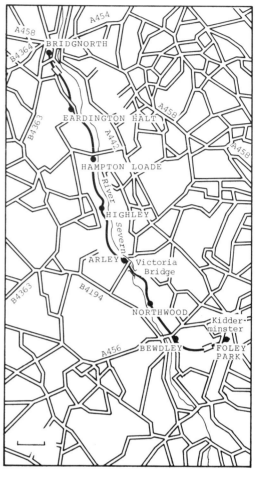

Since 1974 the S.V.R. has run passenger services from Bridgnorth to Bewdley. This is Hunslet 0-6-0 No. 193, now Shropshire, *with the noon service to Arley.* (G. Scott Lowe)

Bridgnorth on the Severn Valley Railway. Stanier 8F 2-8-0 No. 8233, in original L.M.S. livery, has hauled ten-coach trains on many occasions. Here, running tender-first, it crosses G.W.R. 4-6-0 Hinton Manor.

Valley Railway has a large concentration of Great Western motive power. No fewer than five of the 4-6-0 type, three 'Manors' and two 'Halls' have been saved for posterity and four of these restored to working order. The 78XX or 'Manor' class was introduced by the G.W.R. in 1938 as a lightweight, 'go-anywhere' passenger engine capable of working on lines where the 'Halls' and 'Granges' were too heavy. Thriftily reusing the motion and wheels of old 43XX 2-6-0s, the 'Manors' swiftly established a useful

reputation, particularly over the lines of the old Cambrian system. Nos. 7812 *Erlestoke Manor* and 7819 *Hinton Manor* have similarly performed well at the head of S.V.R. trains, whilst No. 7802 *Bradley Manor* awaits its turn for restoration. No. 4930 *Hagley Hall* appropriately takes its name from a nearby stately home and is one of several S.V.R. engines to have been passed for mainline running over B.R. tracks. Sister engine No. 6960 *Raveningham Hall* is in fact one of F. W. Hawksworth's improved 'Modified Hall' class and was restored at Steamtown, Carnforth, before coming to the Severn Valley.

One of Churchward's impressive 28XX class No. 2857, an example of Britain's first 2-8-0 heavy goods engines, has been rescued from

ABOVE: *Just as the 2-6-2 tank was the usual South Wales mainline locomotive, so the 0-6-0 tank was the choice for shunting and trip work. Port Talbot Railway saddletank No. 813, built in 1901, operated from Duffryn Yard depot until purchased by Backworth Colliery in 1934.* (David Williams)

BELOW: *B.R. 2-6-4 tank No. 80079 accelerates away from the permanent speed restriction at Sterns, near Eardington, with a train of G.W.R. Collett coaches. This useful locomotive was obtained in scrap condition from Woodhams' yard at Barry, South Wales.* (Bill Sharman)

Gordon the blue engine is not a character from one of the 'Thomas the Tank Engine' stories but a real live steam performer on the Severn Valley Railway. The locomotive carries the colours of the Longmoor Military Railway in Hampshire and is an example of Britain's first class of 2-10-0.

Barry scrapyard and restored to working order. And what a stirring sight she makes at the head of a long, long train of preserved G.W.R. goods wagons. A smaller and more modern goods engine is No. 3205, one of C.B. Collett's 2251 class 0-6-0s. Built at Swindon in 1946, she was originally shedded at Gloucester to work local passenger and freight services in the Ross, Hereford, Cheltenham and Swindon area. She was transferred to Worcester in 1956, and actually worked on the Severn Valley line until her withdrawal from service. She was then bought by the 2251 Preservation Group, and restored at Buckfastleigh in 1965–6. She was subsequently towed to the Severn Valley, and hauled the first public passenger train on the opening day in May 1970.

The Great Western contingent on the S.V.R. is completed by Collett Mogul No. 9303, large Prairie tanks Nos. 4141, 4150 and 5164, small Prairie No. 4566 and 0-6-0 pannier tanks Nos. 5764, 7714 and 1501. This last engine is an example of the final G.W.R. class to be introduced. Built at Swindon in 1949, she is distinguished from the earlier G.W.R. types by having outside cylinders. This more modern design was by the Great Western's last Chief Mechanical Engineer, F.W. Hawksworth. These engines were built for shunting and moving coaches to and from stations for express trains. No. 1501 was based at Old Oak Common, and worked stock to and from Paddington.

Also carrying G.W.R. colours is 0-6-0ST No. 813. This interesting engine was built by Hudswell Clarke of Leeds in 1901 for the Port Talbot Railway in South Wales, The G.W.R. absorbed the independent railways of South Wales in 1923 and many of their engines were 'Swindonized' in the 1920s, being rebuilt with standard Great Western boiler fittings etc. No. 813 was sold to Backworth Colliery in Northumberland in 1934. In 1968 it was purchased for preservation and moved to the S.V.R.

Two famous West Coast route locomotives stand side by side at Bridgnorth shed. No. 5000 is the prototype of William Stanier's famous 'Black 5' mixed traffic 4-6-0 class. The elegant old Victorian single-wheeler is Cornwall, *the London and North Western express engine of 1847; now back in the National Railway Museum. (Paul Barber)*

Naturally, the L.M.S. is well represented on the Severn Valley Railway and several of its modern designs, showing strong Swindon influence, make a fascinating comparison with the G.W.R. products. One of the best known engines is No. 8233, a 8F class 2-8-0 designed by Sir William Stanier. She was built in 1940 by the North British Locomotive Co. at Glasgow to operate in France on war work, but with the collapse of France she was delivered to the L.M.S. In 1941 she was requisitioned to serve in Persia, and it was not till 1952, after a further spell on the Egyptian State Railways, that she returned to England, to work on the Longmoor Military Railway. Before the end of steam on British Railways she returned to the Glasgow district, and was finally acquired by the 8F Locomotive Society. She came to Bridgnorth in

January 1969, and has given reliable service ever since. She was one of the locomotives selected to take part in the Rail 150 cavalcade at Shildon in August 1975.

Two examples of Sir William Stanier's famous 'Black 5' 4-6-0s are also based at Bridgnorth. In fact one is the class prototype, No. 5000 herself, on loan from the National Collection. No. 45110 *RAF Biggin Hill* was built at the Vulcan Foundry in 1935. Shedded at Holyhead, she worked fast passenger and freight trains to Chester, Birmingham, Manchester, Liverpool and London. She was purchased for preservation at Ashford, Kent, but was moved to the Severn Valley for complete restoration when the Ashford centre closed.

There are three useful Ivatt L.M.S. 2-6-0 Mixed Traffic engines, one being the sole survivor of his 4MT design, No. 43106, built by B.R. in 1951 to the L.M.S. design. The other two are the neat 2MT class locos Nos. 46443 and the green-liveried No. 46521. This latter engine sports a very fine Canadian chime whistle which echoes melodiously down the valley.

Far from its native L.N.E.R. comes the Gresley K4 class 3-cylinder 2-6-0 No. 3442 *The Great*

8

On the Severn Valley Railway, L.M.S. Ivatt class 2MT No. 46521 in correct British Rail livery (it was built by B.R. in 1953 to the L.M.S. design). The inscription on the bridge reads: 'Victoria Bridge' and then from left to right across the arch, 'Messrs. Brassey & Co., Contractors', '1861. John Fowler, Engineer' and 'Cast and erected by the Coalbrookdale Company'. The bridge featured in the 1979 version of The Thirty-Nine Steps. *(David Idle)*

Marquess. The K4s were the last engines to be specially designed for service on the West Highland line from Glasgow to Fort William. On withdrawal, *The Great Marquess* was bought for preservation by Viscount Garnock and for several years was based in Leeds working special trains for enthusiasts.

Wearing its distinctive royal blue livery and representing the Longmoor Military Railway is No. 600 *Gordon*, an example of Britain's first class of 2-10-0 goods engines. This was one of 150 such locomotives developed for wartime use over lightly laid track and one of the very few members of the class not to see service abroad; *Gordon* spent its working life on the L.M.R. and passed to the S.V.R. in 1971.

The Severn Valley Railway is extremely fortunate in possessing the largest collection of preserved carriages and wagons in the British Isles. Complete passenger-carrying rakes of vehicles are available for service representing the Great Western, L.M.S. and British Railways, whilst a growing number of teak-bodied Gresley L.N.E.R. vehicles is undergoing restoration.

The area around
Although the Severn Valley Railway runs through attractive countryside, it is also associated with a whole variety of industrial remains. The town of Ironbridge, for example, set on the steep limestone slopes above the River Severn, received its name because it was the site of the world's first iron bridge, built in 1778. It was designed and cast by the famous ironmaster Abraham Darby, at his foundry in nearby Coalbrookdale. Its single cast-iron span is of 100 feet. Today, the bridge, weakened by 200 years of traffic, is limited to foot passengers only.

At Coalbrookdale itself is the Museum of Ironfounding. Here Abraham Darby pioneered

9

The Ivatt class 4MT 2-6-0s were introduced in 1947 but were not immediately successful owing to initial poor steaming. The only survivor, No. 43106, is seen here at Eardington with the 15.45 Bridgnorth to Bewdley train. (Steve Owen)

the use of coke as a fuel for iron smelting in place of charcoal. The museum exhibits early iron castings, and a selection of some early cast-iron rails. There are also some early locomotives and stationary steam engines, together with a collection of machinery used in the manufacture of iron goods.

Further south is the well-known canal town of Stourport. The story runs that James Brindley, looking for an outlet to the Severn for his Trent and Mersey Canal, selected the then thriving town of Bewdley. The residents felt that the new-fangled canal would lower the tone of their town, and opposed his plans. Accordingly Brindley moved to Stourport, where a series of docks, wharves, and warehouses was built. Much business followed, and Stourport thrived while Bewdley declined. Today much of

Stourport's Georgian charm remains, including the warehouses built by the canal company.

Nearby is Tickenhill Manor, originally a medieval building given to Roger Mortimer by Edward IV. The Manor is faced with Georgian brickwork, but the interior shows glimpses of the earlier house. The Great Hall for example, has much Tudor work and the beams date from the thirteenth century.

Bridgnorth is not known merely for its railway. It is an old town with building dating from the twelfth century. There are some remains of the castle keep, destroyed by Cromwell's forces in 1646. The castle grounds are now an attractive park. The church of St Mary Magdalene was designed by the civil engineer Thomas Telford in the early nineteenth century in the then fashionable Italianate style.

At Shrewsbury is Rowley's House, containing the City Museum, which has a variety of exhibits dating from Roman times to the nineteenth century. There is also a military museum at the Sir John Moore Barracks which features the County Regiment, The Shropshire Light Infantry.

Great Central Railway

Of all the railway preservation projects, one of the most ambitious has been the return to steam on the former Great Central. The Main Line Steam Trust (as the preservation group was originally called) set out to fulfill the dream of many steam enthusiasts: not merely to recreate the lost age of steam on relatively short branch lines, but to acquire a section of a former main line, and restore it to steam running. The line chosen for its activities was the former Great Central route, from Loughborough south towards Leicester. That line had finally been abandoned and closed by British Rail on 5 May 1969. It had been decided to retain the former Midland Railway's route to Loughborough, via Leicester to St Pancras, and reduce Marylebone to the status of a commuter terminus. The base of operations was the $3\frac{3}{4}$-acre site at Loughborough Central Station, which was leased to the Trust. In 1977 the Trust bought the track from Loughborough to Rothley for nearly £250,000.

There was a double irony that the Great Central should have been chosen, for the G.C.R. was the last main line to be built in Britain, with much scepticism from those who thought it unnecessary. It had only been opened to passenger traffic in March 1899, providing a direct route from Marylebone to Rugby, Leicester, Nottingham, Sheffield, Yorkshire and Lancashire. It was aptly named, for a plan of the Company's lines in 1922 resembles the letter *T*. There was the main line running almost due north from London. It had virtually no branches or east–west offshoots until it reached the North Midlands. There, routes broke off due west to Liverpool and Manchester, and due east to Lincoln, Grimsby and Cleethorpes. The railway continued north as far as Doncaster and Wakefield. The Great Central was to continue as a main-line trunk route, with a well-deserved reputation for fast, comfortable and frequent express trains, for over sixty years. In its halcyon days under British Railways, the line boasted such named expresses as the *Master Cutler* and the *South Yorkshireman*. In 1923 the Great Central had, of course, been absorbed into the L.N.E.R.

A journey down the line
As the train leaves Loughborough's Great Central Station, it is tempting to put the clock back two decades – to the happier days of the mid-1950s when a beautifully turned out A3 *Prince Palatine,* or *Solario* perhaps, might have been pulling away from here on an express to London Marylebone, calling only at Leicester and Rugby. But those golden days are gone and the train will now only travel as far as Rothley, via Quorn and Woodhouse. Rothley is just to the north of Leicester. The journey is some $5\frac{1}{2}$ miles.

But it is still an enchanting journey through the beautiful Leicestershire countryside. In the old days, very fast running was the general rule between Loughborough and Leicester. The railway was built for high speeds – no gradient was more testing than a gentle 1 in 176, and the alignment and curvature allowed speeds of up to 80 m.p.h. Alas, the present speed restrictions permit only a fraction of that as the train travels the two miles from Loughborough to Quorn and Woodhouse through gently rolling countryside.

Quorn is an ideal spot to explore the Leicestershire hunting country. The village of Woodhouse lies only 1 mile away, while the famous

The railway preservation event of 1981–82 was the return to steam of the Great Northern Railway single No. 1 on the G.C.R. (L. A. Nixon)

For many years the L.N.E.R. B1 class 4-6-0s were the mainstay of services on the Great Central mainline, so it is fitting that both preserved examples of the class are to be found on today's G.C.R. at Loughborough. This is No. 1306 Mayflower *displaying its apple-green livery. (John Gardner)*

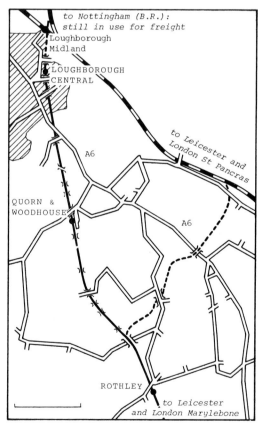

local landmark, Charnwood Beacon (818 ft) is a further 2 miles on. Quorn station is a simple island arrangement, with the tracks running either side of a single platform with umbrella awnings. It is a typical example of a Great Central rural station. Like so many of its kind, Quorn was closed when the Beeching Axe was wielded in the early 1960s.

Leaving Quorn, the train chunters gently on, with the local beauty spot of Chuddon Wood on the left and the wild Charnwood Forest region away in the distance on the right. This is the territory of Lady Jane Grey, the tragic queen whose short reign finished at the scaffold. There opens up a tremendous view, a beautiful patchwork of arable farmland, scattered copses, and then the more heavily wooded countryside as the train approaches Swithland Reservoir (one of the reservoirs which provides Leicester with its water). From the viaducts which take the railway across Swithland, some of the

An L.M.S. 5MT 4-6-0, now named 3rd Volunteer Battalion, The Worcestershire and Sherwood Foresters Regiment, *No. 5231 was built in 1936 and withdrawn from Carnforth shed in 1968. It is clear that the M.L.S.T. track is a true main line, built with gentle gradients and curves. Sadly, the line has been reduced to single track as £125,000 would have been needed to purchase the second.*

loveliest views of all are to be seen. Far to the right lies Swithland Hall, the ancestral seat of the Earl of Lanesborough, the G.C.R.'s President. For the ornithologist the fringes of the reservoir provide a natural home for a remarkable variety of birds.

As the first houses on the left come into view, the train is nearing Rothley Station, reaching the last hundred yards of its journey. Rothley Station is an industrial site not to be missed. It has been carefully restored so that it is almost as it was when opened in 1899 - even down to the gas lighting. A refreshment room is provided, and to remind the visitor of its Victorian origins, the waiting room is decorated with a portrait of Queen Victoria. Rothley Station is also an ideal base for an excursion - the village of Rothley lies one mile away, and Swithland Reservoir can be more closely explored from here. One of

Leicester's most popular picnic spots - and a place well worth a visit - is the highly attractive Bradgate Park, about three miles away. Although the route was originally double track throughout till B.R. days, one set of lines was lifted, and for most of the journey trains operate along a single line.

Stock

Since the Trust was set up to preserve a Great Central Railway it is fitting to begin an examination of the locomotives operating along the line with one of its former engines. The only G.C.R. express locomotive which has survived for preservation is the 4-4-0 No. 506, *Butler-Henderson*. It was built at the company's Gorton works in Manchester in 1919 to the designs of John G. Robinson. The class were known as 'Improved Directors', as they were a revised version of the original Director class of 1913. No. 506 was named after the Hon. Eric Butler Henderson, a board member of the G.C.R. The engine has since been thoroughly repainted and is now resplendent in the green livery of the Great Central, lined out in white and black, with deep red frames and lower splashers. The engine needed a certain amount of mechanical attention before it was put into service again;

it is at present on loan from the national collection at York. In its career this loco must have headed many expresses through Loughborough on its way to Manchester from London.

The mainstay of services during the final years of the G.C.R. mainline were Stanier's excellent 'Black 5s'. So it's appropriate that one of the class, No. 5231, is present at Loughborough and has already put in much useful work on the preserved line. In 1976 at Quorn Station, No. 5231 was named *3rd (Volunteer) Battalion, the Worcestershire and Sherwood Foresters Regiment*. It is a good choice of name, as many of the larger L.M.S. express locomotives were named after regiments of the British Army.

Another loco, one representing the L.N.E.R., is No. 4744, an 0-6-2 tank engine. Built in 1921, she started life on the Great Northern, and was used for hauling suburban trains out of King's Cross. There were special condensers fitted (the pipes visible at the top of the side tanks are part of this apparatus) to reduce steam and smoke in the long tunnels to Moorgate. This engine, now restored to its L.N.E.R. livery, was formerly held on the Keighley and Worth Valley Railway.

Also representing the L.N.E.R. are two of Thompson's B1 class Mixed Traffic 4-6-0s. Like the 'Halls' on the Great Western, they were general-purpose engines and came to be a fairly numerous class – some 410 in all. For a few years in the late 1940s they were the staple express engine along the Great Central before being replaced by the Black 5s when the line passed to the Midland Region. No. 1306 *Mayflower*, resplendent in L.N.E.R. apple-green livery, was formerly based at Steamtown, Carnforth, before moving to the G.C.R. to become a regular performer on the trains to Rothley. The other B1, No. 1264, was rescued from Barry scrapyard and is very much a long-term restoration job.

In fact today's Great Central Railway has laid down what might be described as a long-term investment programme in mainline steam motive power. For in its well-equipped depot at Loughborough a considerable number of exciting restoration projects is being undertaken. When completed, these will give the railway an abundance of mainline and express steam locomotives to haul its trains. The largest and most ambitious restoration concerns the Pacific No.

71000 *Duke of Gloucester*.

The class 8 was designed after nationalization by R.A. Riddles. The engine was completed in 1954 and was intended as a prototype for a standard B.R. express locomotive. But a decision was then taken to switch to diesel and electric traction and so this was the only one of its type ever built. *Duke of Gloucester* saw good service on the West Coast line from Euston to Glasgow for some six years. It was withdrawn in 1962 for preservation by British Rail, probably because of its unique cylinders and valve gear (the latter being an improvement on the British Caprotti type) which were the most efficient on any simple expansion steam locomotive in history. However, after some considerable time, B.R. changed their minds and decided to scrap the locomotive. One of the outside cylinders, complete with valve gear, was sectioned and placed on display in the Science Museum in South Kensington. Eventually, the locomotive appeared in the scrapyard at Barry, South Wales, minus the other outside cylinder. It remained there until 1973 when it was purchased by members of a trust fund set up to secure the engine's future. Restoration is proceeding well, though naturally it is a very costly exercise. Two new cylinders have been cast and machined and Caprotti valve gear parts have been obtained from all over the world. When No. 71000 takes to the rails again under her own steam, it will be one of the greatest achievements by amateur railway preservationists.

There is another 4-6-2 undergoing restoration, No. 34039 *Boscastle*. The engine was built for the Southern Railway in 1941 and numbered 21C139 as part of the West Country class. Some were rebuilt under B.R., involving the removal of the distinctive 'air-smoothed' casing. As a result of the modification, they were 4 tons heavier but much more reliable and economical. *Boscastle*, during part of its varied career, headed the Golden Arrow service to Dover from Victoria.

The Great Western is also to be represented on the railway. No. 6990 *Witherslack Hall* is one of F. W. Hawksworth's 'Modified Halls', completed in 1948. They were medium powered general-purpose engines. This loco was selected in 1948 to take part in exchange trials and was

This is another view of the G.C.R. with both tracks in place prior to the lifting of the down line. The train consists of four British Rail Mark I corridor coaches and an L.N.E.R. Gresley buffet car and is headed by the Hunslet 0-6-0 saddletank Robert Nelson *which used to shunt at Littleton Colliery, Staffordshire. (Paul Barber)*

run over the Great Central network to assess the efficiency of various company's locomotives. It spent most of its life in the Oxford area, before being withdrawn in 1966.

Also of G.W.R. origin is the 2-8-0 No. 5224 with side water tanks. She is entering strange territory, going to the Great Central, although in

15

ABOVE: Butler-Henderson, *built in 1919, is the only Great Central express loco to have survived. It is now back on loan from York.* (Colourviews)

LEFT: *Rothley is the present southern terminus of the G.C.R. This small country station now sees activity unprecedented in its history as locomotives run round their trains before returning to Loughborough. Class N2 0-6-2T No. 4744 is the centre of attention here.* (Paul Barber)

the heyday of steam Great Western engines were no strangers to Leicester. No. 5224 and her sister engines were designed for the Great Western by their Chief Mechanical Engineer, George Jackson Churchward. Built in May 1924, she weighs over 82 tons, and spent most of her working life in the South Wales coalfield, working the short heavy-haul coal trains from the pits in the valleys to the ports and factories.

Another former denizen of Barry scrapyard, and a perfect match for *Duke of Gloucester*, is the B.R. 9F class heavy freight locomotive No. 92212. The 9Fs were closely associated with the Great Central during its last years and put up many fine performances at the head of the Annesley to Woodford freights. No. 92212 is making good progress towards its return to working order.

The railway's passenger-carrying fleet consists of standard British Rail carriages all completed in the 1950s. They are mostly corridor vehicles, though there are some examples of compartment suburban stock. Several carriages are being repainted in their original red and cream livery. A first-class restaurant car is used for special evening departures offering five-course meals on board, and there are also two former L.N.E.R. catering vehicles. One is a buffet car built in 1937 to a Gresley design, which has since been modernized inside by British Rail, and the other a buffet/restaurant car built in 1938 for the *Flying Scotsman*. This carriage has been rebuilt as simply a buffet. A full dining service is offered on two midday trains; the evening meals on the named trains in the summer.

Other L.N.E.R. Gresley teak-bodied vehicles

17

ABOVE: *The solitary standard class 8P Pacific was No. 71000* Duke of Gloucester, *here seen at Birmingham New Street on a Crewe running-in turn in 1960. The engine, built in 1954, is now the subject of an ambitious restoration scheme at Loughborough, G.C.R.* (John Warr)

LEFT: *This is No. 71000 in November 1968 at Barry scrapyard. Many parts are being manufactured for the restoration, which is following the original designs.* (C.M. Whitehouse)

include a travelling Post Office set comprising Tender and Sorting coaches. These are put to spectacular use, normally behind *Butler-Henderson*, to exchange mailbags at speed when passing the lineside T.P.O. equipment installed at Quorn. Here is a railway letter service with a difference!

Bulmer's Railway Centre

In 1968, the cider makers H. P. Bulmer decided to establish a railway centre near their premises at Hereford. The show piece was to be the celebrated Great Western locomotive *King George V*, together with five Pullman coaches formerly used on the Southern Railway's Golden Arrow and Bournemouth Belle. These comprise the 'Bulmer Cider Train'.

For their centre, Bulmer's were able to make use of the Moorfield Depot of the former Midland Railway. The track layout is a triangle, which enables engines and coaches to be turned round. On the waste land enclosed by these lines are the remains of the original Midland sheds.

King George V was the prototype of a famous class. In July 1927, soon after completion, she was shipped to America to represent British locomotive design at the Baltimore and Ohio Railroad Centenary. She still has her large brass bell on her buffer beam in commemoration of

ABOVE: Clan Line *pounds up the last mile to Church Stretton summit, Shropshire, with an enthusiasts' special returning from Chester to Hereford.* (David Williams)

BELOW: *G.W.R. 'King' 4-6-0 No. 6000* King George V *leaves Hereford for Shrewsbury and Chester with the 'Deeside Venturer' on 4 October 1980. Thirty of the Kings were built from 1927 to 1930 and No. 6000 is presently the only active survivor, having been restored with the help of Bulmers the cider makers. This engine heralded the return of steam to Britain's main lines in 1971.* (David Williams)

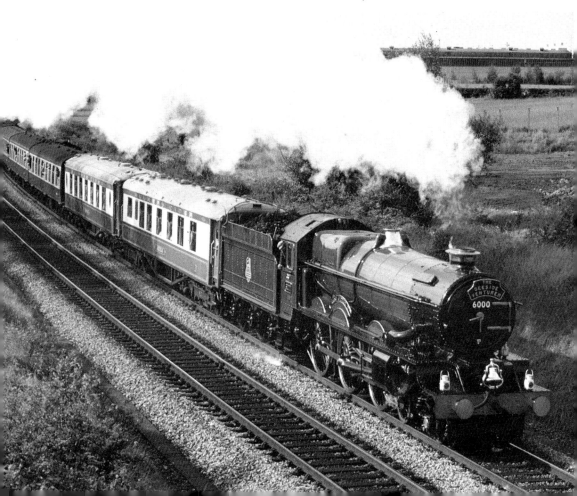

Princess Elizabeth makes a fine show as she leaves Hereford at the head of a special train for Shrewsbury. Arguably one of the most elegant express steam locomotives ever built, the Princess is based at Bulmers Steam Centre. (Rex Coffin)

that visit. On her return to Britain *King George V* was restored for normal express running, and on occasion for royal trains and other prestige runs. When withdrawn from service in 1962, she had covered nearly two million miles, and, being scheduled for preservation, was stored at Swindon. In 1968 Bulmer's offered to pay for her complete restoration, provided she could then be housed and steamed at their Hereford headquarters. Since B.R. withdrew their ban on steam running, *King George V* has been able to

work enthusiasts' specials over certain lines in the Western Region.

Since 1968 other preservation societies have based their locomotives here, among these being the Merchant Navy Class Preservation Society's Bulleid Pacific, No. 35028, *Clan Line*. A fine example of her class, she was built in 1948. Under B.R. she worked such famous trains as The Golden Arrow and The Atlantic Coast Express, and on one occasion, near Axminster, achieved an authenticated 104 m.p.h. She was withdrawn from service in 1967 and immediately acquired by the Society. She took part in the Shildon cavalcade in 1975, and now hauls enthusiasts' specials.

Another famous locomotive stored here is the London Midland and Scottish Railway's *Prin-*

The cider works special featuring Pectin *the popular Peckett pulling a brakevan-load of passengers along the Hereford sidings.* Pectin *formerly worked for the British Aluminium Company at their Burntisland works in Scotland.* (E. L. Crookes)

cess *Elizabeth*, which belongs to the Princess Elizabeth Locomotive Society. Designed by Sir William Stanier, a 4-6-2, she is one of a class designed for the fast London–Glasgow trains, and introduced in the 1930s. In 1936 *Princess Elizabeth* ran non-stop from London to Glasgow (401 miles) in 353 minutes. She continued to work on this route till withdrawn in 1962 and

bought by the Society: until 1976 she was kept at the Dowty Railway Preservation Society's premises at Ashchurch, but is now based on Hereford. On occasion she too hauls enthusiasts' specials.

These three are the star exhibits at Bulmer's, but there are other locomotives too: one steam tank engine, the 0-4-0 saddle tank *Pectin*; and a diesel, *Cider Queen*.

The Worcester Locomotive Society store two of their locomotives here: the G.W.R. 0-6-0 pannier tank No. 5786, and a 0-6-0 saddle tank *Caernarvon*, which comes from Stewart and Lloyd's steel works at Corby.

21

Birmingham Railway Museum

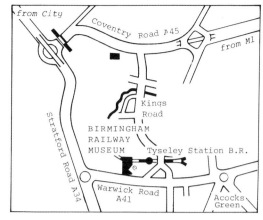

The Birmingham Railway Museum at Tyseley, whose full title is the Standard Gauge Steam Trust, is not simply a place where visitors go to look at objects in glass cases; it is a working museum where fully operational steam engines are housed between runs and where rescued locomotives are restored and maintained. The museum is situated on a spacious site behind the existing British Rail diesel depot. It consists of two large sheds, the Upper Shed, which houses the toolroom, and the New Shed, which acts as

A contrast in styles at Tyseley. The maroon engine is LMS Jubilee class 4-6-0 No. 5593 Kolhapur *which makes an interesting comparison with the rounded lines of Peckett 0-4-0ST No. 1. The latter is not of Great Western origin, but is in G.W.R. livery to resemble engines that used to shunt in Swansea Docks. (*Birmingham Railway Museum*)*

the heavy workshop. The former contains a variety of powerful lathes, and milling and grinding machines, while the latter contains a huge wheel-turning and axle lathe weighing over forty tons. In addition there are various smithies. All this equipment, and the technical skills which it involves, has meant that Tyseley Depot is able to offer comprehensive repair and restoration facilities for steam engines.

No. 7029 Clun Castle *is an impressive performer and for many years has been Tyseley's regular mainline engine. The double-chimneyed* Castle *was one of the final batch of its class to be built and was completed under B.R. auspices at Swindon in May 1950. (*Birmingham Railway Museum*)*

Since B.R. ended steam running in the late 1960s, enthusiasts have been hard-pressed for lines and sheds to run and maintain their engines. This need produced a solution in Tyseley. It now contains a wide variety of locomotives from many companies. These include the Great-Western-designed *Clun Castle, Albert Hall,* and *Thornbury Castle,* together with a number of 0-6-0 pannier tank engines. Equally impressive, in its crimson livery, is the ex-L.M.S. express locomotive, Jubilee class 4-6-0 *Kolhapur.*

The railway museum stands as an example of enthusiast achievement. It also represents a degree of co-operation between B.R., the City of Birmingham, and amateur supporters.

The necessity of a depot such as this for the continued and successful running of steam is quite clear. In normal service a locomotive usually ran for about 100,000 miles before being thoroughly overhauled, which overhaul involved stripping down the engine and removing the wheels and frame. The process needs much heavy equipment and a high degree of skill. Engines selected for preservation, though the pick of the bunch, were obviously at the ends of their useful lives with B.R. Consequently, they have required either immediate attention, or were due for overhaul in the immediate future. Tyseley has been developed to tackle this maintenance and renovation for enthusiasts lacking expertise or equipment to do the work themselves. The sort of routine work which is undertaken at Tyseley includes the removal and

renovation of all mudhole doors, washout plugs, water gauges, safety valves and boiler tubes. The boiler is then filled with steam to check its strength and the accuracy of the gauges. Other parts requiring special attention include the wheels and their flanges together with the brake and draw gear.

Birmingham itself, as an industrial city, possesses many fine relics of industrial growth: the railway museum is but one. The Science

Raising steam in the workshop at Birmingham Railway Museum. (Alan J. Wood)

Museum is the complement of Tyseley, and contains an early English steam engine built in 1784. It also houses a whole variety of the kind of mechanical apparatus which made Birmingham one of the most important manufacturing towns of Europe in the nineteenth century.

Market Bosworth Light Railway

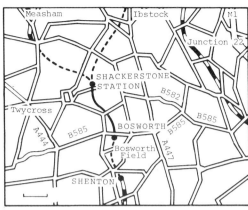

Shackerstone was once the junction station for the Moira West–Nuneaton line and a branch to Coalville and Loughborough. In its heyday six trains each way passed through plus the Loughborough service operated by motor trains (1922), but passenger services ceased as early as 1931 (except for excursions which continued until about 1960). The then Midland Railway Society acquired use of the charming but by then utterly derelict station at Shackerstone in 1970. Under the title of the Market Bosworth Light Railway, services began operating over the $2\frac{3}{4}$ mile section of line from Shackerstone to Market Bosworth in 1979.

The line runs alongside the Ashby Canal

The scene at Shackerstone station, operational headquarters of the Market Bosworth Light Railway, on a typical Sunday afternoon. Bagnall 0-6-0ST No. 2 prepares to take out the two-coach train which the diesel shunter has just brought into the platform. (Paul Barber)

25

A big Stephenson and Hawthorns 0-6-0 sidetank marshalls a demonstration goods train in the departure platform at Shackerstone. (Phil Wood)

through rural shires countryside. The southern-most station, still to be rail-connected, is Shenton which lies in the middle of the Battle-field of Bosworth, now being developed by the County Council as a tourist centre. The line is intended to connect the battlefield with the museum at Shackerstone. As the 500th anniversary of the Battle of Bosworth Field falls in 1985, there is an obvious incentive for the railhead to be pushed southwards by this date.

Stock
Eight steam locomotives, all of industrial origin, together with six diesels, make up the M.B.L.R. motive power. The oldest engine in the col-lection is Borrows 0-4-0 well tank *The King*, built in 1906. Passenger services are usually main-tained by Giesl ejector-fitted Bagnall 0-6-0ST No. 2 whilst a further Bagnall is held in reserve. Two large ex-power station Robert Stephensons and Hawthorns 0-6-0 side tanks are undergoing restoration and should be very suitable for when services are extended to Shenton.

The company owns a number of B.R. Mark I coaches, which, together with a pair of Park Royal diesel multiple-unit trailer coaches acting as observation cars, make up the regular passenger trains. The majority of the goods vehicles date from the pre-nationalization period and are used on engineering and maintenance trains.

The society's headquarters at Shackerstone also contain a fine museum with many relics on display including signal apparatus, signs, tickets, badges and photographs.

The Foxfield Light Railway

The Foxfield Light Railway is a $3\frac{1}{2}$ mile standard gauge line running from Dilhorne Park station to Blythe Bridge (Caverswall Road) station adjacent to the former North Staffordshire (Stoke–Derby) Railway, which it joined at a junction four hundred yards west of Blythe Bridge station. The railway was built in 1893 to connect Foxfield Colliery, Dilhorne, with the North Staffordshire Railway. The colliery closed in 1965 and with it the railway, but both were purchased by Tean Minerals Ltd who occupy the colliery buildings. The Foxfield Light Railway Society Ltd are now the owners and operators of the line.

The operational length of the line now starts at Dilhorne Park station and runs through Dilhorne Wood, past the seventeenth-century Stansmore Hall to circle the foot of Blakely Bank Wood and cross the Caverswall–Dilhorne road by a gated level crossing. Continuing downhill, there is a further straight section and deep cutting spanned by the Caverswall–Blythe Bridge road overbridge, and a little further on passengers get a view of the thirteenth-century Caverswall Castle. The railway terminates at Blythe Bridge (Caverswall Road) station where

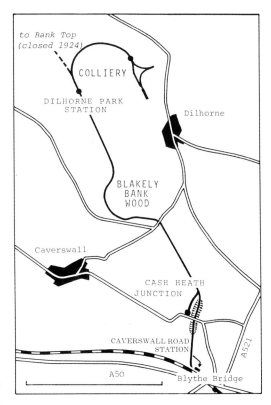

The powerful Bagnall 0-4-0ST Hawarden *from Shelton steelworks prepares to bank a train up the gradient at Foxfield. (*Phil Wood*)*

ABOVE: J. T. Daly, *a Bagnall 0-4-0ST built in 1931, at work in its native Staffordshire climbing away from Foxfield with a train for Blyth Bridge. The air-conditioned observation coach is an ex-Midland scenery van. The Bagnall has now moved on to become the only steam motive power on the Alderney Railway, Channel Islands.* (Geoff Monks)

BELOW: Henry Cort, *built in 1903 and the oldest engine at Foxfield, hauls a one-coach train towards the summit.* Henry Cort *is now rarely used on passenger services.* (R. Crombleholme)

the Society is developing a new terminus complex.

Stock

Appropriately, the railway is operated with a number of industrial tank engines. The oldest is Manning Wardle 0-6-0 saddle tank *Rhiwnant*, built in 1895. There are three Bagnalls, two 0-6-0STs, *Topham* (1922) and *Lewisham* (1927), and an 0-4-0 saddletank, *Hawarden* (1940). There are two Avonside locos, both 0-6-0STs; a Stephenson & Hawthorn 0-4-0 crane tank *Roker* (1940), three 0-4-0ST Pecketts, *Henry Cort* (1903), *Ironbridge* (1933) and No. 11 (1947). There is a Hunslet 'Austerity' 0-6-0ST, *Wimblebury* and a Barclay 0-4-0ST, *Little Barford*, which was the last steam locomotive in regular commercial operation in Greater London. A Barclay fireless loco and four small diesel locos complete the fleet.

For passenger services, the Society has a post-war L.M.S. bogie coach as well as a trio of B.R. Mark I carriages (1957), but has older and more unusual stock, including four L.M.S. bogie scenery vans, two converted to observation cars and one to a refreshment van. There is a wide range of goods stock, including a Smith Rodley steam crane.

Dean Forest Railway

The Dean Forest Railway Society was formed by enthusiasts in 1970 when the then goods-only branch from Lydney Junction to Parkend, in the Forest of Dean, first came under threat of closure. The Society began collecting funds and equipment, to be ready when the line actually closed, so that they could recommence a steam service. Since the line itself was not available, the Society rented and cleared part of the old station at Parkend, painted the goods shed, and relaid a siding. Some wagons, including a G.W.R. 'Toad' brake van, were purchased from Avonmouth Docks, and when a group of members bought *Uskmouth I*, a small Peckett saddletank, short steam-hauled trips became possible and the first of many Open Days was held in October 1971.

As the collection of rolling stock grew, activities became increasingly restricted by lack of space at Parkend and as B.R. continued to retain the branch for ballast traffic, the Society explored other ways to expand its operations. Investigations led to the discovery of the overgrown site of an old mine at Norchard, near

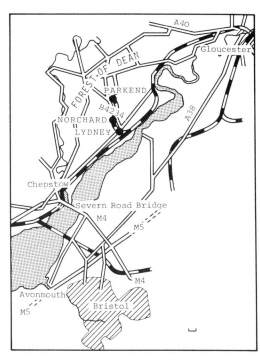

*Down in the forest, something stirs. It's the resurgence of the Great Western Railway as Prairie tank No. 5541 operates the push-pull shuttle service at Norchard. (*Dean Forest Railway*)*

Peckett 0-4-0ST Uskmouth 1 *heads an ex-G.W.R. auto-trailer into Norchard station. The Dean Forest Railway is poised to re-open the Lydney to Parkend branch. (*Phil Wood)*

Lydney. This had the potential to become an attractive steam centre, and its lineside location was also ideally situated to become, in due course, the main branch depot. The area was completely derelict, so during the Summer of 1974 preliminary clearing and levelling was done by bulldozers from the Army Apprentices College at Beachley.

Planning consent was granted in 1975 and the search for buildings and track started, as all these had been removed from Norchard some years previously. Track was purchased from a variety of places: B.R. sidings, docks and even a quarry all yielded useful items which were eventually relaid to the plans drawn up by the Society. Various railway buildings were obtained, and level-crossing gates formed an entrance, with a gatehouse alongside them, incorporating an office and toilets. One of the original Severn & Wye Station buildings, a wooden structure which had survived as an office was donated to the Society. Set up on prefabricated concrete platform sections, it formed a station ready to receive its first trains.

With much more space than at Parkend, the centre offers pleasant wooded surroundings and a steam run of several hundred yards, which extends beyond the former colliery outlet on a riverside formation, independent of the branch line.

The ballast and coal traffic ceased in May 1976, after which British Rail carried out a minimum amount of maintenance on the line, so that it remained available for any resumption of traffic.

In January 1978, all the locomotives and vehicles from Parkend were formed into a train behind G.W.R. 'Small Prairie' tank No. 5541 and proudly steamed down to Norchard, although a B.R. diesel had to lead the cavalcade. From Easter that year Steam Open Days commenced at Norchard and with over 10,000 visitors in the first season rising to over 25,000 in 1980, the Society had established itself as one of the major tourist attractions in the Forest of Dean.

With the Norchard centre firmly established, the Society was quickly able to consolidate its position by extending the running track, laying more sidings and adding to its rolling stock collection.

The future security of the Norchard site was assured when early in 1980 terms were agreed with Lydney Park Estate to purchase the complete site. Towards the end of 1980 the Lydney to Parkend branch was declared 'closed to traffic' by British Rail and negotiations were started during December 1980 with the B.R. Property Board for the purchase of the branch line. At the same time a private company named the Dean Forest Railway Company Ltd was formed, with the intention of converting to a public company and making a public share issue when negotiations were completed.

A large amount of work will be required to bring the branch up to passenger-carrying standard, but it is envisaged that services over at 'least a small section of the line could commence within possibly a year to eighteen months of the completion of the purchase'. At Norchard, work will carry on to improve and add to the facilities already in existence to enable it to fulfil its long-term intentions of being the branch depot.

Stock

Amongst the growing collection of rolling stock at Norchard are no less than three G.W.R. 'Prairie' tanks, and a fourth has been bought to provide a source of spares. No. 5541 was bought by the Forest Prairie Fund from Barry scrapyard in 1972 and restored to working order four years later. Sister engine 5521 also came from Barry, having been purchased originally by the West Somerset Railway before being resold to two Dean Forest Members in 1980. No. 5532 is the similar engine to be used for spare parts. 'Large Prairie' tank No. 4121 joined the three smaller 2-6-2Ts at Norchard in 1980, having also made the journey from Barry. Great Western Pannier tank No. 9681, a representative of a class which was used almost exclusively in the final years of steam operation in the Forest of Dean, it was rescued from Barry scrapyard in 1975 and is undergoing a thorough restoration to working order.

There are two Hunslet 0-6-0STs; the larger, an 18″ 'Austerity' type, has been named *G.B. Keeling* after the General Manager of the old Severn & Wye Railway. The smaller (16″) engine is known as *Jessie* and took an unusual route into active preservation, having been a static exhibit in a park in Cardiff for fifteen years, fitted with steps and railings to allow children to climb all over her. Apart from the small Peckett 0-4-0ST *Uskmouth I*, the railway has three diesel locos, the largest being ex-B.R. Drewry No. 03.062.

In readiness for running a passenger train service over the branch, the railway has bought a rake of B.R. bogie coaches, including two of the experimental XP64 series of vehicles. Most of the other passenger coaches are of Great Western origin, including two push-pull Auto Trailers. Similarly, most of the goods rolling stock hails from the G.W.R.

Quainton Railway Society

The Quainton Railway Society was formed in 1969 as a working railway museum of locomotives and rolling stock together with equipment of all kinds as used until the 1950s. The Society originated from the London Railway Preservation Society, formed in 1962. Over the years it has built up an extremely large and impressive array of exhibits. Quainton itself is of interest in that it was the place where the Great Central and Metropolitan Railways met. Many of the locos and some of the rolling stock reflect these two companies, but there are other main-line and industrial engines, for the aim of the society is to make their collection as comprehensive as possible.

Quainton Road station's heyday can fairly be said to have lasted from 1899, when the Great Central Railway's London extension brought expresses from Manchester and Sheffield thundering through on their way to Marylebone, until 1935 when the former Oxford & Aylesbury Tramroad (the Quainton to Brill branch) closed. Services on the main line continued to decline and the station was closed to passengers in March 1963. The last main line passenger train over the old G.C.R. line steamed through Quainton Road on 5 September 1966, after which the track between Rugby and Aylesbury was lifted, except for a single line through Quainton which remains to this day for freight working from Bletchley.

For three years, Quainton Road stood derelict,

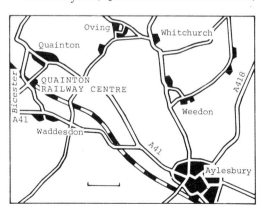

*The London Railway Preservation Society formed in 1969 the Quainton Railway Society which is based on the sidings at Quainton Road station (B.R. still uses the through-line for goods), the place where the Great Central and Metropolitan Railways met. Its particular speciality is old coaches: this train of vintage G.N.R. and G.C.R. six-wheelers is hauled by L. & S.W.R. 2-4-0 tank No. 0314, a well tank loco (the water tank slung between the wheels) built in 1874. (*John Gardner*)*

the only life coming from the occasional passage of goods trains to and from Aylesbury via the Calvert spur line. But on 4 April 1969 a new chapter of activity in the station's life began as preserved engines started to arrive. Today there are over forty locomotives on the site, most of them steam, but including a few diesels. Over a third of this total is either operational now or have worked under their own power at Quainton in the past ten years.

Stock

Appropriately, the Metropolitan Railway is represented by their No. 1, a handsome 0-4-4T built in 1898. This is one of a small class of seven

locomotives (Metropolitan Railway class 'E') which for more than twenty years dominated the Aylesbury services until the introduction of the 'H' class 4-4-4 tanks in 1920. On the formation of the London Passenger Transport Board in 1933, No. 1 became L.T. No. L44 and carried this number until withdrawal in 1964. Notable events for No. 1 during its working career included hauling the first passenger train over the Uxbridge line on 4 July 1904, the last steam train on the Chesham branch in July 1960 and appearing in the Metropolitan Centenary Parade at Neasden on 23 May 1963. No. 1 arrived at Quainton in September 1970 and has undergone an extensive overhaul before emerging once again in Metropolitan lined maroon livery.

No fewer than five ex-G.W.R. locos are to be found at Quainton including examples of the largest tank and tender engine types ever built at Swindon. No. 6024 *King Edward I* was purchased from Barry scrapyard and moved to Quainton Road in 1973. Since then it has been completely dismantled down to its component parts and is undergoing a major rebuild. 2-8-2T No. 7200 is the prototype member of its class and also arrived at Quainton from Barry scrapyard. The 72XX class were rebuilt from earlier 52XX 2-8-0 Tanks, the frames being lengthened at the rear to accommodate a trailing pony truck, whilst the bunker and back water tank were both enlarged to give the engine an extra 700 gallons of water and two tons of coal. The engines were used on mainline haulage of heavy mineral traffic.

No. 6989 *Wightwick Hall* is one of F.W. Hawksworth's 'Modified Hall' class 4-6-0s. By altering the 'Hall' design with full-depth plate frames at the front end and a new type of plate-frame bogie, Hawksworth produced a much stronger and more workmanlike engine than the Collett members of the class.

Two pannier tanks, Nos. 7715 and 9466, complete the G.W.R. collection at Quainton. No. 7715 was purchased from London Transport in 1970 when it was numbered L.T. No. L.99. It is an example of the 57XX type, Britain's most numerous class of locomotive – in all, 863 of them were built. No. 9466 is, in contrast a much larger and more modern

0-6-0PT, having taken to the rails after nationalization in 1952. By the time the last of the 210 locomotives of the 94XX class entered service in 1956, dieselization was already gathering momentum on B.R. and the class as a whole was destined for a tragically short life. Fifty of them, barely worn, were sold for scrap in 1960 and No. 9466 made the journey to Woodhams scrapyard at Barry in October 1964. After purchase for preservation and arrival at Quainton, it has been undergoing a major restoration to working order.

Doyen of the Quainton collection is L.S.W.R. Beattie 2-4-0WT No. E0314. This charming old engine dates from 1874 when it was built for use on the Waterloo suburban 'services. When replaced on these trains by the much larger Adams 4-4-2 Tanks in the 1880s, most of the class were withdrawn, though thirty were converted into tender engines and three were drafted down to the West Country. Here, they soon made the Wenford Bridge mineral line in Cornwall their home. The sharp curves on this line prevented the use of larger, heavier engines and the three Beattie tanks handled almost all its traffic for over 60 years. The Quainton engine was rebuilt and reboiled several times during her long lifetime and has carried a variety of numbers. Starting her career as L.S.W.R. No. 314, she became successively 0314, E0314, 3314 and 30585, the last being her B.R. identity. Purchased for preservation in 1963, the engine was initially stored at Bishops Stortford before moving to Quainton and being restored to working order in 1976 at the ripe old age of 102! Known simply as 'The Beattie', No. E0314 is the mascot and emblem of the Society.

Quainton is also the home for three modern L.M.S. Ivatt Light Mixed Traffic engines. 2-6-0 tender engine No. 46447 and its 2-6-2T derivatives. Nos. 41298 and 41313 were introduced in the postwar years under the L.M.S. and construction continued after nationalization. In fact, all three preserved engines were built in B.R. days. Although modest in size, these useful little locos incorporated several features developed for use on the heaviest express engines, including self-cleaning smokeboxes, rocking grates and self-emptying ashpans. Their designs also formed the basis of the Riddles B.R. Standard 2MT classes numbered in the 78XXX and 84XXX series.

Quainton is perhaps best known for its large and varied fleet of industrial steam locomotives. Significant examples are: *Sir Thomas*, a handsome Hudswell Clarke 0-6-0 side tank which is the officially preserved representative of the former Oxfordshire Ironstone Company's fleet. Barclay 0-4-0 Fireless locomotive No. 2243 which has been restored to working order and is steamed from time to time, taking its supply secondhand from one of the larger engines: *Sydenham*, one of the famous Aveling & Porter geared engines looking like a road traction engine on rails: *Coventry No. 1*, a large, well-proportioned 0-6-0 side tank built by North British in 1939 to a much earlier design by Neilson Reid; Peckett 0-4-0 side tank No. 1900 – a miniscule engine only 5 ft 4 in. high which demands footplate crews both agile and small of stature, and which usually carries a headboard proclaiming it to be the smallest standard gauge engine in the British Isles. There are three of the interesting chain-driven, vertical-boilered Sentinel locomotives, the oldest of which was actually owned by the Great Western Railway for a short while.

The Society has a very interesting and historic collection of coaches. There is a Great Northern six-wheeled third-class brake carriage, built in 1895. Other historic carriages include an L.N.E.R. Gresley-designed BSK coach, No. 41384, built in 1936; an L.C.D.R. first-class four-wheeled coach built in 1880; an L. & N.W.R. first-class kitchen/dining car No. 77, built in 1901; and an L. & N.W.R. six-wheeled passenger brake, No. DM 279982, built in 1891.

The Society holds a number of open days on bank holidays. Rides are then available, when the engines are in steam. The nearest railway station is Aylesbury, and there is occasionally a charter d.m.u. service from there to Quainton station.

Chasewater Light Railway

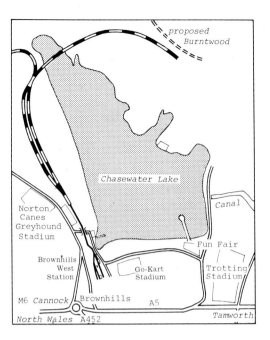

The Chasewater Light Railway was first leased from the National Coal Board in 1965. At the time it still constituted part of the truncated remains of the former Cannock Chase and Wolverhampton Railway, built in 1856, and an extension of the Midland Railway's Walsall Wood branch opened in 1884. The Chasewater line's operators are very conscious of the great tradition of British minor railways and the railway reflects something of the spirit of prewar light railways of the Colonel Stephens group. In fact a portrait of the Colonel hangs in the waiting room at Brownhills West station.

Most of the rolling stock and equipment owned by the railway is of considerable antiquity, though passengers are nowadays likely to find themselves travelling in former diesel multiple-unit trailer coaches – albeit propelled along by a steam locomotive. On special occasions, however, the vintage coaches are brought out.

Currently being restored is a Manchester, Sheffield and Lincolnshire Railway six-wheeler, which was taken over as a rotting hulk. It dates from about 1890. A superb example of restoration is provided by the sole surviving vehicle from the Maryport and Carlisle Railway, a six-wheeled carriage built in 1879. There is also a former Great Eastern full brake coach, No. 44, built in 1885, as well as a number of other vintage coaches, mostly from the Midland Railway.

OPPOSITE ABOVE: *Peckett superpower at Quainton! 0-4-0 saddletanks* Hornpipe *and* 2105 *double-head the train of coaches. (*Phil Wood*)*

OPPOSITE BELOW: *Doyen of the Chasewater Light Railway is Neilson saddletank* Alfred Paget. *Supplied originally to Gartsherrie Ironworks in Scotland, the little engine recently celebrated its working centenary amid suitably industrial surroundings at Chasewater. Here it heads a passenger train at Brownhills West. (*John Gardner*)*

The line runs around the edge of Chasewater Pleasure Park, which features a fine lake, go-kart stadium and fun fair. Ultimately it is hoped that the railway will operate along a 2-mile stretch (purchased from B.R. in 1978) with proper station facilities at each end to enable a regular passenger schedule to be introduced. A particular feature is a narrow $\frac{1}{4}$-mile causeway across the end of the lake.

Stock
Eight industrial steam locomotives plus four diesels provide the motive power for the line. In recent years passenger trains have been hauled by the oldest engine in the collection, built in 1882, Neilson 0-4-0ST *Alfred Paget*, and by Barclay 0-4-0ST *Invicta* (1946), Peckett 0-4-0ST *The Colonel* (1914) and Hawthorn Leslie 0-4-0ST *Asbestos* (1909). The only six-coupled locos in the collection are two Hudswell Clarkes, the ancient No. 15, a saddletank built in 1895 and the modern *Whit No. 4*, a side tank built in 1949. The society possesses a fine collection of small relics, tickets, plates and other railway memorabilia. Many of these items are displayed inside the railway's 1909 L.N.W.R. travelling Post Office vehicle.

35

North Staffordshire Steam Railway Centre

'Owd Knotty', otherwise the North Staffordshire Railway, was a line of immense character
and very much a family concern. Very few of
the larger railway companies could equal the
aesthetic charm of its station architecture, fewer
still could claim the formation of a staff social
association after the 1923 grouping, and none
could claim to have been immortalized by
musical documentary. Small wonder, then, that
a preservation society should come forward,

Austerity 0-6-0 saddletank Josiah Wedgwood,
*painted in the old North Stafford livery of Madder
Lake, carries out some shunting at the Cheddleton
headquarters. (*Tom Heavyside*)*

wishing to perpetuate the memory of the
'Knotty' in more tangible, living form.

The North Staffordshire Railway Company
has established its headquarters at Cheddleton
station in the picturesque Churnet Valley.
Cheddleton is situated on a B.R. freight-only
line carrying bulk sand traffic from quarries at
Oakamoor; a further two miles to Alton Towers
and on to Uttoxeter has been lifted.

At Cheddleton sidings have been laid to
accommodate the preservation company's
stock, as well as a short running line over which
a visitor shuttle service is operated, trains
terminating in the station's recommissioned bay
platform. Operations are controlled from the
former Elton Crossing signalbox which has been
moved to Cheddleton and recommissioned.

Stock
The working steam engine is one of the familiar

Hunslet 'Austerity' 0-6-0STs painted in 'Knotty' madder lake livery and named *Josiah Wedgwood*. Undergoing restoration are two ex-B.R. locomotives purchased from Woodham's scrapyard at Barry. These are L.M.S. 4F class 0-6-0 tender engine No. 4422, built in 1927, and British Railways Standard 4MT class 2-6-4 tank No. 80136. Both are long-term projects but will prove to be very suitable motive power should access ultimately be obtained to the Oakamoor line.

Passengers are carried in a pair of B.R. Mark I mainline coaches and there is a small collection of goods vehicles.

The area around

The Churnet Valley is renowned for its natural beauty and visitors to the station can readily sample the pleasant scenery and places of interest within a short radius of the museum. The picturesque Cauldon Canal runs parallel to the railway and is only a short walk away from the station. The passenger-carrying narrow boat 'Royal Jubilee' operates along the Cauldon Canal throughout the summer season and enquiries about booking should be made at Cheddleton station. A well-restored flint mill and church (St Edward's) are located in Cheddleton village, with Coombes Valley nature reserve nearby. The area is honeycombed with pleasant walkways and the station is situated on the Staffordshire County Council leisure drive.

The well-known tourist attractions of Alton Towers and Rudyard Lake are within easy driving distance of the museum. The station building at Cheddleton is both beautiful and imposing, built in the Jacobean style reputedly by the famous architect Pugin and is protected as a listed building by the Department of the Environment. An attractive souvenir shop and museum rooms are situated at platform level in the main building with the railway offices above. Light refreshments are available from either the shop or one of the carriages located in the bay platform area. Cheddleton is being restored to represent a typical country station of the old 'Knotty' railway and the museum contains authentic relics and items of interest from the original North Staffordshire Railway.

Whipsnade and Umfolozi Railway

Opened in 1970, this splendid narrow-gauge railway was created from scratch as a commercial venture, and is operated by Pleasurail. It allows close-quarter viewing of species like white rhinos, bison and camels, uncaged in the animal paddocks of Whipsnade Zoo. It is an imaginative answer to the problem of helping visitors to the Zoo see as much as possible of the wildlife there.

The first stage went only to the white rhino enclosure. The rhino came from Umfolozi in Zululand, hence the railway's name. They soon grew used to the 2 ft 6 in. gauge steam locomotives, and so in 1973 the railway was extended to its present length of about 2 miles. (The animals are now so used to the railway that train crews often have to persuade sleeping rhinos that the best place to take a nap is not on the permanent way!)

The railway forms an irregular oval, with trains starting and finishing at the twin-platform Whipsnade Central station next to the dolphinarium. Fairly considerable engineering

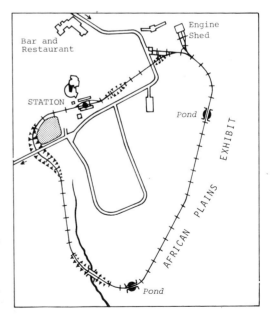

ABOVE: *Whipsnade's smallest engine* Excelsior *at the railway's original terminus platform with a train of open-sided coaches. (*Phil Wood*)*

BELOW: Conqueror *accelerates a train away from Whipsnade Central station at the start of a trip round the animal enclosures. (*Tom Heavyside*)*

works were necessary (the Zoo is on top of the Dunstable Downs), and the line features a short tunnel, two level crossings, steep gradients, and several cuttings and embankments.

Much of the line's equipment and rolling stock came from the Bowater paper-mill railway at Sittingbourne (part of which has been preserved as the Sittingbourne and Kemsley), which was last used for industrial purposes in 1969. The three 0-6-0 tanks, *Chevallier, Conqueror* and *Superior*, were built by Manning Wardle, Bagnall and Kerr-Stuart respectively, in 1915, 1922 and 1920. (*Conqueror* fell into the dock at Bowater in the 1953 flood.) The fourth steam loco is the oldest (1908), the 0-4-2 *Excelsior*, built by Kerr-Stuart. Passengers are carried in coaches rebuilt from pulp wagons.

On static display is the 3 ft 6 in. gauge 4-8-0 No. 390 from the Zambesi Sawmills, built in Glasgow in 1896, and a Rhodesia Railways sleeping car. These items were presented to artist David Shepherd (of Cranmore) by President Kaunda, and then transported over 12,000 miles to Whipsnade.

The railway usually operates with steam but two 100 h.p. Fowler diesels are used for shunting, and sometimes haul off-peak trains.

The Leighton Buzzard Narrow-Gauge Railway

During World War I supplies of sand from Belgium dried up, and pits near Leighton Buzzard were opened to meet the need. Increased output demanded improved transport, and $4\frac{1}{2}$ miles of 2 ft gauge railway was laid down between Churchways and Pages Park and opened for traffic in 1919. Motive power was at first by steam but latterly till the pits were closed in 1969, petrol-driven ex-W.D. locomotives were used.

The Leighton Buzzard Narrow-gauge Railway Society was formed in 1968 in anticipation of the line's closure, and ran their first passenger train – diesel hauled – on 3 March 1968. In June their first steam engine arrived, and was run along the line. (Trains now start from Pages Park Station in Billington Road.) This first engine was

Kerr Stuart 0-4-0 saddletank Pixie *stands by the water tank at Pages Park station on the Leighton Buzzard Narrow-Gauge Railway.* (Phil Wood)

Chaloner, which has a vertical boiler and was built by De Winton & Co. of Caernarvon in 1877, for work in slate quarries in the Nantille Valley, North Wales. She remained there until bought in 1960 by Mr Alfred Fisher, who overhauled her. She is claimed to be the oldest narrow-gauge engine in England, and the last working example of an industrial type once common in North Wales. She has been on loan to the National Railway Museum for several years.

Chaloner is No. 1; No. 2 is *Pixie*, a 0-4-0 saddle tank, built in 1922, which worked in Devon County Council roadstone quarries till 1955. She was bought and overhauled by the Industrial Locomotive Society, and began service at Leighton Buzzard in 1969.

Rishra, No. 3, was built in 1921 for service in India. She hauled coal trains from a wharf on the Hooghly river to the boiler house of the Pulta Pumping Station at Barrakpore, north of Calcutta, and after long negotiations was restored by the apprentices of the Hooghly Dock and Engineering Co. She was then shipped back to England, and first ran there in October 1972.

The Doll is No. 4. A 0-6-0 tank engine built by Andrew Barclay in 1919 for work in an

Watching gnomes gather in the Park as an Elf *and a* Pixie *pause at the platform. The 'little people' are all part of the charm of the Leighton Buzzard Narrow-Gauge Railway. (J. Horsley)*

ironstone pit in Oxfordshire, she was later transferred to a foundry in Bilston, where she had very rough treatment. Purchased by the I.L.S. in 1972, she is in the process of being restored, in the hope that she may once again be steamable.

The Society has two other steam engines and eighteen diesels, mostly W.D. types, and offers a regular scheduled service on Sundays, Easter to September, and Bank Holiday Saturdays and Mondays in addition; there are 3 miles of track now in use.

Future plans include the building of further passenger rolling stock, and the setting up of a museum of the local sand industry.

Besides being an ancient market town of considerable interest, Leighton Buzzard is also within reasonably easy reach of such places as Woburn Abbey, Whipsnade Zoo, the Stagsden Bird Gardens, and the Shuttleworth Aircraft Museum at Old Warden near Biggleswade.

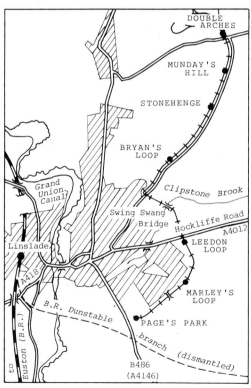

40

The Cadeby Light Railway

Cadeby is a small Leicestershire village not far from Market Bosworth (from which the famous battle of 1485 took its name). The narrow-gauge railway there is entirely the inspiration of the Rector, the Rev. E. R. Boston. It runs round the grounds of his rectory.

In 1962 he bought the Bagnall saddle tank *Pixie*, No. 2090, from Staveley Minerals who had no further use for her in their quarry. Following *Pixie's* arrival, a trackbed was prepared and track laid. This involved clearing away vegetation and laying down ballast delivered from the nearby Cliffe Hill quarry. The railway was fortunate in receiving much of its track free, as a gift from Cadeby quarry. Track-laying went on from early summer through to September by which time a station and most of the upper curve had been completed. *Pixie* had not

Bagnall 0-4-0 No. 2090 of 1919 on the Cadeby Light Railway. (T. J. Edgington)

worked for some time; she therefore needed a thorough overhaul. New slide bars, new crossheads and fresh piston rings were fitted. The boiler was carefully examined and given a stiff hydraulic test. The first steam run was in April 1963, and the locomotive proved to be in fine working order. That summer witnessed the completion of the 400-yard line between Cadeby and Sutton Lane Stations.

Since then, many more locomotives have been acquired; part of the permanent way has been relaid with 40-lb rail replacing the lighter, original track. Besides the engine *Pixie*, the Railway now has two other steam locomotives: both are 0-4-0 tanks, but of very different appearance. *Margaret* is one of the classic Hunslet saddletanks built for use in the Penrhyn Quarries in North Wales in 1894. The other engine was built by Orenstein & Koppel in 1914 and is of the German firm's familiar well tank type.

In addition to these steam-powered engines, the Railway has acquired several diesel locomotives. These include Motor Rail 'Simplex' Diesel, No. 3874. This engine was built in 1929

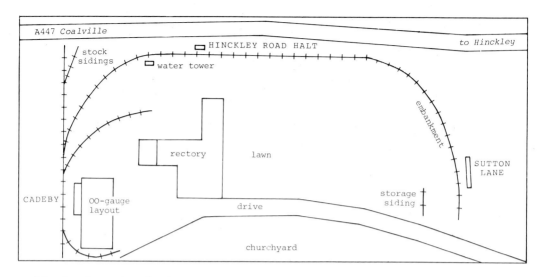

and is of a class originally designed to run in France during World War I. No. 3874 was rescued from the Birmingham, Tame and Rea District Drainage Board in 1965. Another early 'Simplex' diesel owned by the Railway is No. 5853, constructed in 1934. It is universally known by the operating staff as 'The Diesel'; this is now an accurate description, as the original petrol engine was replaced in 1958 and a Dorman 20 h.p. diesel substituted. Also to be seen is No. 1695, *Lilleshall*, a Baguley petrol-driven engine finished in 1928; Motor Rail Diesel No. 5609, built in 1931; and a Hudswell Clark diesel No. 558, completed in 1930. This last engine is curious in that it was designed with a dummy chimney of a steam type. (It is rumoured that these were fitted to these locomotives because the works manager was a keen steam enthusiast and had very dogmatic views as to the proper appearance of engines.) The three open wagons which serve as passenger carriages have all come from the R.A.F. railway at Fauld. They have since been smartly turned out in grey-and-black livery with red fittings.

There are two bonuses to be found at the railway; one is a collection of traction engines and the other a fine model railway. The latter is housed in a wooden shed situated behind Cadeby station. It represents the South Devon section of the Great Western Railway between Newton Abbot and Totnes. The actual countryside around Dartmoor is faithfully reproduced, although the junction station of Olton Prior is imaginary. The main line is worked on the basis of the 1938 timetable, with the clock speeded up by a ratio of 8:1, permitting the day's schedule to be completed in only 3 hours. The railway boasts a large number of G.W.R. locomotives, including Kings, Castles, Stars, Manors and Granges, together with the ubiquitous pannier tanks. Twenty engines are required to fulfil the demands of the timetable. The line has taken over a decade to build, so far, and much work still remains to be done. In the rectory itself there is a very comprehensive collection of railway relics ranging from nameplates to tickets and luggage labels.

The traction engine collection includes the steam roller *Thistledown*, built by Aveling and Porter, and *Fiery Elias*, a Foster traction engine built in 1929. Both are in full working order. *Fiery Elias* is a single cylinder 7-h.p. engine capable of hauling 16 to 20 tons, while *Thistledown* is a 5-h.p., ten-ton steam roller built in 1903. She worked for Leicester County Council until 1960, and has since been well restored.

The Cadeby Light Railway is probably the smallest steam-worked narrow-gauge railway in the world. The line is open to the public on the second Saturday in the month, and other days by arrangement.

Midland Railway Centre

Created by the amalgamation of the Midland Counties, North Midland and Birmingham and Derby Junction Railways in 1844, the Midland Railway grew by extension and further amalgamation to be the third longest in Great Britain and one of the best managed systems in the world. Because of its wide ownership of joint lines, its crimson lake trains, unsurpassed for comfort and catering, were to be seen in England, Wales, Scotland and Ireland and in more towns and cities than those of any other company. It was engineered with imagination and most of its stations were architectural gems.

The railway enjoyed an enviable reputation as a pioneer. This was established in the 1870s, a notable decade during which the Midland became the first to introduce third class on all trains, to abolish second class, to upholster third class and to operate Pullman cars, setting standards of comfort which the other railway companies were forced to emulate, although not always with success. Many Midland features were continued by the London Midland & Scottish Railway after 1923 and, indeed, by B.R.

after 1948. Such a railway, which gave so much to our social, economic and industrial history, is worthy of a lasting memorial.

In July 1969 the then curator of Derby Museum, Mr. Arthur Thorpe, F.M.A., put forward a scheme to commemorate the Midland Railway in the form of a working, living museum, illustrating the history and development of the Midland Railway and its successors. At the outset it was recognized that the magnitude of the scheme was such that volunteer support from the public was essential and in 1969 the Midland Railway Project Group (now the Midland Railway Trust Limited) was formed to provide it.

At the commencement of the project, a number of redundant railway lines in or around Derby were considered on which to establish the centre. The choice eventually made was part of the ex-Midland Railway line from Ambergate to Pye Bridge. The only passenger station actually on the line was at Butterley, which

One of the most beautiful express locomotive types ever to run in the British Isles were the Midland Railway 'Spinners'. No. 673 operated for a while on the Midlands line at Butterley. (Phil Wood)

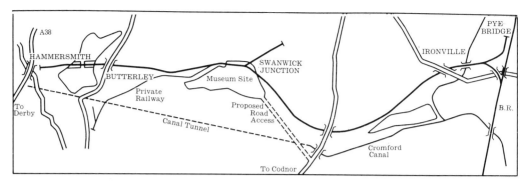

opened on 1 May 1875 and closed on 16 June 1947, although excursion traffic continued into the sixties. On 23 December 1968, the section of line from Ambergate to Swanwick Junction was closed completely and the remainder of the line to Codnor Park Junction became a private siding to the Butterley Company Works.

The reasons for the selection of this particular length of line for the Midland Railway Centre fell into three categories. Firstly, the line is located centrally between the high population centres of Nottingham, Derby, Chesterfield and Sheffield. Secondly, part-way along the line there were the remains of a pit tip that could be reclaimed in such a way as to allow the creation of a substantial living museum complex on a 57-acre site alongside the railway line. Thirdly, the scheme fitted in with a linear green belt and leisure area, designated by the local planning authority. Hence, there were good long-term reasons for the selection of this length of line.

Although the railway line for the Midland Railway Centre had been selected, it was 1973 before members of the Trust could actually commence work on site. The first four years were spent gathering items from around the country that were of relevance to the Midland Railway, these relics then being put in store in or around Derby. The items collected ranged from station masters' uniforms to railway turntables, from signal boxes to rolling stock. At long last, work actually started 'on site' in September 1973, but it was a daunting prospect that faced the volunteer members of the Midland Railway Trust. Most of the track had been lifted, all the original station and platforms had been demolished, no other structures existed and mains services had long since been disconnected.

The decision was taken to make the site of the old Butterley Station the initial base for the project and everything that can be seen there today has been built, laid, made or transported there since those early days. By 1975, the site had progressed sufficiently to allow the first of what was for a while to be a regular feature, these were Steam Open Days when locomotives were steamed and items were on display to the public. Unfortunately it was to be several years before a passenger service could commence.

From 1975 onwards, time was devoted to restoring and preserving items of historical significance to the Midland Railway in addition to providing the basic facilities required for train operation and the visiting public. This included further track laying, the installation of run-round loops and ground frames and watering and coaling facilities. A significant advance was made in 1978 when the first stage of what will eventually be a 300 ft long carriage shed was brought into use, providing much needed accommodation. After a lot of legal complications, procedures were put in hand during January 1980 for obtaining a Light Railway Order – a statutory instrument that is a prerequisite to moving passenger trains. This lengthy procedure was concluded during July 1981 and coincided with the completion of the first mile of operational track to the satisfaction of the Department of Transport Railway Inspectorate. Finally, with the transfer of land from British Railways to the Derbyshire County Council and subsequent 99-year lease to the Trust, the wheels were able to turn.

The first passenger train to mark the new era departed from Butterley Station at 11.30 a.m. on 22 August 1981. The official opening took place

Somerset and Dorset 2-8-0 No. 13809, complete with Pines Express headboard, makes light work of its ten-coach load.

the following week. Following the opening of the line, efforts are being concentrated on general lineside improvement and the construction of the basic museum shell at Swanwick on the site of the old Britain Colliery. In its initial stages it will be used as covered storage for rolling stock and essential workshop accommodation but ultimately it will house the already vast and ever-growing collection of static exhibits, both large and small.

A journey down the line
The first notable item on entering the Midland Railway Centre is the station building. The original Butterley Station was demolished when the line closed but fortunately a similar disused building existed at Whitwell in North Derbyshire. The Trust acquired the building and then set about the laborious task of taking it apart, stone by stone, moving it to Butterley and rebuilding it. This long and difficult task should

be completed in the near future. Once through the booking office, the visitor walks onto the platform which has also been rebuilt by the Trust as the original was demolished along with the station.

Walking under the bridge to the former goods yard reveals much of interest. On the former cattle dock can be seen coaching stock under restoration and at the side of the dock are two coaches containing model railway displays. The first is an historic Midland Railway arc-roofed coach which now houses a display by the East Midland E.M. Gauge Society. Opposite this over the level crossing is the picnic area and the footpath along the top of the cutting to Swanwick which provides excellent opportunities for photography. The area beyond the buffet is used for locomotive maintenance.

The air of nostalgia begins straight away, the guard's whistle blows, the green flag is waved, an answering whistle from the locomotive and the journey begins. The locomotive has to work hard to pull the train out of Butterley Station and a glimpse of the rolling stock in the yard is seen before the train enters the cutting. The line climbs steeply through the cutting and the beat of the hard working steam locomotive can be heard. At the end of the cutting, the line levels out and the storage sidings and shed at Swanwick can be seen on the righthand side. The train then descends the gradient to Swanwick Junction Station. This will be the headquarters of the Centre and much building work can be seen in progress. Many more items of interest are stored at Swanwick and a walk up to the storage shed is strongly recommended to view the historic items on display. Passengers may break their journey here if they wish.

On the journey beyond Swanwick Junction visitors should look out for Jessop's monument on the hill to the right and below in the Golden Valley, the Codnor Park Reservoir and the industrial hamlet of Ironville, built by the Butterley Company to house its workers. Many of these cottages have now been restored. The present line terminates at Ironville within sight of the main Erewash Valley line of British Rail.

On the return journey after pausing at Swanwick Junction we make a spirited non-stop run through Butterley and across the Butterley Reservoir. This pleasant stretch of water was built to feed the Cromford Canal, which passes under it in a tunnel, and is now used for leisure activities. It is a very popular fishing spot and the wildlife of the reservoir is also of note. The railway crosses the water on an impressive stone embankment and, shortly after the crossing, Hammersmith Station is entered. The railway now terminates here since the building of the A38 trunk road cuts the line. Originally it ran to the main line at Ambergate. Hammersmith was the junction of a branch to Ripley and the space occupied by this junction is now used by the Trust. Two impressive stone platforms have been built as the first stage of the station and the rest of the site is used for storage by the signal and telegraph department.

In a short while, the locomotive has run round the train and is ready to return to Butterley Station.

Stock

No visitor can fail to be impressed by the authentic L.M.S. atmosphere created by the large collection of locomotives and rolling stock,

nearly all of which reflect Derby ancestry.

Oldest of all the historic Midland Railway locomotives is the beautifully restored express passenger locomotive completed to the designs of Matthew Kirtley at Derby in September 1866. Built specifically for hauling passenger trains to King's Cross station, then the Midland's London terminus (courtesy of the Great Northern Railway), she is typical of the period, with outside cranks to the driving axles and double frames. Rebuilt at various dates she was finally withdrawn from service by the L.M.S. in August 1947, appearing at the Stephenson Centenary celebrations at Chesterfield in 1948. She was preserved at Derby Locomotive Works until 1964 and later still at Leicester's temporary Stoneygate Museum, before moving by road to the Midland Railway Centre in 1975. She has since been repainted by apprentices at Derby Carriage and Wagon Works.

If the Trust has a 'standard' class of locomotives, it can fairly be said to be the popular L.M.S. 'Jinty' 0-6-0 tanks, of which there are four at Butterley. Developed from a Midland Railway design of 1899 this large class of 422 locomotives was widely used over the whole L.M.S. system on shunting line freight and passenger duties. They were built between the years 1924 and 1931 and most survived to be taken over by British Railways, the last one being withdrawn in the 1960s.

Nos. 16440 (latterly 47357) and 47327 were both recovered from Woodhams at Barry Docks, and the former was rebuilt in Derby Locomotive Works, being steamed again for the first time in June 1973. It was later restored in authentic L.M.S. passenger livery although the class never enjoyed such luxury being demoted to plain black all their working lives! No. 47327 is at present dismantled and being gradually restored to working order as funds allow and will eventually be painted in representative L.M.S. black livery. The third locomotive, 47445, was sold out of service to Hargreaves (West Riding) Ltd and finished its normal working life at Crigglestone, near Wakefield, before being acquired for preservation in June 1970. This locomotive is also dismantled and awaiting restoration.

The spare boiler, 2022, began life as 16647 and was converted for stationary duties at

Dating back to 1866, Midland Railway 2-4-0 No. 158A is based at Butterley. (John Gardner)

Darlington in September 1965. It was recovered from Red Bank carriage sidings, near Manchester, in 1972 and parts have already been incorporated in 16440. Its frames may well be used as a basis for the restoration of the third locomotive of this basic motive power group.

The largest locomotive present is the elegant Stanier Pacific No. 6203 'Princess Margaret Rose'. The design of this class has been called 'a landmark in locomotive history' since these engines represented a major step forward for L.M.S. locomotive policy. First of the second batch, 6203 emerged from Crewe Works in July 1935 and began to work on the West Coast main line being allocated to Polmadie (Glasgow); Camden (London); Edge Hill (Liverpool) and Crewe Depots. She attained a record speed for the class of 102.5 m.p.h. near Leighton Buzzard in May 1936, and was further distinguished by being the only Stanier Pacific to be repaired at Derby, that being in 1951–2.

She was withdrawn from Carlisle Kingmoor shed in October 1962 with 1,494,484 miles to her credit and was purchased by the late Sir Billy

Butlin for display at his Pwllheli holiday camp. She was offered on loan to the Trust in April 1974 and was moved through the camp over several weekends and then by rail to Derby for storage, arriving at the Centre in October 1974.

Following the formation of British Railways in 1948, R.A. Riddles was given the job of co-ordinating locomotive design and producing a range of standard locomotives of all classes incorporating the best features of the old major four companies. No. 73129 is an example of the class 5 4-6-0 Mixed Traffic tender locomotive, and is one of the last batch of steam locomotives built at Derby Works. She is fitted with British Caprotti rotary cam valve gear, as were thirty others of the class which totalled 172 locomotives in all.

The class as a whole worked on all six regions of B.R. and as new 73129 was allocated to Shrewsbury after completion at Derby in 1956. She later moved to Patricroft Depot, Manchester, in September 1958 and spent the remainder of her short working life there on express passenger and latterly also freight, duties. Withdrawn from service in December 1967 she fortunately found herself as one of the large group of scrap locomotives in Woodham's yard at Barry and languished there until selected for preservation at the Midland Railway Centre. Following purchase by Derby Corporation she was moved overnight by rail in company with other locomotives. She moved by rail to the Midland Railway Centre on 14 February 1975 since when the long process of restoration has begun.

No. 4027 is one of the ubiquitous 'Derby 4s', or Fowler 4F class 0-6-0 goods engines; a large class originally introduced by the Midland Railway in 1911. Equally at home on stopping passenger or freight workings, the locomotives were 'maids of all work' and were to be found all over the L.M.S. system. Most lasted to be taken over by British Railways and the last one was withdrawn from traffic in the 1960s. No. 44027, as it was under the B.R. numbering system, was itself withdrawn from Workington motive power depot in November 1964 and was placed in store at Preston Park, near Brighton, awaiting restoration. After much hard work, which has included a full boiler internal examination with re-tubing, the engine was steamed again on 1 December 1979 after 15 years of inactivity and made its first public appearance on New Year's Day 1980 at a Centre Open Day. It is in regular use taking turns hauling passenger trains on the Trust's line and is painted in L.M.S. unlined black livery. This engine starred in the Rainhill Trials Celebrations in May 1980.

It has often been said that the L.M.S. should have adopted a more modern goods engine design in the 1920s, instead of continuing to build the 4Fs right up until 1941 when a total of 772 were in service. Curiously enough, Sir Henry Fowler had designed a very suitable heavy freight 2-8-0 for the Somerset & Dorset Joint Railway in 1914 and six of these were built by the Midland Railway at Derby in that year. However, neither the Midland nor the L.M.S. adopted the design for their own use, though a further five engines for S. & D.J.R. use were supplied by Robert Stephenson & Co in 1925. No. 13809 is one of this batch. A handsome, powerful machine, she is restored to L.M.S. unlined black livery and shares duties hauling passenger trains at the Centre with occasional excursions on to B.R. metals to haul specials. This locomotive also appeared at the Rainhill

Trials Celebrations in May 1980.

Amongst the smaller industrial steam locomotives housed at Butterley are the sole-surviving locomotive built by Markham of Chesterfield, an Andrew Barclay 0-4-0 Crane Tank, and a Nasmyth Wilson 0-4-0ST built in 1894. There are also two significant diesel-electric locomotives: No. 12077 built in 1950 to an L.M.S. design, and No. D4 Great Gable, one of the celebrated 'Peak' class locomotives introduced under the B.R. Modernization Plan in the late 1950s.

Few, if any, preservation sites outside the National Railway Museum, can claim such a historic collection of rolling stock. At present the Trust has no less than four 6-wheeled coaches which together with the 2-4-0 No. 158A give a view of rail travel prior to 1900. Two of these coaches have been restored to their Victorian glory, from rotting shells, and now they are a credit to all involved in the mammoth job of restoration. The collection covers some 90 years of carriage building and the progress over these years can be seen at the Centre with examples of stock from each decade.

Much of the work on this side is far more long term than the locomotives and to ensure a complete collection many bodies have been obtained from throughout the country as long-term projects. Among these are no less than three Pullman cars imported by the Midland Railway from the U.S.A. in 1873. Although it will be many years before these can be completely restored, they are of much interest in their present condition.

Several of the coaches have become temporary homes for shops, the buffet, a model railway and so on, providing much needed accommodation for these facilities, prior to the vehicles' complete restoration. It was at the Rocket 150 celebrations where this side of the Midland Railway Centre's preservation skills was shown. Sleeping car 612 and vestibule coach M7991 were externally restored for staff use, and the latter had only arrived at the Centre a matter of weeks earlier in a very poor condition. These two, although not on public display, were ambassadors to the rest of the preservation movement and they received many favourable comments.

WALES

Introduction: Narrow-Gauge Railways in Wales

It was probably in North Wales that railways first became an attraction for visitors on holiday. There was a passenger coach, or coaches, to carry tourists on the 1 ft 11½ in. gauge Festiniog Railway as early as the 1840s, long before that line had steam locomotives. Horses pulled trains up the long continuous gradients, and gravity took them downwards.

The particular attraction of the F.R. for visitors was that fine views could be seen from its course high among the mountains. Later, steam locomotives were introduced, and regular passenger trains followed (the first in Britain on a gauge less than standard). The F.R. blossomed out into a small-scale main line which became a prototype for narrow-gauge railways throughout the world; visitors came to see it as an engineering marvel. By 1895 Baddeley and Ward's guide to *North Wales* was commenting '. . . though the wonder has somewhat worn off, still no orthodox tourist visits Wales without taking a turn . . . on the "Toy" railway.' The epithet 'Toy' was to be disdained by future generations of railway enthusiasts, but by 1895 several other narrow-gauge or 'Toy' railways had been built in Wales and were finding in tourism a useful way of supplementing ordinary goods and passenger traffic. More were to follow, and the Snowdon Mountain Railway was being built specifically for tourist traffic, to take holiday makers to the summit of the highest mountain in England and Wales.

During the 1930s Welsh narrow-gauge lines lost most of their local passengers to faster, more convenient, buses. Those lines that continued to run passenger trains did so almost entirely in summer only, for holiday visitors, to whom the twin attractions of small trains and mountain scenery were as enticing as ever. It was on lines known to holiday visitors, the Talyllyn and the Festiniog, that the railway preservation movement commenced in the 1950s. People on holiday started to come not only to travel on these railways, but also to help re-open and run them, voluntarily.

Most of the Welsh tourist railways have joined to form the Narrow Gauge Railways of Wales Joint Marketing Panel. This publishes a combined timetable sheet for the Ffestiniog, Welshpool and Llanfair, Talyllyn, Vale of Rheidol, Llanberis Lake, Snowdon Mountain, Brecon Mountain, Gwili, Fairbourne and Bala Lake lines. It also arranges for 'Narrow-Gauge Tourist Tickets' to be issued, which gives seven days unlimited travel on all these lines except the Snowdon.

Many of these railways have links with the Association of Railway Preservation Societies. The preservation movement as a whole benefits greatly from the expertise provided by well-established undertakings such as the Ffestiniog, and the Welshpool and Llanfair, and these in turn benefit from sound financing and safe operation and publicity of newer preserved railways.

Meanwhile, in north and mid-Wales, the 'Great Little Trains of Wales' (to use the collective name coined by the joint marketing panel) have become one of the Principality's most popular attractions for visitors.

They are all, those that operate a regular tourist service, *little* trains, that is to say, narrow-gauge. The standard-gauge preserved

1

railway in this part of the world is limited to the Llangollen Railway, now operating trains again on a long-dismantled line. On the other hand, several British Rail lines in north and mid Wales have their own scenic attractions and are worth travelling for their own sake, although trains are not, of course, steam-hauled. Notable are the Conwy Valley line (from Llandudno Junction to Blaenau Ffestiniog) and the Cambrian Coast line (Dovey Junction to Pwllheli). The latter links several of the little trains.

Though small, most of the little railways that were built up to the time of World War I were not made that way to attract custom, like a later generation of miniature railways. They were made narrow-gauge because such railways can traverse sharp curves and this, in a mountainous region, meant smaller civil engineering works and, in turn, cheaper construction. Narrow-gauge railways also meant small, cheap locomotives and rolling stock and low running costs. Many of them were built to provide mines and quarries with an outlet.

The Ffestiniog Railway

The line and its history
The purpose of the Ffestiniog Railway was to link slate quarries around Blaenau Ffestiniog with the harbour at Porthmadog (or, as it was known until recently, Portmadoc). This is about 13 miles to the south-west and some 700 ft lower. The line was built by the Ffestiniog Railway Company, and opened in 1836. The first steam locomotives were introduced in 1863, two small 0-4-0 tanks with tenders for coal. Many strange designs had first been considered, for much contemporary opinion held that it was impracticable to build locomotives at all for so narrow a gauge. In 1865, four-wheeled passenger coaches were acquired, and the line passed by Board of Trade inspector for regular passenger traffic.

Blanche, *a Hunslet 0-4-0 saddletank built in 1893, was used by the Penrhyn Railway. The Ffestiniog purchased it in 1963. (*D. R. Stopher*)*

Double-Fairlie locomotive Merddin Emrys *entering Minffordd on the first stage of its journey up to Blaenau Ffestiniog.* (R. Crombleholme)

This was a remarkable feat, for, since the 'gauge war' between 7 ft and 4 ft 8½ in. gauges, it had been illegal to construct a passenger railway of any gauge other than standard.

The Ffestiniog Railway really caught the public imagination, however, when rapidly increasing traffic obliged it to introduce more powerful motive power, *Little Wonder*, a double-ended 0-4-4-0 built to Fairlie's patent, carried on two bogies and having the appearance of two locomotives back-to-back – a compact but powerful machine. The type had been tried elsewhere, but it was on the F.R. that it was first really successful. Shortly afterwards the F.R. introduced the first bogie coaches to be used in Great Britain. Behind all this lay the Spooner family: James Spooner was the engineer who built the line, Charles Spooner, his son, introduced steam traction and developed the railway. The slate trade flourished and the

railway prospered with it.

And when the slate trade eventually declined, the railway did too. Tiles became cheaper, and standard-gauge railways built direct to Blaenau Ffestiniog took much of what traffic was left. Local year-round passenger traffic (except for quarrymen's trains) ceased in 1930, and all passenger traffic was suspended at the outbreak of war in 1939. In 1946 the railway, overgrown, closed for freight too.

It became a lot more overgrown during the next few years, for the Act incorporating the Company was so old that it included no provision for legal abandonment and dismantling and the company could not afford to obtain such powers from Parliament.

The re-opening
The Ffestiniog Railway Society Ltd originated from a public meeting called by seventeen-year-old L. A. Heath Humphrys in Bristol in 1951. The intention was to re-open the railway with voluntary support. Investigations showed that the Company was heavily in debt, which would

3

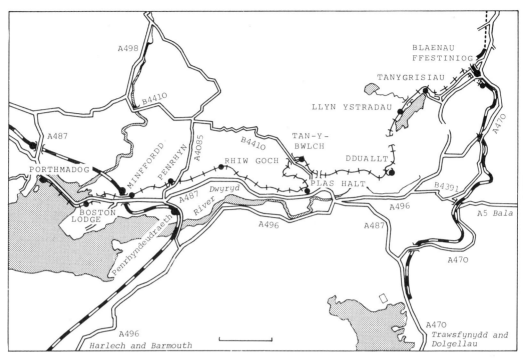

make it expensive to obtain control. The society sought a wealthy patron, and eventually found him in A. F. Pegler, who purchased a controlling interest in the Company in 1954, and then set up a trust to hold the controlling shares. The original trust was superseded in 1964 by the present one, called the Ffestiniog Railway Trust, which is a registered charity.

After Pegler obtained control, Company and Society agreed to work together to re-open the railway. This was not an easy task, for during eight years of dereliction, the railway had become so overgrown with brambles, rhododendrons, and even small trees, that it was for much of its length no longer possible to walk along it. The undergrowth had to be cut back, and this was done sufficiently for works trains, hauled by internal-combustion-powered locomotives, to traverse the whole line in 1955; to make the track safe for passenger trains, much more work was needed.

Re-opening the F.R. has thus been done by stages: Porthmadog to Boston Lodge (1 mile) (which houses the railway's works) in 1955; to Minffordd (2 miles from Porthmadog) in 1956; to Penrhyndeudraeth ($3\frac{1}{4}$ miles) in 1957; and to

Tan-y-bwlch ($7\frac{1}{2}$ miles), the half-way point, in 1958. There was then a pause for consolidation; the next station, Dduallt ($9\frac{1}{4}$ miles) was reached in 1968.

A big obstacle prevented re-opening of the next section. In 1955, after control of the railway had changed but before any of it had been re-opened, electricity authorities obtained powers to submerge part of the course of this section of the line beneath a reservoir for a hydro-electric power station. The F.R. had an immensely long legal battle to obtain compensation: eventually, in 1971, it received £106,700 on grounds of lost operating profits.

This sum has not been enough to pay for building a deviation line. Work started, however, in a small way, in 1965, and in 1978 the

Mountaineer was saved from the scrap merchant in 1964 when the Tramway de Pithiviers à Toury in France was closed. Built in 1917, the 2-6-2 Alco tank is seen here entering Tan-y-Bwlch cutting. The darkness of the smoke is partly due to the fact that the Ffestiniog locos are oil-burning – a change made because of the fire risk from the sparks of coal-burners. (C. M. Whitehouse)

4

The bustle of narrow gauge activity as trains cross at Tan-y-Bwlch. (Jarrolds)

line was re-opened to Tanygrisiau (12¼ miles). The final crowning achievement came on 25 May 1982 when the first Ffestiniog train steamed triumphantly into the brand new interchange station at Blaenau Ffestiniog. Now it is a simple matter for passengers arriving from the North Wales coast on Conwy Valley line diesel trains to step across the platform and join the F.R. train for the spectacular 13-mile journey through to Porthmadog. This major railway engineering achievement is fully in the spirit of the great narrow-gauge pioneering traditions of the F.R. and has been made possible by additional funding from the Wales Tourist Board and the Manpower Services Commission. Equally significant has been that a large part of the work has been done voluntarily: this has meant that volunteers have excavated large amounts of rock to make cuttings and dumped the spoil to form embankments.

The railway proper is operated by a mixture of permanent staff, temporary staff and volunteers. On any particular train the driver is almost certain to be on the permanent staff, the fireman is probably a volunteer, and the guard and buffet car attendants might be either permanent staff or voluntary, or temporary staff too.

A journey down the line
A trip on the Ffestiniog Railway generally starts at Porthmadog. As with all the railways in this section, the train service is geared to visitors on holiday, and so is most intensive in high summer, and less so in spring and autumn. Even out of season, there are trains at weekends and over Christmas; the only periods during which there is no public train service at all are from mid-November until Christmas, and from the New Year until mid-February.

Porthmadog station shows its origin by being at the harbour; the building is partly old, partly new-and-in-keeping. It includes the booking office, the railway shop which sells books, souvenirs and models, and the self-service restaurant. Immediately on leaving the station, the railway runs along the Cob, an early nineteenth century sea wall. On clear days, the mountains of Snowdonia, including Snowdon itself, can be seen to the north. At the end of the Cob comes Boston Lodge Works: passengers get a brief glimpse of scenes of industry within. Minffordd is an interchange station with B.R.'s Cambrian Coast line; after another mile or so the railway takes up the hillside-shelf formation which continues, with few interruptions, as far as Dduallt. The line climbs gradually; the floor of the valley is eventually left far below, and the views are magnificent: wooded hillsides, mountain streams, steep slopes, rivers, lakes, the distant sea and a far glimpse of the silhouette of Harlech Castle.

The old line passed through a long tunnel beyond Dduallt. This is now blocked, and its far portal is submerged below the normal water level of Llyn Ystradau reservoir. So the deviation has immediately to gain height: it does so by a spiral, unique in Britain. It climbs round a curve of approximately 220 degrees, crosses over the original line by a new bridge at the approach to Dduallt station, and continues to curve and climb, taking up a new course parallel to the old but higher up the hillside. A new

Ex-Penrhyn Railway Linda *heads a train into Tan-y-Bwlch. These 0-4-0STs have been converted to oil-burning 2-4-0 tender engines. (Jarrolds)*

tunnel about 310 yards long follows, bored through rock by miners employed by the company during 1975–6; beyond it the route runs above the shore of the reservoir, past the power station, and falls gently to Tanygrisiau. From here to Blaenau is only a short distance over somewhat easier gradients under the shadow of the great slate-bearing mountains.

Stock

Ffestiniog passenger traffic has grown rapidly: during the years 1940 to 1954 inclusive it was zero, but in 1975 there were 441,000 passenger journeys. Locomotives and rolling stock have increased in proportion. The first steam locomotive used by the new regime was the 0-4-0 tank, *Prince*. In theory this locomotive is one of the originals: in practice she (or *he* – it is difficult to conform to the usual convention of referring to locomotives as *she*, when faced with such a name) has been rebuilt so many times that little if any of the original remains. The 1946 closure

interrupted one of the rebuildings: a new boiler, delivered but not fitted, was something of a godsend to the new regime, which completed re-assembly in 1955. A further rebuilding has just taken place.

The F.R. had three other double Fairlies after *Little Wonder*, and two of them survived in 1955. Both were subsequently overhauled and used and both, eventually, became due for rebuilding again. This has meant provision of two new double boilers. One of the locomotives, *Merddin Emrys*, was rebuilt in 1970; with the other, *Earl of Merioneth*, so much new work is being incorporated that she is regarded as a new locomotive incorporating some old parts. The original locomotive stock has been supplemented by two 0-4-0 saddle tanks, *Linda* and *Blanche*, from the Penrhyn Quarry Railway (which have been rebuilt as 2-4-0 saddle tanks, to make them ride better, and with superheaters and piston valves to make them more efficient); and by *Mountaineer*, a 2-6-2 tank built in the U.S.A. in 1917 for British military light railways in France: she subsequently ran for the Tramway de Pithiviers à Toury until 1964, when that line closed. She was then

Merddin Emrys *skirting Llyn Ystradau and approaching the summit of the Ffestiniog's deviation line to Tanygrisiau. (*Norman Gurley*)*

bought by the present writer and brought to the U.K. Like the other locomotives, she now belongs to the Ffestiniog Railway Company.

All steam locomotives in use have been converted to burn oil instead of coal. Conversion was almost immediately followed by the oil crisis and rapid escalation in the price of oil: this the railway has met by modifying the locomotives to burn a mixture of waste oil and diesel oil (instead of pure diesel oil). The conversions, prompted by the need to eliminate sparks which set fire to lineside forestry, proved their worth during the 1976 drought when, if the locomotives had still burned coal, trains would have had to have been cancelled beyond Penrhyndeudraeth so as to avoid the forestry area. Several small diesel locomotives are used for works trains and some off-peak passenger trains.

The great historic interest of the coaches on the line in 1955 was matched only by their state of dilapidation. They included four-wheelers from the 1860s and bogie coaches from the 1870s, but none had been used or maintained for the previous fifteen years. Those that were repairable (which eventually proved to be most of them) were gradually rebuilt and brought back into service. To them were added coaches from other long-closed lines – the Welsh Highland and Lynton and Barnstaple Railways – which had fortunately survived; subsequently, many new coaches have been built. F.R. coaches carry first- and third-class passengers: first is both more expensive and very much more comfortable. Many of the first-class seats in recently-built coaches came from withdrawn standard-gauge Pullman Cars. There are licensed buffet cars and observation cars included in most trains.

Photography
Despite the mileage of film exposed at it, the Ffestiniog Railway is not an easy line to photograph. It is particularly dangerous to attempt to

ABOVE: Earl of Merioneth *at Tanygrisiau waiting to leave for Porthmadog.* (Tom Heavyside*)*

BELOW: Blanche *heads a train along a dry-stone embankment typical of the F.R.* (P. J. G. Ransom*)*

reach vantage points by trespassing along the line, for clearances are tight – often only a few inches between train and rock cutting. But the line is unfenced across the Cob, with a footpath alongside. Main roads cross the line near Boston Lodge and Penrhyndeudraeth, and minor roads run near to it between these points. It seems likely that Dduallt will become a favoured photographic location. The little hill in the centre of the spiral belongs to the railway company, and is a picnic site with a viewpoint: photographers are able to alight at Dduallt to photograph the trains as they circle around them.

The area around

It is worth remembering that however impressive the Ffestiniog Railway may seem, it was originally but a small part of the distribution system of the slate industry. To put it into context, there are two other visits to make in the vicinity.

The Llechwedd Slate Caverns at Blaenau Ffestiniog show how slate was quarried or, to be precise, mined. Visitors enter the mine on a small train hauled by a battery-electric locomotive. Parts of the old workings are illuminated: life-size dummy miners appear to be hewing rock. Elsewhere the train emerges briefly into daylight before plunging underground again. The effect is dramatic.

Porthmadog was in the past as famous, if not more so, for its sailing ships as for its railway. These ships distributed Ffestiniog slate throughout the world. The Porthmadog Maritime Museum enables visitors to see something of this end of the industry: situated in an original quayside slate-storage shed are displays and artefacts, and alongside the quay (and accessible to visitors) is the ketch *Garlandstone*. She is not a Porthmadog-built ship (none is known to survive), but she did trade to Porthmadog, and her spars and black hull contrast markedly with modern yachts and motor cruisers, giving an idea of what the harbour once was like.

The Talyllyn Railway

The line and its history

James Winton Spooner, elder brother of Charles Spooner of Ffestiniog, was the engineer who constructed the Talyllyn Railway. This line of 2 ft 3 in. gauge was opened in 1866 to link slate quarries at Bryn Eglwys, near Abergynolwyn, with Tywyn, where an interchange station, now called Wharf, was built alongside a siding of the coastal standard-gauge line. This was itself then new – original Talyllyn plans were to go to Aberdovey harbour.

Like the Ffestiniog Railway, the Talyllyn Railway was laid out on continuous down gradient, but it does not seem that gravity was ever used regularly to power trains. However, the Talyllyn Railway Company did develop one delightful custom dependent on gravity: visitors who wished to return to Tywyn late in the evening, say after climbing Cader Idris, after the last train had gone, could arrange to have an empty slate wagon left for them at Abergynolwyn – and in this they would embark to trundle gently homewards through the dusk.

From this it can be appreciated that the Talyllyn was not, for much of its life, a busy line. When it was built, however, it was well and substantially equipped with what were then modern locomotives and rolling stock, in anticipation of both heavy slate traffic and of passenger traffic. The railway company was a subsidiary of the Aberdovey Slate Co., which had been formed to exploit Bryn Eglwys quarry, and had re-equipped the quarry on a grand scale, in the belief that it held large reserves of good quality slate, and perhaps gold as well.

Both these beliefs proved to be unfounded, though slate quarrying on a limited scale continued until the late 1940s. The railway was still operating then, but since the 1860s no new locomotives or passenger carriages had been added, and the track too, except for one short section, was laid with the original rails. The railway had become a remarkable antique, and it was also very dilapidated indeed. Furthermore the railway company was not nationalized in 1948, unlike most other railway companies,

A timeless scene on the Talyllyn Railway as No. 1 heads up the valley near Brynglas with two of the line's original coaches. (R. Crombleholme)

for the T.R. was no longer considered important for transport. Its absence from the transport bill drew it to the attention of the author and engineer the late L. T. C. Rolt, who approached the owner to find out what could be done to perpetuate the railway.

The owner, of both railway and quarry, was Sir Henry Haydn Jones, who had purchased them in 1911 and intended, despite closure of the quarry, to continue to run the railway during his lifetime. This, sadly, was not very long, for he died in 1950.

The formation of the Preservation Society
The Talyllyn Railway Preservation Society was formed at a public meeting in Birmingham in October of the same year. A committee was appointed which included L. T. C. Rolt, J. H. Russell, P. B. Whitehouse, and P. J. Garland. The intention was to revive the railway by

public subscription, and run it with volunteers. This concept was entirely novel, and the pioneers had no idea that they were starting a movement which would become national, and indeed worldwide. Rather, they had a daunting task ahead of them, and were far from confident of success: P. J. Garland recently told the author that he agreed to become Honorary Treasurer because, as an accountant, he felt that someone with practical experience of liquidation would be needed before many months had passed! He is now President of the Society.

Lady Haydn Jones, Sir Haydn's widow, had inherited the railway company shares and she very kindly agreed to give them to a new holding company, called Talyllyn Holdings Ltd, controlled by the Preservation Society. In effect this meant that the Society was able to run the railway, without having to pay for it. This was fortunate, for there was much else to be paid for over the next few years.

Under Society operation, the numbers of passengers carried on the railway rapidly increased. This brought both revenue and

11

No. 3 Sir Haydn, *a 0-4-2 transferred from the Corris Railway on its closure in 1948, crosses the major engineering feat of the Talyllyn – the Dolgoch viaduct.* (T. J. Edgington)

problems: for a time equipment was deteriorating from wear and tear more rapidly than the Society could improve it. This vicious circle was changed only when the Territorial Army relaid a mile of track as a training exercise.

The number of passenger journeys was 15,628 in 1951, and 165,232 in 1977. Though there have been ups and downs, the figures have tended to increase, and this has meant many changes and improvements. Where once a single train, going up and down the line, could carry all the traffic, there are now sometimes three on the move at the same time. So, as well as additional locomotives and rolling stock well-suited to their task, this has meant heavy rail, proper ballast, passing loops, signal boxes, electric train staffs, colour-light signals and a

telephone system – all things unknown in Sir Haydn's day. It has also meant re-equipped and extended workshops, and rebuilt stations. But the original locomotives and coaches, two and four in number respectively, are maintained to their traditional appearance, even though they now incorporate many new parts, and the new buildings harmonize with their surroundings. The track, the gauge, the route, the scenery and the steam are still the same.

Actually the route is not quite the same: it has been extended. Beyond Abergynolwyn passenger station there continued the 'mineral extension'. For $\frac{3}{4}$ mile, to sidings at the foot of a rope-worked incline which led to the quarry, this extension ran along the hillside among forest-covered mountains, and it was an early ambition of the society to open this section for passenger traffic. But restoration of the Tywyn to Abergynolwyn section had to come first, and then much work was needed to rebuild the extension to passenger rather than freight standard. It was

Douglas, the Barclay well tank heads a train of enclosed bogie coaches. (P. J. G. Ransom)

a proud day when, on 22 May 1976, the T.R.'s Nant Gwernol Extension was opened.

The Railway today

The Talyllyn Railway therefore now extends from Tywyn to Nant Gwernol. It is best to join trains at Tywyn Wharf, for Nant Gwernol has no road access (though there are footpaths), and in any case the line is seen to best advantage during the journey into the hills rather than away from them.

At Tywyn Wharf the Railway Shop has an extensive range of books and souvenirs; refreshments are available, and the Narrow-Gauge Railway Museum contains many exhibits from narrow-gauge lines, both passenger-carrying and industrial. The museum is an entity distinct from the railway, but related to it.

The railway traverses Tywyn by a half-mile cutting, to reach Tywyn Pendre station. Here are the railway's works, and locomotive and carriage sheds. After Pendre the line climbs steadily through farmland past Rhydyronen station ($2\frac{1}{2}$ miles), while the hills close in gradually, as far as Brynglas ($3\frac{1}{4}$ miles). Here the route takes up a hillside shelf formation on the south side of the narrow valley of the stream called Afon Fathew. The hills on either side grow steadily higher, and just before Dolgoch Falls station (5 miles), the railway crosses a ravine by a three-span brick viaduct. At Dolgoch Falls station, locomotives usually take water, which gives photographers their opportunity, and many passengers leave the trains altogether to visit the waterfalls.

At Abergynolwyn ($6\frac{1}{2}$ miles) the grey-stone station building, though it looks old, was completed only in 1969; it includes a refreshment room. Many down trains from Nant Gwernol to Tywyn pause here for long enough for passengers to sample it.

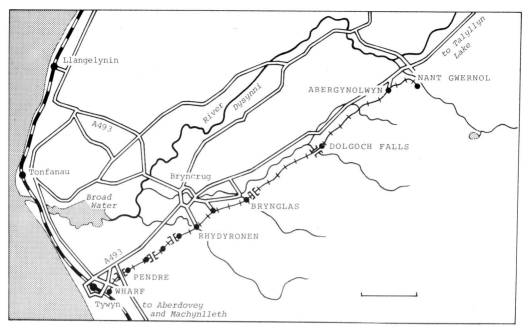

The valley through which the T.R. runs from Brynglas almost to Nant Gwernol is straight, but as the train approaches Abergynolwyn the sides of the valley come closer together and the valley floor rises towards the railway. But then, when the train leaves Abergynolwyn, the valley is seen to widen again, and its floor falls away. The cause of the latter feature is an accumulation of glacial moraine, an ice-age relic; as a consequence of the two features together, the finest views on the railway, looking up the continuing valley to the mountains beyond, are revealed to passengers on the extension.

Stock

When the T.R.P.S. took over in 1951, all of the Talyllyn Railway's locomotives and passenger coaches were over eighty years old. The locomotives were 0-4-0 tank *Dolgoch* which was (just) in working order, and 0-4-2 saddle tank *Talyllyn*, which was not and had been placed, worn-out, on a siding beneath a hay barn. There were four four-wheeled passenger coaches and one four-wheeled brake van, which included a ticket window from which the guard could issue tickets at stations en route. All these five vehicles could be entered from one side only and all station platforms were on the north side

of the line, a feature which continues to this day.

Both *Dolgoch* and *Talyllyn* were in due course rebuilt, and they and the original coaches and van continue to operate. An immediate need to supplement the original stock was met by obtaining from British Railways two locomotives, a brake van and several coal wagons from the Corris Railway. This line, fortunately of the same unusual 2 ft 3 in. gauge, had been closed in 1948, but the stock had remained at its station at Machynlleth, not far from Tywyn. The locomotives, both 0-4-2 saddle tanks, were named on the Talyllyn *Sir Haydn* and *Edward Thomas*, after the T.R.'s former owner and traffic manager respectively. Another steam locomotive, a 0-4-0 tank of industrial type, was presented to the railway in 1953 and named *Douglas*. In 1969 a similar but larger locomotive, built only in 1950 and scarcely used, was purchased from the Irish Peat Board. It was a 3 ft gauge locomotive, and is being rebuilt as a 0-4-2 tank for the 2 ft 3 in. gauge. Several diesel locomotives are used, almost exclusively for works trains.

No. 1 about to depart from Tywyn Wharf station with a train for Nant Gwernol. (Phil Wood)

No. 2 Dolgoch *on an up-train at Dolgoch Falls* station. (Rimmer Photography*)*

The Vale of Rheidol Railway

The line and its history

Though the Talyllyn Railway was engineered by a member of the Spooner family, the Vale of Rheidol Railway vindicates better the techniques they demonstrated on the Ffestiniog. It was opened in 1902, to link Aberystwyth with Devil's Bridge 11¾ miles to the east, and for the final four of those miles its 1 ft 11½ in. gauge enables it to twist and turn along a shelf cut on the steep side of the Rheidol gorge. In this location a standard-gauge line would have been very much more expensive to construct.

The railway was built to carry minerals (lead ores and so on), tourists, and ordinary passengers and freight traffic, in roughly that order of importance. In those prosperous Edwardian times it prospered too, so much so that the independent Vale of Rheidol Light Railway Company was taken over in 1913 by the Cambrian Railways Co. So the V. of R. line descended to the Great Western Railway in 1922 and, in due course, to British Railways in 1948. By then it had long-since ceased to carry freight; passenger trains ran only in summer for tourists, and had been suspended completely from 1940 to 1944 inclusive. In 1968, when the rest of British Rail had gone over to diesel and electric traction, the V. of R. line became not only B.R.'s only surviving narrow-gauge section, but also its only surviving steam-worked line. And so it continues.

The V. of R.'s fortunes under B.R. have varied. In the 1950s with its main-line maintenance standards, and particularly its track, it was an example to volunteers on the Talyllyn and Ffestiniog Railways as they struggled to recover their railways from years of decay. But publicity for the V. of R. was conspicuous by its absence – for example, winter timetables, as I recollect them, regularly included in the V. of R. table the forbidding statement 'service suspended', without any indication that the service would start up again in the summer: 'service suspended', in timetable-ese, was generally a euphemism for 'line closed completely'. In the late 1950s, B.R.,

Corris Railway passenger coaches could not be obtained from British Railways, for the Corris line had lost its passenger service in 1931 and the coaches were then dispersed. But the body of one which had been used as a garden shed was eventually recovered, rebuilt and put back into use; and bodies of two coaches from the Glyn Valley Tramway (closed in 1935), which had also survived, were similarly obtained and rebuilt. The first supplements to the coaching stock were open toast-rack quarrymen's coaches from the Penrhyn Quarry Railway: these were in poor condition and did not long survive, but there are now several four-wheelers built by the T.R. and based on the Penrhyn design, with added roofs. More important are several bogie coaches built at Tywyn to a handsome and substantial design which, though modern, complements the traditional lines of the locomotives.

Among all the stock new to the line, the original stock is now somewhat diluted. The flavour of the past can be recaptured, however, when the T.R. runs from time to time a special vintage train of the original stock.

16

spurred on perhaps by the success of other Welsh tourist lines, started to publicize the Vale of Rheidol, named the locomotives, and re-introduced Sunday trains. Traffic increased.

Then in the 1960s, as a consequence of London Midland Region electrification, former G.W.R. lines in the Birmingham area were transferred from the Western to the London Midland Region, and so were their extensions to Chester and North and mid Wales. These routes soon afterwards suffered a decline in services from which they have never fully recovered. The Rheidol was included in the transfer, and by the end of the 1967 season was looking very down at heel. Locomotives which a few years before had been spotless were now filthy, and their nameplates had been removed for fear of theft. The last remaining passing loop, at Aberffrwd, $7\frac{3}{4}$ miles from Aberystwyth, had been lifted, and the increase in the number of passengers was levelling out just at a period when on the Ffestiniog Railway, for instance, passenger traffic was increasing more rapidly than ever.

A group of railway enthusiasts with practical experience on preserved lines negotiated with B.R. for purchase of the Rheidol, with a view to running it properly. B.R. was at first willing to sell; then, for political reasons, the proposed sale was cancelled.

However B.R. started to develop the line itself. A big improvement was made at Aberystwyth. The narrow-gauge line was diverted into the main station, to terminate in the 'Carmarthen bay' formerly occupied by standard-gauge tracks used by trains for the closed Aberystwyth–Carmarthen line. At the same time, narrow-gauge tracks were laid into the former standard-gauge locomotive shed, a substantial building then standing vacant. This not only enabled the V. of R. locomotive shed – a cramped and isolated corrugated-iron building dating from the opening of the line – to be vacated, but also provided extensive under-cover winter storage for coaches, which had previously been lacking. So the stock was better protected from both weather and vandalism.

Locomotives and coaches were repainted in B.R. blue livery, locomotive names were replaced, and local railway management intensified publicity for the line. The idea for formation of the Narrow Gauge Railways of Wales Joint Marketing Panel came from B.R.'s area manager at Machynlleth, in whose domain the Rheidol lay. A souvenir and refreshment shop was opened at Devil's bridge. The reward for all this was an increase in the number of passenger journeys from 95,500 in 1969 to 179,000 in 1975, an all-time record for the line.

A decision to end the inclusion of the Vale of Rheidol within B.R.'s corporate identity was taken in 1980 and as a first step to restoring the line's character, locomotive No. 8 *Llywelyn* was painted in full G.W.R. livery. Three of the line's wagons, used for engineers' trains, were restored to 1902 V. of R. livery, whilst a named

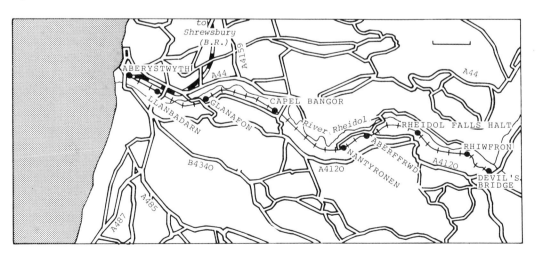

ABOVE: *Two of the Vale of Rheidol 2-6-2 tanks caught in an off-duty moment in the former standard gauge locomotive shed at Aberystwyth. This is now British Rail's one and only steam motive power depot. (*Phil Wood)

LEFT: *No. 7* Owain Glyndwr *stands at the former Carmarthen line platform at Aberystwyth. Both locomotive and rolling stock are shown in B.R. 'Corporate image' blue livery – now being dispensed with in favour of more traditional colour schemes. (*Jarrolds)

OPPOSITE: *No. 8* Llywelyn, *also in plain blue livery, pauses at the water tank just outside Devil's Bridge station after the energetic climb up the valley. (*Jarrolds)

*Looking from the old standard gauge shed towards the mainline (Aberystwyth) station and the V. of R. terminus. The loco is No. 7 Owain Glyndwr, one of only two narrow gauge locos built at the G.W.R. Swindon works. (*Andrew Roberts*)*

train, *The Welsh Dragon*, complete with headboard, was inaugurated. All passengers on the line are issued with souvenir tickets. These innovations were so well received by the public that the line's oldest locomotive, No. 9 *Prince of Wales*, emerged in 1982 resplendent in its original yellow ochre livery complete with lining and crests. This gesture marked the engine's eightieth birthday and again resulted in much favourable publicity for the V. of R.

In 1970 the Vale of Rheidol Railway Supporters' Association was formed to promote and popularize the line, and provides an unusual, possibly unique, example of B.R. and railway enthusiasts getting together for such a purpose. Its committee of eight members includes two appointed by British Rail and six elected by the

Association's own members, who numbered 350 in 1976. Members publicize the line and organize party visits to it. They can visit the shed at Aberystwyth by arrangement, and have the use of a standard-gauge camping coach there.

The line today

The Vale of Rheidol line itself, after leaving Aberystwyth terminus, runs parallel to the standard-gauge for $1\frac{1}{2}$ miles, to Llanbadarn station. Then the main line bears away to the north and the V. of R. continues eastwards along the floor of the Rheidol valley, crossing the river by a timber viaduct. There are in total seven intermediate stations and halts at which trains call by request. In the first $5\frac{1}{2}$ miles, the steepest gradient is 1 in 105, but then stretches of 1 in 50 start to alternate with level sections, and from Aberffrwd the gradient is 1 in 50 continuously for 4 miles to Devil's Bridge. The line winds along a shelf cut on a steep and wooded hillside, and offers views of a cascading river far below, and traverses side gulleys by means of strikingly tight horse-shoe curves.

The phenomenon known as the Devil's Bridge is in fact three bridges of various ages, one above the other, spanning a chasm. To be precise, the bridge attributed to the Devil is the lowest and oldest of the three. They are found by turning left on leaving the station and walking a few hundred yards along the road. There are also waterfalls to be viewed and visited.

Stock

Three locomotives work the V. of R.: No. 7, *Owain Glyndŵr*; No. 8, *Llywelyn*; and No. 9, *Prince of Wales*. All are 2-6-2 tanks, and powerful for the gauge. No. 9 is the oldest, and was built for the opening of the line. Nos. 7 and 8 were built for it by the G.W.R. at Swindon in 1923 and No. 9 (then G.W.R. No. 1213) was rebuilt there so as to be almost identical to them. The name *Prince of Wales* was carried by the locomotive when owned by the original V. of R. company, and re-instated by B.R. when the other two locomotives were named. The coaches now in use include bogie observation cars, with sides open above the waist, and closed bogie coaches. The latter were built by the G.W.R. as late as 1938, incorporating components from earlier coaches; the former also date from 1938 or, in some instances, 1923. The Vale of Rheidol line is operated entirely by paid staff, and drivers, for instance, alternate between driving steam locomotives on the narrow-gauge line and diesel trains on the standard.

Photography

The course of the upper part of the railway makes it difficult to reach and photograph, but there is an overbridge at the approach to Devil's Bridge station, and elsewhere a rough road leads to the level crossing and station at Aberffrwd, where locomotives take water and provide a photographic opportunity. Between Llanbadarn and Aberffrwd several minor roads run close to the railway and also offer photographic potential.

The Welshpool and Llanfair Light Railway

The line and its history

The early history of the 2 ft 6 in. gauge Welshpool and Llanfair Light Railway has much in common with that of the Rheidol. Both came under the wing of the Cambrian Railways, and so passed in due course to the G.W.R. and then to British Railways.

The W. & L. was opened in 1903 and linked Welshpool, where there was an exchange station with the standard-gauge, with Llanfair Caereinion, $9\frac{1}{2}$ miles to the west. It was built and owned by the independent Welshpool and Llanfair Light Railway Company, but was operated from the start by the Cambrian. The G.W.R. therefore started to work the line in 1922, and absorbed the local company the following year. Passenger services ceased in 1931; although the countryside through which the railway passes was and is very pleasant, it lies outside the main tourist area of North and mid Wales. General freight traffic continued: the line eventually became the last non-preserved narrow-gauge railway to carry public freight traffic in Great Britain. It was finally closed in November 1956.

Preservation

Following the Talyllyn and Ffestiniog examples, a preservation society was formed the same month. Support was slow in coming forward and negotiations with B.R. and the Ministry of Transport were long drawn out, though working parties of volunteers were permitted on the line from 1959. In 1960 the preservation society was replaced by the Welshpool and Llanfair Light Railway Preservation Co. Ltd, and in 1962 B.R. was authorized to lease to the preservation company the line from Raven Square, on the western edge of Welshpool, to Llanfair. The company has since been able to purchase it outright.

One of the causes of delay had been that the line, commencing at the standard-gauge station on the east side of Welshpool, had to traverse the town and in doing so crossed several streets

The low-slung former gasworks shunter Dougal *is an economical station pilot at Llanfair Caereinion. Here it shunts a Zillertalbahn coach. (*Jarrolds*)*

on the level without gates. Authority to reopen this section could not be obtained and it has been dismantled. The preservation company was able to use it for a time for works trains.

So the preservation company based itself on Llanfair, and in 1963 re-opened the $4\frac{1}{4}$ miles to Castle Caereinion. In 1964 it re-opened a further $1\frac{1}{4}$ miles to Sylfaen, though towards the end of the season trains had again to terminate at Castle Caereinion because of poor condition of the track beyond. The following winter floods severely damaged the viaduct over the River Banwy, about $1\frac{1}{2}$ miles from Llanfair, a disaster, for the company could ill afford repairs. During the 1965 season a shuttle train service ran between Llanfair and Heniarth Gate ($1\frac{1}{4}$ miles) only, until viaduct repairs were completed in mid-August. The train service was then re-sumed as far as Castle Caereinion; resumption of trains to Sylfaen had to wait for a full overhaul of the track throughout, and was delayed until

1972. The Welshpool extension was opened on 18 July 1981 and adds $2\frac{3}{4}$ miles to the railway, including the 1-mile long 1-in-29 climb up Golfa Bank. This is a very scenic part of the railway, twisting and turning to climb up the valley of the Sylfaen. It is also a testing piece of line to operate!

The line today
The railway is now operated almost entirely by volunteers, who are members of the pre-servation company, with only a few paid staff. It is not as busy as some of the other Welsh lines, which makes it pleasant for people who do go to it. Train services are not so extensive either, but there are two or three trains each way daily throughout the summer, at weekends in spring and autumn, and daily during the Easter and Spring Bank Holiday periods. Road travellers can conveniently include a visit to the W. & L. while going to or returning from lines further west, and unlike those lines, the W. & L. is within easy range of the Midlands.

Llanfair Caereinion station has a buffet and railway shop, and locomotive sheds and repair works, built by the preservation company be-

Kerr Stuart 0-6-2T Joan *heads a train of Austrian Zillertalbahn four-wheel coaches on the approach to Heniarth station.* (Welshpool & Llanfair Railway)

cause the original shed was located on the section now dismantled, in Welshpool. Most of the way to Heniarth Gate, the line close by follows the tree-lined north bank of the River Banwy, and an isolated watering point enables locomotives to take water. Beyond the viaduct, the line follows the south bank of the river, crosses a tributary by a stone-built viaduct and reaches Cyfronydd (2¼ miles). Here the river diverges to the north, and the railway continues in an easterly direction up a side valley. The countryside is typical of the Welsh borders – no mountains, but cultivated hills and valleys interspersed with woodland – not spectacular, but pastoral and pleasant. Castle Caereinion was

originally the mid-point of the line. At Sylfaen the railway comes alongside the main road from Llanfair to Welshpool (though parking space is limited, and intending passengers are advised to make for Llanfair or Raven Square). Beyond Sylfaen the line enters its most attractive and demanding section, although from the locomotive crew's point of view, going down the bank to Welshpool is mostly a case of keeping a sharp look-out and applying the brake. Coming back up the 1-in-29 is a different matter though!

However, there is a short climb at 1-in-50 away from Sylfaen until the summit of the line is reached at approximately 6 miles from Llanfair. From the summit (600 feet above sea level) the line falls at 1-in-63, crossing the steep and picturesque minor road to Castle Caereinion via Coed-y-Cwm Farm and enters Golfa station. The

23

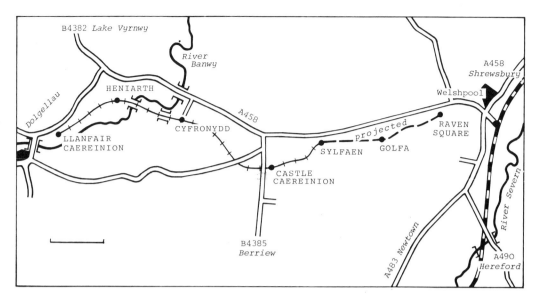

station **stands** at the top of the famous Golfa incline, in its day the steepest section of the Cambrian Railways worked by passenger trains and among the steepest in the British Isles.

The cosmopolitan atmosphere of the W. & L. is here epitomised by Joan *(imported from Antigua) with the Sierra Leone coaches. (*Ralph Cartwright*)*

From Golfa the line runs high up on a bank above the Sylfaen Brook, curving repeatedly among the trees to obtain the easiest route, but still having to fall some 300 feet in two miles. The railway is now passing through the Powis estate and there are fine views of the magnificent woods surrounding Powis Castle which stands on the hillside opposite.

No. 10 Sir Drefaldwyn *came from Austria in 1970, having been built for German service in World War II. The train is of Austrian and British stock. (*Ralph Cartwright*)*

Below the level crossing with New Drive, with its fine black and white lodge on the right, the gradient becomes a gentle 1-in-320 for another furlong with a final $\frac{1}{4}$-mile at 1-in-43 until Welshpool (Raven Square) is reached. This is a brand-new station constructed for the reopening of the lower section of line in 1981. The fine brick-built signalbox is the first of a complete set of station buildings and engine shed planned for the site.

The railway was one of the first to be built under the provisions of the Light Railways Act 1896, and is in many ways a typical light railway. It has few bridges, but many level crossings (without gates across the road), and it has few earthworks but many sharp curves and steep gradients, which enable it to follow, so far as possible, the lie of the land.

Stock

Two locomotives, identical 0-6-0 tanks, were built by Beyer Peacock for the opening of the line, and worked it alone throughout its pre-preservation existence, until 1956. Fortunately both survived closure and, after a period in store, first one and then the other were obtained by the preservation company and returned to the line.

The original passenger coaches were less fortunate: they were scrapped a few years after passenger services were withdrawn. This meant that the preservation company had to obtain coaches from elsewhere, and it also judged it necessary to augment the locomotive stock. Without main-line maintenance facilities to fall back on, it has to rely on members working in their spare time, so locomotive overhauls are inevitably protracted. In any event, additional locomotives have been an attraction to visitors.

There were no other public railways of 2 ft 6 in. gauge surviving in Britain to form a source

25

ABOVE: Monarch, *the Bagnall-Meyer articulated locomotive, is a powerful but temperamental addition to the W.& L.'s motive power.* (Jarrolds)

LEFT: *One of the line's original Beyer Peacock 0-6-0 tanks heads a train westwards over the reconstructed Banwy bridge.* (Jarrolds)

of supply. Fortunately for the W. & L., though, the Admiralty ceased to use its 2 ft 6 in. gauge Lodge Hill and Upnor Railway in Kent in 1961, and the W. & L. was able to obtain from it rolling stock which included five bogie coaches. Four of these were rather primitive, of covered toast-rack type, but the fifth was a comfortable saloon coach built only four years previously!

More coaches were obtained in 1968. These are four four-wheeled coaches which came from the Zillertalbahn, a 760 mm gauge railway in the Austrian Tyrol. Short and tubby in appearance, with slatted wooden seats, these coaches are pleasant, but typical of a railway tradition very different to that of Britain. They did, however, solve the W. & L. railway's immediate passenger-carriage problem, and a fifth similar coach has since been obtained from the same source.

All the charm of the unexpected encounter with a narrow gauge steam train at a rural level crossing is summed up in this picture of No. 1 The Earl entering Castle Caereinion station. (David Idle)

The first additional steam locomotive suitable for passenger trains was *Monarch*, an articulated 0-4-4-0 tank obtained from Bowaters' papermills railway in Kent by a member of the preservation company in 1966, and then donated to the railway. Large and powerful – too much so for light trains – she spent several years first stored and then under overhaul, but she entered revenue-earning service in 1974.

Before *Monarch* entered service, another steam locomotive was already hauling passenger trains. This was 0-8-0 tank No. 10, *Sir Drefaldwyn* – the name is Welsh for Montgomeryshire, in which county the W. & L. was situated before the recent re-organization of local government. She complements the Austrian coaches for she was purchased in 1969 from the Styrian Provincial Railways and entered service on the W. & L. in 1970. She was built in France in 1944, to a German military railway design; she spent her working life up to 1969 in Austria.

British builders of steam locomotives formerly had a thriving export business, particularly with British colonies and the W. & L. has now brought back to Britain two locomotives representative of the trade. The first is *Joan*, a 0-6-2 tank built in 1927 by Kerr Stuart, and bought by a group of W. & L. members from the Government Sugar Factory of Antigua in the West Indies; the second is 2-6-2 tank No. 85 of the Sierra Leone Government Railway. That system is now closed, but No. 85 was built by Hunslet as recently as 1954; with her the W. & L. was able to obtain four modern bogie coaches built in England in 1961.

The preservation company has also had a succession of diesel locomotives, large and small, for works trains.

Photography
Running through open countryside, the W. & L. is not a difficult line to photograph. There are vantage points at or near most stations and level crossings. Other tourist attractions in the neighbourhood include Powis Castle, and boat trips on the Shropshire Union Canal at Welshpool.

The Snowdon Mountain Railway

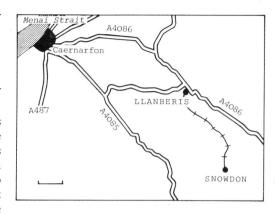

The line and its history

Of all the old-established railways in this section, the Snowdon Mountain Railway has the least complex history. This rack railway was built in the 1890s, on principles developed in Switzerland, to carry tourists from Llanberis to the summit of Snowdon. It continues to do just that. The company owning and operating the line, originally the Snowdon Mountain Tramroad and Hotels Co. Ltd, is now Snowdon Mountain Railway Ltd.

The railway has always been unique as the only mountain rack railway in the British Isles, and it has gained distinction by sticking to steam power while most Swiss rack railways have been electrified.

Oddly enough, there was an early intention to electrify the Snowdon. That same 1895 guide book referred to in the introduction to this section, published while the railway was being built, describes it as 'the new Electric railway' and adds 'powerful steam locomotives are to be used *at first*' [author's italics]. They still are!

In the Abt rack system used on the Snowdon railway, pinions beneath the locomotives engage with two toothed racks laid between the rails, to propel the locomotives onwards and upwards, up gradients too steep for normal adhesion working. On the Snowdon railway, the gradient is in places as steep as 1 in $5\frac{1}{2}$, which is another British record for a locomotive-worked line.

A train arrives on Snowdon summit. Coach and engine are always uncoupled for safety reasons, and so the engine is always below the coach. The racking is clearly visible. (David Idle)

This portrait of locos taken at the Llanberis shed clearly shows the slope of the boilers on the 1895-designed Swiss-built engines. (P. J. G. Ransom)

Descending locomotives are braked by the rack and pinion, too.

The opening day in 1896 was marred by a disaster. The locomotive of the first descending train left the rails, possibly at a point where frost had distorted freshly laid track, and became disengaged from the racks. It fell into a ravine and was damaged beyond repair. The driver and fireman jumped clear and were unharmed, and the carriages forming the train, which as a safety precaution had not been coupled to the locomotive, were stopped safely by their own brakes – but not before a passenger had jumped out and been fatally injured.

The line was closed, and guard rails, of inverted-L shape, were laid on either side of the racks; grippers were fitted beneath the loco-motives which would engage with the guard rails, should a locomotive attempt to leave the rails, and prevent pinions from disengaging from racks. The railway re-opened for the 1897 season and there has been no similar incident subsequently.

The line today

To avoid disappointment, it is essential to consider what weather conditions are likely to be at the summit before making a trip up the Snowdon Railway. The summit is 3,561 feet above sea level. On a fine day it is a superb place with magnificent views; on a wet, windy, cloudy day it is most unpleasant. On any day, conditions are more severe than in the valley below.

The starting point, the Snowdon station at Llanberis, is at the south-east end of that village; it has a restaurant, a shop and a buffet. Trains comprise a single coach and a locomotive

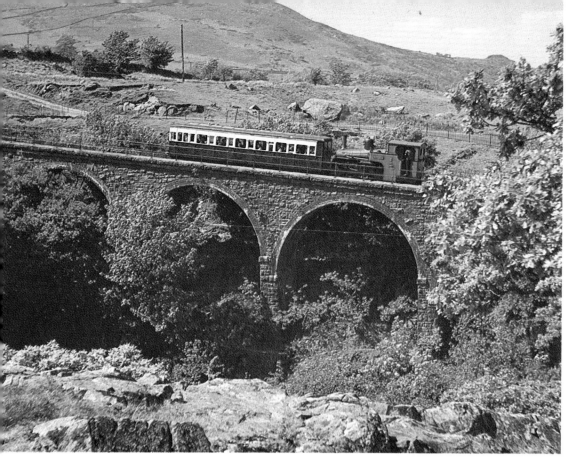

*And this is the easy bit! A Snowdon train crosses the stone viaduct shortly after setting out from Llanberis station. (*Noel Habgood*)*

(which, on the uphill journey, pushes it). Each coach carries up to about 60 people, and at busy times trains run in convoy, but there is still sometimes a queue of passengers at Llanberis. The train leaves the station past the locomotive shed and works; the first few hundred yards, on a gradient of 1 in 50, are deceptively easy: one wonders what all the fuss is about. Then the coach rears up as it reaches the first steep section, where the gradient is 1 in 6, and the locomotive starts to work in earnest, with appropriate sound and fury (although travelling at about 5 m.p.h.). The Snowdon Railway is a fine line for locomotive noises: sitting in a down train at a passing loop and listening to an up train approaching, one would suppose it to be the Cornish Riviera at 90 m.p.h.

That first steep section takes the line across a stone viaduct; then the railway, which has so far been heading south-west, curves gently through 90 degrees to take up the south-easterly alignment which continues most of the way to the summit. There are three intermediate stations (none of which serves any built-up area) which have loops for trains to pass. At places where the gradient eases, passengers looking ahead sometimes experience the curious optical illusion that the track goes over a hump and then downhill. In fact, the upward course is continuous, and as the train climbs, ever more spectacular views are (on a fine day) revealed, to culminate in the very extensive panorama of mountain and sea obtainable from the top. The summit station is of course the highest station in the British Isles; a café adjoins it.

The distance from Llanberis to Snowdon Summit is about 4¾ miles, with a vertical climb of 3,140 ft, and the journey takes one hour, up or down. Fares are not cheap: rack-railway fares never are, anywhere. Such lines are expensive to run. In spring, when ice and snow still cover the top of the mountain, trains terminate short

*Further up the mountain the scenery is wilder and more spectacular. A train attacks the gradient under a stormy sky. (*Phil Wood*)*

of the summit, and fares are comparatively inexpensive. Trains do not run in winter.

Stock

The seven locomotives used on the Snowdon Mountain Railway were all built by the Swiss Locomotive Works of Winterthur, Switzerland. They are typical of rack locomotives built by that company, even to the gauge, which is 80 cm (2 ft 7½ in.). They came in two batches, Nos. 2 to 5 built in 1895 and 1896, and Nos. 6 to 8 built in 1922 and 1923. All have boilers inclined in relation to the frames, so that boilers are approximately level when going uphill. No. 4, *Snowdon*, was rebuilt by Hunslet Engine Co., Leeds, in 1961–2, and in the process almost all the main components were renewed.

The coaches are all bogie coaches. Originally all were open-sided above the waist, with curtains to keep out the worst of the weather. In recent years all have been given glazed windows.

A visit to the Snowdon Railway could well be combined with a visit to the Llanberis Lake Railway and the North Wales Quarrying Museum, both described later.

Photography

The footpath from Llanberis to the summit follows the railway fairly closely, so photographers can ascend by early trains and descend on foot to photograph following trains. For car-borne photographers, a rough, narrow and steep road from Llanberis leads to an under-bridge about a mile up the line. At Llanberis station, the upper section of the car park overlooks the locomotive shed and provides a vantage point for photographing locomotives standing on its approach tracks: it is normally only here that it is possible to take a photograph which shows clearly the front of a Snowdon locomotive, unobscured by a coach.

The Fairbourne Railway

The line and its history

The Fairbourne Railway, two miles of 15 in. gauge line, originated as a 2 ft gauge horse-drawn tramway in 1890. At this time the village of Fairbourne was being built as a seaside resort, and the initial purpose of the tramway was to carry building materials. Very soon, however, it started to carry passengers also, between Fairbourne station on the Cambrian Railways, Fairbourne Beach, and Penrhyn Point at the foot of the Mawddach estuary, whence there was, and still is, a ferry to Barmouth. The line functioned in useful but unspectacular manner with horse-drawn trams for the next twenty-five years or so.

In 1916 the horse tramway was purchased by Narrow Gauge Railways Ltd. This company was associated with Bassett-Lowke Ltd the famous model engineers and, in spite of its name, built and operated miniature railways: that is to say, small railways whose size was intended to attract custom, using locomotives which were, more or less, scale models. Favoured locations were seaside resorts and, prior to World War I,

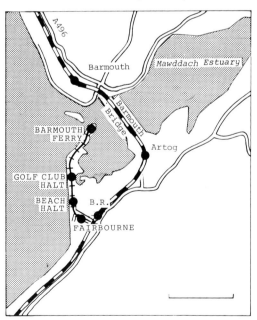

international exhibitions. In 1915 N.G.R. Ltd had taken a lease on the closed Ravenglass and Eskdale Railway in Cumberland, and was by stages narrowing the gauge to 15 in. and re-opening it. It repeated the operation at Fairbourne. The line was relaid to 15 in. gauge and became known as the Fairbourne Miniature Railway. A Bassett-Lowke miniature 4-4-2 and open-air four-wheeled coaches were provided to work it.

The miniature line passed through several changes of fortune, operator and rolling stock until the start of World War II. During that War the line was closed; it was badly damaged by the weather and the military.

What was left was purchased in 1946 by new owners from the Midlands. Track was relaid, the locomotives (one steam, one petrol) and the coaches were overhauled, and the line was re-opened in 1947. The venture was successful and since then there have been a great many developments: more and better locomotives, both steam and internal combustion, more and better coaches, some open-air, some closed, and much-improved stations. In 1976 an extension at Penrhyn Point was opened to bring the line closer than ever to the ferry landing.

In 1958, after several years of improvements, the word 'miniature' was dropped from the title, and the operating company became Fairbourne Railway Ltd.

The Railway today

Visitors arriving by road and rail encounter the Fairbourne Railway at its Fairbourne station. This immediately portrays the scale of improvements under the present ownership. The earlier station, a roadside run-round loop from which tracks continued into a locomotive shed, is now reduced to the status of sidings. Intending passengers first cross its tracks by board crossing and then cross a bridge over a stream to enter the new station, built in 1956. An overall roof spans four tracks, and the whole building is used to store rolling stock under cover in winter. A buffet and shop are adjacent, and those parts of the station area not covered by track or building have become a garden of traditional railway-station smartness.

After leaving the station, trains cross

Siân *departs from Fairbourne for the two-mile journey to Barmouth Ferry station.* (H. Sykes)

another bridge over the stream and then run alongside a straight road in a westerly direction for about a quarter of a mile to the beach. There the line turns sharply northwards. The juxtaposition here of seaside holiday houses, beach, and 15 in. gauge railway is reminiscent of the Romney, Hythe and Dymchurch Railway. There are request halts at Bathing Beach and Golf House, and a passing loop, installed in 1952 at approximately the mid-point of the line to enable a frequent train service to be run, with two trains in use simultaneously. Beyond the passing loop the railway runs by sand dunes and shingle beds to Penrhyn Point, which has fine views up the Mawddach Estuary to the east, with Barmouth Bridge in the foreground and the mountains beyond.

Stock

The stock of steam locomotives, which before World War II was never more than two, and often only one, is now four. Pride of the line are two handsome 2-4-2 tender locomotives: *Siân* (Welsh for *Jane*) which was built specially for

the line in 1963, and *Katie*, built in 1950 but purchased by the railway only in 1965. They are similar in appearance and, appropriately for a line which has dropped 'miniature' from its title, are scarcely miniature machines. Certainly they have no known prototype, and are way over scale for models of standard-gauge locomotives built for 15 in. gauge. The proportions of their cabs are such that the driver, sitting in the tender, is as likely to look forward over the cab roof as through the cab windows, and the design represents perhaps a half-way stage between a miniature locomotive and a full-size locomotive for the gauge. In any event, they are handsome, well-proportioned machines, well suited to their work.

The other two steam locomotives are miniature locomotives. One of them, the Bassett-Lowke-built 4-4-2 *Count Louis*, has been on the Fairbourne line since 1925. The fourth steam locomotive is 4-6-2 *Ernest W. Twining*, built in 1949.

Since the 1930s some trains have been hauled by internal combustion locomotives; there has been a succession of these, of which the survivors are 0-6-0 diesel *Rachel* and Bo-Bo diesel *Sylvia*.

Katie, one of the attractive 2-4-2 tender engines specially developed for the Fairbourne line, sets out from the terminus. (Phil Wood)

Coaches are a mixture of open-air and fully-enclosed types. Some of the open-air coaches have end screens to protect passengers from locomotive exhausts, and some are articulated

in rakes of three. A buffet car is taken to Penrhyn Point each day to serve refreshments there.

Photography
Absence of fences alongside the railway makes it easy to photograph. The combined trip from Barmouth Quay by ferry (motor boat) and then over the railway makes an unusual excursion.

The Llanberis Lake Railway

The Llanberis Lake Railway, though opened only in 1971, has antecedents of much more extensive history. It was built on the track-bed of part of the 4 ft gauge Padarn Railway, which from 1843 to 1961 carried slates from Dinorwic Quarry, Llanberis, to Port Dinorwic on the Menai Strait. Railway and port were owned by the quarry company, which also had an extensive system of 1 ft $10\frac{3}{4}$ in. gauge lines serving the Quarry itself. This was claimed to be the largest slate quarry in the world, and its railway system, operated by attractive little 0-4-0 saddle tanks, most of them built by Hunslet, was well-known to railway enthusiasts.

The locomotives, rolling stock and track of the 4 ft gauge line were sold for scrap after closure (with the exception of a few items which went to museums), but the first two miles of its route lay alongside the attractive lake called Llyn Padarn, and this gave rise to ideas of using it for a tourist railway. Matters became urgent in 1969 when the quarry company went into liquidation and its assets were put up for auction. A. Lowry Porter, a physiotherapist with experience as a volunteer on the Ffestiniog Railway, called a meeting which set up the Llanberis Lake Railway Society. This made successful bids at the auction for three of the surviving steam locomotives and one diesel, all of 1 ft $10\frac{3}{4}$ in. gauge.

In the meantime the old Caernarvon County Council had placed a preservation order on the Quarry's very extensive Victorian workshops, with a view to turning them into a museum – as has subsequently been done. The locomotive shed, forming part of the works, has been made available to the new railway, providing it with the valuable feature of ready-made covered accommodation for storage and repairs. The county council also acquired the track-bed of the old 4 ft gauge line alongside the lake and made it available to the railway.

Promoters of the new line decided it should be built to the common gauge of 1 ft $11\frac{1}{2}$ in., rather than the quarry's unique gauge of 1 ft

$10\frac{3}{4}$ in., to suit any further locomotives and rolling stock which might be obtained. The locomotives obtained from the quarry company were in due course modified to fit, when they were overhauled. Coaches were built at Llanberis. Just over a mile of the old track-bed was cleared of bushes and trees, and 1 ft $11\frac{1}{2}$ in. gauge track was laid on it. The Llanberis Lake Railway Co. Ltd was formed, with the intention that local capital and local labour (in an area of high unemployment) were to be used.

Opening day was fixed for 28 May 1971 and the railway was ceremonially opened on that day by T. Mervyn Jones, chairman of the Wales Tourist Board. But the opening train carried no passengers: shortly before the ceremony a coach had become derailed. Examination showed that new track had settled under the weight of locomotive Dolbadarn, and that the suspension of the new coaches was not flexible enough for them to pass over the defective section safely. There was no time to check the whole line before the opening ceremony, so to avoid risk of a further derailment, to a passenger train, it was arranged that the opening train would make a demonstration run, empty – which it did,

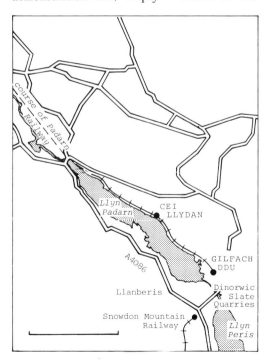

without trouble. Subsequent examination of the track showed no further defects and a pre-booked passenger special ran the following day. But it was decided to rebuild the coaches to a better design and at the same time operate a diesel locomotive up and down the line to iron out any further weaknesses.

Public passenger train services eventually started on 19 July 1971. During the following winter the line was extended to its full length, and more locomotives and coaches have been added at intervals. Steam locomotives on the line in 1978 included three from Dinorwic quarry and two 0-4-0 tanks imported from Germany. Recently, too, the railway has had much winter freight traffic in connection with a hydro-electric power scheme, for which electric cables were laid in a trench alongside the line.

The line today

Visitors to the Llanberis Lake Railway turn off the main road almost opposite the mountain railway station at Llanberis, down a side road which leads to the lake railway's terminus at Gilfach Ddu.

For almost its entire course the railway runs close to the lake. Despite the proximity of old

Dolbadarn, a 0-4-0 from Dinorwic Quarry, hauling a train of Llanberis Lake Railway-built coaches at Cei Llydan. (T. J. Edgington)

quarries, the railway runs through rural sur-roundings, with a steep hillside on one side of the line and the lake on the other. There is no road along this shore of the lake, so only rail passengers get the very fine view back across the lake to the Snowdon range of mountains. There is a passing loop at Cei Llydan and the line terminates at Penllyn: there is no station here and visitors join trains only at Gilfach Ddu. Return trains do, however, call at Cei Llydan where passengers may alight, and there is a lake-side picnic place.

Photography and the area around

Visitors to the Llanberis Lake Railway should certainly not miss the North Wales Quarrying Museum in the former quarry workshops adjoining Gilfach Ddu station. The Museum is a joint venture of the County Council (formerly Caernarvonshire, now Gwynedd), the Depart-ment of the Environment and the National Museum of Wales. Original equipment of the workshops forms the bulk of the exhibits, much

Leaving Gilfach Ddu. It is clear that the trackbed was built for the 4 ft gauge. (P. J. G. Ransom)

of it in its original location. The fitting and blacksmith's shops, iron and brass foundries, pattern makers' workshop and store, and an enormous water wheel, combine to give a vivid impression of the interior of a Victorian engineering works.

Pleasant footpaths starting from Gilfach Ddu have been laid out through the oak woods which cover the hillside here. One of these crosses a bridge over the railway, which is a useful vantage point for photographers. The Cei Llydan halt is also useful for photography.

The Bala Lake Railway

The line and its history

Closure under the Beeching Plan of the very picturesque standard-gauge line from Morfa Mawddach (Barmouth Junction) to Ruabon prompted several ambitious proposals for preservation. These eventually resulted in two separate undertakings, both of which are now open for passenger traffic.

The Bala Lake Railway runs from Llanuwchllyn for four-and-a-half miles, mostly alongside Bala Lake (the largest natural lake in Wales), to Bala (Llyn Tegid) station at the lake's north-eastern extremity. This railway is notable among Welsh tourist lines as being primarily the result of local initiative. It originated with a public meeting held at Bala in April 1971. A company was formed: Rheilffordd Llyn Tegid Cyf, or in English Bala Lake Railway Ltd, and £10,000 was raised from shares sold locally. A supporting group, the Bala Lake Railway Society, has also been formed.

The new railway was laid to a gauge of 1 ft 11½ in. on the track-bed of the old line. Work started at the station of Llanuwchllyn, and the first section, a little over a mile to a temporary terminus at Glanllyn, was opened on 13 August 1972. The line was subsequently extended by stages: Bala (Llyn Tegid) was reached in 1976. There are hopes of extending the line still further towards Bala town.

The line today

Llanuwchllyn station includes the platforms, station buildings and signal box of the former standard-gauge station. New sheds for storage and maintenance of locomotives and rolling stock have been added. The station building includes the original booking office, which still displays the last (1965) timetable of the former standard-gauge line, and a new refreshment room. Here, after train time, the author found a relaxed atmosphere – nothing much happening and a murmur of Welsh in the background – reminiscent of the Talyllyn of twenty years ago.

Train services run throughout the summer and at weekends in spring and autumn. Gener-ally, steam locomotives are used only at weekends. Leaving the station, the railway has a long stretch of straight track; then it comes beside the lake shore which it follows, more or less, as far as the other terminus. Hills rise up from the south side of the line. At Llangower, 2¼ miles from Llanuwchllyn, is a picnic place with access to the lake. Bala (Llyn Tegid) station comprised in 1978 little more than a platform and run-round loop, close to the B4391 road from Bala to Llanfyllin.

Stock

When the Bala Lake Railway was opened, it used a small four-wheeled diesel locomotive. In 1973, however, a handsome Bo-Bo diesel locomotive was built for it by Severn-Lamb Ltd, with a Leyland engine: this is named *Meirionydd*. Regular steam haulage started in 1975 after the arrival of the 0-4-0 saddle tank *Maid Marian*. This locomotive was built by Hunslet in 1903 for Dinorwic Slate Quarries Ltd and is typical of her type: she was bought for preservation in 1968 by the Maid Marian Locomotive Fund and ran on the Bressingham and Llanberis Lake railways before coming to Bala. Her performance on the B.L.R. has been good, and she has been joined by sister engines *Holy War* and *Jonathan*. Both *Maid Marian* and *Holy War* have been rebuilt with cabs since their arrival at Llanuwchllyn. A fourth locomotive of the same type, *Alice*, has also arrived on the railway, but in what amounts to 'kit form'!

Purchased at the same time as *Holy War* whose first owner removed all easily removable parts and abandoned the frames, tank and boiler at the top level of the quarry. The cylinders, wheels, motion etc, came to Llanuwchllyn as spares with *Holy War*. The boiler, frames and tank were purchased and removed from the quarry by the West Lancashire Light Railway who used the boiler on *Irish Mail*. The frames and tank arrived at Llanuwchllyn in 1977. The rebuilding of this locomotive as an 0-4-2T with tender is a long-term project. By way of contrast to the Quarry Hunslets, there is also a diminutive Kerr Stuart 'Wren' class 0-4-0ST, *Ashover*, as well as a private collection of over a dozen internal combustion locomotives.

The Bala Lake Railway runs in an attractive lakeside setting. **Maid Marian** *and her train enhance the view near Llanuwchllyn. (*Jarrolds*)*

The first coaches were two bogie toast-rack coaches with open sides. They have been joined by three compartment bogie coaches, two bogie saloons and two semi-open saloons, all purpose-built for the line.

Photography and the area around
The line is not difficult to photograph, for it runs in many places close to the road along the south shore of the lake. Apart from the lake itself there are few other specific attractions for tourists in the vicinity, but Bala is a pleasant small town in an attractive hilly district. If one wished to have a holiday staying in a central location to visit all the 'Great Little Trains' in turn, Bala would be as good a base as any.

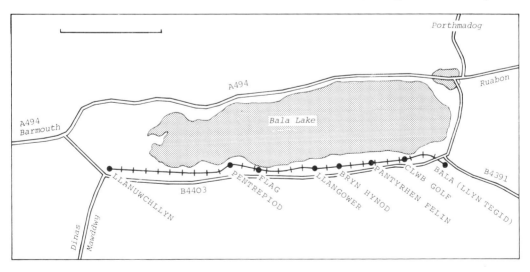

Llangollen Railway Society

The Llangollen Railway Society, originally formed in 1972 as the Flint and Deeside Railway Preservation Society, is the only standard-gauge steam line operating in North Wales. It is based at Llangollen Station, and was on the former Great Western Railway from Ruabon to Bala, which then connected with the Cambrian Coast line at Barmouth. The connection at Ruabon was with the company's main line from Paddington to Chester and Birkenhead. The Bala Lake railway, as it was originally called, connected at Corwen with the L. & N.W.R.'s line south from Rhyl and Denbigh. Unfortunately both of these routes were scheduled for closure under the Beeching report, and the line to Llangollen stopped passenger running in 1965. The track was lifted shortly afterwards, and the land sold to the local authority.

It was felt by local enthusiasts that this famous Eisteddfod town situated in the picturesque valley of the River Dee would be bound to attract sufficient visitors to make a steam railway financially viable. It would also provide an interesting transport comparison with the Welsh branch of the Shropshire Union Canal which had its dock and turning point in the town. (An interchange should also be possible at Berwyn Halt.) Accordingly, money was raised and negotiations opened. The first plan was to purchase the station at Llangollen and the $3\frac{1}{2}$ miles of track on the way west to Corwen. The Society's ultimate aim is to re-lay the line to this junction, via Carrog, Glyndyfrdwy and Berwyn. Berwyn, $1\frac{1}{2}$ miles out from Llangollen, is the terminus for the initial passenger service planned. This will be a journey of some ten miles through some of the remotest Welsh uplands. It is an ambitious project, but promises to be a marvellous ride when completed.

The Society received the keys for Llangollen Station in June 1975. Since then much work has been focused on the restoration of the station buildings. When the Society took over, they were dilapidated in the extreme. Today they are smart, and in good order, and a refreshment room and shop have been provided. In addition,

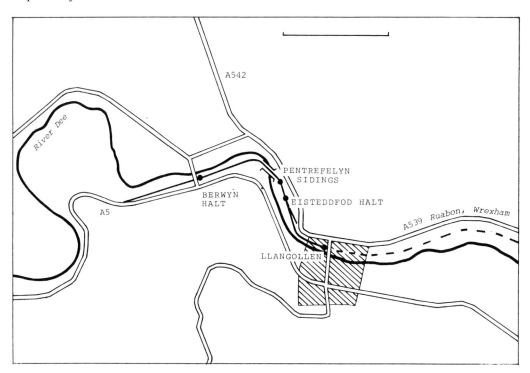

the station and goods areas have been re-laid with track, which has been extended for half a mile in the direction of Corwen with track donated by Shell Oil. The original signal box, situated at the end of Platform 1, has been preserved, and controls the points and movement of trains in the area. The station was officially re-opened on 13 September 1975, after months of intensive clearance work, when a diesel ran the length of one section of track.

RIGHT: *The attractive Llangollen station has regained much of its G.W.R. splendour.* Austin 1 *stands at the platform; the Fowler diesel is nearer the camera.* (T.A. Parkins)

BELOW: Austin 1 *in close-up after five years of restoration work during which the loco was completely re-tubed and vacuum brakes fitted.*

41

*At the beginning of its passenger-carrying career, the Llangollen Railway offers a ride by the River Dee with magnificent scenery to come when it extends towards Corwen. (*Llangollen Railway Soc.*)*

Stock

The Society has acquired a number of saddle tanks and a deal of rolling stock. Most of the locomotives have arrived as gifts from firms who have switched to diesel traction. The first steam engine to be restored on the line is the Kitson 0-6-0 saddletank *Burtonwood Brewer*. This locomotive was built in Leeds in 1932 to the designs of Manning Wardle & Co., whom Kit-sons had absorbed in 1926. It was acquired from British Leyland at Longbridge, Birmingham, and formerly carried the name *Austin I*.

In addition the following locomotives are undergoing restoration on the railway: Hudswell Clarke 0-6-0T, *Richboro*, built in 1917; Hunslet 0-6-0T, No. 1234, also built in 1917; Peckett 0-4-0ST, No. 2084, built in 1948; and G.W.R. 0-6-0 Pannier tank No. 7754, which was obtained from the National Coal Board in South Wales. The first train to be hauled on the Society's line was headed by the Fowler diesel, 0-4-0 named *Eliseg*.

For operating its passenger services, the railway has two B.R. Mark I suburban coaches which once saw service on the Kings Cross suburban trains. There are also a pair of G.W.R. Brake third bogies coaches dating from 1938; a former G.W.R. 'Toad' goods brake van, No. 17407, built in 1940; and a varied selection of goods rolling stock.

Six years of hard work at Llangollen were crowned with achievement on 26 July 1981 when the railway ran its first steam passenger trains under special authorization from the Railway Inspectorate pending completion of the Light Railway Order formalities. The railway operates on Sundays and public holidays from Spring Bank Holiday onwards. Despite an objection from the County Council who were worried that the presence of the railway might hamper road improvements proposed on the last two miles of trackbed before Corwen, the Society is still optimistic that it will ultimately run trains at least as far as Carog, eight miles from Llangollen. Meanwhile, track is being laid on the next $\frac{3}{4}$-mile of trackbed towards Berwyn, where it was hoped services would reach during 1983. This will involve crossing the River Dee on a plate girder bridge.

There is a Llangollen Railway Rolling Stock Group. Membership is open to the public and is available by purchasing one or more shares in any item of stock subsequently purchased by the Society. A number of locomotives and passenger coaches have been selected for possible preservation, when they and the funds become available.

The area around
Llangollen, besides being the site for the International Musical Eisteddfod, every summer, has a number of historic buildings. On a hill overlooking the town are the remains of Castle Dinas Bran. There is a beautifully decorated eighteenth-century timbered house, Plas Newydd. It was the home of the 'Ladies of Llangollen', two Irish women who settled here, drawing famous visitors because of their eccentricities.

The River Dee which flows through the centre of the town is spanned by a fine fourteenth century stone bridge, built by a Bishop of St Asaph.

The Gwili Railway

The line and its history
While steam 'tourist' railways originated and indeed proliferated in North Wales, South Wales remained something of a blank on the preserved-railway map. This blank was partly filled with the opening in 1978 of the first section of the Gwili Railway.

Historically the line has respectable antecedents. It commenced its existence not on the narrow gauge but, by contrast, on the broad. Brunel's broad gauge is so much associated with

Gwili Railway: hilly, open country. (P. G. Wright)

Peckett 0-4-0 Myrddin/Merlin *(the engine is bilingually named, one each side) was built in 1939. This inaugural train, one d.m.u. trailer, ran on the Gwili Railway in March 1978. (Gwili Railway Co.)*

the West Country and the lines thither that one tends to forget that it extended also far into South Wales, and when the Carmarthen and Cardigan Railway was promoted in the late 1850s, it was built on the broad gauge. So much of it as was built, that is: for the line never reached Cardigan, and at this stage got no closer than Llandyssul. In due course, however, the Manchester and Milford Railway was opened and extended, despite the ambitions indicated by its name, from Pencader, on the C. & C. near Llandyssul, to Aberystwyth: later still, the standard-gauge C. & C. and the M. & M. were successively taken over by the Great Western Railway, and Carmarthen to Aberystwyth became one of that company's secondary main lines.

Its passenger service was eventually withdrawn about 1964, but much of the southern part of the line remained in existence for freight traffic for several years thereafter. So when the Gwili Railway was promoted to bring back the nostalgia of steam to this part of South Wales, it was able to purchase nearly $1\frac{1}{2}$ miles of track northwards from Bronwydd Arms (the first station out of Carmarthen), and 8 miles of track-bed extending from Abergwili, on the outskirts of Carmarthen, past Bronwydd Arms to Llanpumsaint. This purchase was completed on 8 November 1977; the Gwili Railway Co. Ltd's Light Railway Order, covering the whole of this section, had come into force five days earlier. Supporting the company is the Gwili Railway Preservation Society.

The line today
The section over which train services run at present is from Bronwydd Arms northwards for $1\frac{1}{2}$ miles to a new halt made at Penybont. Throughout its length, the line follows the

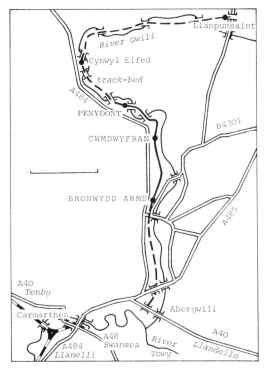

Welsh Highland Railway

The Welsh Highland Railway is of special historic interest as it was run for a period by the legendary Colonel Holman F. Stephens, was opened in 1923 but operated for only fourteen years before complete closure. It joined the existing Porthmadog-Croesor Junction section of the Croesor Tramway (built some sixty years earlier) with the North Wales Narrow-Gauge Railway which ran from Dinas Junction, on the L.N.W.R. Caernarvon-Afon Wen branch, to Rhyd-ddu at the foot of Snowdon. Plans to link these two railways had been in hand before World War I but hostilities prevented implementation until almost ten years later. However, within eighteen months of being surveyed in January 1922, the work was completed, and it became possible to make a narrow-gauge journey of over 40 miles, starting from Dinas Junction, connecting with the Ffestiniog Railway at Porthmadog and continuing on that line through to Blaenau Ffestiniog. Indeed, for the dedicated traveller, a complete round trip was possible by changing onto the L.M.S. branch train at Blaenau and journeying via Llandudno Junction and Caernarvon, back to Dinas Junction again!

Unfortunately, the new railway was never a success. The slate industry was declining and, at the same time, rural bus services were at their zenith. The Welsh Highland service was slow and unimaginative and despite the scenic attractions of the Aberglaslyn Pass near Beddgelert, it never achieved the popularity of its elder neighbour, the Ffestiniog. Indeed, with the Ffestiniog eventually leasing the W.H.R. and both lines coming under Colonel Stephens' management, the newcomer very nearly brought about the downfall of the F.R. as well.

Passenger trains ceased to run after the end of the 1936 season and freight traffic came to an end the following year. The line remained in a state of growing dereliction for four years before the Ministry of Supply requisitioned the remains for use in the war effort. Demolition took place during 1941–2 and two years later the company was compulsorily wound up.

But the line and its history continued to

attractive valley of the River Gwili. During the summer of 1978, frequent trains ran at weekends only; the first public services between Bronwydd Arms and Cwmdwyfran started on 30 April, although they had run since 25 March over just half a mile of track. During that first season, 20,000 passenger journeys were recorded.

Stock
During 1978 the train was a stumpy 1939-built Peckett 0-4-0 saddle tank named *Merlin* (or *Myrddin*), hauling a single coach which was formerly a British Rail d.m.u. trailer car. The Railway subsequently bought four B.R. Mark I coaches, two being compartment vehicles and the others a buffet car and a griddle car. Apart from *Merlin* there are four other industrial saddletanks present, whilst the largest locomotive is G.W.R. 4-6-0 No. 7820 *Dinmore Manor*. This is yet another example rescued from Barry scrapyard and constitutes a long-term restoration project.

The W.H.R. inaugurated its services with diesel power. **Kinnerley** *at Porthmadog.* (T. Heavyside)

fascinate railway enthusiasts and a plan to build a new railway over the old W.H.R. route was first mooted in 1961. A company, the Welsh Highland Light Railway (1964) Ltd, was formed three years later. However, negotiations to acquire the trackbed from the official receiver have been repeatedly delayed. The death of the original company's liquidator, road-widening schemes, and even the reorganization of local government are among the reasons for these delays.

Despite these setbacks, the present company has continued working towards its goal and in 1973 was allowed occupation of its present site, Beddgelert Siding, Porthmadog, where slate used to be transhipped from narrow gauge to standard gauge wagons. Passenger operation commenced on 2 August 1980 and over 7,000 passengers were carried during the ensuing short season. The following summer, on 18 July 1981, the railway was officially opened by Councillor Roberts, Chairman of Gwynedd County Council. Although some legal problems remain, the company hopes to start rebuilding the next section of line between Pen-y-Mount and Pont Croesor, a distance of $1\frac{1}{2}$ miles. Sufficient materials for a substantial portion of this distance are on hand, and the extension could be in use by 1984.

Stock
Pride of place goes to *Russell*, a 2-6-2 tank built by Hunslet in 1906 and the only survivor of the original W.H.R. locomotive stock. *Russell* has been joined by two Bagnall 0-4-2 tanks re-imported into this country from the Rustenberg Platinum Mines in South Africa. When restored, these will take on the names of two of the old N.W.N.G.R. locos, *Snowdon Ranger* and *Moel Tryfan*. There is also a large Peckett 0-4-2T, *Karen*, and a pair of Orenstein & Koppel 0-6-0 well tanks, *Nantmor* and *Pedemoura*, both of characteristic German outline.

About a dozen small diesels are also available, and up to the end of the 1982 season it was one of these that hauled the passenger train service. However, steam traction is promised from 1983 onwards.

Brecon Mountain Railway

The Brecon Mountain Railway is constructed almost entirely on the trackbed of the Brecon & Merthyr Railway. This railway, opened in 1859, originally ran from Newport to Brecon. Becoming part of the Great Western Railway under the Railways Act of 1921, the line continued to serve the area until closed for passenger traffic in 1962. The present railway is the brainchild of Tony Hills, the former proprietor of a North Wales engineering business, who in 1972 set about looking for a suitable site to build a new 2 ft gauge railway in a part of the country that did not already have such an attraction. Several sites were investigated before the choice finally went to the former Brecon and Merthyr Railway.

Narrow gauge rails by the reservoir at Pontsticill. Sybil *is in the foreground as the East German 0-6-2T passes. (*Brecon Mountain Railway*)*

Reconstruction of the railway between Pant and Pontsticill involved the construction of a 600-yard deviation at Pant, necessitated by the original alignment being unobtainable. Building this deviation involved excavating 3,000 cubic metres of rock. Since closure by B.R. three bridges had been removed and replacement of these has been necessary. Pontsticill station site was cleared and landscaped and the railway buildings erected. Two miles of track have been laid and ballasted, rail and timber coming from various parts of Britain. Ballast, 1,200 tons of it, has been obtained from a local quarry.

For all but about a mile of its length, the line runs within the Brecon Beacons National Park, which means there are fairly restrictive planning requirements on any buildings that are needed. An example of this is the railway workshop at Pontsticill, which has been stone-faced using materials recovered on demolition of the original island platform.

Certain buildings at Pontsticill, the operating centre of the railway, remain from B.R. days: the station house – extended and modern-

East German 0-6-2 tank Graf Schwerin-Löwitz *at Pant station. The quality of the restoration work and coachbuilding can be seen. (*Tom Heavyside*)*

ized – and the signalbox, which still needs a lot of restoration. However, being within a National Park has many virtues, not the least being the views from the railway which at times are breathtaking. Over most of the run, the background is dominated by Pen-y-Fan, at 2906 feet the highest point in South Wales. In the foreground are the Taf Fechan and Pentwyn Reservoirs which have a combined length of over three miles.

Construction of the first two miles of line began in 1978 with site clearance and drainage. From the outset, the railway employed a small, permanent labour force which is supplemented at weekends by volunteers, mostly members of the Brecon Mountain Railway Association – a body not financially linked with the railway company. Track-laying, using rail obtained from the Longmoor Military Railway, started at Pontsticill and progressed southwards towards Pant. Financing of the railway's construction was helped largely by a £50,000 grant from the

Wales Tourist Board. The Brecon Mountain Railway opened for traffic on 8 June 1980, operating an hourly schedule at weekends.

Stock

Since the opening, services have been in the hands of two steam locomotives – Quarry Hunslet 0-4-0ST *Sybil* dating from 1903, and the handsome Jung 0-6-2T *Graf Schwerin Löwitz*, formerly No. 99.3353 of the Deutsche Reichsbahn, the East German State Railways. Originally, she had been built for the Mecklenburg-Pommersche Schmalspurbahn, an extensive 600 mm gauge network near the present border with Poland, which finally closed in 1969.

Still to be restored to operating condition are Orenstein & Koppel 0-4-0 well tank No. 12722 of 1936 from a Hamburg stone quarry and two small vertical-boilered 0-4-0 tanks from North Wales slate quarries. But dwarfing all these engines is the mighty Baldwin Pacific tender engine No. 61269, built in 1930. This loco worked for the Eastern Provinces Cement Company in Port Elizabeth, South Africa, until damaged in a shunting accident and bought for preservation in the U.K. Passenger rolling stock of suitable standards for the new line was not readily available so the railway is constructing its own distinctive carriages with end balconies. These are built on the bogies and chasses of ex-South African Railways freight wagons. Three of these forty-seater vehicles have so far entered service.

Services operate daily from the beginning of May to the beginning of October. Trains commence running at 11 am and continue until dusk. A weekend, Saturdays and Sundays, service operates from October until December and during the schools autumn half-term trains operate daily between 12 noon and 3 pm. Workshop facilities at Pontsticill are open for inspection by the public on the first Sunday in October and entrance to the workshops is free to railway passengers.

Eventually it is intended that the railway be extended further into the Brecon Beacons National Park to a terminus at Torpantau and completion of this section will mean the line passing through the highest railway tunnel in Great Britain.

LANCASHIRE
AND THE NORTH-WEST

The Ravenglass and Eskdale Railway

This fascinating 15 in. gauge line links two valleys, Miterdale and Eskdale in West Cumbria, and runs from Ravenglass on the coast, to Dalegarth, some three miles from the celebrated Hard Knott Pass.

The line and its history
It was opened in 1876 as a 3 ft gauge line, to serve a group of iron mines in Eskdale. The output of these mines did not come up to expectations and the line was bankrupt in less than a year. It remained thus until the closure of the last mine forced complete abandonment in 1912.

The line lay derelict till 1915, when its remains were leased by Narrow Gauge Railways Ltd, a concern in which Messrs Bassett-Lowke, the model-makers, had a large interest. N.G.R. re-gauged the track from 3 ft to 15 in., and a train service was resumed using miniature locomotives built by Bassett-Lowke, together with locomotives and coaches built some twenty years before by Sir Arthur Heywood for his private railway at Duffield in Derbyshire. The Bassett-Lowke engines were scale models built for exhibition, and proved to be too lightly constructed to stand the hard slogging needed on the switchback R. & E. line. The Heywood engines, though strongly built, were already some 20 years old and past their prime. However, one of the Heywood engines, a 0-8-0 named *Muriel*, was rebuilt in 1926–7 as a 0-8-2 using *Muriel*'s chassis with a new boiler and firebox. She was renamed *River Irt* and is still in regular service.

In 1925 the line was taken over by Sir Aubrey Brocklebank, Chairman of the Cunard Steamship Line. He expanded the quarries at Beckfoot, and enlarged the crushing plant at Murthwaite to provide extra revenue from freight for the little line. After his death however, his successors took little interest and the line deteriorated. They sold it to the Keswick Granite Co. in 1948. The Granite Co. ran down the quarries but kept the railway running. In 1958· they put it up for auction. It was eventually bought by Mr Colin Gilbert, a Manchester stockbroker, who put up the bulk of the money on behalf of the newly formed Ravenglass and Eskdale Railway Preservation Society. Since then freight traffic has been abandoned, and an all-the-year-round passenger service run.

The line is operated by a permanent staff under the Manager, Mr Douglas Ferreira,

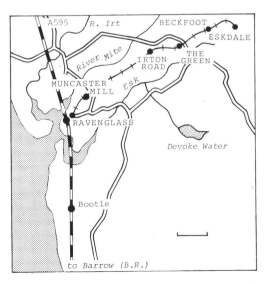

assisted by voluntary help from Preservation Society members.

A journey down the line

The time allowed for the 7-mile journey is 40 minutes. This may seem excessive, but it must be remembered that this is a miniature railway, and the line abounds in sharp curves and stiff gradients. Drivers have to know the road thoroughly in all weathers, and the peculiarities of their engines too, if they are to get the best out of them and keep time.

Leaving Ravenglass we drop down to Barrow Marsh alongside the River Mite, dive under the main road and reach Muncaster Mill Halt. The mill waterwheel has been restored and will probably be turning as we pass. The interior machinery is being gradually restored too, and is open for visitors' inspection.

From the Halt, a stiff climb begins on a long S-bend through Miteside woods; our engine begins to bark with effort up gradients varying sharply between 1 in 42 and 1 in 79. The scenery is striking, and the local names are fascinating not only here but all along the line. Beyond Miteside Halt, with its shelter made from a boat, we come to Katie Caddie Gates, Katie Caddie Curve, Creep Cutting, and then a minor summit known to enginemen as 'The Top'. It is not line summit by any means; merely one of the many with which this line abounds. A gentle drop to Murthwaite follows. On the right, built into the hillside and now heavily overgrown, is all that remains of the stone-crushing plant and former workshops of the R. & E.R. The plant is now demolished, and scrub has taken over, but ten and more years ago the place was, so to speak, littered with history, relics of former locomotives and rolling stock, now put aside for proper preservation.

From Murthwaite there is a gentle climb through Horsefall Wood to Rocky Point, where the line circumnavigates an outcrop. Our engine works hard again up the 1 in 47 to Walk Mill summit, where, ahead, Scafell looms up in the distance, and our track, straight for once, dips and rises like a fairground switchback. Down, down we go to the Big Stone, then up again and sweep round into Irton Road Station, some four miles from Ravenglass. This is the half-way point, and there is usually a train from the other

direction waiting to pass us.

From Irton Road to the Green is a half-mile – but a very pretty one – and in this short distance we pass from Miterdale into Eskdale. The Green is now a charming station, made so by the work of the Yorkshire Branch of the Preservation Society. It was not always thus however. It was once a ramshackle place with a dilapidated hut and grass-grown platform. Local legend has it that a neighbouring farmer went to a sale and bought a second-hand hen house. It was to be delivered by rail on a certain day. On the appointed day he sent a boy to fetch it. Arrived at the station the boy loaded up the only hut he could find. . . .

Leaving the Green, the line curves under the road, and climbs sharply to Hollinghow Woods, over 1 in 36. With a heavily loaded train, a good start is needed to avoid stalling on the bank, particularly in wet weather. We twist and turn through the woods on a ledge, higher than and some distance from the valley road. About a quarter-mile further on, and still in the woods, we reach Fisherground Corner, so called because the farm of that name is below us on the right. A short sharp gradient follows, and on the left, supported by two concrete columns, is a water tank made from an old steel wagon body which is filled from a hillside stream. This still serves as an emergency water supply for thirsty locomotives.

On again past Spout House Farm, we come to Gilbert's Cutting. In pre-preservation days the line made a sharp S-bend here to get round an outcrop. It was a splendid place for photography, but bad for railway operation, as the curve had to be negotiated carefully. In 1963, Mr Gilbert paid for a cutting to be dug through the outcrop.

From this point on, we are near to, and still above, the road which keeps us company for the next half-mile or so. Soon we pass the former Beckfoot quarry, long abandoned and shrouded in trees. A quarter of a mile ahead is Beckfoot Halt. This request stop is mainly used by visitors staying at the former Stanley Ghyll Hotel, which is now a centre run by the Y.H.A. It is the building on our right as we pass the Halt and on the other side of the road. Beckfoot Wood lies ahead, and the line runs beside a lane

2-8-2 River Mite *on the turntable at Eskdale (Dalegarth) against the magnificent backdrop of the Cumbrian mountains. The locomotive was built as recently as 1966.*

leading to some cottages. Drivers say this can be a tricky stretch. The gradient is stiff (though not the stiffest on the line) and it can be slippery in wet weather. Little sunlight can penetrate the trees, and even if the rest of the line be dry this part is apt to remain damp and greasy. Leftward among the trees on the other side of the lane are the remains of bothies in which miners of the 1870s lived before proper accommodation was built for them.

Once at the summit, we coast down past the cottages and into Eskdale terminus first opened in 1926. There are two tracks in the station, with a turntable at the end. The main platform is on the right, with a building housing a refreshment and waiting room, a shop and the booking office. A spacious car park and picnic area is in the field behind. This is one of the many improvements put in since preservation. That the Railway is now a go-ahead concern is obvious. During the last ten years two new locomotives have been built, the greater part of

the line relaid. The track layout at Ravenglass has been greatly improved and effectively signalled, saloon coaches provided to ensure passenger comfort during bad weather, and an awning erected to provide much needed shelter on the bleakest part of the station at Ravenglass. The greatest advance of all has been in the matter of train control.

Train control by radio. Through the years the R. & E.R. has tried many methods, but none, however satisfactory they may have been elsewhere, was really suited to the conditions under which the R. & E.R. has to work. Then someone came up with the idea of radio control. A scheme was evolved, and it has been in use successfully for some years now.

The system briefly is this: each locomotive is equipped with a radio transceiver and there is another unit in the control cabin at Ravenglass.

Between the two terminal stations are three loops where trains can pass each other, at Miteside, Irton Road Station, and Fisherground. Some distance ahead of each loop, a disc with a zig-zag line on it is prominently displayed on a post beside the line. On reaching this, the driver calls up Control, identifies himself, states his

3

position, and asks for instructions. He may be told to pass through the loop without stopping; on the other hand if the controller has another train approaching in the opposite direction he will instruct the driver to halt in the loop and let it pass. This process is repeated for every train in each direction throughout the day's timetable.

From his timetable graph before him on the desk the controller knows where every train *ought* to be at any given moment. Now, with his radio telephone, he knows where they all *actually are* – which can sometimes be a very different thing. With this system, emergencies can be anticipated and prompt action taken so that mishaps do not in fact happen. The system is still in its infancy. The R. & E.R. is the pioneer of it in this country.

Stock

The Railway now has five steam locomotives. When in the early 1920s it was clear that the Bassett-Lowke models were not really up to the job, Henry Greenly designed *River Esk* as a freight engine to handle the stone traffic. She is a 2-8-2, the first engine of that wheel arrangement ever built in this country. She was built by Davey Paxman of Colchester in 1923. She is a miniature locomotive built to a scale of 4 in. to the foot. At one stage in her career she was given a steam tender with a 0-8-0 chassis. This was not a success, so the tender was mounted on two four-wheeled bogies instead, and the steam chassis stored away in case it might some day come in useful. *River Esk* has been a capable performer ever since, and is a very handsome engine. Until 1966 she wore a green livery, but in 1967 she was given a coat of blackberry black lined out with red and white, and now looks even better.

For some twenty-five years, *River Esk* and *River Irt* carried the brunt of the traffic, for they were the only two steam engines on the line. *River Irt* is the oldest 15 in. gauge locomotive in active service anywhere; for she, as we mentioned above, is a rebuild of Sir Arthur Heywood's *Muriel* of 1894. She was powerful and reliable but certainly no beauty! Her miniature cab gave her driver little protection. She was given a larger one in 1972, and her chimney was

lengthened in proportion. This gave a bonus of better steaming, and it also improved her looks. She wears her former green livery with red and black lining.

In 1967 *Esk* and *Irt* were joined by *River Mite*. She was built by Clarkson of York on – wait for it! – *River Esk*'s steam-tender chassis which had been thriftily stored away 33 years before. Naturally she had her teething troubles, but 16 years of service has proved her worth. She was first painted Indian red – but is now a shade of vermilion.

The centenary year of the railway saw yet another locomotive added to the stud. This is *Northern Rock*, designed and built at Ravenglass. The only part not made there was her R. & E. R. standard boiler, supplied by an outside firm. She went into service in April 1976, and has been at work ever since, and shown herself to be a powerful engine. She is painted in a yellowish shade of green known as muscat, and lined out with red and black.

As if to prove that it is still in the forefront of ingenuity, the R. & E.R. added another steam locomotive to its stock at the end of 1981. At first sight *Bonnie Dundee* is a straightforward 0-4-2T, of pleasing narrow-gauge appearance. But it is, in fact, a 'Ratty' rebuild of a former 2 ft gauge gasworks 0-4-0 well tank with inside frames built by Kerr Stuart in 1900.

Modifications included swapping over the frame plates to allow the 15 in. gauge driving wheels, obtained from a Muir Hill tractor locomotive dismantled several years ago, to be fitted between them. The side tanks are the one-hundred-year-old galvanized iron remains of the Heywood 0-6-0T *Ella*, and have been fitted in addition to the well tank to give the loco enough water for the 14-mile round trip. Entirely new are the axles, outside cranks, connecting rods and smokebox, while the rear frames have been extended by nine inches to give more footplate space. So *Bonnie Dundee* is a masterpiece of R. & E.R. improvization and adaptation – and fully in the traditions of this railway!

Since the early 1920s the R. & E.R. has used internal combustion locomotives (i.c.l.'s) alongside their steam engines. As we have seen, the 0-6-0 named *Ella*, was, when withdrawn, can-

In the fine surroundings of the Mite valley 2-6-2 Northern Rock *heads for Ravenglass with a train of modern enclosed bogie stock.* (Nick Stanbra)

nibalized into a petrol locomotive. The remains, now a tool van, are usually to be seen on a siding just outside Dalegarth station.

The i.c.l.'s were used as standby locomotives for hauling relief trains in summer and works trains in winter. They still perform these functions, and in addition tackle the winter passenger service, for at that season the steam engines are regularly under repair.

The i.c.l.'s most in evidence to summer visitors are three: first *Shelagh of Eskdale*. She is named after a local historical character, and is a diesel-hydraulic locomotive built in 1968 by Curwen and Severn-Lamb, painted royal blue.

A petrol-driven engine built in 1929 has given yeoman service. She was built to resemble as far as possible a steam tank engine and her

exhaust was surrounded by a steam-engine-type chimney. Not unnaturally she was known as *Pretender*. Not long ago it was feared that her much-repaired engines were past further repair and that she would have to be scrapped. The R. & E.R. engineers, however, are nothing if not resourceful. They replaced her ailing petrol engine with a diesel salvaged from a boat sunk in Ravenglass harbour. This has given her a new lease of life and everyone now calls her *Perkins*. She is painted Brunswick green with orange and black lining.

A further powerful double-bogie diesel locomotive, *Lady Wakefield*, was added to stock in 1980.

A twin-car diesel set can generally be seen during the day in Ravenglass station. The cars are painted aluminium colour, and both carry the Silver Jubilee device. This is the R. & E.R. Silver Jubilee train, added to stock during 1977. The train is very successful, and is used for light

5

relief trains, small party bookings, and V.I.P.s visiting the line. The cars are excellently sprung, and their riding has to be experienced to be believed.

The coaches found at Ravenglass are a mixture of opens and saloons. The latest batch of saloon coaches was built and delivered between 1966 and 1974; the opens are mostly older. In fine weather, trains are made up of opens, with saloons used on rainy days. More often than not it is wiser to use both, but it is noticeable that the opens fill up first. The saloons have excellent observation windows, but the open coaches give by far the best view of the countryside during the run.

The area around
Ravenglass, Irton Road, and Dalegarth are ideal centres from which to set out by car or on foot, to explore the countryside.

Muncaster Castle is one mile from Ravenglass. The castle itself is mainly Victorian, but parts of the medieval castle remain. There is a fine collection of furniture and pictures, ornamental gardens to wander in, and a nature trail to follow.

Ravenglass itself was a Roman port; a 'Roman Trail' has been laid out to follow.

A *Roman road* ran from Ravenglass over Hard Knott Pass and Wrynose Pass to the Roman station near Windermere, and there is a Roman fort still to be seen on the slopes of *Hard Knott*. Not too far away by car is *Wastwater*, and further away in an easterly direction are *Coniston* and *Windermere,* and the beauty spot of Tarn Hows.

In the same neighbourhood, but 2 miles south-east of Hawkshead is Hill Top, Sawrey, the home of Beatrix Potter. From there it is not far by car to Grasmere and Rydal Water. Rydal Mount was the house in which the poet Wordsworth lived for the last 37 years of his life.

Grizedale Forest Wild Life Centre is well worth a visit. It is 3 miles south of Hawkshead on the road to Satterthwaite.

Henry Greenly's masterpiece River Esk *nearing the end of its journey at Ravenglass with a trainload of passengers. (*Phil Wood*)*

The Lakeside and Haverthwaite Railway

The line and its history
The Lakeside and Plumpton Branch Railway was opened by the Furness Railway Company on 1 June 1869; after almost a hundred years of continuous running, it was closed at the end of 1965.

From the beginning it was associated with Windermere tourism. This business reached a peak during the inter-war years, when special excursions were run from London, Blackpool and Leeds. After World War II, the traffic became narrowly seasonal; lack of winter trade led Dr Beeching to recommend the closure of this line to passengers in the early 60s; a freight service continued until 1967. The Lakeside Railway Estates Company was formed in that year in the hope of reviving the whole line. Later, when this was found to be impossible, they settled for the three miles between Lakeside and Haverthwaite. In 1970 they were granted permission by British Rail to start renovating the permanent way; from then on locomotives and coaches began to arrive. On 2 May 1973, the line was opened for the conveyance of passengers by the late Bishop of Wakefield, the Rt Rev. Eric Treacy.

The line today
The actual line now open to the public runs from the terminus station, Lakeside on Windermere and runs roughly south-west to Haverthwaite. Between these two lies Newby Bridge Halt, recently restored by the Blackpool Branch of the Society. There are two short tunnels at Haverthwaite; both are unlined, being cut through solid rock. Haverthwaite is the headquarters of the line, having not only spacious goods yards for storage of stock, and car parking, but being alongside the main A590 road. The railway is single-track throughout, with a run-round loop at each terminal station.

Stock
The line's principal motive power is provided by the two 4MT class 2-6-4 tanks. Designed by

7

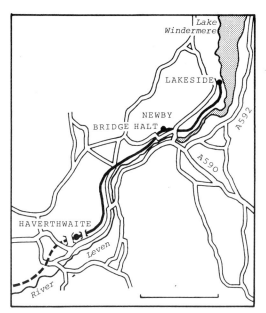

Charles Fairburn for the L.M.S in 1944, they were intended for light passenger and goods duties. No. 2073 was built in 1950, and No. 2085 in 1951. They were built in Brighton for work on the Southern Region. No. 2073 did not require much restoration, being ready for service within six months. No. 2085, however, needed more extensive repairs, and complete re-tubing. She was not ready for five years. No. 2073 has been painted in the livery of the London and North Western Railway, that is blackberry black. No. 2085 has been repainted in the livery of the Caledonian Railway, a bright mid-blue.

However, the most regular performers on the line are the 0-6-0 tank engines of which there are five. Perhaps the hardest workers are the two Hunslet 'Austerity' tanks, *Cumbria* and *Repulse*. *Cumbria* was purchased from Army service at Long Marston depot and arrived at Haverthwaite in very fine condition. *Repulse*, built in 1950, worked for the National Coal Board and can be distinguished by its Giesl ejector chimney. Both engines have, of course, been fitted with vacuum brake equipment.

Another regular tank steamer is No. 14, *Princess*. She is an 0-6-0 saddle tank manufactured by W.G. Bagnall of Stafford in 1942. On completion, *Princess* was sent to perform shunting duties for the Preston Corporation on the banks

of the River Ribble. She has since been renovated and had vacuum braking gear fitted. Unlike the Hunslet, this tank has outside cylinders and visible driving gear. Similar in external appearance are the two Hudswell Clarke 0-6-0s, now numbered 5 and 6. No. 5 was built in Leeds in 1929 and No. 6 at the same place some ten years earlier. They have both had chequered careers, but came together in the 1960s to work at the Byfield Ironstone Company's pits in Scunthorpe; when these pits were closed down in 1969, the locos were purchased for the Lakeside Railway.

There are no fewer than five 0-4-0 saddle tanks, two each from Peckett and Barclay and one from Avonside. Also from Andrew Barclay is an interesting 0-6-0 Fireless dating from 1917.

The railway has an impressive diesel fleet of six locos, perhaps the most interesting being the L.M.S. prototype machine No. 601 of 1945 vintage. More familiar in outline are the two B.R./Drewry 03 class shunters Nos. 03 072 and D2117, both built in 1959. The oldest of the diesels is L.H.R. No. 16 *Fluff*. The bodywork was constructed by Hunslet of Leeds in 1937 but the engine is a Fowler 44 h.p. diesel. She is used for shunting, and for light works trains. The other two locos also originated with Fowlers of Leeds. One was built in 1948 and retains its original mechanical transmission, whilst the other was extensively rebuilt by Thomas Hill of Rotherham in 1961 and now resembles one of their Vanguard types with hydraulic transmission.

Finally, there is the tiny petrol-driven four-wheeled *Rachel*, No. 9 on the Railway. Manufactured in Bedford by the Motor Rail and Tram Car Company in 1924, she was originally used as a shunter in a paper mill in Burneside. She was purchased by a member of the Lakeside Railway Society and transferred to the line in 1973. *Rachel* is an exceptionally compact loco; she is powered by a 40 h.p. Dorman Engine, and weighs a mere 10 tons.

The Railway also possesses eleven coaches. These, with one exception, are all of British Railways origin. The Society purchased eight standard coaches to run their passenger service. There are six regular side-corridor second-class coaches; four are numbered E24248, E24377, E24381, and E24731 and were built

Resplendent in Furness Railway livery, the Austerity saddletank Cumbria *approaches Newby Bridge. (*Tom Heavyside*)*

in 1953; the others, E24449 and E24799, were built in the following year. In addition, they have purchased a 'BSK' and a 'BSO'. The former, No. E34181 built in 1951, matches the other six, but has only four compartments and a luggage and guard's brake compartment as well. The 'BSO', E9218 built in 1953, is of similar design to the 'BSK' except that it has a central corridor with open seating, with a guard's and luggage compartments. This carriage has now been converted into a buffet car. The luggage compartment is used as a bar, and the guard's compartment as a kitchen. Coach No. E70361 is a former L.N.E.R. Gresley-designed parcels van with a brake and guard's compartment, built at York in 1936. (It is significant in that it was one of the first of his carriages to be constructed in metal; previously teak had been used.)

There are many and various wagons on the Railway. One of the more outstanding is the Esso oil tank. It was presented by the Esso Company who had previously restored and repainted it. It is now used as an emergency mobile water tank in case of fire. In 1972 a goods brake van was

purchased for £120. It was formerly used on the L.M.S., constructed at Derby in 1947, and has since been painted grey with a black frame. There are also some box vans, including a G.W.R. van and a Southern Railway van, both of 12 tons. There is also a bogie bolster wagon capable of handling long and heavy loads, together with a Conflat wagon and a general-purpose five-plank wagon.

The area around
Lake Windermere itself is well worth visiting; it is England's largest lake, being some ten miles from north to south. During the nineteenth century, the lake became noted for sailing, and a number of yacht clubs were established. B.R. boats run a service between Lakeside and Ambleside, and provide a fine way of viewing the lake. The railway runs in connection with these sailings with a daily timetable from June to mid-September, and a weekend service from May to the end of October.

OVERLEAF: *The only two former L.M.S. Fairburn 2-6-4 tanks are to be found on the Lakeside and Haverthwaite Railway. Here No. 2085 lifts a train past Backbarrow. The engine is in Caledonian Railway livery. (*Alan Middleton*)*

9

Steamtown

Steamtown Railway Museum is located at Carnforth in Lancashire, six miles north of Lancaster and Morecambe. Carnforth was once an important railway junction: three important pre-grouping Companies met here, the London and North Western, the Midland, and the Furness Railways. Built on the site of the formerly large marshalling yard and locomotive depot, Steamtown covers some twenty-three

BELOW: *A cross-section of Steamtown's motive power being prepared for its day's work. Visible are* Flying Scotsman, Sir Nigel Gresley *and a* Barclay saddletank. *(*Phil Wood*)*

acres, including over three miles of track. Besides the sheds for storing the locomotives, there are good facilities for servicing and running them. The working coaling plant is capable of holding 150 tons of coal; there is an ash disposal plant, a seventy-foot vacuum turntable (particularly valuable in view of the limited space available), and a 75,000-gallon water storage tank. There are also carriage and wagon works, and a machine shop. The whole system is controlled from a restored Midland Railway signal box removed from the Settle and Carlisle line. For the visitor there is a gift shop and a cafe and ample free car parking. Steamtown has a fine collection of engines and carriages selected from a wide area. Main line express locomotives have been preserved from the L.N.E.R., G.W.R. and Southern Railway

Two famous front-ends at Carnforth. The two L.N.E.R. Pacifics have made this former L.M.S. shed their home. (Geoff Silcock)

Companies, while the L.M.S. is prominent among the unnamed engines. The company has also succeeded in building up a fine collection of smaller industrial locomotives and their more modern diesel counterparts. In addition, they have acquired an interesting group of steam engines from Europe. Ever since the ban on steam-hauled trains was lifted by British Rail in 1971, the Steamtown depot has repeatedly supplied the locomotives required to haul these specials. Their authorized route is from Sellafield, through Barrow, Carnforth, Skipton, and thence over the Settle and Carlisle line to Carlisle itself.

Locomotive stock
Probably the best-known engine housed at Steamtown is No. 4472, *Flying Scotsman*. After

finishing her time with British Rail, *Flying Scotsman* was purchased by Alan Pegler in 1963. He had her extensively overhauled and repainted in her apple-green L.N.E.R. colours, and she worked private excursion trains for six years. He then took her to America on a trade mission promoting British goods. Though she successfully travelled over 15,000 miles around the United States, the crossing to the West Coast and San Francisco produced financial difficulties for Mr Pegler. In 1973 Mr W. H. McAlpine purchased No. 4472, and since her return to Britain, she has been shedded here, and has powered numerous steam specials. *Flying Scotsman* was completed in 1923 and exhibited at the Wembley Exhibition. In 1928 she became famous for hauling the first non-stop train from King's Cross to Edinburgh. On a trial run in 1934, she became the first British steam engine to achieve an officially recorded 100 m.p.h. This famous engine has carried as many as six numbers in her lifetime. She was Great Northern

S.R. 4-6-0 No. 850 Lord Nelson *heads a railtour train over Ais Gill viaduct on the Settle and Carlisle line, Royal Wedding Day, 1981. (*David Wilcock*)*

No. 1472, then L.N.E.R. No. 4472, named *Flying Scotsman*. In 1946 she was re-numbered '502', then '102'. On nationalization in 1948 her new number was '60103'. Up to her official withdrawal from B.R. in January 1963, she had travelled 2,080,000 miles, most of this along the L.N.E.R. East Coast main line in express passenger service.

The other famous L.N.E.R. engine is a Gresley Pacific, No. 4498, named after her designer Sir Nigel Gresley. The A4 class were among some of the first streamlined locomotives produced for the fast East Coast run to Scotland to rival the L.M.S. in the west. This class of locomotive holds the world speed record for steam, 126 m.p.h. This was achieved by No. 4468 *Mallard. Sir Nigel Gresley* has often topped 100 m.p.h. and also holds the British record for

post-war steam running with passenger trains.

Representing the Southern Railway, and immediately recognizable by her smoke deflectors, is No. 850, *Lord Nelson*. Designed by R. E. Maunsell in the 1920s, this 4-6-0 class was introduced to supersede the lower powered *King Arthur* locos. They suffered some teething troubles, however, and it was not until after World War II that they ran really smoothly, when fitted with multiple blast pipes. These were the engines which hauled the famous boat trains from Waterloo to the South Coast and pulled the excursion trains crowded with Londoners seeking the sun and sea.

Also from the Southern is rebuilt Bulleid 'Merchant Navy' class 4-6-2 No. 35005 *Canadian Pacific*. This engine was rescued from Woodham Brothers' yard at Barry and is undergoing a complete overhaul which is, of necessity, a long-term project.

Proudly displaying L.M.S. maroon colours is the famous three-cylinder 'Jubilee' class 4-6-0

13

No. 5690 *Leander*, always a firm favourite at the head of mainline steam specials. This loco was withdrawn by B.R. in March 1964 and sent to Barry scrapyard. It was purchased for preservation in 1972 and overhauled at the B.R. workshops in Derby. *Leander* returned to steam in August 1973 and has hauled many trains over B.R. tracks, based first at Dinting and subsequently at Carnforth. Between August 1980 and February 1982 the locomotive underwent a major overhaul on the Severn Valley Railway and has since returned to its mainline duties.

Sister engine No. 45699 *Galatea* is also present at Carnforth, having also been rescued from Barry scrapyard, but is currently in an unrestored, stripped-down condition.

Equally well-known, but not as glamorous, are the three 'Black Fives'. These 4-6-0 loco motives were designed by Sir William Stanier for the L.M.S. to work all kinds of train. They were first introduced in 1935, and from then on worked goods and passenger trains. These engines were superbly designed and popular with their drivers. They were un-named and wore a plain black livery with red lining. The Steamtown trio are Nos. 44871 and 44932, both dating from 1945, and No. 45407, built in 1937.

A particularly eye-catching locomotive at the Museum is No. 6441. Painted in L.M.S. maroon-and-black and lined in yellow, this engine is a striking exhibit. The 2MT 2-6-0 class was originally designed by H. G. Ivatt for the L.M.S. for secondary duties, but was so successful that they continued to be built by B.R. after nationalization. In fact, No. 6441 was not built until 1950, at Crewe. She then spent most of her working life in Lancashire on local passenger services, including the 'Lake Windermere Cruise' starting from Morecambe. (The engine was purchased by Mrs Beet, who used to watch the loco running past her house when running between Carnforth and Hest Bank.)

In addition, Steamtown also has a comprehensive collection of tank engines designed for shunting duties, suburban and branch-line

Flying Scotsman *at Ganton hauling an enthusiasts' special from Scarborough to York. The engine was later overhauled for a tour of North America and Canada in 1969–73. (P. N. Trotter)*

15

Lord Nelson at rest during a visit to Liverpool Road station, Manchester, in 1980. Part of the National Collection, the Southern 4-6-0's operational base is Steamtown. (Tom Heavyside)

passenger trains and light goods work. Included in this category is No. 1300. Built in 1896 for the Lancashire and Yorkshire Railway, this 0-6-0 tender locomotive was withdrawn from service in 1960 as B.R. No. 52322 and has now been restored to full working order. Two G.W.R. tank engines are present; both have been purchased from Woodham Brothers, Barry, in scrap condition. They are 0-6-2T No. 5643 and 0-6-0PT No. 9629.

In contrast to the British express locomotives, two of the finest continental Pacific classes have found a home at Carnforth. From France comes No. 231 K22, originally built for the Paris, Lyons and Mediterranean Railway in 1914. Originally

shedded at Avignon, she hauled expresses between Paris and the Riviera. She was extensively rebuilt in 1937 and allocated to the Northern Region, often hauling the 'Flèche d'Or' between Calais and Paris. She epitomizes all that was best in French steam engineering.

The German express engine is No. 012 104-6. Again a 4-6-2, she was completed in 1940 by Schwarzkopf in Berlin as a streamlined express engine. Having been damaged by British bombing in 1944, the streamlined casing was removed in 1951 and she was converted to oil firing in 1957. She is noticeably German, particularly distinguished by the shape of her smoke deflectors.

The exciting atmosphere of a steam shed at night is recreated in this view of L.M.S. Black 5 No. 4767 standing under Steamtown's coaling plant. (David Wilcock)

There is also a fine collection of smaller, industrial locomotives collected from various sites throughout the country, twenty in all. The locos in regular use are No. 1, *Coronation* and No. 2, *Cranford*. This engine is fitted with vacuum brake gear and so is suitable for hauling passenger coaches. One of the more unusual is *Gasbag*, an engine formerly used by Eastern Gas; it is particularly curious in that the four wheels are linked by chain drive. One of the – literally – more colourful is *Jane Darbyshire*, a 0-4-0 steam-powered tank loco built in 1929. She is now painted purple with red fittings and wheels. She was meant to be called 'J. N. Darbyshire', but the signwriter working on her name boards misheard his instructions and named her 'Jane' instead! Of similar design is *British Gypsum*, another 0-4-0 tank completed in 1953; she is bright red. Also of note is *Glenfield*. Completed in 1902, *Glenfield* is a 0-4-0 tank loco with a crane mounted on top of her boiler. She is a working engine, and performs many useful functions in the Steam-town Museum. She is painted in black and light green, and lettered in cream.

Particularly of note is Steamtown's oldest inhabitant, *Lindsay*, built in 1887. She is one of the very few locomotives built by the Wigan Coal and Iron Company. Now fully restored to working order and resplendent in lined-out maroon livery, *Lindsay* takes her turn hauling passenger trains the length of the Carnforth site.

Steam haulage for passengers at Carnforth is not confined to the standard gauge. A fine 15 in. gauge line now runs the length of the site (approximately half a mile) and visitors can enjoy a run on this line in open coaches behind a Guest Pacific loco built in 1946, before return-ing from Crag Bank station on the standard gauge train.

Ex-London and North Eastern Railway class A4 4-6-2 No. 4498 Sir Nigel Gresley *heads a fourteen-coach railway enthusiasts' special train northwards out of Sheffield at Wincobank Junc-tion. This locomotive was bought by enthusiasts and, based at Carnforth, is hired for specials. Six A4s are preserved, two of them across the Atlantic.* (Gavin Morrison)

ABOVE: British Gypsum, *painted a rich red, has been used at rallies and carnivals. (G. Brocken)*

BELOW: *Since Carnforth was one of the last steam M.P.Ds. in the country, the Museum company was able to take over equipment in good condition. Carnforth has two L.M.S. 5MT 4-6-0s: No. 44932 (1945) and No. 45407 (1947). (T. J. Edgington)*

Rolling stock

Steamtown has a fine collection of coaches, selected from many companies to complement their steam engines. They have a particularly fine collection of 'official' coaches, saloon coaches fitted with observation sections, dining facilities and lounges, so that senior railway officials and directors could inspect their companies in a comfortable fashion. The North Eastern Railway's Directors' Saloon No. 305 is now in its original bright maroon. It still has the original carpets and upholstery on the armchairs and sofa. It has a clerestory roof, and is a fine example of Edwardian coach building.

It was also possible to purchase or hire a private saloon from railway companies. One of these is also preserved here, Great Western saloon 'Stapleford Park' No. 9004. It is a particularly attractive coach finished in the classic chocolate-and-cream livery of the Great Western, with a whitened roof and gold lettering along the sides. Steamtown also houses a Great Eastern teak-finished Chairman's saloon, complete with balcony, lounge, diner, kitchen,

Lindsay, Wigan's pride and joy, accelerates past Selside signal box with the Crag Bank shuttle service at Carnforth. (David Wilcock)

toilet and shower bath; a luxurious coach indeed.

Carnforth is also the base for two other major organizations operating trains of Pullman cars over B.R. tracks. Firstly, there is the Steam Locomotive Operators Association (S.L.O.A.), who are the principal coordinators of all steam-hauled tours run over British Railways metals. Their stock consists of seven First Class Parlour cars, the 'Hadrian Bar' car, which is fitted out as a mobile shop, and a Pullman Second Kitchen car. All the S.L.O.A. Pullmans are B.R.-era vehicles built in 1960–61 and usually run with the two S.L.O.A. B.R. Mk I Corridor Brake Composite coaches.

Secondly, there is the exotically-named Venice-Simplon Orient Express Company, whose stock of vintage Pullman cars is overhauled and restored at Steamtown. The V-S.O.E. train operates from Victoria station on the Southern Region in connection with the luxury Orient Express train running through to Venice from the Channel ports.

Not to be missed either is the Museum's

21

OPPOSITE: *Stanier class 5 4-6-0 No. 5305 acce-lerates away from Garsdale. It is operated by the Humberside Loco Group and has been based variously at Hull, York and Carnforth.* (Jarrolds)

ABOVE: *Jubilee 4-6-0 No. 5690* Leander *on the Hope Valley line at Chinley East Junction with the 'Leander Envoy' special train.* (Bob Green)

model railway display. This aims to suggest what some of the actual exhibits would have looked like when in regular use in various parts of the country. The display is designed to represent Berkhamstead on the L. & N.W.R. and L.M.S. main line at two different periods – first in the 1920s, and second in the late 1930s. Both models have appropriate locomotives and rolling stock. There are approximately fifty locomotives, a hundred coaches and around two hundred wagons operating on the model: it is a fine scenic display.

The area around
Not so far from Carnforth itself there are two old houses of historical interest. Borwick Hall is a fine Elizabethan manor house standing within its own grounds and has not been altered substantially since its construction, in 1595, around an earlier structure. It also possesses some fine gardens. Leighton Hall is a later construction. It consists of an eighteenth-century core, on which is superimposed the then fashionable Gothic style, in the early nineteenth century. The house is still in the possession of the Gillow family who have resided there for many generations; the house contains a fine collection of domestic furniture and pictures.

Steamport (Southport)

Steamport is being developed as the Railway and Transport Museum for Merseyside in what was once the Motive Power Depot of British Railways at Derby Road, Southport. It is intended that Steamport will be a working museum in the sense that the majority of the larger exhibits will eventually be fully restored and functioning for the enjoyment of visitors.

The project is run by members of Steamport

Steamport (Southport) was once an M.P.D.–Southport Derby Road. Stanier L.M.S. 5MT 4-6-0 No. 44806, named Magpie *after an association with the TV programme, stands in the shed behind some of the industrials. (Tom Heavyside)*

(Southport) Ltd, which is a voluntary organization and registered as a charity. The company was originally formed as the Southport Locomotive and Transport Museum Society in 1971. The Motive Power Depot at Derby Road had been disused since 1966 when the last steam locomotives at Southport were withdrawn from service. It had been thoroughly stripped by British Railways and subsequently vandalised so that not a door, window or pane of roof glass was left unbroken. There was no water, electricity or other services, the shed and yard were full of rubble and, worst of all from a railway point of view, no track remained on site.

While negotiations for the lease of the building went on, members of the Society engaged in various fund-raising activities and slowly began to clear the shed, restore services and start laying track. Lengths of track were salvaged and

*Lucy the small Avonside meets No. 5 the large Peckett at Southport. (*Tom Heavyside*)*

transported from redundant industrial sidings in St Helens. Six pairs of doors were rescued from the former electric stock repair shops at Meols Cop and were hung at the end of the shed.

By 1973 agreement had been reached with British Rail on the lease of the shed and the first locomotives, buses and other exhibits were moved to the site. In addition, agreement was also reached on a rail connection between B.R. and Steamport enabling further rolling stock to arrive at the shed on their own wheels. The museum opened to the public on Spring Bank Holiday 1974 and since then the number of exhibits has steadily grown as more track has been laid and more of the shed brought into use.

The largest locomotive preserved here is the former L.M.S. Stanier-designed 4-6-0 No. 44806, *Magpie*, built in 1944. More modern is the Riddles 2-6-0, No. 76079 (4MT class) which was completed in 1957. From Woodham Brothers' yard at Barry have come L.M.S. 'Jinty' 0-6-0T No. 7298 and G.W.R. 2-6-2T No. 5193,

the former having been restored to full working order in time to take part in the Rocket 150 Cavalcade at Rainhill in 1980. The most venerable locomotive on display, though as yet unrestored, is the famous mersey Railway 0-6-4T *Cecil Raikes*, on loan to Steamport from the National Collection. In addition, there are eight industrial saddle tanks; three Pecketts, two Hunslets, a Hudswell Clarke *Waleswood*, the Avonside 0-6-0ST *Lucy* and the Barclay 0-4-0ST *Efficient*. A Sentinel geared, vertical-boiler steam locomotive, *St Monans*, contrasts its modern styling with diesel locomotives from Fowler, Ruston Hornsby and Thomas Hill as well as a Greenwood and Batley battery electric loco. Representing the first generation of mainline diesel locomotives introduced by B.R. under their modernization plan is Class 24 No. 24.081.

A wide variety of passenger and goods rolling stock, much of it with Merseyside connections, has been assembled. There are also historic vehicles housed at Steamport and they include four trams, a Bradford trolleybus and several vintage motor buses.

25

The Isle of Man Railway

Midway across the Irish Sea, about equidistant from England, Scotland and Northern Ireland, lies the Isle of Man. It is sufficiently distant from the mainland to give it the isolated atmosphere of a mountainous little independent king- dom – which it is. The people, Government, customs. language and money, not to ment- ion the cats, are notably different from the count- ries nearest to the island.

The majority of visitors to the Isle of Man still arrive by sea at the capital Douglas, which just over a century ago took over the responsibility of being the island's administrative centre from Castletown. Douglas takes its name from the confluence of two rivers, the Dhoo and the Glass. The Railway station stands on the site of a marsh where these rivers met at the head of the creek where old Douglas stood. The present impressive facade of the railway premises on Bank Hill is not the original station of 1873, which was a small wooden affair, but dates from the progressive years when the Railway Com- pany anticipated a growing tourist business and provided a large station to meet the demands. It is the largest narrow-gauge railway station in the British Isles.

Today, with part of the railway system closed down, some of the bustle and reason for the existence of this miniature mainline terminus with its handsome booking hall, extensive plat- forms and more-than-adequate workshops, has gone with changing times, but it still recalls the era when over a million passengers a year were carried. Even at the present day when steam railways are popular with visitors, these passen- ger figures remain unassailed!

History of the line
The island's railway system dates from the 1870s when recommendations were made that

The authentic narrow gauge charm of the Isle of Man Railway is perpetuated by its use of the original Victorian engines and coaches. No. 4 Loch, built in 1874, is the oldest working loco on the island. (Jarrolds)

26

Douglas and Peel should be linked by a railway built to narrow-gauge, which was proving to be the pattern in developing overseas countries. Lines to Port Erin and from Peel to Ramsey would follow. An Isle of Man Railway Company was formed but money was short and when work could begin, the Manxmen employed deserted the site each season to go herring fishing! So the contractors had to call in navvies from Ireland and Wales to finish the work. The Peel line opened first, in 1873, followed by the more difficult route to Port Erin in 1874. Together they proved so expensive that the Company asked the Government if it would lend money to begin the Ramsey line. When this request was turned down, it was decided to drop the scheme. Naturally, the inhabitants of the island's second biggest town were not pleased at this and they promoted their own Manx Northern Railway, employing Scottish contractors to connect Ramsey with the I.M.R. at St John's. This line opened in 1879.

Some of the Northern directors promoted the Foxdale Railway to carry lead from the important mines there, over their own M.N.R. and to ships at Ramsey harbour. Foxdale had been one of the richest mining districts in the kingdom but its best days were past and the lead traffic was a flop. Before long the M.N.R. (which had some curious agreements with the Foxdale line)

was on the verge of bankruptcy. Luckily, the Government stepped in and I.O.M.R. absorbed its northern neighbour in 1904.

Rail traffic over the entire system (with the exception of the Foxdale branch) remained high until the 1950s. Thereafter it began to decline with the corresponding growth of road traffic. By 1965 the loss of railway business to the buses, plus the wearing out of much of its equipment caused the complete closure of the system. However, in 1967 it arose Phoenix-like under a new regime headed by the Marquis of Ailsa. Frequent services ran again, old liveries blossomed forth and some of the engines were rebuilt with new boilers. Alas, it was all too good, and too expensive, to last. Lord Ailsa relinquished his control after two seasons and local control was resumed, though now only the Douglas to Port Erin line was in operation. Eventually, the Manx Government stepped in and 'nationalized' the railway in 1977.

Stock

All the locomotives now running on the railway were built by Beyer Peacock and Co. of Manchester and are of the 2-4-0 side tank type. Only five locomotives remain on the railway – many of their sisters can now be found in museums. Most of the working locos still carry the attractive lined green livery reintroduced in the Ailsa

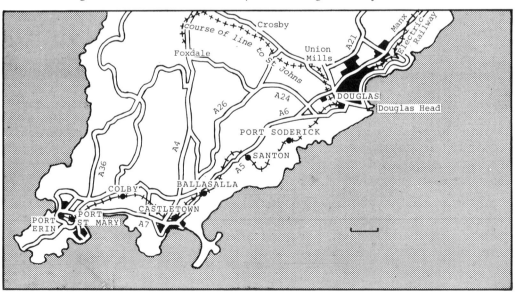

This picture clearly shows the distinctive design of the Isle of Man Railway 2-4-0s. The sidings in which they stand are less used now and only two platform faces of Douglas are in use.

era, but engine No. 4 *Loch* is painted in the dark red colour scheme of the nationalized Isle of Man Railways group. It has also been fitted with a classically elegant bell-mouth brass dome cover appropriate to the time when it was built (1874).

In 1961 the I.M.R. bought two modern diesel railcars from the County Donegal Railway Joint Committee in Ireland. They are not normally used for passenger traffic but if thus employed they do so running back-to-back like Siamese twins as the I.M.R. has no turntables to turn a single-unit car round. The two railcars were by Walker Bros. Ltd of Wigan, built in 1950 and 1951, together with the ex-Great Northern Railway of Ireland (Dundalk Works) which built the carriage portions. They were C.D.J.C. Nos. 19 and 20 and have retained these numbers on the Isle of Man.

The carriages include some very old survivors from the last century which have been modernized and upholstered. The I.M.R. Company's original ones were carried on four wheels; later

they were 'close-coupled' semi-permanently together in pairs. Later still, the pairs were put on to new bogie underframes and at first a gap could be seen between the two individual bodies in the middle. The old wheels and frames from the four-wheelers were made into wagons and vans so that nothing was ever wasted. The former Manx Northern Railway had six-wheeled carriages but none of these is now in use; it also had two bogie carriages for through-services to Douglas and both these survive. Among the later modern carriages are some saloons with big observation windows and – except for their smaller size – the compartment stock is very little different from that used on the mainland. The Isle of Man was always far ahead of the mainland railways in providing bogie passenger vehicles and had electricity lit coaches when in England they were still using gas or oil-lit four- and six-wheelers.

Other railways and attractions

Visitors to the Isle of Man should on no account miss a journey on the Manx Electric Railway which since 1893 has provided a service up the east coast of the island between Douglas and Ramsey. It is a particularly picturesque route, moving inland before Laxey and crossing a large

*Loch leaving Douglas with the 16.05 train to Port Erin. This service is the last survivor of a once extensive network of routes and is justly popular with enthusiasts. (*J. A. Bodfish*)*

viaduct, which provides a clear view of the famous Manx waterwheel. The cars are brightly painted in red and white with light brown, with the large side panels in varnished teak. Trains are usually arranged as a motor car with a trailer.

At Laxey there is a mountain railway, a 3 ft 6 in. gauge electric line running up to the summit of Snaefell. There is a centre rail to help prevent derailment and assist braking. An in-teresting collection of historic exhibits from the Isle of Man's electric railways and tramways has been brought together in the Electric Railway Museum near the station at Ramsey. There is a railway museum at Port Erin. The I.M.R.'s first engine, *Sutherland*, laid down in 1873, is there, as is the last, *Mannin* (1926). There is also the Royal Carriage together with a host of memora-bilia, including tickets, photographs, signs and signals.

Castletown has a transport museum of a different kind. It is a nautical collection, and is housed in a three-storeyed boat-house almost 200 years old. Among the exhibits is a schooner-rigged yacht, the *Peggy*, which dates from 1791.

Dinting Railway Centre

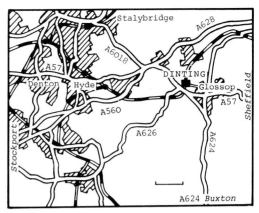

The Dinting Railway Centre, operated by the Bahamas Locomotive Society, is based in the former Great Central engine shed, at Dinting on the B.R. line between Manchester Piccadilly and Glossop. The society was formed early in 1967 in an effort to secure the L.M.S. Jubilee class 4-6-0, No. 5596 *Bahamas*, for preservation - hence the title. The loco was purchased, and then sent for restoration by the Hunslet Engine Company of Leeds. In 1968 the Committee of the Society began to search for a home for their newly restored locomotive. Dinting was ideal and with generous assistance from a Society member and encouragement from Glossop Council the site was purchased from British Rail. Since that time a great deal of work has been undertaken to improve the services offered. An Exhibition Hall, capable of housing up to nine mainline locomotives has been constructed, a picnic area

*Dinting shed plays host to the visiting L.M.S. Black 5 4-6-0 No. 5305, owned by the Humberside Loco Preservation Group. (*R. Crombleholme*)*

created, road access, car park, refreshment and shop areas built. There is also an extensive steam-operated miniature railway which has been constructed by members of the Buxton Model Engineering Society.

Stock
Bahamas has been joined at Dinting by several other famous mainline express engines. The most venerable of these is the L.N.W.R. 2-4-0 *Hardwicke,* veteran of the great Railway Races to the North, built in 1892 and on loan from the National Collection. Also from the West Coast

*The distinctive lines of the L.N.W.R. Webb coal tank No. 1054 are evident as it emerges from Dinting shed. The loco was restored to working order in 1980. (*Tom Heavyside*)*

route comes No. 6115 *Scots Guardsman*, one of the famous taper-boiler 'Royal Scots', now appropriately painted in L.M.S. post-war lined black livery. From the rival East Coast route is a pair of L.N.E.R. Pacifics. No. 19 *Bittern* is one of Sir Nigel Gresley's great streamlined A4 class 4-6-2s, built in 1937. No. 532 *Blue Peter* was actually completed at Doncaster under British Railways in 1948, but is one of A.H. Peppercorn's A2 class Pacifics designed in the final years of the L.N.E.R. and therefore finished in apple-green livery.

On loan from the North Western Museum of Science and Industry is the former Great Central 2-8-0 No. 102, completed in 1911. Dinting is also host to the L.N.E.R. 0-6-2 'Coal Tank' dating from 1888. This engine was restored to working order to take part in the Rocket 150 Cavalcade at Rainhill in 1980.

The Society also has several coaches, most of which originated with the L.M.S. They include a medical officer's saloon, No. 45017 built in 1923. The Society's plans for the future aim to provide the North-West with a fully operational steam locomotive museum, and a stabling point for preserved locomotives which can then be used for specials on British Rail's territory. The centre is open most weekends and weekdays throughout the year, while special steam open days are arranged at Easter and on Bank holidays in the summer. Brake-van rides are offered when locos are in steam.

The North Yorkshire Moors Railway

Yorkshire is a very fortunate county; not only does it have Britain's largest static railway collection, in the National Railway Museum at York, but it can also boast of having two of the country's major preserved standard-gauge railways within its bounds.

The line and its history
The larger of the two is the North Yorkshire Moors Railway, whose beginnings can be traced back to the tiny seaport of Whitby a century and a half ago. In those days, the only connection between Whitby and the rest of the country – other than by sea – was the often impassable turnpike road over the bleak and desolate moors. By the time that the Whitby and Pickering Turnpike Road Act became due for renewal in 1826, the more far-sighted residents of Whitby were thinking of a railway as an alternative. Various schemes were suggested, one of them being for a line to connect Whitby with the newly opened Stockton and Darlington Railway. Robert Campion, the author of this scheme, had a route surveyed and reported on it at a meeting early in 1831. It was discussed at another meeting two months later together with a further scheme, favouring a line to Pickering. A committee was formed to look into both and Campion's surveyor, Thomas Storey, was engaged to survey this alternative route.

Not being entirely satisfied with Storey's surveys, the committee finally called in George Stephenson, the 'father of British railways', and asked him to examine and report upon the two

schemes. Stephenson reported in favour of the Pickering route at a meeting held a year later at Whitby's Angel Inn. The report was received with great enthusiasm; a share list was opened on the spot, and before the close of the meeting, £30,000 of the estimated £48,000 cost of construction had been subscribed. Unhappily, Stephenson's estimate was to prove wildly inaccurate, and the final cost of the line came to

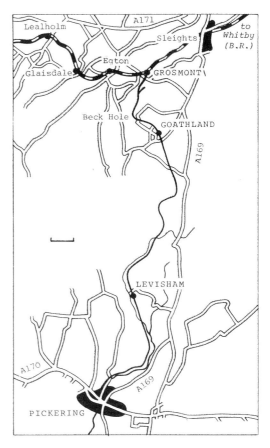

ABOVE: *Lambton Railway No. 29 attacks the 1 in 49 gradient to Goathland. (*R. Crombleholme*)*

LEFT: *The ultimate development of the N.E.R. 0-6-0 was class P3 (L.N.E.R. J27). No. 2392, the last of the class, was rescued for the N.Y.M.R. and is seen here in the Shildon Cavalcade. (*David Williams*)*

OPPOSITE: *K1 2-6-0 No. 2005 and Lambton tank No. 5 on the gradient to Goathland.*

a staggering total of over £105,000. In the Angel Inn that day hopes ran high, and on the crest of the wave of enthusiasm the committee pressed on. Application was made to Parliament, and on 6 May 1833, the Whitby and Pickering Railway Act received the Royal Assent. The first step forward had been made, despite the fact that the legalities seem to have been done in such haste that one section of the Act approved the use of steam locomotives, and another one forbade it!

Work now started in earnest. The first sod was cut in September 1833, and by June 1835 sufficient progress had been made for a regular

Grosmont motive power depot on the North Yorks Moors Railway with, from left to right, N.E.R. 0-6-0 No. 2392 (built 1923), Lambton 0-6-2 tank No. 29 (1904), No. 2005, an L.N.E.R. K1 class 2-6-0 built in 1949, and Black 5 (L.M.S. 5MT 4-6-0) No. 5428, named Eric Treacy *after the former Bishop of Wakefield, the railway photographer. (John Hunt)*

service to be started from Whitby to Grosmont. Finally, on 26 May 1836, the ceremonial opening of the whole line took place. Church bells and a procession through the streets of Whitby started the day, and when the first train arrived at Pickering it was greeted by a crowd of no less than seven thousand people supported by the music from five bands. That is no mean feat for a quiet country town. After the celebration lunch at the Black Swan, the official party returned to the Angel Inn at Whitby, and the celebrations went on until the early hours of the following day.

The first trains bore little resemblance to their steam-hauled counterparts of later years. Horses provided the motive power, and passengers travelled in what was virtually a road coach on railway wheels. (One of these is pictured in oils in Whitby Museum.) Freight was carried in horse drawn wagons too; the stones for Waterloo Bridge, Somerset House and many other famous buildings travelled the first few miles of

The other tank from Lambton Colliery, No. 5 (built 1909) nears Beck Hole on the North Yorkshire Moors Railway. (John Hunt)

their journey to London over the metals of the Whitby and Pickering Railway.

During the first few years of its existence, the line prospered, carrying some four thousand people each month at a fare of four shillings (20p) inside or three shillings (15p) outside. One of them, Charles Dickens, described it as a 'quaint old railway along part of which passengers are hauled by a rope'. He was referring to the 1500-yard-long incline between Beck Hole and Goathland: since its gradient of 1 in 15 was too steep for horses, the coaches were hauled up by means of a cable.

In 1836, Whitby solicitor Henry Belcher published a book entitled *The Scenery of the Whitby and Pickering Railway*. Three years later he persuaded the railway company to run special trains to Grosmont in connection with a fête to raise funds for a new church there. The trains from Whitby started at 9.00 a.m. and ran at hourly intervals. The fare was reduced from 9d to 6d ($3\frac{3}{4}$p to $2\frac{1}{2}$p). Trains in the opposite direction ran as required, the first one leaving Pickering at 5 a.m., and the fare was 1s 6d instead of 2s 3d. The first cheap railway excursions had arrived.

Despite these promising beginnings, the fortunes of the line began to decline in the early eighteen forties. A network of railways had rapidly spread over the country; the 'Railway Mania' had begun. The outstanding figure in the railway world at this time was George Hudson, a financial manipulator whose dubious dealings had given him control over an empire of small railways. One of Hudson's companies, the York and North Midland Railway, opened a line from York to Scarborough in 1845, with a branch to Pickering. In the same year, the directors of the W. & P.R. sold the line to the Y. & N.M.R. for £80,000.

Hudson was not the sort of man to let the grass grow under his feet, and the line from Whitby to Pickering was soon doubled and joined to the York and North Midland. Steam engines were introduced to the line in 1846, and the first reached Whitby a year later. Having been designed for horse-drawn traffic, the line abounded in sharp curves; special short-wheelbase engines, known as 'Whitby Bogies', were built to work the line, together with four-wheeled coaches (instead of the six wheeled ones by then coming into use). Rapidly acquiring the nickname of 'Whitby Bathing Machines', these coaches ran from Whitby through to London and became notorious for their rough riding. Further amalgamations took place over the ensuing years, both before and after the collapse of Hudson's empire in 1849. By 1854, both the W. & P.R. and the Y. & N.M.R. had become part of the newly formed North Eastern Railway.

The Beck Hole incline remained a thorn in the side of the railway operators. The N.E.R. decided to bypass it, by building a deviation between Grosmont and Goathland. This was completed in 1865. The hindrance to through locomotive working was thus eliminated, although the 1 in 49 gradient which replaced it was and still is one of the steepest in the country. In 1872 the incline once again came into use, when a 750-yard length of 43 in. gauge track was laid on it, in order to test a mountain railway locomotive built at Leeds and destined for Brazil.

In 1908 part of the old line was re-opened, from Grosmont to the foot of the incline. A summer service of railcars was introduced. This ran until the advent of World War I in 1914, carrying holiday-makers from the coast to the moors.

After the war, the railways were merged into four groups: in 1923, the N.E.R. became part of the London and North Eastern Railway. When the four groups were nationalized the L.N.E.R. became British Railways (Eastern Region). Nationalization did not lead to continuing prosperity for the Pickering and Whitby line. In 1964, the Beeching Report recommended that all three lines to Whitby should be closed. A very strong case was made for the retention of rail connection to Whitby, and extremely vigorous local opposition was aroused. Finally, only a modified form of the Beeching plan was adopted. The lines from Whitby to York and to Scarborough were abandoned in 1965; the line to Middlesbrough was left open. For the first

time in one hundred and twenty-nine years, trains no longer ran between Whitby and Pickering. The short length between Whitby and Grosmont, however, was kept open, since it is part of the line to Whitby from Middlesbrough.

Preservation
The Whitby–Pickering line lay neglected for two years. The track became rusty and overgrown; paint peeled from deserted stations and signal boxes. But in June 1967, Mr Tom Salmon of Ruswarp called a meeting at his home. From this small beginning emerged the North Yorkshire Moors Railway Preservation Society, with the avowed intention of re-opening the line. Public meetings were held, and membership grew. Its prestige and status became such that even British Rail was prevailed upon to grant a six-month reprieve on the lifting of one line of the track. The membership continued to grow, area groups were formed, and in the first year of the Society's existence, £8,000 was raised. By now B.R. was prepared to give permission for restoration work to begin. One Sunday in November 1968 the level crossing gates at Grosmont were repainted; three months later a small saddle tank locomotive, on loan to the society, steamed proudly from Pickering to Goathland, cheered on its way by hundreds of well-wishers. The Whitby and Pickering Railway was coming to life again.

Negotiations with B.R. continued. The society was reconstituted as the North Yorkshire Moors Historical Railways Trust. With the support of the local authorities and the English Tourist Board, it was able to purchase the trackbed from Grosmont to Pickering, together with the actual track as far as Ellerbeck. Thanks to the many individuals and organizations who lent locomotives and rolling stock to the railway, the Trust was now able to run privately chartered steam-hauled trains between Grosmont and Ellerbeck. These boosted both the membership and the income of the railway. By 1973 the Trust, with a membership then of 9,000, had managed to purchase the track from Ellerbeck all the way to Pickering. With the transfer of a Light Railway Order from B.R., all was in order to run a public service.

Lambton tank No. 29 just above Beck Hole between Grosmont and Goathland on the North Yorkshire Moors Railway. (G.W. Morrison)

Eight years previously, Mr and Mrs F. F. Clough had travelled on the last train to Pickering; on Easter Sunday 1973, they came from North Wales to ride on the first public train on its return from Pickering to Grosmont. The Whitby and Pickering Railway, under its new name of North Yorkshire Moors Railway, was well and truly back in business.

Nine days later, on 1 May, the railway was officially opened by H.R.H. the Duchess of Kent. At Whitby the Duchess unveiled a plaque at the Angel. She went on to unveil a further one at Grosmont station, and then journeyed to Pickering on the inaugural train. A large crowd awaited her, and she there unveiled a third plaque at the Black Swan.

Access
The journey time by rail from Whitby to Grosmont is seventeen minutes; from Middlesbrough it is one hour. Visitors arriving at Grosmont find it very easy to change from British Rail to the North Yorkshire Moors Railway as both railways use the same station. (In the days of horse traction, the station was a stone building to the east of the present line: it is still there and, although it is now the local Post Office, the doors of the old stables can still be seen. The present station was built when the line changed to steam. For some years before the town's first Methodist Church was opened in 1867, Station Master Robert Ingham allowed the station to be used as a place of worship.

A journey down the line
Leaving Grosmont the train passes over the level crossing where the gates were so enthusiastically painted in 1968; it then crosses the River Murk Esk and plunges into a short tunnel dating from 1845. Alongside the line is a foot path, which after crossing the river passes through the narrow tunnel originally used by the old

7

During the Jubilee weekend of 1977 Lambton No. 29 leaves Grosmont for Goathland over the level crossing. (Valerie Burns)

horse-drawn railway. To the left of the tunnel entrances is the church of St Matthew; it was in aid of the building fund of this church that Henry Belcher organized the first excursions. His work is recalled by the east window, which is dedicated to his memory.

Once through the tunnel and past a newly built engine shed, Deviation Signal Box marks the start of the notorious Beck Hole incline, part of which can still be seen on the right-hand side of the railway. Up to this point the train has been proceeding fairly gently, but now the bark of the exhaust increases as the engine begins to climb. The Murk Esk is crossed once more and as the train leaves the valley floor and the wooded banks of the Esk behind, it turns sharply to the left into the valley of a tributary, the Eller Beck. Still climbing, it crosses the Beck three times in rapid succession. One bridge, at Water Ark, crosses a separate footbridge over the river at the same time. Sweeping on below a road bridge

and past the tiny village of Darnholm, the railway enters a cutting blasted from the solid rock. The staccato beat of the exhaust echoes back, until the driver shuts off steam and with a rumble of wheels and a screech of brakes, the train rolls to a halt at Goathland. Many steam trains terminate here but those who wish to may change to a modern diesel railcar for the rest of the journey to Pickering.

South of Goathland, the route of the original line appears to the right and joins the present one, still climbing towards Summit Signal Box, the highest point on the line. Over the moors to the left, the majestic scenery is topped by the three radomes of Fylingdales Early Warning Radar Station, like a row of gigantic golf balls.

Once past the signal box the line descends, crossing Lyke Wake Walk, a forty-mile trail across the moors between Osmotherly and Ravenscar, and enters the environmentally unique area of Fen Bog, and the valley of Newton Dale. Some 22,000 years ago, water escaping from glacier lakes in Eskdale built up in Fen Bog before bursting forth and scouring out the deep trench of Newton Dale. To the

ABOVE: *Lambton and train start to climb the Esk Valley from Goathland on the N.Y.M.R. Former courses of the railway can readily be seen on the valley floor. (P. J. G. Ransom)*

BELOW: *The epitomy of the N.Y.M.R.: the 1947 Black 5 No. 4767 – the only one with Stephenson link motion – approaches Eller Beck with a train from Pickering. (G. W. Morrison)*

average traveller, the tiny stream gurgling through the woods and the reedy swamp of Fen Bog, where the water laps up against the railway embankment, give little indication of the awesome deluge that once thundered along carrying millions of tons of earth and rock. The geologist, however, can find ample evidence of what happened from the strata exposed in the valley sides: rocks from pre-glacial times to modern Oxford clay can readily be identified.

No road runs along Newton Dale, and the wide panoramic windows of the railcars provide the best way to see the unspoilt countryside and the wildlife that it supports. Man has left some interesting items too: there are the ruins of Carter's House, which served as an inn to the navvies who built the line and Skelton Tower, an architectural folly built by the Rev. Thomas

Skelton, a local eccentric. A little further south, the Raindale Inn served as a changing point for horses. Today it is used as a field study centre, and has been renamed 'The Grange'. Part of Levisham station, on the edge of Levisham Moor and the railway's first road contact since leaving Goathland, is also used as a field study centre; after that the only buildings before Pickering are a few cottages at Farwath, built to house the platelayers who maintained the track. Drivers were instructed to stop there to pick up and set down platelayer's wives as required; it was their only contact with the outside world. Newton Dale widens out here to become the Vale of Pickering, taking its name from the market town eighteen miles by rail from Grosmont. Pickering is the southern terminus of the North Yorkshire Moors Railway (as it was of the

BELOW: *Levisham station from No. 29, about to cross with No. 2005 (which is reverse-running), with the North Yorkshireman.* (John Hunt)

OPPOSITE: *Great Northern saddletank No. 1247 darkens the sky on the approach to Goathland with a heavy train.* (Patrick Russell)

ABOVE: *Acquired by the North Eastern Loco Preservation Group in 1982,* Joem *is a member of the J72 class built in 1949 to the 1898 N.E.R. design. (*David Wilcock*)*

OPPOSITE: *Bursting into the sunlight from Grosmont tunnel and complete with commemorative headboard, Lambton No. 29 makes a fine showing. (*Maurice Burns*)*

Whitby and Pickering) and is headquarters of the Railway Trust. The station is listed as a building of special interest, and like the stations at Grosmont and Goathland contains a gift shop and has refreshment facilities.

Stock
It is perhaps appropriate that a line which was engineered by George Stephenson should have running on its metals an engine named after the great man. This engine, No. 4767, was one of the last of the famous L.M.S. 'Black Fives', built in 1947. Together with several other N.Y.M.R. engines, it took part in the Rail 150 celebrations of the 150th anniversary of the Stockton and Darlington Railway at Shildon in 1975, where it was named *George Stephenson* by the Rt Hon. William Whitelaw, M.P. The choice of this name for this particular engine was apt as it is the only one out of a class of 842 engines that was built with Stephenson's link-motion valve gear. Like many of the engines on the line, No. 4767 is privately owned, but it is in the care of the North Eastern Locomotive Preservation Group, whose engines form the backbone of the railway's motive power, and whose volunteer members form the nucleus of the railway's locomotive staff. As its name implies, the Group's main interest lies in its North Eastern Railway locomotives, typical of goods engines in the north-east during the last fifty years of steam.

The N.E.R. Raven three-cylinder 0-8-0s (L.N.E.R. class Q7) were usually on Tyne Dock to Consett mineral traffic. No. 63460, standing in South Shields station, is in the National Collection and is based on the N.Y.M.R. (John Warr)

No. 2238 is an enormous eight-coupled engine of class T2, built in 1918. No. 2392, of class P3, with its six coupled wheels is not much smaller: although of N.E.R. design, it was actually completed in 1923 by the L.N.E.R. History has a habit of repeating itself and the group's third engine, a K1 class 2-6-0, No. 2005, although an L.N.E.R. engine, was actually built by British Railways in 1949.

Other engines in which the group takes an interest are two 0-6-2 tank engines which were built for the privately owned Lambton Colliery Railway in the first decade of the century. They are bigger than the small shunting engines normally associated with industry, and their greater power and larger coal and water capacity enabled them to haul long trains of coal wagons from the inland collieries to the coast. They are easily distinguishable by their low semi-circular cab roofs, designed to enable them to negotiate the restricted clearances beneath the coal staithes at the harbour.

A further locomotive is on loan to the group

from the National Collection; this is N.E.R. three-cylinder 0-8-0 goods engine No. 901, Sir Vincent Raven's largest and most powerful freight engine.

No. 5428 is a sister engine of *George Stephenson* but with standard Walschaerts valve-gear. It has been named *Eric Treacy* after the late Bishop of Wakefield, the railway enthusiast.

Far from its native South of England is S.R. S15 class 4-6-0 No. 841 *Greene King*, which is a useful performer on N.Y.M.R. trains. This engine was formerly housed on the Stour Valley and Nene Valley lines in East Anglia and took part in the 1975 Shildon Cavalcade. *Greene King* was a former inhabitant of Barry scrapyard as was another Southern engine on the N.Y.M.R., No. 34010 *Sidmouth*, a Bulleid light Pacific of the 'West Country' class which is in need of a complete overhaul before it can steam again.

The North Yorkshire Moors Railway is also the home for a large fleet of ex-B.R. mainline diesel locomotives, principal among them being two 'Deltics', Nos. 55009 *Alycidon* and 55019 *Royal Highland Fusilier*. In recent years there has been a high incidence of diesel haulage on N.Y.M.R. trains, so prospective visitors are recommended to check by telephone first to see whether steam motive power is in use.

There is a large collection of coaches and other items of rolling stock. The observant visitor will find many vehicles of interest, ranging from B.R. diesel multiple units, and B.R. coaches built in the late fifties, to a Great Northern Railway coach of 1898; from a Shell-Mex tank wagon built during World War II to a snow plough from Edwardian days.

In addition to the regular services (see A.R.P.S. listings) many special trains are run. These include evening 'National Park Scenic Specials' from Pickering to Goathland, and specially chartered 'Disco Specials', which provide musical evenings to cater for all tastes. Licensed buffet cars are included on all special trains as well as on many service trains.

Combined rail/coach tours to the North York Moors National Park Centre at Danby Lodge are available in various forms and include catering services at several levels for those requiring them.

The Keighley and Worth Valley Light Railway

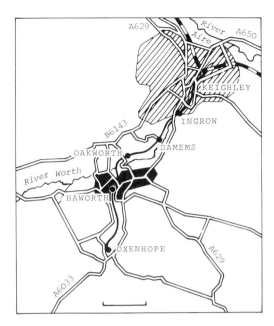

The line and its history

Sixty miles south-west of Grosmont, the town of Keighley lies astride the main line between Leeds and Carlisle. The Leeds and Bradford extension of the Midland Railway reached Keighley in 1847 and two years later was extended to meet the East Lancashire Railway at Colne. A scheme for a Manchester, Hebden Bridge and Keighley Junction Railway, which would have run through Haworth and down the

The smallest and earliest 0-6-0s of the L. & Y.R. fleet were the 'Ironclads' of 1887. No. 52044 was the last survivor, here seen on a 'Ninetieth Birthday' steaming. (J. G. Mallinson)

Just how uphill the K. & W.V.R. is can be seen here as Polish Railways 2-8-0 No. Tr 203.474 climbs towards Haworth with a six-coach Easter Monday train. (R. S. Greenwood)

Worth Valley to Keighley, had been put forward in 1845 but this, like many others proposed during the years of the Mania, came to nothing.

In 1861 a civil engineer, John McLandsborough, visited Haworth, and was surprised to find that the Worth Valley had no railway line. He drew up plans for a line connecting Keighley to Haworth and Oxenhope which were so well received by a number of influential men in the area that a deputation was sent to meet the directors of the Midland Railway and discuss the scheme with them. There were fifteen mills in the Oxenhope area and many more along the proposed route, all of which were potential customers. Knowing this, and anticipating the opening up of slate and free-stone quarries in the valley, the Midland directors gave the plan their blessing, and agreed to operate the line in return for half of the receipts. The deputation reported back to a

meeting at Haworth where it was revealed that the building of the railway would take about a year and would cost some £30,000. The subsequent prospectus issued by the newly formed Keighley and Worth Valley Railway Company very prudently specified a share issue of £36,000. In a similar way to that of the inaugural meeting of the Whitby and Pickering Railway, a share list was opened on the spot. By the end of the meeting, a sum of £31,340 had been subscribed; almost identical to the one subscribed twenty-nine years earlier in Whitby. By another coincidence the ultimate cost of the K. & W.V.R. equalled that of the W. & P.R.: £105,000. Parliamentary approval for the line was duly sought and granted; the company was incorporated by the Keighley and Worth Valley Act of 1862. Mr J. S. Crossley, C.E., F.G.S., engineer of the Midland Railway, was appointed engineer for the line; it was, however, John McLandsborough, whose services had been retained by the company, who did most of the work.

The next stage began; land was purchased for a double-track railway, although only a single line was planned in the first instance. Tenders were invited for its construction; of the ten subsequently received, that of John Metcalfe of Bradford (£21,940 7s. 4d.) was accepted. Work commenced with the ceremonial cutting of the first sod at Haworth by Isaac Holden, the company Chairman on 9 February 1864. However, the contractor was to have difficulty in getting possession of the land. Prices ranged between eighty and one hundred pounds per acre, but even at these figures the owners seemed reluctant to part with their property. In the end it took three years to build the five-mile line. There were three further causes for delay. The most quoted reason is that a cow 'ate the plans': two surveyors working on the line adjourned for lunch, leaving what were reputed to have been the only set of plans in existence in the corner of a field; on their return they were horrified to find that a cow had trampled their theodolite beyond repair, and had reduced the plans to an indecipherable pulp.

A far more serious delay occurred during the digging of a tunnel under the Halifax road at Ingrow. A vein of shifting sand was struck. So

Lancashire and Yorkshire Railway 0-6-0 saddle-tank No. 752 pauses at Platform 4 at Keighley station to contemplate its working centenary. This finely restored veteran was built in 1881. (David Wilcock)

much sand ran out of the workings that one end of the newly built Wesley Place Methodist Church, which stood nearby, subsided. (The chairman of the railway company, Isaac Holden, was doubtless embarrassed by this, since he had laid the church's foundation stone a couple of years previously!) The building had to be demolished and re-sited further away from the tunnel. A legal wrangle followed and after four years, some £2000 damages were awarded against the company. Finally, the contractors failed to supply an adequate labour force: the company had to enforce a penalty clause in the contract, claiming for 309 days at £20 per day.

Finally, early in November 1866, the line was completed throughout. Two weeks later, the

West Riding of Yorkshire suffered from storms of extreme severity. Forty yards of embankment were washed away at Damems; there was a landslip at Haworth Station, and much more minor damage. After repairs the date was set for the Grand Opening on Saturday 13 April 1867. It rained!

The flag-bedecked engine rumbled out of Keighley station with the inaugural train of seven coaches and a guard's van. Once out of the station and on the steeply graded curve over the river, the engine slipped to a standstill on the wet rails (this was to be repeated many times over the years). The resourceful driver ran the train back through the station, and making a running start succeeded in climbing the bank. Again between Oakworth and Haworth the engine slipped to a halt: this time the train had to be split and taken to Haworth in two sections.

So started the Keighley and Worth Valley Railway. It was solid and dependable, hard-working and prosperous.

In 1883 Keighley Station was rebuilt on a new

17

ABOVE: *The Stephenson and Hawthorns 0-6-0ST Samson enters Oakworth station.* (G.W. Morrison)

OPPOSITE: *A double-headed train on the K. & W.V.R. crosses Mytholmes Viaduct. The locomotives are B.R. standard class 4 4-6-0 No. 75078 and ex-Corby 0-6-0ST Samson.* (J. Winkley)

site to accommodate the Great Northern Railway's double-track line from Halifax, which ran alongside the Worth Valley line for its last mile into Keighley. In 1892, the somewhat suspect wooden viaduct over Vale Mill Dam between Oakworth and Haworth was replaced by a deviation over several new bridges and through the newly constructed Mytholmes Tunnel.

The heyday of the line was the years just prior to World War I. By the time of the grouping in 1923, when the Midland Railway became part of the London, Midland and Scottish Railway, the decline had already set in. Coal traffic to the mills dwindled as steam power gave way to electricity; materials began to come in by road and finished goods left the same way.

After nationalization in 1948, the line became part of British Railways (Midland Region), although later transferred to the North Eastern Region.

Preservation

By the mid 50s, the line running at a loss, the question of its closure was referred to the Transport Users' Consultative Committee in 1959. The Keighley Borough Council persuaded the Committee that a more intensive passenger service would be more remunerative. In June 1960 diesel multiple units took over the line, giving an extra sixty-six trains a week. But this did not have the desired effect, and the last passenger train ran on 30 December 1961; freight services lasted for a further six months. Strong local feelings were aroused by the withdrawal of the passenger services, and three months after the last passenger train ran Mr G. R. Cryer called a public meeting. Encouraged by the example of the Bluebell Railway in Sussex, where for two years a dedicated group of amateurs had been successfully running a steam operated public service over five miles of former

18

The distinctive air-smoothed shape of a Bulleid Pacific, in this case City of Wells *at Keighley. This locomotive has proved a superb mainline performer on B.R. special trains. (*Graham Scott-Lowe)

British Railways track, the meeting formed the Keighley and Worth Valley Railway Preservation Society, with the object of re-opening the line.

Preliminary approaches were made to B.R., and Haworth Station was rented as a headquarters and museum. A special train was chartered to run over the branch just before the freight service was withdrawn; then followed a series of lengthy negotiations with British Railways. By early 1964 the Society was given permission to carry out maintenance work on the line. Later on it was allowed to keep rolling stock there, and the first locomotive (a diminutive saddle tank) arrived by road in January 1965. More items arrived and British Railways authorized

the running of works trains to haul them up the branch and to facilitate track clearance and maintenance. An operating company, the Keighley and Worth Valley Light Railway Limited, was formed in 1966 and finally reached agreement with B.R. to purchase the line for £45,000 and to lease Platform 4 at Keighley Station for a period of 25 years. A Light Railway Order was obtained in due course, and the Inspecting Officer of the Ministry of Transport gave approval for the line to be re-opened on 29 June 1968. A short ceremony was held at Keighley, at which the Mayor cut a tape and declared the line again open. The inaugural train double-headed by two beautifully restored steam engines, stormed up the gradient from the station in splendid style (unlike its predecessor of a hundred and one years previously). The faith of the founders of the K. & W.V.R.P.S. had been vindicated; once again the valley echoed to the sound of steam engines working hard uphill.

Access

The Railway is easily reached by both public and private transport. Keighley Station is served by local rail services from Leeds, Bradford, Skipton and Morecambe, as well as by some of the Leeds–Carlisle expresses. West Yorkshire bus services from Bradford and Leeds to Keighley pass the station, and other bus services connect directly with most towns in the area. Visitors by car from Bradford and Leeds using the A650 to Keighley will find a large free car park close to the station. The A6033 from Hebden Bridge passes through Oxenhope and joins the A629 from Halifax and Huddersfield near Haworth. From this junction the A629 continues down the Worth Valley, through Keighley, to Skipton. Car parking is available free at Oxenhope and Oakworth, and for a small charge at Haworth.

As might be expected in a town of sixty thousand there are plenty of places to eat in Keighley. The station itself has a buffet in the summer months and similar facilities are provided at Haworth and Oxenhope during busy periods. When the railway buffet car is not running in one of the trains, it is open for service in Haworth yard, whilst inside the station a

20

Big Jim, the American-built S.160 class 2-8-0 designed for wartime use in Britain, was purchased from Polish State Railways for use on the K. & W.V.R. Here it is at Oxenhope. (John Sagar)

confectionery counter sells sweets, crisps and minerals and there is a well stocked bookshop. The same sort of services are available on a reduced scale at Keighley and Oxenhope.

A journey down the line
'Uphill' is the key word; once out of Keighley station, the line climbs continuously on an average gradient of 1 in 75 all the way to Oxenhope, 330 feet above its starting point. From the station, the line curves sharply to the right over the River Worth, on a gradient of 1 in 66 which for a short length steepens to 1 in 58, the steepest gradient on the whole line. The gradient eases appreciably after about half a mile. Shortly after this a gap appears in the

industrial back streets which have bounded the line so far: this marks the site of the junction with the old Great Northern line, closed in 1967. The brick then closes in again, and almost at once Ingrow station is reached. The one-hundred-and-fifty-yard Ingrow Tunnel follows, above and to the east of which stands the second Wesley Place Methodist Church. After the tunnel, the built-up area is left behind, and the track winds and climbs as it follows the River Worth to Damems. The station here was reputed to have been the smallest on the Midland Railway; it can only accommodate one coach. Beyond it, on a gradient of 1 in 64, the new company has built a passing loop to allow up and down trains to pass enabling a more intensive service to be worked in peak periods. Train movements through the loop are controlled by a signal box brought from Frisinghall on the Bradford–Shipley line. On becoming redundant the complete box was transported by

21

road to Oakworth before being taken by rail to Damems.

Beyond the loop, the line enters a narrow cutting, emerging to run into Oakworth Station. The station is half a mile below the village, and is typical of that of a Midland country branch line; it has been kept in Edwardian condition, complete with gas lamps. It achieved fame in 1968, when the B.B.C. used it to film Edith Nesbit's book *The Railway Children*; E.M.I. used it too when making the film of the story. Leaving Oakworth over a level crossing, the line curves first to the left and then to the right, crosses a three-arch viaduct over the River Worth and plunges into Mytholmes Tunnel. It emerges in the valley of the Bridgehouse Beck, which it follows for the rest of the way through Haworth to Oxenhope.

Haworth has achieved fame out of all proportion to its size, for the Rev. Patrick Bronte became curate of the Church here in 1820. Here, on the remote windswept moors, in a village of grim stone cottages, the three Bronte sisters, Charlotte, Emily and Anne, lived. Haworth attracts thousands of people every year to visit the Bronte Museum in the old Parsonage, and to see the old village.

Haworth Station is the headquarters of the railway, and the old goods yard is now the maintenance depot for the line's rolling stock. From here onwards the curves in the line become generally less severe as the valley opens up onto the barren moors, although the final bend tightens as it takes the railway into Oxenhope. This is the terminus, and there is a large museum where coaches and locomotives not in service are displayed.

Stock
The K. & W.V.R.'s collection of over thirty locomotives is one of the largest in the country. The two oldest main-line locomotives in the collection are both 0-6-0 engines from the former Lancashire and Yorkshire Railway; the elder of the two, No. 752, was built as a tender

Steam superpower on the climb away from Keighley. They are both British-built 2-8-0s: L.M.S. 8F No. 8431 and W.D. No. 1931, the latter reimported from Sweden. (Gavin Morrison)

The work that goes into restoration. LEFT : *Looking along No. 75078 (a standard B.R. 4MT, built 1956) in 1973. (*G. W. Morrison*)* OPPOSITE : *The same loco being prepared for a boiler inspection at Haworth Yard in 1978. (*R. S. Greenwood*)*

BELOW : *No. 43924 (Midland Railway No. 3924) is a 4F built in 1920. Fully overhauled in 1977, it is seen here in 1978 hauling freight on an enthusiasts' weekend. (*G.W. Morrison*)*

engine in 1881, but rebuilt as a saddle tank fifteen years later. The other, No. 957, was not built until 1887, and survived in its original form to become British Railway's 52044. No. 957 is a veteran of the cinema screen; she appeared in *The Private Life of Sherlock Holmes* and again as the *Green Dragon* of the fictitious 'Great Northern and Southern Railway' in *The Railway Children*. There are two other L. & Y.R. engines on the line, both tiny 0-4-0 shunting engines known colloquially as 'Pugs'. One has been restored to its original L. & Y.R. livery whilst the other retains its B.R. unlined black.

The Midland Railway is represented by one of its standard 4F goods engines built at Derby in 1920. This engine, No. 3924, deserves a place in the annals of preserved steam locomotives. Not only was she the first of many engines to be rescued from the Barry 'Graveyard', but she was also the first engine from there to be restored to working order. One other pre-grouping engine is to be found at Haworth. Originally No. 85 of the Taff Vale Railway, she became No. 426 of the Great Western Railway in 1922. Five years later she was put up for sale and being of a similar size and type to the Lambton engines, two of which (see above) are operating on the North Yorkshire Moors Railway, she was purchased for use at the Lambton colliery, her cab and bunker being cut down to conform with the restricted loading gauge.

Pannier Tank L89 came from the Great Western Railway by way of London Transport. Built at Swindon in 1929 as one of the 862-strong 57XX class she was bought by London Transport in 1963 and worked engineers' trains over the London Underground System until acquired by the K. & W.V.R. in 1970. Painted light brown for her appearance in *The Railway Children*, she has since reverted to the maroon livery that she carried under London Transport ownership.

The L.M.S. class 5s, the famous 'Black Fives', are represented by No. 45212. One of the equally numerous and very similar looking heavy freight engines of the class 8F 2-8-0s completes an L.M.S. trio. During World War II, hundreds of Austerity 2-8-0 freight engines based on the 8F class were built for army service overseas. After the war one of these, along with nearly two hundred others, was sold to the Netherlands. She was re-sold in 1953 to the Swedish State Railways and equipped by them for work north of the Arctic Circle. She returned to Britain and the Worth Valley in 1973. She is the only remaining member of her class in Britain.

Another Austerity type built during and after the war was a heavy 0-6-0 saddle tank. Many were later sold to the L.N.E.R. where they were known as class J94; the Worth Valley has several, together with two similar but larger engines, known on the railway as 'Uglies'.

A further wartime mass-produced design,

this time of American origin, was the U.S. Army 0-6-0 'switcher' or shunting engine. Many were shipped to this country for service on the continent. After the war the Southern Railway bought fourteen and modified them for use in the Southampton Docks. One of these, No. 72, resplendent in light-brown livery with a silver smoke box, helped to haul the society's inaugural train. Still wearing her colourful livery she has since been equipped for oil firing and named *Vulcan*, after her builders, the Vulcan Ironworks of Pennsylvania. The other engine on the first train was No. 41241, a 2-6-2 class 2MT tank engine, of L.M.S. design built by B.R. She wears British Railway's mixed traffic lined black livery.

Also of functional American outline is the 2-8-0 wartime locomotive No. 5820. This is one of Major Marsh's celebrated S160 class, which were built in large numbers to suit the British

loading gauge but were used extensively on the European mainland, both during the war and afterwards. This particular example was purchased from Polish State Railways and restored to its wartime livery for use in John Schlesinger's film *Yanks*. Of special note, too, is the Southern Railway Bulleid Pacific locomotive No. 34092 *City of Wells*, which has been painstakingly restored to working order after languishing in Barry scrapyard, and has headed many excursions over B.R. tracks since.

BELOW: *This L. & Y.R. 0-6-0 No. 52044 kept in B.R. livery was built in 1887 and is the oldest mainline engine on the K. & W.V.R. Seen here between Haworth and Oxenhope.* (G. W. Morrison)

OPPOSITE: *Ivatt class 2 2-6-2 tank No. 41241 with a Keighley to Oxenhope train.* (R. Bastin)

The Yorkshire Dales Railway

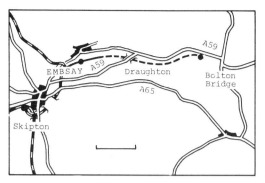

The line and its history

The Midland main line from Leeds to Carlisle passes through Skipton, some nine miles north-west of Keighley. During the last century proposals were made in 1846, 1856 and again in 1858 for a 'Wharfedale Railway' to link Skipton with Ilkley. These came to nothing, although in 1865 the Otley and Ilkley Joint Railway did reach Ilkley from the opposite direction. The Skipton–Ilkley route was proposed again in 1873, received Parliamentary approval in 1883, and was finally built and opened by the Midland Railway in 1888. A nine-mile branch to Grassington, from a junction near Embsay, was approved in 1897 and built in 1902. It lost its regular passenger service as early as 1930 although holiday excursions continued to run until 1967, the line having been kept open to serve the limestone quarries at Swinden.

The Embsay Junction–Ilkley line closed in 1965 under the auspices of the Beeching plan,

Passengers huddle under the awning at Embsay as Barclay saddletank No. 22 braves the downpour with a Yorkshire Dales train. (David Wilcock)

and three years later, when it seemed likely that the line to the quarry would be closed, the Embsay and Grassington Railway Preservation Society was formed to try to save it. Changing its name a year later to the Yorkshire Dales Railway Society, it rented the eighteen-acre site at Embsay Station. With the arrival of its first locomotive in 1970, the Embsay Steam Centre came into being. The quarries at Swinden have since been extended, giving the Grassington Branch a new lease of life. Consequently the Society has had to change its aims and is now extending eastwards along the old track-bed towards Ilkley. The ultimate hope is to reach Bolton Abbey, some three-and-a-half miles away, in easy stages; the first stage is the one-and-a-half miles to Holwell Bridge; the second a further mile to Draughton.

*One of the few Yorkshire Engine Co. locomotives preserved in working order brings a varied train of stock into Embsay station. (*Tom Heavyside)

The Y.D.R. began the 1980s the best possible way – with the granting of a Light Railway Order. So nowadays visitors can enjoy a regular train service running from Embsay station down to the junction with the Grassington branch and back, running non-stop through the station and up the half-mile or so of newly relaid track, before returning once again to Embsay.

At Embsay junction the Yorkshire Dales line is once more permanently reconnected with the national railway system. In fact, the Y.D.R.'s permanent way gang installed the points themselves, under the supervision of a B.R. inspector. This was the first time that amateur enthusiasts have been entrusted by British Rail with making a permanent junction on one of their main running lines. This connection has already been put to good use, as a diesel multiple-unit shuttle service has been inaugurated to carry passengers from Skipton to connect with Y.D.R. Steam Open Days. Though small in stature, the Yorkshire Dales Railway is big in spirit and is already generating its own particular atmosphere – somewhere between

that of the traditional English branch line and the more 'grass roots' charm of a Colonel Stephens light railway.

Stock
The Yorkshire Dales Railway has brought together a collection of eighteen industrial steam locomotives, most of them built in Leeds by Hudswell Clarke and Hunslet, though Barclay, Peckett and the Yorkshire Engine Co. are also represented. About half a dozen of the engines are available for regular traffic and have been restored to a very high standard indeed. A $9\frac{1}{2}$ in. gauge live steam miniature track runs alongside the station approach road and is the home of *King Tut*, a freelance 2-4-2 tender engine built by Stephen Smith in 1932.

Side by side with a six-wheeled coach built in 1896 as the personal saloon of Sir Vincent Raven, Locomotive Superintendent of the North Eastern Railway, are a number of British Railways Mark I bogie vehicles of the type now rapidly being withdrawn from main line service. They have been joined by a rake of four L.N.E.R. Gresley teak-bodied bogie coaches of 1935 vintage which usually form the working train set.

National Railway Museum York

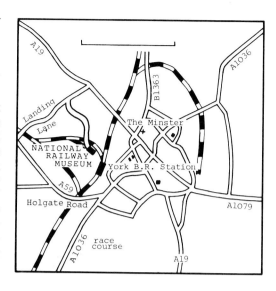

Even though it is not a working line, no account of steam railways could possibly omit the National Railway Museum at York. The original railway museum consisted of two parts: the small relics were in part of the original York station and the large exhibits were in the former York and North Midland locomotive works off Queen Street, and most of them stayed in those rather cramped quarters till the opening of the N.R.M. in 1975. After nationalization, the Museum of British Transport was set up at Clapham in South London, containing both road

BELOW: *The Chinese National Railways 4-8-4 No. 607 is swung ashore at London Docks after its return to this country.* (Science Museum)

OPPOSITE ABOVE: *A galaxy of colourful historic locomotives viewed from the museum gallery. In*

the foreground Midland Railway Compound No. 1000. (Jarrolds)

OPPOSITE BELOW: *The handsome N.E.R. class M express engine No. 1621.* (Jarrolds)

and rail transport exhibits. Under the Transport Act of 1968, the Museum's future became the responsibility of the Department of Education and Science as part of the Science Museum, and the British Railways Board was directed to provide a single home for the railway collections at both Clapham and York.

Originally, York North Loco Shed consisted of four adjacent roundhouses, but two were demolished in 1957–8 to make way for a new diesel depot. The other two remained unaltered and have now been converted into the museum's main display hall; the larger exhibits are stationed around its two turntables. The twenty-four roads around the larger table are used to display locomotives and one of them has had its pit deepened to enable visitors to walk upright beneath the engine on show above. The turntable itself has been kept in its original open form, with one road connecting it with the smaller twenty-road table, which has been

On the turntable is N.E.R. 0-6-0 No. 2392, on loan from the N.E.L.P.G. and built 1923. Mallard, *the record-breaking A4 Pacific is back right.*

decked into give better public access to the items of rolling stock grouped around it. Direct connection to the main line through the diesel depot enables the exhibits to be changed from time to time. An associated new building has been erected on the Leeman Road frontage, and there are an entrance hall, lecture theatre, refreshment room, shop for souvenirs and books, offices and stores as well as a gallery running the full length of the main hall.

Stock

Exhibits are rotated so visitors must not expect to be able to see any one item. The locomotives range from the Shutt End Colliery's *Agenoria* of 1829 to *Evening Star*, the last locomotive to be built for B.R. (in 1960). Pride of place must go to the L.N.E.R.'s streamlined *Mallard*, holder of the world speed record for a steam locomotive, 126 m.p.h. The N.E.R.'s No. 910 also holds a record: built in 1874 at Gateshead, she is the only engine to have taken part in the 50th, 100th and 150th anniversary celebrations of the Stockton and Darlington Railway. She is one of the original engines in the Queen Street

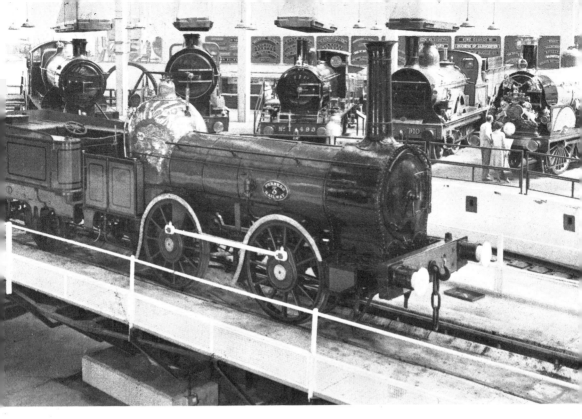

ABOVE : *Old 'Copperknob', built in 1846 for the Furness Railway stands gleaming on the N.R.M. turntable. (National Railway Museum)*
BELOW: *L. & N.W.R. No. 790, Hardwicke was built in 1892 and took part in the Railway Race to the North in 1895, covering the Crewe-Carlisle section at an average 67 m.p.h. Hardwicke was withdrawn in 1932, and went to the Clapham Museum as part of the National Collection. She is seen here being prepared for the 'Rail 150'.*

Museum. Another Queen Street original is G.N.R. 'Single' No. 1, which was removed from the museum in 1938, overhauled, and steamed as part of a campaign to publicize the Flying Scotsman. Later in that year, before returning to the museum, she was chartered by the Railway Correspondence and Travel Society to haul the first-ever rail tour. London, Brighton and South Coast Railway *Gladstone* of 1882 is a further Queen Street veteran. Bought in 1927 by the Stephenson Locomotive Society, she was restored to her original livery before being presented to the museum.

Many people consider that the South Eastern and Chatham Railway D class engines were the most handsome ever built, both in form and livery. The Museum is fortunate to possess the last survivor, No. 737, beautifully restored to her original condition. Also from the south is

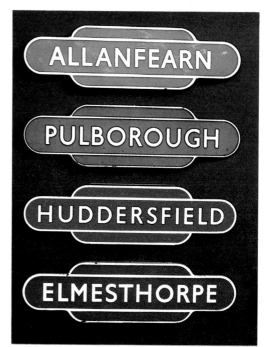

ABOVE: *The magnificent Gresley V2 Green-Arrow with the Norfolkman railtour. (Bob Green)*

RIGHT: *Totem-style station nameboards (early British Rail.) (Jarrolds)*

BELOW: *In the main hall, a replica 1st class coach of the 1830s and a chaldron wagon. (Jarrolds)*

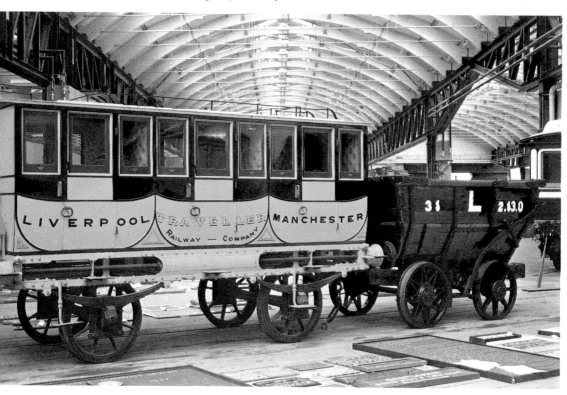

Duchess of Hamilton made a welcome reappearance on mainline trains during 1980. It is seen on a special working to commemorate 150 years of railway mail trains (David Williams)

Southern Region rebuilt Merchant Navy class, No. 35029, *Ellerman Lines*; one of the most fascinating locomotives in the collection, which has been sectioned to show the internal construction; her wheels and motion are electrically driven to demonstrate how they work.

Rolling stock

Rolling stock held includes replica Liverpool and Manchester Railway coaches of 1830, Royal saloons and travelling Post Offices as well as representatives of more everyday coaches. Goods vehicles are represented on a smaller scale and there are two working sets of points that can be demonstrated, one manual and one electrical. The small relics sections cater for everything from buttons to station name boards and from signals to silverware.

The Middleton Railway

The line and its history

In the Hunslet area of the great industrial city of Leeds can be found the Middleton Railway. Conceived originally in 1755 as a wooden tramway to carry coal, the various private agreements between the colliery owner Charles Brandling and the local landowners were superseded in 1758 by the first Act of Parliament to sanction the building of a railway.

In 1808, John Blenkinsop was appointed to be Brandling's agent; three years later he patented a rack-rail method of locomotive traction. Mathew Murray of the Round Foundry at Holbeck near Leeds was commissioned to build a locomotive incorporating the patent, and in June 1812 the resulting engine was tested and found to be capable of doing the work of sixteen horses. Together with a similar engine it worked successfully for over twenty years, even though one of them had to be rebuilt after blowing up in 1818 and killing the driver. (According to George Stephenson, who gave evidence about the accident, the driver had been 'in liquor' and had overloaded the safety valves.) The Brandling collieries changed hands in 1834, and shortly afterwards the new owners reverted to horse traction. Steam reappeared in 1866 after a further change of ownership although it was still on the original gauge of 4 ft 1 in.; the change to standard gauge was not made until 1881.

The National Coal Board inherited the Middleton when the mines were nationalized after World War II. In 1958 when the track needed wholesale renewal and the collieries were losing money, it was decided to close the line. Whilst haggling over the future of the railway went on between the N.C.B. and the City Council, who opposed the closure plan, the railway celebrated its bi-centenary in June 1958 with a special passenger train. The protagonists finally rea-

Not a scene from rural Yorkshire but, incredibly, a steam train at work on the Middleton Railway, barely a mile from Leeds city centre. (David Wilcock)

A line-up of Middleton stock against a typically industrial background: Bagnall 0-4-0 Matthew Murray *(built 1943),* Hudswell Clarke 0-4-0 Henry de Lacy II *(1917),* Hawthorn Leslie 0-4-0 No. 6 *(1935) and Peckett 0-4-0 No. 2003 (1941).* (Tom Heavyside)

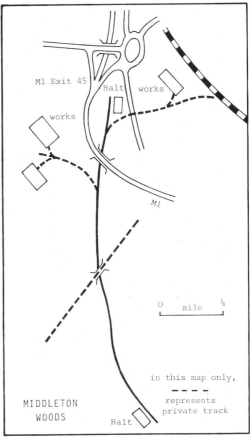

ched a compromise which led to the section of the line from Parkside Junction to Broom Pit being retained and restored; when, in 1959, the Leeds University Union Railway Society was looking for a stretch of line to use as a railway museum, the disused part of the Middleton was an obvious choice. The University authorities were not too keen on the idea, but the enthusiasts, led by Dr R. F. Youell, persevered and founded the independent Middleton Railway Preservation Society. The ownership of the abandoned section had passed into many hands and much further negotiation was required before agreement was finally reached. Notwithstanding this, the line was re-opened in June 1960 (giving free rides at the traveller's risk) making the Middleton the first preserved standard-gauge railway to run a passenger service; it beat the Bluebell Railway to the title by just two months.

Although not the original intention, the idea began to develop of restoring the line to its original role as a goods carrier. Two of the companies who had previously used the railway, Claytons and Robinson & Birdsell, agreed to support the venture in return for a regular daily service. This started in September 1960 and has run ever since. Diesel-hauled freight trains run every evening during the week, and a steam-hauled passenger service runs on Saturdays, Sundays and Bank Holidays from Easter until the end of October; trains leave at half-hourly intervals between two and five p.m. The part of the line now operated for passengers is a one-mile section starting at Tunstall Road Halt. Travelling south from there the line to the B.R. exchange sidings trails back on the left, and then the railway plunges through a tunnel under the M1. Emerging the other side, a further line trails back, this time to the right, leading to Robinson & Birdsell's scrap yard and to Claytons' works yard where the Middleton's locomotives have been kept since the railway's inception. A little further on the track goes under the bridge which formerly carried the G.N.R. branch to Beeston Junction and then passes the site of that railway's exchange sidings on the left, used by B.R. locomotives up until 1967. The line terminates at Middleton Park.

Stock
The Middleton has several basically similar 0-4-0 saddle tank industrial engines. These include Peckett No. 2003 *John Blenkinsop*, Hudswell Clarke No. 1309 *Henry de Lacy II*, and Bagnall No. 2702 *Matthew Murray*, named after the line's first locomotive builder. Also to be found are two former L.N.E.R. engines, Sentinel No. 59 (which ended its 'main-line' career as B.R. No. 68153), and an 0-4-0 tank, No. 1310, built for the N.E.R. in 1891. This latter engine belongs to the Steam Power Trust 65 as does a rather quaint-looking tank engine built for the Danish State Railways in 1895.

Diesel locomotives used for freight workings include a pair of early Hudswell Clarkes, *Carroll* and *Mary*, a Hudson-Hunslet, *Courage*, and a small Fowler. There is also an assortment of wagons and cranes to complete the collection of this unique railway, which since 1962 has been protected by the National Trust because of its historical value.

The North of England Open Air Museum, Beamish

Beamish Hall in County Durham is the home of the North of England Open Air Museum. 'Beamish', as the museum is usually known, was established in 1970 by a joint agreement of most of the larger local authorities of the North-East as 'an open air museum for the purpose of studying, collecting, preserving and exhibiting buildings, machinery, objects and information illustrating the development of industry and the way of life in the North of England'. Local Government re-organization in 1974 made it necessary for a revised agreement to be drawn up and signed on behalf of the four new County Councils of the North East; Northumberland, Tyne and Wear, Durham and Cleveland.

The site extends over two hundred acres of woodland and rolling countryside and is being transformed into several areas, each one covering some aspect of the former way of life in the North East. The Home Farm, part of the original estate, acquired a steam engine to drive its machinery in 1870. The chimney and engine house survived and a stationary steam engine built in Middlesbrough in 1852 has been obtained to power it so that the threshing machine, chaff-cutter and sawbench can work once more.

A typical North-Eastern colliery is being constructed, complete with a vertical winding engine built in 1855 and originally installed at Beamish Colliery. Steam for the engine is supplied by two Lancashire boilers brought from Shotton. A 'coffee-pot' vertical-boilered locomotive built in 1871 shunts wooden 'chaldron' wagons from Seaham Harbour, and nearby can be found Beamish's *pièce de résistance*, *Locomotion*. This is a full-size working replica of George Stephenson's famous engine of 1825 which worked on the world's first steam-hauled passenger railway, the Stockton and Darlington. The replica was built as a training exercise by apprentices from all over the area for the Railway's 150th anniversary celebrations in 1975. (The original *Locomotion*, together with

Railway antiquities at Beamish. N.E.R. J21 class 0-6-0 No. 876 (built in 1889) stands between Stephenson tank Twizell *of 1891 and the Forcett Railway coach dating from 1867. (*Phil Wood*)*

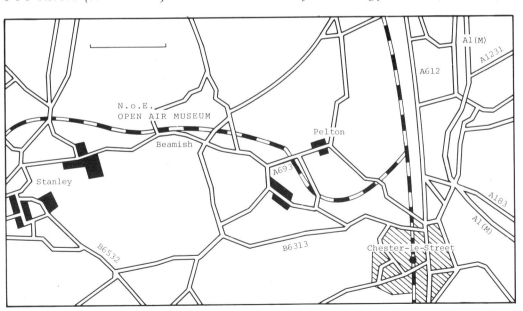

The replica Locomotion *steams regularly across the Beamish site. Also making a brave show is restored industrial 0-4-0 tank No. 18 built in 1863. (*North of England Open Air Museum*)*

Derwent, a later engine from the S. & D.R., can be found at North Road Station Railway Museum in Darlington. See page 45.)

Wagons from the colliery will be rope-hauled up an incline to a coal staith by means of the Warden Law engine from Hetton Colliery. From here connection is made with a rebuilt section of the N.E.R. leading to a typical country station. This is Rowley station, opened in 1867, on the Stanhope and Tyne Railway, west of Consett. It has been dismantled stone by stone and rebuilt at Beamish. A yard, complete with a small loco shed, signal box, goods shed, coal drops and weighbridge, completes this part. Route mileage is about one mile, but actual track mileage is nearly twice that. Nine steam locomotives are in store or in process of being restored for use on the line. The principal one, already on the line, is N.E.R. C class 0-6-0 goods engine, No. 876 (B.R. No. 65033 of class J21) whilst the oldest is the Hetton Colliery locomotive built by George Stephenson in 1822. A stalwart performer is the little Lewin 0-4-0 tank built in Poole in Dorset in 1863, now restored to its original side-tank condition, but once familiar to many people as a saddletank, shunting under the coal staithes at Seaham Harbour. Five N.E.R. coaches are being rebuilt for use on the railway, together with a representative collection of goods rolling stock, including a snow plough.

A half-mile electric tramway provides a passenger service during the summer, and the largest item in the collection, a 100-ton steam excavator, is occasionally steamed. Hundreds of other items, both large and small, all add up to give a fascinating glimpse into a past era.

Those requiring refreshments are adequately catered for by the 'Simpkins Tea Room' and there is the added attraction of the 'Bobby Shafto' pub during the summer season.

Beamish is still in the development stage. Many exhibits have yet to be installed or restored to working order, and many more will be added to the collection as time goes on. Working exhibits, such as *Locomotion*, the steam excavator, a steam hammer, and so on, are demonstrated from time to time and details of these and other events, which include Horse Driving Trials, Reliability Trials and Commercial Vehicle Trials, can be obtained from the Museum.

At Home Farm visitors can see traditional northern farm animals, exhibitions and a large collection of farm implements and carts. There are also demonstrations of pottery-throwing, hand printing, bread baking, 'proggy' mat-making and smithing.

A society has now been formed of those interested in this project, known as Friends of the North of England Open Air Museum and has a membership of 800.

The Bowes Railway

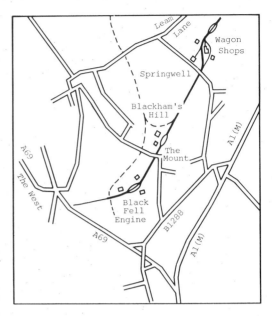

The Bowes Railway is a former colliery railway, laid down to carry coal from the Northumberland pits to the rivers of the North-East for shipment by coast to London and the South-East. It is often forgotten that in mining districts large networks were owned not by the mainline companies, but by the collieries themselves. This line was originally, until 1932, called the Pontop and Jarrow Railway. The oldest section was designed by George Stephenson, and ran from Mount Moor Colliery via Springwell to Jarrow itself. At its fullest extent the railway was fifteen miles long. During its history it has served as many as thirteen separate collieries. It was linked to a section of the Pelaw Main Railway in 1955, thereby including a further three mines within its orbit. Pelaw is also a stop of the former N.E.R. line between Newcastle Central and South Shields. Jarrow Station is to the east on the south bank of the River Tyne.

The railway had seven rope-worked inclines, and three locomotive-operated sections. It was not merely concerned with the shipment of coals, and for a time ran a passenger service. However, closures in the 1970s prompted conservationists and preservationists to look into the question of rescuing parts of this industrial railway. By 1974 only the section from Monkton to Jarrow was still in use, under the National Coal Board. With the closure of the line between Kibblesworth and Springwell Bank Foot, the Improvement Committee of the Tyne and Wear County Council considered a restoration project. In March 1976 the County Council completed the purchase of the length of track from Black Fell Bank Head (near the former Mount Moor Colliery) to Springwell Bank Head, a distance of 1¼ miles, together with the lineside buildings, winding engines, and forty-one wooden wagons. This section, part of the 1826 line, consists of two inclines (685 metres at 1 in 15 approximately and 1070 metres at 1 in 70 approximately) operated by the Blackham's Hill Engine, which are thus the only preserved rope inclines in the world. This was followed in September 1977 by the purchase of the railway's engineering and wagon shops at Springwell with much of their machinery, at the eastern end of the preserved section. The whole railway, its buildings and machinery, is now a scheduled Ancient Monument protected by the Department of the Environment. The Tyne and Wear Industrial Monuments Trust, a registered charity set up in 1975 and run by volunteers, is the Council's agent in restoration work and in operating the Railway for the public. Public passenger operation commenced on 1 July 1979 in a provisional form, but following the granting of a Light Railway Order in 1981, an extended service now carries visitors between the workshops complex and the rope-hauling demonstrations at Blackham's Hill.

The Trust also has a locomotive coal wagon, three brake vans, a reel wagon and a Kibblesworth Drift bogie wagon. There are two saddletank locomotives, both 0-4-0s built by Andrew Barclay of Kilmarnock. No. 22 was built in 1949 and is the only steam locomotive purchased new for the Bowes Railway still surviving. *WST* is a slightly smaller loco dating from 1954 which was acquired from the British Gypsum Company's Cocklakes works in Cumbria. The railway is reached by bus from Newcastle and Sunderland and is close to the A1(M).

41

The Tanfield Railway

Tanfield Railway is being built on a 3-mile section of the former Tanfield Wagonway. This was the most famous of Tyneside's early wooden railways, opened as early as 1725. It was an advanced engineering enterprise, a worthy forerunner of the nineteenth century's steam railways. Amongst its original features were the Causey Arch, the world's first railway bridge, and the Causey Embankment, 100 feet high and both still in existence today. The new line is being laid on a section of the old wagonway between Sunniside and East Tanfield, last used in 1962.

Sir Cecil A. Cochrane is a 0-4-0 saddletank. Built in 1948, it here trails a four-wheeled balcony saloon. (A. Thompson)

The essential industrial character of the wagonway is to be preserved, but of course the new line is for passenger-carrying. Locos have been selected from private manufacturers who had an established connection with the North-East. Coaches are both vintage and of comparatively modern designs, with a number of rebuilds from various sources. All are four- or six-wheelers and constructed from wood.

Particularly noteworthy are saloon coaches Nos. 1 and 4. At first sight these balcony-end four-wheelers look like the coaches supplied at the turn of the century to pioneer British Light Railways, such as the Lambourn and Rother Valley. This is intentional – the Tanfield line is very close in spirit to this earlier generation of minor railways and the saloon coaches have been built by the Tanfield volunteers themselves to lend the correct atmosphere. Tanfield is the home for one of the best collections of industrial steam locomotives in the country,

most of them having been built locally on Tyneside. The oldest is Black Hawthorn 0-4-0ST *Wellington*, built in 1873, and there is also an R. & W. Hawthorn 0-4-0ST of 1884 vintage. More typical are the Hawthorn Leslies and Robert Stephenson and Hawthorn four and six-coupled saddletanks, of which the newest example was built in 1954.

There are four Andrew Barclay locomotives of which perhaps the best-known is 0-6-0 side tank No. 17, a long-time favourite from the Waterside colliery system in Ayrshire, but now in need of a major rebuild before she steams again. The standard of restoration achieved at Tanfield is very high indeed and the working locomotives and stock are a credit to all concerned. Train services now operate over a mile of track between Marley Hill and Sunniside, where a small terminus station has been built.

With a pedigree stretching back beyond the original Tanfield Wagonway of 1725, today's Tanfield Railway is the culmination of over three centuries of history. The ultimate plan is to extend the line right back to East Tanfield stopping on the way at the Causey Arch. This will give a total run of three miles over some stiff

Veteran Tynesider at Marley Hill shed is this R. W. Hawthorn 0-4-0ST South Durham Malleable No. 3 *dating from 1884. (*Phil Wood*)*

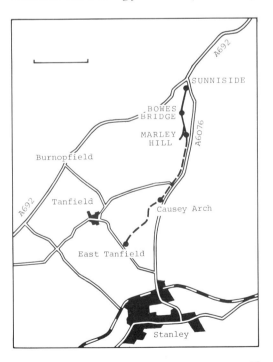

43

ABOVE: *Those industrious Geordie lads at Tanfield preparing yet another saddletank for action. It is a Tyneside product by Hawthorn Leslie – works No. 2859 built in 1911.* (Paul Barber)

LEFT: *It could be a scene from the Golden Age of British light railways in the 1920s, but in fact this is a contemporary view on the Tanfield Railway. No. 21 at Sunniside terminus.* (A. Thompson)

1 in 40 gradients – reminders of the horse-drawn days when these were rope-hauled inclines. Much of the Tanfield line's charm stems from the energy and warmth of the Geordie character – it most surely ranks as one of England's friendliest railways – and in recognition of its achievements the railway won the 'Steam Past' Award in 1981.

Darlington Railway Museum

It is fitting that the principal station on one of Britain's first steam railways (the Middleton Railway was the first to use steam locomotives successfully for commercial purposes, in 1812) should have become the site for a local railway museum. On 27 September 1825 the first train was run from Shildon, via Darlington to Stockton. It was a mixture of mineral wagons, filled with either people or coals, together with the Company's carriage, aptly named *Experiment*. The line had been laid under the direction of George Stephenson with the assistance of his son Robert. Though this inaugural service proved to be immensely popular, the Directors did not institute a passenger service till 1833, and the railway remained a freight-only concern, although some passengers were horse-drawn.

The first steam engine to run along the line, on the opening ceremony, was *Locomotion No. 1*. Designed and constructed under the supervision of Robert Stephenson (though not with close attention), *Locomotion* continued to work on the railway till 1846, and sporadically after that. The company then sold the engine in 1850 for scrap when technology's advance had made it obsolete. Fortunately *Locomotion* was rescued from the breakers' yard, and sent to work as a pumping engine at Lucy Pit, Crook. The North Eastern Railway, which had absorbed the Stockton and Darlington, reclaimed the engine in 1857, realizing its historical importance. It was restored ready to be placed on display. They exhibited *Locomotion*, together with No. 25, *Derwent* (a 0-6-0 built in 1845), in their new Darlington Station. They were both placed on stands alongside the buffer stops in the central concourse, as mementoes of the

*The fine structure of Darlington North Road station, now a museum. (*N. E. Stead*)*

45

Company's history. In 1925 the L.N.E.R. decided to hold a centenary celebration to commemorate the opening of the Stockton and Darlington. *Locomotion* was taken from display to take part in the parade of steam engines. However, the company cheated. It appeared to watchers that *Locomotion* was steaming as she raced along with smoke billowing from her chimney. In fact an electric motor had been fitted in the tender, and cotton waste soaked in oil was burning in the firebox.

With the opening of this new museum in the former Darlington North Road Station, both *Derwent* and *Locomotion* have been moved from their old home in Darlington Bank Top. In addition, the museum houses two other N.E.R.

Derwent is a Stockton and Darlington Railway heavy goods engine of 1845, now in safekeeping at Darlington. (N. E. Stead)

locomotives, both vintage engines. There is the 0-6-0 No. 1275, built in 1874, and the 2-4-0, No. 1463, built in 1885. *Derwent* was withdrawn from service in around 1865, having worked on the S. & D. for twenty years. After working on colliery lines, No. 25 was presented to the N.E.R. in 1895 and was then placed on display alongside *Locomotion*.

Additionally, there are three small industrial steam locomotives, all with North Eastern connections. The venerable, vertical-boilered 0-4-0 tank No. 17 was built by the Thornaby-on-Tees engineering firm of Head Wrightson and Co., whilst the little 0-4-0ST *Met* came from Hawthorn Leslie of Newcastle in 1909. The Bagnall fireless locomotive, whilst built in Staffordshire, worked at the Darlington factory of Patons and Baldwins Ltd.

Darlington North Road Station, situated on the line west to Shildon, has been rebuilt several times. It is a simple building, but distinguished

ABOVE: *The atmosphere of rail travel in the 19th century: the building is an S. & D.R. original and all the exhibits have links with the north-east.* (Darlington Railway Museum)

RIGHT: *Stephenson's* Locomotion *has pride of place.* (Darlington Railway Museum)

for the unusual roof structure. The two bays were supported by a row of iron columns erected down the middle between the tracks. It lay in an exceptionally dilapidated state for a number of years while funds were being raised for its restoration and conversion into a museum. Certainly the Shildon railway parade, organized to commemorate the 150th anniversary of the S. & D., helped to highlight its condition. Darlington Bank Top Station is on the main East Coast line between York and Newcastle, and there are local services from each, as well as express trains from King's Cross.

The Lincolnshire Coast Light Railway

North-east Lincolnshire possesses what at first sight is a vintage narrow-gauge railway. However, although the locomotives, rolling stock and track are indeed of vintage origin, the railway itself dates back to only 1960. The Lincolnshire Coast Light Railway Company Limited was formed by a group of railway enthusiasts in April of that year; by the end of August it had laid and opened a half-mile line from North Sea Lane, Humberston to Humberston Beach. Six years later the line was relaid on a new alignment, and was extended for a further half-mile to South Sea Lane, near to the centre of the Humberston Fitties Holiday Camp.

*The Lincolnshire Coast Light Railway is rarely operated by steam. This is diesel No. 4 with an Ashover Railway coach. (*T. J. Edgington*)*

The original track came from the Nocton Estate Light Railway, an agricultural line near Lincoln, which in turn had obtained it from a World War I dump at Arras in France; it is of 60cm (approximately two-foot) gauge. Most of the extension track came from the Penhryn Railway in Wales. Gradients are non-existent, and the railway's diminutive motive power copes quite easily with the one-coach trains. There are two steam locomotives, an 0-6-0 saddle tank built in 1903 called *Jurassic*, formerly owned by the Rugby Portland Cement Company, and an even older 0-4-0 saddle tank, *Elin*, dating back to 1899. Passengers are catered for by three bogie coaches, two from the Ashover Light Railway and one from the Sand Hutton Railway near York. A handful of diesel locomotives and an assortment of wagons completes the railway's rolling stock.

Traffic consists mainly of holiday-makers, and consequently the railway runs only from Whitsun until the end of October. Diesel haulage is used during the week with steam normally taking over at the weekends.

SCOTLAND

Museums and Preservation in Scotland

Interest in old locomotives and other 'bits and pieces' linked with railways has been strong in Scotland at least since the 1850s when Alexander Allan, Locomotive Superintendent of the Scottish Central Railway, had one of the primitive Dundee and Newtyle Railway's 0-2-4 locomotives, *The Earl of Airlie*, restored and photographed before it was scrapped.

The first locomotive to be preserved in Scotland, however, came from over the border. This, the oldest steam locomotive in existence, is the *Wylam Dilly*, William Hedley's first locomotive, built for colliery service at Wylam near Newcastle in 1813. She was in operation till about 1867, when she was purchased by Hedley's descendants who presented her to the Royal Scottish Museum in Edinburgh in 1882 where she still is. All conventional railway locomotives can trace their descent from this, the first practical locomotive to run with smooth wheels on smooth rails. Her locomotive neighbours in the Royal Scottish Museum are some superb working models of British and foreign locomotives, made in the museum workshops, but the Museum also owns a narrow 2 ft 6 in. gauge electric locomotive from the Winchburgh Oil Works, West Lothian, which is at present in store. The Museum has also lent its largest locomotive to the Scottish Railway Preservation Society (see below).

The practical interest in the setting up of an industrial museum which found expression in the setting up of the Royal Scottish Museum, also found expression in the setting up of the

Kelvingrove Museum in Glasgow, Scotland's great industrial city. Neither the original Kelvingrove House nor its magnificent successor was really suited to the display of heavy machinery, though a few full-size stationary steam engines were preserved for a time in the grounds. The opportunity to tackle something bigger came when Glasgow's tram service, once the envy of the world, came to an end in 1962. A horse tram had been set aside when the tramways had been electrified in 1901, and this was joined by a selection of electric trams, restored to earlier forms of liveries in the paintshop of what had been the tramway workshops in Albert Drive. The popular success of this Transport Museum, which included a few horse drawn vehicles, some Scottish-built cars and a fine collection of bicycles, encouraged expansion, and it was indeed fortunate that the Museum was enabled to step in when British Railways policy on the preservation of steam engines in Scotland abruptly changed, and to take into care four locomotives which had been maintained in running order for the working of special trains. Two of these had been set aside by the London, Midland and Scottish Railway in the 1930s when the distinctive locomotives of the old Scottish railway companies were fast disappearing. Both are exceptional. Caledonian Railway No. 123 was built as that railway's exhibit at the Edinburgh International Exhibition of 1886. With her large single pair of driving wheels she was unusual on a Scottish line but she was very swift, and starred in the 1888 race to the North between the East Coast and West Coast routes. On the hilly Carlisle–Edinburgh section she managed to run the $100\frac{3}{4}$ miles in $102\frac{1}{2}$ minutes, for long a record. Thereafter she was used to haul special saloons, and ran ahead of the Royal Train as pilot engine to ensure the safety of the route. Ending her days on the level Perth–Dundee lines she was withdrawn in 1935 and restored to her original Caledonian blue livery. Her companion in the paint shop in the former Caledonian Railway's St Rollox workshops was Highland Railway 4-6-0 No. 103, the first locomotive of that wheel arrangement to run in Britain, and forerunner of a highly successful type that hauled all classes of trains on Britain's railways till the last days of steam.

When in 1957 the Great Western's *City of Truro* was brought out of York Railway Museum, and restored to working order, her public appearances were such a success that Mr James Ness, General Manager of the Scottish Region of B.R. put No. 123 through St Rollox Works, and she, very successfully, ran special trains over the next few years. Then in 1959 a Scottish Industries Exhibition was organized in Kelvin Hall, Glasgow, and Mr Ness, with an eye to publicity as well as sentiment, had No. 103 restored to working order. She was magnificently repainted in 'Stroudley's Improved Engine Green' (actually yellow), the colour remembered by her designer's daughter. Nos. 123 and 103 were joined by Great North of Scotland Railway 4-4-0 No. 49 *Gordon Highlander*, which had been withdrawn two years earlier, and North British Railway 4-4-0 No. 256, *Glen Douglas*, withdrawn from traffic for restoration. These four locomotives, together with *City of Truro*, imported for the occasion from Swindon, ran a series of special trains from Scottish towns and cities to Glasgow for the Exhibition. These ran to Kelvin Hill Station on the old underground Glasgow Central line, and proved extremely popular with the public and with enthusiasts. For the next seven years the quartet worked enthusiasts' specials all over Scotland, No. 103 having a special triumph in 1965, the centenary year of the Highland Railway, when she ran under her own steam to Inverness, and then worked a series of public special trains from Inverness to Nairn (the oldest section of the Highland Railway). There was strong public pressure to keep her in Inverness but back she came to the Lowlands to be moved with her sisters into the Transport

Museum at Glasgow in 1966. The four locomotives preserved there were joined by two others. Caledonian Railway No. 828 is a 0-6-0 heavy goods engine built in 1899. She was withdrawn in 1963, and bought by the Scottish Locomotive Preservation Fund, formed by a Glasgow-based group of railway enthusiasts, chiefly members of the Stephenson Locomotive Society. No. 828 was restored to exhibition condition, though not working order, in Cowlairs Works, Glasgow, before she was moved into the Museum. This engine was moved back out of the Museum in 1980 and may now be seen on the Strathspey Railway. Its place in the Museum was taken by the tiny Glasgow-built Chaplin vertical-boilered shunting loco.

Glasgow and South Western Railway No. 9 was very much the 'poor relation' at first. Withdrawn in 1934 and sold to a colliery in North Wales, she survived to become the only Glasgow and South Western Locomotive. She was presented to the Museum by the National Coal Board in 1965. Dirty black, with a home-made chimney and patched tanks, she looked a sorry sight when first moved into the Museum. Her thorough 'facelift' included a wooden chimney made in a shipyard, and 'cosmetic' treatment of her tanks. Restoration was completed with a coat of G. & S.W.R. green, making her one of the most attractive exhibits in the Museum. Later this quintet of main-line locomotives was joined by an industrial shunting engine. This is a fireless locomotive, charged with steam from a stationary boiler, latterly used at the Dalmarnock, Glasgow, Power Station of the South of Scotland Electricity Board. She was installed in 1969.

Complementing the full-sized exhibits is a 4mm scale model of Carlisle Citadel station, operated at weekends; some fine models of Scottish built locomotives; a collection of early rails showing the evolution of the railway; and a remarkable collection of railway relics. Even the Museum Tea Room is dominated by railways with fine paintings of two early viaducts, collections of locomotive works plates, and gauge 1 model locomotives and rolling stock, and a carpet with representations of No. 123 and *Glen Douglas*.

Trams are by no means forgotten – the

Most of the locomotives now in Glasgow Transport Museum were active on main line steam specials in the early 1960s. Caledonian Railway 'Single' No. 123 is seen at the head of an excursion to the Bluebell Railway. (John Gardner)

Glaswegians' love of the 'caurs' is legendary – from the original horse-drawn tram of 1894, to the Cunarder, the story of the trams can be seen and times-past recalled. Also to be seen are commercial vehicles, ranging from a steam-powered traction engine to road rollers.

On 14 December 1979 a new gallery featuring the Glasgow Underground Railway was opened. This is in the form of a reconstruction of the old Merkland Street station and includes two of the old cars.

The Scottish Railway Preservation Society

The realization that the eleventh hour was at hand, and that all too soon locomotives and other relics of the old Scottish railways would disappear, was certainly behind the raising of a fund to purchase C.R. No. 828 (see above) by a group which at first had had much more grandiose schemes to preserve a representative selection of Scottish locomotives. It was also behind the formation of the Railway Preservation Society in England. This also had grand aims which included the setting up of branches all over Britain. It arranged a public meeting in Edinburgh in November 1961. Those present decided not to form a branch of the R.P.S., but to found instead the Scottish Railway Preservation Society in co-operation with its progenitor. The aims were straightforward: 'to acquire relics of the railways of Scotland, to restore them to original condition wherever possible, and to display them to the public either in use on a line or in a static display.'

The curious, slightly comic, but real rivalry between Scotland's capital and its chief manufacturing centre be-devilled the early history of railway preservation in Scotland. The S.R.P.S. and the S.L.P.F. went their separate ways, and for a time it seemed that the Glasgow group might dominate. The sparks in the S.R.P.S.'s aims 'to acquire relics and to display them in use', however, were slowly fanned into a flame. With remarkable faith the still-new Society leased in 1964 an old transhipment shed in Springfield Goods Yard, Falkirk, as the large relics museum, and Murrayfield Station, Edinburgh (now demolished) as a small relics museum. The good-natured tolerance and support of British Rail was, in retrospect, obvious in their taking on trust an untried group of enthusiasts. The 300 ft-long transhipment shed had been built for the collection and sorting of iron castings for onward shipment for the many foundries in and near Falkirk. It had some years previously been badly damaged by fire. When the Society took it over it was partly roofless, and the wooden platform running the length of

the building was largely a charred mass. With axe, saw, and sweat the rubbish was cleared and the first large relics made their appearance. These were: an ex-Great-North-of-Scotland ballast wagon of 1880, a primitive but interesting vehicle; and Caledonian Railway 0-4-4T, No. 419. She had been withdrawn in 1962 as B.R. No. 55189, and was one of a numerous class used for suburban and branch-line traffic all over the Caledonian and later L.M.S. system in Scotland. She was purchased by the S.R.P.S. with the help of a generous loan from an English member, Mr W. E. C. Watkinson, who also paid for her restoration at Cowlairs Works. It was the need to house No. 419 which really forced the S.R.P.S. to take on Falkirk, and it was the preservation of No. 419 which made many enthusiasts accept the S.R.P.S. as a genuine preservation society. A night glimpse of 419 at Eastfield locomotive shed gleaming darkly in her rich Prussian blue was the author's real introduction to the S.R.P.S., the beginning of a love-hate relationship that has lasted for more than a dozen years.

Another locomotive which came the way of the Society was *Ellesmere*. This tiny machine was built in 1861 by Hawthorn's of Leith, founded by the better-known Newcastle firm of R. & W. Hawthorn to build locomotives for Scottish Railways. Overtaken in the manufacture of main-line locomotives in the 1850s by other firms, the concern turned to the building of small industrial locomotives, mainly of the 'well tank' type which have the tanks for water between the frames. *Ellesmere* is one of these. As her name suggests she was built for service in Lancashire, and when she was withdrawn in

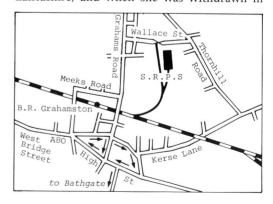

Early days at Falkirk as volunteers polish up Caley tank No. 419 whose preservation gave a vital early boost to the success of the S.R.P.S. (S.R.P.S.)

1957, a group of enthusiasts secured her for preservation. It seemed sensible to preserve her in Edinburgh, and so she was brought up to Dalry Road Locomotive Shed. She languished there, and in various other storing places, until presented to the S.R.P.S. in 1963. Even then she did not finally reach Falkirk until 1966. As there was no apparent possibility of restoring her to working order, and in view of her historical interest (she is the oldest surviving Scottish-built locomotive) the Royal Scottish Museum has acquired her from the Society for eventual display in Edinburgh.

Before *Ellesmere* reached Falkirk the collection there had begun to grow. A Caledonian Railway goods brake van was bought from the N.C.B. by two members, and arrived in September 1965. It was soon joined by a much more exotic vehicle, the only Royal Coach owned by a Scottish Railway Company. It was built as a First Class Saloon in 1898, and was used by King Edward VII, Queen Alexandra, and the Prince of Wales (later George V), on a number of occasions between 1902 and 1910. The L.N.E.R. transferred the vehicle to the Engineers' Department in 1924, and an end-observation window was inserted. This most attractive vehicle, with a beautifully panelled interior, a kitchen compartment, and a tiny guard's compartment, was in a scrap yard when the Society decided to try to save it. Unfortunately, the agreement between B.R. and the scrap dealer did not allow resale to the Society. For a time the situation looked black, but Sir Malcolm Barclay Harvey, historian of the G.N.S.R. used his influence to secure the release of the saloon, and generous donations by members and others paid for it. It has now been professionally repainted in its original red-and-cream livery.

The Society has, since its formation, been represented at many exhibitions all over Scotland. Its first excursion north of the Highland line was to Inverness for the Highland Railway Centenary Celebrations in 1965. A feature of

At the Falkirk depot of the S.R.P.S. near Grahamston station, work proceeds on Maude, *North British 0-6-0 No. 673, built in 1891. On the right is* City of Aberdeen, *a 0-4-0 saddletank used on street tramways from Aberdeen gas works to the railway yards. Behind* Maude *are a Shell/BP tank wagon dating from 1897; the Barclay 0-6-0 No. 20, largest of the locos saved from the Wemyss Coal Company's private railway; Caledonian Railway 0-4-4 No. 419 (1891). (S.R.P.S.)*

the festivities was an auction of railway relics at which the Society secured some small items. Mr W. E. C. Watkinson bought the largest relic, a six-wheeled H.R. coach which had been converted for departmental use, for the Society. It was then completely restored externally, and partially renovated inside at Lochgorm Works, Inverness. Meticulous attention to detail was a feature of the work done at Lochgorm, genuine H.R. fittings being used wherever possible. One source of door handles and interior parts

was a H.R. coach converted to a Scout Hut in a Glasgow suburb. Mr Watkinson also bought a very early (c. 1870) four-wheeled coach which had been used as a bothy by platelayers at Inchlea Crossing on the H.R. main line. On removal to Falkirk it was found to be in remarkably good condition. After some years in store there, the coach was moved to the Strathspey Railway for restoration.

With this little group of vehicles, a rusty iron shed, and no proper public access, the Society held its first open day at Falkirk late in 1965. B.R. kindly hauled the stock out of the shed on the Friday, and positioned it nicely for photography. Unfortunately it rained for most of the day, damping the spirits of those hardy enthusiasts and others who turned up. However towards evening the sun came out to shine on members trying to push the vehicles back into the shed. Unfortunately, although most of the stock was returned, one of the locomotives could not be persuaded to move, despite the use of pinchbars and crowbars. With darkness, the

Carving a niche in railway history, North British Railway 0-6-0 Maude *heads for Rainhill with a pair of Caledonian Railway coaches in 1980. (*Phil Wood*)*

attempt was abandoned and B.R.'s diesel shunter had to give the necessary push on Monday morning.

With its first public display, the Society began to win the confidence of industrialists and members of the public. The Carron Iron Company, in 1966, gave the S.R.P.S. one of its dumb-buffered wagons, the last in service in Scotland.

It had always been the Society's intention to acquire a North British Railway locomotive. The first choice was a 0-6-2T (L.N.E.R. N15) of a type used for shunting, banking and short-distance goods trains, but this had little appeal; accordingly attention shifted to a J36 (a 0-6-0 tender locomotive). This most successful class of engine was built between 1888 and 1900, and fifty were sent to France during World War I. On their

return the N.B.R. named them after battles and generals. By 1963 the only named member of the class still running was *Maude*, B.R. No. 65243, and in the following year an appeal was launched for money to buy her. By the end of 1965 the fund stood at £36 but a concentrated appeal brought the total to £800 by July 1966, when the locomotive was withdrawn. A world shortage of copper forced the scrap price of the locomotive up and up, always ahead of the Society's fund raising. Finally negotiations were entrusted to Captain Peter Manisty, Chairman of the Association of Railway Preservation Societies. Captain Manisty arranged a 'package deal' for three locomotives wanted by members of the A.R.P.S. *Maude*'s price was £1250, and a determined last-minute appeal raised enough money to secure her, and she was moved to Falkirk in January 1967. The locomotive had been run into the ground, and although some initial restoration work was taken in hand, it became apparent that a thorough overhaul, together with replacement of the tender tank

The S.R.P.S. specializes in goods vehicles and old coaches (which are used on railtours). This selection of goods stock is hauled by Neilson 0-4-0 Kelton Fell, built in 1876 and donated to the Society by the National Coal Board in 1968. A G.N.S.R. ballast wagon is followed by a bulk grain van of the Leith General Warehousing Co., a dumb-buffered mineral wagon of the Carron Company (i.e. the buffers are not collapsible, but solid; here a wood beam), and a Caledonian Railway 6-wheeled brake van. (S.R.P.S.)

was essential. From 1976 on, a determined effort was made, and *Maude* was re-steamed in 1978. Since then, *Maude's* greatest achievement has been her epic, unassisted return journey from Falkirk to the Rocket 150 Cavalcade at Rainhill in 1980. The gallant little engine made the entire 500-mile round trip under her own steam and without a B.R. diesel pilot loco being attached; she was the only loco at Rainhill to achieve this feat.

Later in 1967 the first of a steady stream of Scottish standard-gauge industrial locomotives made its way to Falkirk. This was the 'Fairfield Tram', an electric locomotive used between 1940 and 1966 to move raw materials from the Govan goods yard to the Fairfield ship-building yard along Govan Road. Originally this was a tram route, and when the trams were replaced by trolley buses in 1958 the single collector was replaced by trolley poles. The locomotive was offered first to the Glasgow Museum of Transport, who declined it, but suggested that the S.R.P.S. might take it. It was moved to Falkirk by road, and is being restored by a group of tram-minded members. Fitted with batteries, it can and does operate on open days.

Other locomotives which appeared at Falkirk in 1967 were a Peckett 0-4-0 saddle tank presented by Colville's Ltd to the Locomotive Club of Great Britain (which found a temporary resting place at Falkirk before being moved to the Club's depot at Sittingbourne), and the

L.N.E.R. 4-4-0 Morayshire heads a S.R.P.S. railtour train composed mainly of preserved historic coaches high above the waters of the Firth of Forth on the world's most famous railway bridge. (David Wilcock)

Society's first diesel locomotive, a standard Ruston and Hornsby DS88 four-wheeled shunter presented by J. and A. Weir, papermakers of Kilbagie, Clackmannanshire.

The diesel brought life to Falkirk and ended the Society's forced reliance on B.R.'s good nature for movement of stock. Late in 1967, however, the Society received word of an even better present - its first steam locomotive in working order. No. 13 had, for some years, been the oldest working locomotive in Scotland, and preliminary approaches had been made to her owners, the N.C.B., about her acquisition. Built in Glasgow as *Kelton Fell* for an iron-ore railway in Cumberland, she had nevertheless spent most of her life in Scotland. On her withdrawal, the

N.C.B., through Mr W. Rowell, Area Director, and Mr J. D. Blelloch, Chief Engineer of the Scottish North Area, presented her to the Society. The Presentation was made at Gartshore 9/11 Colliery in February 1968.

No. 13 was soon steamed by S.R.P.S. members, but disaster soon struck when a crank pin broke. Replacement was no easy matter. She had to be jacked up and her wheels dropped, the pin pressed out, and a new pin made and pressed in. While the locomotive was wheel-less the opportunity was taken to carry out a complete overhaul and repaint, and when No. 13 emerged from the shed resplendent again as *Kelton Fell*, she was the first of the Society's steam locomotives to be completely restored. A renaming ceremony was performed in March 1976 by Mr Blelloch, now Chief Engineer of the N.C.B.

No. 13 was soon joined by another N.C.B. locomotive, No. 1. Built as *Lord Roberts* in 1902 for the Coltness Iron Company, this engine is a large 0-6-0 tank used for heavy ironworks shunting. Used at Bedlay Colliery between 1955 and 1968, No. 1 broke a crosshead and was withdrawn from service. Another approach to the N.C.B. was successful, and No. 1 came to Falkirk late in 1968. There she lay until 1976, when work started on her overhaul.

The efforts to acquire locomotives, and *Maude* in particular, had diverted attention from the rapidly vanishing stock of older types of coaches and wagons on B.R. and in private ownership. When the B.R. preserved locomotives were moved into Glasgow Museum, there was no room for the two ex-C.R. coaches which had been restored to run behind No. 123. After being left in store for some time they were eventually offered for sale at £1000 each. At that price the S.R.P.S. was not interested, though the Bluebell Railway bought one of the pair. The A.R.P.S. again negotiated a package deal in which the S.R.P.S. secured the remaining coach for £500. Curiously enough, the Bluebell's coach came to the S.R.P.S. in 1974, though it had been sadly neglected and required extensive replacement of the metal sidepanels.

1968 was the year of the wagons. One of these came from Gartsherrie Ironworks, Coatbridge, with spares for No. 13, and remained at Falkirk. The Scottish Tar Distillers Ltd gave a square tank wagon built as long ago as 1877, three more conventional tank wagons came from Shell and Briggs of Dundee, and two bulk grain hopper wagons were sold to the Society for a nominal sum by Robert Hutchison and Co., the Kirkcaldy maltsters. With a group of four wagons purchased from the Admiralty in 1969, and a further three acquired in 1971, these form one of the most comprehensive groups of wagons owned by any preservation society.

1969 was the year of the coaches. During the previous year the Society had become involved with the Highlands and Islands Development Board in discussions about operating the railway between Aviemore and Boat of Garten.

The prospect of being called on to run a railway stimulated interest in acquiring coaches of historic interest and also more modern examples which would be easier to keep in service. Two pre-grouping coaches were located at Bundeath Admiralty Armaments Depot, and as the internal train service there had ceased, they were obtained for a very modest sum. Structurally, both were in poor condition, and they had no vacuum brake gear, so they have had a low listing for restoration, though some work has been done on the smaller of the two, a G. & S.W.R. corridor coach.

The two modern coaches bought in 1969 were a compartment coach, of L.N.E.R. design though built to B.R.'s order in 1951, and a second-class 'open corridor' built by the L.M.S. in 1946. In the following year two more modern coaches of L.M.S. design were bought. By that time the Society had realized its aim of owning coaches from all the Scottish pre-grouping railways, with the exception of the N.B.R. N.B.R. coaches of a variety of types, in many locations, had been carefully examined by S.R.P.S. members, but none appeared satisfactory. However, a former invalid saloon, converted in 1957 to an engineers' saloon, was purchased in 1972. It has since been refitted with a corridor connection at one end, and has been repanelled and repainted in N.B.R. livery.

While the Society was buying these coaches, and increasing its wagon collection, more locomotives were arriving at Falkirk. Clydesmill No. 3, a typical Scottish industrial locomotive, was built by Andrew Barclay and Sons Ltd. of Kilmarnock in 1928 for the Clyde Valley Electric Power Company. She was given to the S.R.P.S. by the South of Scotland Electricity Board late in 1969. Arrangements were made to run her to Falkirk under her own steam, and on a cold January day in 1970 an epic voyage commenced. No. 3 had been in store for two years, and the first attempt to steam her had failed miserably. One of her axle boxes started heating, and at Whifflet two of the accompanying party were despatched to a nearby chemist's shop. At the next stop, Cumbernauld, the offending box was duly dosed with four large bottles of castor oil. It worked! No. 3 steamed happily into Falkirk, driven by a retired driver, Willie Bell. She arrived a trifle late, but was a sight for sore eyes.

In October of the same year, a much larger locomotive came to Falkirk Shed. She was No. 20 of the Wemyss Private Railway, and was one of a number of basically similar heavy 0-6-0 tanks

An impressive convoy of S.R.P.S. rolling stock heads for Shildon in 1975. Pausing at Dunbar station are D49 class 4-4-0 Morayshire *and Caley tank No. 419, plus historic coaches. (*W. S. Sellar*)*

used to transfer coal from mines originally owned by the Wemyss Coal Company to Methil Harbour for shipment or for transfer to B.R. The Private Railway's apparently assured future was cut short by a bad outbreak of fire in Michael Colliery, the most important pit on the line, in 1967. The line lingered on till 1970 though it had been little used during the intervening period.

In the late 1960s the west of Fife had been a stronghold of heavy industrial locomotives and with the prospect of the S.R.P.S. being able to operate a railway, there was inevitable talk of securing one. The Society itself was however fully committed and it was good to hear of the setting up of the Fife Industrial Locomotive Preservation Group - which aimed at preserving a Wemyss engine for service on a preserved line. The chosen engine was No. 20 because at the time of the Michael fire she was being re-boilered and overhauled. Thanks to the generosity of the Wemyss Estates, No. 20 was duly

purchased together with a substantial quantity of spares including a complete set of wheels. Sadly No. 20's trip to Falkirk was not so successful as No. 3's had been. The engine ran hot, damaging her axle boxes and scoring her journals (the parts of the axle which rest in the box). The damage has been repaired sufficiently for No. 20 to be steamed, but she is not as strong as she was, and must be treated with care. The engine is now the property of the S.R.P.S.

The S.R.P.S. withdrew from negotiations with the Highlands and Islands Development Board and B.R. over the Strathspey line in 1971 (see above and further below). While the search for a more convenient alternative went on a policy of retrenchment was adopted at Falkirk. In 1972 the South Scotland Electricity Board kindly donated another Ruston DS88 Diesel shunter from Bonnybridge Power Station, while a third came from the North British Distillery, Edinburgh in 1974, and the North British Saloon made its appearance (see above). By 1973 the Society was actively considering another railway, the Alloa–Dollar branch, which had been retained for coal traffic from the Dollar Mine after passenger services had ceased. With rumours that the remaining locomotives at

11

Woodham Brothers scrapyard at Barry were to be cut up, a group of S.R.P.S. clubbed together to form the Locomotive Owners Group (Scotland) Ltd (L.O.G.S.) to buy a B.R. suburban tank engine No. 80105. The purchase price of £4000 was raised surprisingly quickly, but the cost of removal from Barry to Falkirk (£1400 plus V.A.T.) seemed a stumbling block. At one stage the possibility of shipping the locomotive to Glasgow was investigated, but in the end it proved cheaper to use road transport, and No. 80105 came up the M6 and A80 in fine style, arriving at Larbert in October 1973.

The prospect of acquiring a railway put a premium on fund raising, and to house a sales stand an ex-L.N.E.R. pigeon van was purchased in 1973. This has done yeoman service. Two more diesels were added to the fleet in 1973–74. One was the third Ruston DS88, and the other was a Scottish-built 0-6-0 built by Andrew Barclay in Kilmarnock for the Admiralty in 1941. The most recent diesel is a 165 h.p. Ruston with electric transmission donated by the British Steel Corporation in 1975.

Prospect for the Alloa–Dollar line still seemed bright in 1974, when the Society opened negotiations with the Royal Scottish Museum about *Morayshire*. This locomotive had been bought in 1964 by an engineer, Ian N. Fraser, who had been a pupil of Sir Nigel Gresley. *Morayshire* was restored to her original L.N.E.R. green livery at Inverurie Works in Aberdeenshire in 1964. Mr Fraser then had the problem of finding somewhere to keep her. From 1965 to 1966 she rested in I.C.I.'s Ardeer factory where she was secure from vandals but exposed to a corrosive atmosphere. With no prospect of running the locomotive, Mr Fraser made an agreement with the Royal Scottish Museum that she should go on display there. Until then she was to be stored in an Admiralty Depot at Dalmeny, near the Forth Railway Bridge. She languished there for nine years, and with the postponement of museum development looked like staying there indefinitely. A group of S.R.P.S. volunteers with experience in locomotive restoration approached Mr Fraser, and then the Royal Scottish Museum with a view to restoring her to running order. The target date set for restoration was the Shildon 'Rail 150'

cavalcade to celebrate the 150th anniversary of the opening of the Stockton and Darlington Railway. As *Morayshire* was built at Darlington Works, her appearance there would be most appropriate. A small squad worked on the locomotive from July 1974, but as August 1975 approached the effort was increased. There were a thousand and one tasks to be tackled, and on top of that No. 419, which was to accompany *Morayshire*, had to be overhauled and her tires re-profiled. At times it seemed that the work would never be completed to schedule. A major set-back occurred during the re-wheeling of No. 419 when one pair of wheels was inserted the wrong way round - a simple matter to put right in a well equipped workshop, but difficult in a dark and draughty shed with jacking and packing the only way of lifting the locomotive. However, all was well on the day, and the two locomotives with three restored coaches worthily represented Scotland and the S.R.P.S. at Shildon.

Unhappily the plans to secure the Alloa–Dollar line were hit by the recession and cutback in Local Authority expenditure, and the Society had to fall back on Falkirk where work is actively in progress on the never-ending tasks of restoration and maintenance. The S.R.P.S. also runs rail tours all the year round. A number each year use some of the preserved coaches, which have travelled as far afield as Mallaig and Kyle of Lochalsh.

The Society's ultimate aim to operate a branch line in Central Scotland and recreate the atmosphere of Scotland's distinctive railways finally came to fruition in 1981 with the opening of the Bo'ness and Kinneil Railway (see next section).

This new development parallels the continuing programme of work at Falkirk where the public are always welcome to view the stock preserved and undergoing restoration. There is usually no charge for admission, except on special open days, although of course support for the Society, by membership, is encouraged. There is a large shop selling railway material. Visitors always have a reasonable chance of seeing some movement, although it is usually only with a diesel shunter.

The Bo'ness and Kinneil Railway

Bo'ness (once known as Borrowstounness), an old Firth of Forth port about fifteen miles from Edinburgh, was once the scene of considerable railway activity with a rail link along the foreshore from Kinneil in the west to Carriden in the east.

There was also a passenger service to Polmount, which ended in 1956, and a complex network of some seven miles of sidings around the harbour and dock. The sidings were used to store withdrawn steam locomotives in 1962–63, after which they were lifted and the site grassed over. On that same land, the S.R.P.S have established the headquarters of their new railway. Bo'ness has gone from being a graveyard of steam to a scene of its rebirth.

In July 1978, Falkirk District Council granted the Scottish Railway Preservation Society planning permission for 'the formation of a railway system and the erection of an engine shed and station platform at The Foreshore, Bo'ness'. Work began in May 1979, following a grant

Scotland's brand new steam railway at Bo'ness at last has given the S.R.P.S. a line of their own on which their vast and varied collection of rolling stock can be operated. Barclay side tank No. 24 hauls the opening train into the newly-built station with the Clydesmill Barclay saddletank No. 3 in the background. (Bill Roberton)

from the Scottish Tourist Board.

In two years, a green field site alongside the dock basin was transformed into a living steam railway.

The station buildings came from Wormit (at the south end of the Tay Bridge) which closed in 1969. Society members dismantled the old structure and re-erected it at Bo'ness, after remedial work was done.

Essential services such as water, electricity and drains have been put in and an attractive cobbled road laid.

As well as the efforts of S.R.P.S. members, work has been carried out by men from a Special Temporary Employment Scheme; a bricklaying squad from Community Industry, boys from Polmont Borstal and Royal Engineers Territorials, who spent two weekends in August 1980 laying track as an exercise.

The society's long-term aim is to operate trains along the entire five-mile branch from the town to the former Bo'ness Junction, on the Edinburgh-Glasgow main line. However, British Rail's price of £114,000 for the track was well beyond the society's means.

The S.R.P.S therefore elected to purchase about $1\frac{1}{2}$ miles of track from Kinneil Colliery to just short of a former passing loop at Birkhill, plus a detached section of track over the Avon Viaduct.

This package cost £46,000 and did not include the yard at Kinneil which would have needed to be relaid in any case.

Central Regional Council and Falkirk District Council each agreed to contribute £10,000. The

The Clydesmill Barclay heads a lightweight train along the foreshore at Bo'ness. The coach was built after nationalisation to a postwar L.N.E.R. design. (Phil Wood)

balance has been put up by the Scottish Tourist Board and by the S.R.P.S. itself, which has used up all the society's available cash.

The S.R.P.S will then be able to run trains from Bo'ness to Birkhill, a distance of about three miles once the foreshore line to Kinneil is complete, Kinneil yard relaid and a run-around loop built at Birkhill.

In the future is the relaying of the entire branch to Bo'ness Junction and a new connection with the main line plus the extending of facilities at Bo'ness, such as a maritime museum and a museum of industrial archaeology which, linked to a working steam railway, would put Bo'ness firmly on the tourist map of Scotland.

The railway triumphantly opened to traffic on 27 June 1981 amidst a Spectacular Festival of Transport. Vehicles of every kind, from horse-drawn to hang gliders, launched the railway in grand style, with thousands of passengers carried on the trains during its first weekend of operation.

Stock

Much of the stock now at Bo'ness was formerly housed at Falkirk, and more will be transferred as the scale of railway operations increases. However, the line's largest locomotive was delivered direct to Bo'ness from the docks where it had arrived from Sweden. It is one of the handsome SJ (Swedish State Railways) B class 4-6-0s, No. 1313, built in 1917. This impressive machine has been restored to its original livery of green and silver-grey and dwarfs its native Scottish shedmates.

Services are normally in the hands of the three industrial tank locomotives, Barclay 0-6-0 side tank No. 24 (complete with Giesl ejector chimney), Barclay 0-4-0ST *Clydesmill No. 3* and Hawthorn Leslie 0-4-0ST *Sir John King*.

Only two passenger vehicles have so far been transferred from Falkirk – a B.R.-built brake-composite of L.N.E.R. design and the North British Railway Invalid Saloon, but more coaches will come to Bo'ness as required.

The Strathspey Railway

The Strathspey Railway is undoubtedly the most ambitious railway preservation project in Scotland. It has about five miles of track between Aviemore and Boat of Garten and some track-bed beyond. The scheme had its inception in a schoolboy's letter to the S.R.P.S. in April 1967, suggesting that the Society acquire one of the two lines between Aviemore and Grantown-on-Spey, $12\frac{3}{4}$ and $14\frac{1}{2}$ miles long, to run a summer steam service initially, and eventually a winter service. The schoolboy was the son of a Highlands and Islands Development Board Official, and it was found the the H.I.D.B. was interested in developing a steam-hauled tourist railway on this route. Detailed investigation by the S.R.P.S. revealed that the aim of running to Grantown-on-Spey was impractical, and attention was concentrated on the Aviemore-Boat of Garten section of the line to Forres via Gran-

town. This had been built by the Inverness and Perth Junction Railway and opened in 1863, but had been abandoned for passenger traffic in 1965. The Aviemore–Boat of Garten section was retained to give access to the G.N.S.R. line to Craigellachie till November 1968. This five-mile stretch is well suited to operation by a preservation group, as it is, despite its situation in the heart of the Highlands, almost level; there are no major engineering works. The S.R.P.S. had detailed discussions with the H.I.D.B. and B.R., but though the Board promised substantial help to the Society, the high price demanded by B.R. gave cause for concern. Delays in reaching agreement with B.R., concern about its ability to raise enough money to fulfil its side of the bargain, and the feeling that adequate voluntary help might not be forthcoming, led the S.R.P.S. to withdraw by resolution at its A.G.M. in 1971.

L.M.S. Black Five *No. 5025 runs round its train at Boat of Garten on the Strathspey Railway in Scotland. (*Phil Wood*)*

The decision was, however, not unanimous, and a group of members made an independent approach to B.R. and H.I.D.B. to take over the project. The Strathspey Railway Company Ltd was registered, and reached agreement on price, £44,250, and grant. As a gesture of goodwill, the S.R.P.S. presented the new company with the distillery Pug *Dailuaine* and some wagons, which were at Aviemore and had been given by the Scottish Malt Distillers to the Society.

The Strathspey Company had acquired a very basic railway. The trackwork had been drastically simplified, and the locomotive shed at Aviemore, part of the property acquired, had not only been disconnected, but occupied by a scrap dealer and a joiner. Getting access to the shed at Aviemore has in fact been a serious problem for the Strathspey, and it was not until December 1976 that the first two roads in the shed were re-commissioned, though the re-laying of track to it had started late in 1972.

Stock

The first working locomotive arrived in 1972, a Simplex four-wheeled diesel from Aberdeen Gas Works, presented by the Scottish Gas Board, and this was followed by one of the 0-4-0STs from Granton Gas Works, Edinburgh,

the first working steam locomotive at Boat of Garten. The S.R. named her *Forth*. To provide a focus for voluntary effort on the line, the Strathspey Railway Association was founded in April 1972, the relationship between the Association and the Company being modelled on the pioneer Welsh preserved lines.

Two of the Strathspey Railway's first Directors were Mr W. E. C. Watkinson and Mr Ian L. Fraser, both deeply committed to Railway Preservation. Mr Watkinson's generosity to the S.R.P.S. in its formative years has already been mentioned. When steam traction was finally abandoned by B.R. in 1968, he bought from them a Stanier 'Black Five' 4-6-0, B.R. No. 45025 (L.M.S. 5025), and during 1969 had her overhauled by the Hunslet Engine Co. in Leeds. (She was one of the first, built in 1934.) He intended her for the Aviemore–Boat line, and when the Strathspey Company was formed he promised that this locomotive would be available for work on the line. In the meantime she worked on the Keighley and Worth Valley

OPPOSITE: *Awaiting its return to active service inside Aviemore engine shed is Caledonian Railway 0-6-0 No. 828. This engine was in Glasgow Transport Museum until 1980. (*Bill Roberton*)*

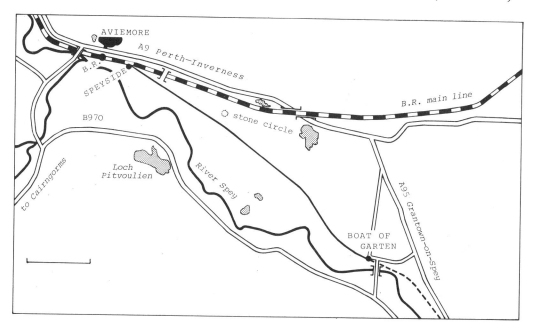

17

Railway, where resplendent in L.M.S. black-lined livery, she attracted a good deal of attention. Eventually she became unfit for further work, and her move north was made via Kilmarnock where she was overhauled by Andrew Barclay and Sons Ltd. She reached Boat of Garten on 29 May 1975 after a ten-hour journey under her own steam. It was No. 5025 which marked the re-opening of the shed at Aviemore on 14 December 1976, by breaking a tape stretched across one of the tracks. The other main line locomotives on the line are mostly of the post-war Ivatt 2MT class 2-6-0 lightweight mixed traffic locomotives which put in useful work in Scotland. The working example is Mr Fraser's engine, No. 46464, built at Crewe in 1950. She spent most of her life working round Arbroath, Mr Fraser's home; where she was known as 'The Carmylie Pilot' because she worked the light railway to the Carmylie Quarries. When she was withdrawn, Mr Fraser bought her from B.R. He offered her to the Dundee Corporation Museum, but unfortunately they could not accommodate her in their Museum and she was too large for any of their stores. She was therefore put under cover in a closely fitting wooden case in a warehouse at Dundee harbour, where she stayed till March 1975 when she too made her way to Boat of Garten. The Company bought a sister engine, No. 46512, from Woodham's scrapyard at Barry, in 1973, and she was moved to Bewdley on the Severn Valley Railway for preparation there before the journey north. A further example, No. 46428, was also acquired from Barry as a source of spare parts.

Undoubtedly the most beautiful engine on the Strathspey Railway is Caledonian Railway goods engine No. 828, resplendent in its brilliant blue livery. It was bought for preservation in 1964 when it was withdrawn from service as B.R. No. 57566. After two years in store, it was restored to 'Caley' livery at Cowlairs Works before entering Glasgow Transport Museum as a static exhibit. It had always been the desire of its owners, the Scottish Locomotive Preservation Trust Fund, to return it to working order, so it was transferred from the museum in 1980 and is now undergoing work to enable it to steam again.

The other locomotives at Aviemore are all industrials. A third Barclay 0-4-0ST came in 1973 from the South of Scotland Electricity Board at Renfrew. The Company named her *Clyde*, and she hauled the first steam train on the railway, a Directors' and Shareholders' Special on 6 April 1974. She was also an attraction at the steam days held during 1974–5. A 0-6-0T has also been secured from the Wemyss Private Railway. The most recent acquisitions are three Austerity 0-6-0STs from English collieries, and a further group of Andrew Barclay saddletanks, mostly obtained from the National Coal Board in Scotland. The principal member of the line's diesel fleet is British Railway's 'Peak' class main-line diesel-electric locomotive No. 44008, now named *Schiehallion*.

The rolling stock on the S.R. has been acquired with a view to economical operation, and is mainly of B.R. standard design. There are, however, coaches of L.M.S. and Great North of Scotland origin. A notable item is a buffet car 'Glenfiddich', once used on the Edinburgh–Glasgow multiple-unit diesel service, and presented to the Company by William Grant and Sons Ltd, distillers of Glenfiddich.

A journey down the line

An entirely new station has been built at Aviemore near the site of the engine shed, Aviemore Speyside. The increased traffic on the B.R. line which has followed from the opening of the Aviemore Centre, means that the original Aviemore station could not provide facilities for the Strathspey Railway without interfering with B.R. services. The new station has a correct 'period atmosphere' because it is being con-structed with material from the disused station at Dalnaspidal, on the main Perth–Inverness line some twenty-five miles south of Aviemore.

Leaving Aviemore, the line runs past Spey Lodge, a railwaymen's holiday home, and out along the heather-clad valley (or 'strath') of the River Spey. Near the lineside are the remains of a stone circle built *c.* 1500 B.C. by the Beaker people – a reminder of more than three thousand years of habitation of the area. The railway then runs through the widening Strath, with the foothills of the Cairngorms to the south and east, and the Monadhliaths to the west of the line. There is no road near the line, only a track leading to a settlement which dates from mediaeval times, Kinchurdy farm, some three miles out of Aviemore. In the open country, wildlife may be seen, particularly deer, hares, and red squirrels.

Unlike many other sections of the Highland Railway, there are no steep gradients on the line, only a slight rise from each terminus to near the half-way point, at the bridge over the track to Kinchurdy. The railway is then only 800 feet above sea level, yet within ten miles are four of the five highest mountains in Britain. After the half-way point, the line descends gently to Boat of Garten, originally the junction for the G.N.S.R.'s Speyside branch, and therefore larger than it might have been. The buildings date largely from the 1860s, and a museum there contains photographs of the line in the past and a model of the station in the 1950s. There are two typical Highland Railway signal boxes. The footbridge is of the original (standard H.R.) design, but the actual structure was moved, like Aviemore Speyside station, from Dalnaspidal.

The Society already owns the track-bed from Boat of Garten onwards for about $4\frac{1}{2}$ miles to Broomhill. Regular passenger services from Aviemore Speyside to Boat of Garten started in 1979 (at weekends from May to September, with mid-week services in 'high season'). After seven years of hard work and sometimes of un-certainty, the Railway's future seems secure.

At Boat of Garten on the Strathspey Railway as Ivatt Class 2MT 2-6-0 No. 46464 is prepared for its next trip to Aviemore (Speyside). The railway has three of this class. (Bill Roberton)

Lochty Private Railway

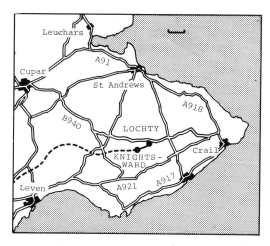

Since 1967 it has been possible to travel behind steam locomotives on summer Sunday afternoons on the Lochty Private Railway, a remarkable line owned by Mr John Cameron. He was one of many Scottish railway enthusiasts thrilled by the use of A4 streamlined Pacific locomotives on the three-hour Glasgow–Aberdeen express trains from 1961. *Union of South Africa*, No. 60009, was already familiar in Scotland, as for many years she had hauled Edinburgh–King's Cross expresses, and had been based at Haymarket Shed. When she was withdrawn from service in 1966, Mr Cameron bought her, originally for preservation in a museum. She bade a triumphant farewell to main-line operation in March 1967, when piloted by a 'Black Five', and hauling a 700-ton 18-coach train, she achieved a record time of 87

Lochty station is the start of a 1¼-mile ride on the Lochty Private Railway. (Fife Railway Preservation Group)

minutes for the 89 miles from Perth to Aberdeen. Shortly afterwards she was removed by road to her new home at the Lochty. Mr Cameron had purchased a farm through which ran part of the route of the freight-only East Fife Central Railway, which terminated in a field at Lochty. He immediately saw the possibility of relaying part of the line for *Union of South Africa*, and accordingly about half a mile of ex-colliery rail was laid by Mr Cameron and

L.P.R.: the loco is a Peckett 0-4-0 from the British Aluminium Company at nearby Burntisland. The 'nameplate' reads 'B.A. Co. Ltd.'. (Fife Railway Preservation Group)

volunteer assistants, who form the Fife Railway Preservation Group.

One advantage of the railway being bordered by land owned by Mr Cameron is that no statutory authority was necessary for services.

In the summer of 1967 No. 60009 was steamed on her own, but in the following year one of the ex-L.N.E.R. 'beaver tail' observation cars built for the pre-war 'Coronation' Edinburgh–King's Cross high-speed service came to Lochty, and a public service was operated. Though Lochty is far from public transport, enough people found

their way there to justify extension to a terminus at Knightsward, $1\frac{1}{4}$ miles from Lochty. No run-round facility exists at this terminal, so the train is gently backed to its starting point. *Union of South Africa* left Lochty in 1973 to 'return to steam' on B.R., but the summer service is still operated by one of the tiny Peckett 0-4-0ST engines from the British Aluminium Company's Works at Burntisland, the Barclay 0-4-0ST *Forth*, formerly on the Strathspey Railway, a similar locomotive, NCB No. 21, which came from Frances Colliery, Dysart in 1981, an Austerity 0-6-0ST from the Wemyss Private Railway, and a Ruston Diesel Shunter from the North British Distillery, Edinburgh. No. 60009 runs occasional excursions, now based at Markinch, Fife.

IRELAND

Railway Preservation Society of Ireland

The Society is the only body in Ireland operating mainline steam engines, and enjoys a close co-operation with the Irish railway companies C.I.E. and N.I.R. No restrictions are placed on routes over which steam can run and the Society's tours are exclusively steam-hauled. The annual tour programme usually comprises one-day outings from Dublin and then Belfast in the spring, followed by the big one – a two-day two-engine all-steam tour from Dublin over part of the C.I.E. system. The summer is the time for the season of four 'Portrush Flyer' steam excursion trains – an accurate recreation of the Ulster excursion train to the seaside. Then, to round things off, another one-day tour is operated in Northern Ireland in September.

The R.P.S.I. was formed in 1964 to obtain some examples of Ireland's steam locomotives and to restore and maintain them in working order. The Society's base is at Whitehead

A much-travelled centenarian, the J15 class 0-6-0 No. 186, provides broad gauge motive power at the R.P.S.I.'s Whitehead depot. The third vehicle is the twelve-wheeled Rosslare Express *tricomposite brake coach. (Charles Friel)*

The lure of steam in Ireland is personified by the elegant sky blue 4-4-0 No. 171 Slieve Gullion *seen here at Londonderry Waterside station on an R.P.S.I. tour. (Charles Friel)*

Excursion Station, built by the L.M.S. (N.C.C.) in 1903 to cope with the day-trip traffic from Belfast. The facilities include a long platform and water tower, together with the original two-road engine shed and the recently added three-road extension built by the members. The Society carries out its own minor repairs, painting and cleaning.

Stock

Pride of place in the Society's collection must go to *Slieve Gullion*, the handsome, high-stepping 4-4-0 in its beautiful Great Northern Railway livery of sky-blue and scarlet. The engine was designed by Clifford and built, as were so many G.N.R. engines, by Beyer Peacock of Manchester in 1913. She was rebuilt by Glover in 1938 and is the last example of the five 'Mountain' class 4-4-0s – a typical Edwardian express engine. These locomotives pulled trains on the Belfast to Dublin and Londonderry lines.

Reminiscent of the L.M.S. 2-6-4 suburban tank classes is the 'Jeep', or N.C.C. tank No. 4. This was one of eighteen class WT engines which were used extensively by the Ulster Transport Authority, later Northern Ireland Railways. Their last task was the hauling of the twenty-wagon two-engine spoil trains on the Belfast-Larne line, and when No. 4 was bought by the Society in 1971 for £1,275 she was the last steam engine still in company service in the British Isles.

There are two J15 class 0-6-0 goods engines from the Great Southern and Western Railway. They are examples of Ireland's largest class of locomotive. In all 111 of this type were built from 1866 onwards at Inchicore to the design of MacDonnell. These locomotives were typical examples of the Ramsbottom/Webb Crewe tradition and were to be found throughout the Great Southern system. They were very successful machines and were mainly used for freight and local passenger workings, with a top speed in the low sixties. No. 186 is now the oldest working steam engine in Ireland, having been built by Sharp Stewart in 1879. Sister engine No. 184 is the saturated steam version of

There's nothing quite like an Irish railtour. Sky blue and scarlet 4-4-0 No. 171 Slieve Gullion *gets underway through the suburbs of Dublin with a heavily-laden train for Sligo. (*Phil Wood*)*

the J15 class. Until the 1940s this locomotive was fitted with the old type of double smokebox doors. Some years ago No. 184 was used in the making of the film *Darling Lili*. Both J15s have since had starring roles in the Michael Chrichton film *The First Great Train Robbery*.

Representing one of Ireland's smaller independent railway companies is the 0-6-4 tank *Lough Erne*, again a Beyer Peacock product. She is the last surviving locomotive of the Sligo, Leitrim and Northern Counties Railway, which had been operated principally by 0-6-4Ts since 1882. It was the last conventional steam locomotive built for any Irish railway and passed to the U.T.A. on closure of the Sligo line. It was purchased privately for preservation in 1970 and has subsequently been bought by the R.P.S.I.

Short passenger trips within the Whitehead depot are usually in the hands of the Hudswell Clarke 0-4-0ST *Guinness*, while in reserve there is the Avonside 0-6-0ST *R.H. Smythe*. This engine ran over the lines of the Londonderry Port and Harbour Commissioners until the late 1950s when she became redundant and was bought by a clergyman. He sold her to the Society for a penny in 1972 and since then the Whitehead locomotive maintenance team have been working hard on overhauling her.

Forming the trains which the Society operates on its railtours are mainly post-war steel-bodied G.N.R. vehicles, but there is also a twelve-wheeled brake/composite coach which once formed part of the G.S. & W.R. *Rosslare Express* out of Dublin in Edwardian days, and a G.N.R. directors' saloon of 1911 vintage.

Each year the Society operates several main-line railtours over the N.I.R. and C.I.E. systems. R.P.S.I. tours are designed for the enthusiast with plenty of photographic and tape-recording opportunities with special stops, runpasts, lineside buses and train-splitting on two-engine tours.

Irish Steam Preservation Society

Shane's Castle Railway

This Society operates a ¾-mile long, 3 ft gauge steam railway in the grounds of Stradbally Hall, Stradbally, County Laois in the Irish Republic. In addition to the railway, the Society has a steam museum in the town of Stradbally, which is opened on request at any time, by prior appointment. Each year the railway is a major attraction during the National Traction Engine Rally held in the grounds of Stradbally Hall at the beginning of August. It is also hoped to operate the line for open days on other days, particularly if there are any other suitable functions in the town, as well as on Easter Sunday and Monday and the last weekend in October.

The Society was founded in 1965 by some local traction engine enthusiasts. The present 3 ft gauge railway was started in 1969 and has been gradually extended since then as far as limited finance and voluntary labour have allowed. The Society organises the National Traction Engine Rally each year and the railway represents the only steam ride available to the public.

Stock
On the Stradbally line, motive power is provided by an Andrew Barclay 0-4-0 tank dating from 1949, hauling a 45-seat 'toastrack' bogie coach. In the museum in Stradbally town is one of the intriguing 0-4-0 tanks built by Spence for the Guinness brewery in Dublin. The engine operated on the 1 ft 10 in. gauge, but could be hoisted onto a 5 ft 3 in. gauge chassis which it drove through rollers, and thus carry out broad gauge shunting. There is a 5 ft 3 in. gauge Drewry petrol railcar on display in the museum too.

The Shane's Castle Light Railway opened in May 1971 and is currently the only narrow gauge steam-operated railway in regular use anywhere in Ireland. The railway runs from the terminus on the edge of Antrim through a largely wooded setting to the ruins of Old Shane's Castle. The area is also a nature reserve, which is jointly managed with the Royal Society for the Protection of Birds. Although the S.C.R. is essentially a tourist attraction, built after all the original Irish 3 ft gauge lines had closed, it is a charming little railway and deservedly popular with its many visitors.

The idea of establishing a railway at Shane's Castle goes back to the post-war years when the relics of a 2 ft gauge military line existed here. This, coupled with the rapid rise of the railway preservation movement in England, inspired Lord O'Neill to start a similar project in Northern Ireland. What has been achieved is the construction of a 1½ mile line which has become the home for an interesting and varied collection of locomotives and rolling stock.

No. 1 *Tyrone* is the oldest locomotive on the line and worked for many years at Larne Harbour for the British Aluminium Company. Built by Pecketts of Bristol in 1904, it is a most picturesque machine and has something of the atmosphere created by Emmett in his *Punch* magazine cartoons.

No. 3 *Shane* is a more modern Barclay 0-4-0 welltank and came to Shane's Castle from Portarlington after being in storage following a relatively short working life. Being much larger than No. 1, it is the principal passenger-hauling engine on the line..

No. 5 *Nancy* is by far the largest locomotive on the railway but is in very poor condition, having been stored in the open for ten years following the closure of the Eastwell Ironstone Quarries in Leicestershire. *Nancy* was built by the Avonside Engine Co. in 1908 specially for ironstone work.

The two diesels, *Rory* and *Nippy*, have much less visual appeal than the steam engines and are

Bringing back memories of Ireland's roadside narrow gauge lines, Peckett 0-4-0T No. 1 Tyrone threads its way through the wooded grounds of Shane's Castle. (Charles Friel)

not commonly used for passenger work. Most of the carriages are of the covered bogie type with sides open above the waist and were built in the Shane's Castle workshops. These have been joined by three former metre-gauge Belgian tramcars from the Charleroi Tramway which came from the Cotswold Light Railway in Gloucestershire.

The S.C.R. has also preserved a few items from the old Irish narrow-gauge lines, such as a Ballymena and Larne coal wagon and the Londonderry and Lough Swilly mobile crane and open wagon. Also on site at Shane's Castle is the rolling stock collection of the North West of Ireland Railway Society. These comprise former County Donegal Railways 2-6-4 tank *Columbkille*, built in 1907 and two of the famous Donegal diesel railcars, Nos. 12 and 18. There is also a C.D.R. J.C. composite coach and a few coach underframes. Plans are under discussion about future developments at the railway which could lead to a more ambitious 3 ft gauge museum arising.

Belfast Transport Museum

The museum houses part of the Ulster Folk Museum collection and covers all aspects of transport. On display are over a hundred vehicles, including railway and tramway examples, also models, equipment and records. The long red-brick building in Witham Street, East Belfast, has been for many years the home of the collection but the exhibits may well be moved to the newly designated rail transport museum site at Cultra, near Hollywood.

Stock

The Irish standard gauge of 5 ft 3 in. is represented by five steam locos, a diesel railcar and a horse tram. From the Belfast and County Down Railway comes 4-4-2 tank No. 30, built in 1901. This is a typical Beyer Peacock design developed from earlier 2-4-2T engines. The class was responsible for the bulk of B. & C.D.R. passenger train haulage. This locomotive became U.T.A. No. 30 and was stored from 1956 to 1961 when it was restored to its original livery and placed on display. From the Great Northern comes 2-4-2T No. 93, one of Clifford's JT class built in 1895 and originally named *Sutton*. For English visitors, the lines of L.M.S (N.C.C) 4-4-0 No. 74 *Dunluce Castle* will be familiar. It was designed by Sir Henry Fowler of the Midland Railway and can be regarded as an Irish version of his L.M.S. class 2P 4-4-0s built contemporarily at Derby.

Pride of place in the museum goes to Great Southern Railway 4-6-0 No. 800 *Maeve*. This locomotive and its two sisters were the crack locomotives of Ireland. Apart from the G.W.R. 'King' class, they were probably the most powerful 4-6-0s in Western Europe and were introduced with a view to speeding up the Dublin – Cork services. The magnificent bronze nameplates were inscribed in Erse after ancient queens of Ireland and the spelling 'Maeve' is the English rendering. Restored at Inchicore Works, Dublin, in 1963 and presented for display in the following year by the C.I.E.

The Great Northern Railway of Ireland distinguished itself by using every form of rail traction on its system over the years – steam, diesel, electric, battery, petrol and horse! So it is appropriate that an early diesel railcar, designated simply as 'E' and dating from 1934, is on display together with the famous Fintona tram. This vehicle became a celebrity in its own right and ran on the ½-mile Fintona Junction to Fintona Town branch in connection with the mainline trains. It was withdrawn (and the horse retired) when the mainline service ceased. The tram carried first, second and third class passengers, though these distinctions were largely ignored!

Steam on the 3 ft gauge is represented by 2-6-4T *Blanche* from the County Donegal Railways in its geranium red livery, Cavan and Leitrim Railway 4-4-0 tank No. 3 *Kathleen* dating from 1887, Portstewart Tram loco No. 2, built by Kitsons in 1883 and Peckett 0-4-0T No. 2 (a sister engine to *Tyrone* at Shane's Castle). The County Donegal is also represented by its pioneer petrol railcar of 1906, as well as a later Drewry car of 1926 and its unique Atkinson Walker diesel tractor *Phoenix*. Lastly, the 1 ft 10 in. gauge Guinness Brewery system is represented by Spence 0-4-0 tank No. 20 of 1905.

GAZETTEER

by Roger Crombleholme

The following pages list all 70 railways described in the main text, and list and briefly describe 92 other sites of interest. These further entries are chiefly minor steam-powered railways offering rides, but some museums and centres of railway preservation, or even single engines of interest, are included. The choice is of necessity selective, but is intended to show the wide range of the steam preservation movement.

Each entry has

Name of Railway or Museum
Brief description
Address
O.S.REF. TO NATIONAL GRID
TELEPHONE
ACCESS, including rail and bus services where possible.

Details

Opening times
Facilities

Symbols used for facilities are:

P   parking
S   shop selling railway items
R   refreshments
M   museum of railway items
pa picnic area
T   timetable for railway appears in British Rail volume
A   timetable is in *ABC Guide*
t   railway issues its own timetable as leaflet

Each entry is numbered. Italic numbers (e.g. *26*, used for sites not in the main text) refer to the endpaper map. Sites with main-text entries have bold numbers (e.g. **96**), which also refer to the map.

National Grid References
Every Ordnance Survey map is overprinted with a grid. In this *Guide*, references are given to four-figure accuracy. The two letters of the reference designate a hundred-kilometre square, the key to which is given on every map. The number then consists of a two-figure 'easting' and a two-figure 'northing', which together specify a one-kilometre square. Eastings come first. Counting starts from 00, not 11, within each lettered square, and runs across (left to right, west to east), and then upwards.

A.R.P.S. Brochure
The gazetteer refers to 'A.R.P.S. listings': these are given in a summary brochure updated each year. It is available from The Association of Railway Preservation Societies (Steam Train Guide), Sheringham Station, Norfolk NR26 8RA. Please send a stamped addressed envelope.

Whilst we have taken every care in compiling this gazetteer, we cannot be held responsible for any in-accuracies – apart from anything else, the details may change. For exact running times, etc., see the A.R.P.S. list or contact the railways directly.

1

THE SOUTH-WEST

1 Lappa Valley Railway
Passenger-carrying 15 in. gauge steam-operated light railway.
St Newlyn East, Cornwall.
O.S. REF. SW 8356
TEL. Mitchell 317

The railway offers a 1-mile ride along the track-bed of the former G.W.R. Newquay-Chacewater line, commencing from Benny Mill, about one mile north-east of St Newlyn East and running to East Wheal Rose Mine.

Operated daily throughout the holiday season.

P   S   R   pa

2 China Clay Industry Museum
A museum of locomotives, rolling stock and historical machinery associated with the Cornish china clay industry.
Wheal Martyn, Trenance Valley, St Austell, Cornwall.
O.S. REF. SX 0054
TEL. St Austell 850362
ACCESS. Bus route No. 529 St Austell to Bodmin. Nearest B.R. station: St Austell (2 miles).

Amongst the locomotives on display are the 4 ft 6 in. gauge Peckett 0-4-0ST *Lee Moor No. 1* and the standard gauge Bagnall 0-4-0ST *Judy.*

Open daily from 1 April to 31 October between 10 a.m. and 5 p.m.

P   S

3 Forest Railroad Park
Dobwalls, Liskeard, Cornwall.
O.S. REF. SX 2165
TEL. Dobwalls (0579) 20325
ACCESS. Nearest B.R. station: Liskeard.

Judy, *the diminutive Bagnall 0-4-0ST from Par Harbour, can now be found at the China Clay Industry Museum. (*Norman Glover)

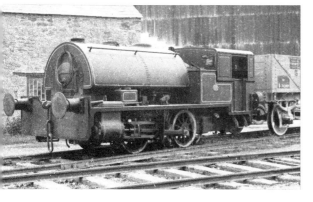

Operates daily from April to October between 10.30 am and 6 p.m. Last admission 5.30 p.m.

P   S   R   M   pa   forest walk   children's playground

4 Dart Valley Railway
Buckfastleigh, Devon.
O.S. REF. SX 7466
TEL. Buckfastleigh 2338
ACCESS. Buckfastleigh station is just off the A38 trunk road, halfway between Exeter and Plymouth. Bus routes Nos. 188 or 189 from Newton Abbot and No. 115 from Totnes.

Services operate over Easter week, then Sundays, May Day Holiday weekend and daily from mid-May to mid-September.

P   S   R   M   T   A   t   pa

5 Torbay and Dartmouth Railway
Paignton Park Station, Torbay Road, Paignton, Devon.
O.S. REF. SX 8860
TEL. Paignton 555872
ACCESS. Torbay and Dartmouth line station is next door to B.R. Paignton Station and the bus station. From South Hams area, make for Dartmouth, then take the ferry to Kingswear station. By public transport: rail from Exeter or beyond, Newton Abbot and Torquay to Paignton B.R. There are frequent local buses to Paignton from the Torbay area itself.

Full daily steam service operates at Easter, then Sundays and daily from mid-May to early October.

S   R   T   A   t

6 West Somerset Railway
Minehead Station, Minehead, Somerset.
O.S. REF. SS 9846
TEL. Minehead 4996
ACCESS. By road, off the main A39 near the seafront. Bus route No. 218 for Watchet or Minehead. The W.S.R.'s own coach meets some trains from Taunton.

Full daily steam service operates from mid-May to early October.

P   S   R   M   t

7 Tiverton Museum
Static steam locomotive exhibit.
St Andrew Street, Tiverton, Devon.
O.S. REF. SS 9512
ACCESS. In centre of town, near Town Hall. Entrance from public car park in Phoenix Lane. Nearest B.R. station: Tiverton Junction (6 miles).

G. W. R. 0-4-2T No. 1442 is on display. Other small exhibits include a large model of a G.W.R. broad gauge 4-4-0T *Lalla Rookh* built c. 1870.

Open all year except Bank Holidays, Monday to Saturday 10.30 a.m. to 4.30 p.m. Admission free.

8 Bicton Woodland Railway

Bicton Gardens, East Budleigh, Budleigh Salterton, Devon.
O.S. REF. SY 0786
TEL. Colaton Raleigh 68465
ACCESS. On A376 Newton Poppleford – Budleigh Salterton Road, slightly north of St Mary's Church. Nearest B.R. station: Exmouth, thence by No. 334 bus on Exmouth-Sidmouth route.

Operates daily from April to October 10 a.m. to 6 p.m.

P   S   R   M

9 Beer Heights Light Railway

Passenger-carrying 7¼ in. gauge steam-operated railway.
Beer Modelrama, Beer, near Seaton, Devon.
O.S. REF. SY 2389
TEL. Seaton 21542 Ext. 36

High on the hillside at the back of the village of Beer is Modelrama, round whose grounds runs the Beer Heights Light Railway, a miniature line built to narrow gauge proportions which runs at present for approximately ⅓ mile from the terminus at Much Natter to White Falls. Future extension is planned to incorporate a tunnel of approx 150 ft in length, diverting the line under the garden, the adjoining lane and car park into the field opposite where there will be a new terminus to be named Little Doing.

The Golden Arrow Pullman Car 'Orion' serves as a restaurant.

P   S   R   A   putting green   children's play corner

10 Seaton and Colyford Electric Tramway

Passenger-carrying 2 ft 9 in. gauge electric tramway.
Riverside Depot, Harbour Road, Seaton, Devon.
O.S. REF. SY 2490
TEL. Seaton 21702
ACCESS. Axminster B.R. station, thence by bus No. 213

The tramway operates along the track-bed of the former L.S.W.R. Seaton branch for 2½ miles as far as Colyton. A 12-minute interval tram service operates at peak periods throughout the holiday season.

P   S

11 Bristol Industrial Museum

Passenger-carrying steam-operated railway adjoining the city's museum of industrial technology.
Princes Wharf, Bristol, Avon.
O.S. REF. ST 5872
TEL. Bristol (0272) 299771 Ext. 290
ACCESS. 5 minutes walk from the centre of Bristol. Nearest B.R. station: Bristol Temple Meads. Car parking adjacent to site in Wapping Road.

A ⅓ mile ride in a G.W.R. 'Toad' brake van between the Museum and the Great Western Dry Dock where Brunel's famous ship, the SS *Great Britain* is on display. Trains are hauled by the Peckett 0-6-0ST *Henbury*. The Museum houses machinery and vehicles associated with Bristol's industrial past.

*The push-pull passenger service at Bitton on the Bristol Suburban Railway. (*Tom Heavyside*)*

Railway operates at intervals throughout the summer season in conjunction with the Industrial Museum. The Museum is open Saturdays – Wednesdays throughout the year from 10 a.m.–12 noon and 1–5 p.m. Admission free.

P   S

12 Bitton Railway Centre

Standard gauge railway preservation centre, featuring steam-hauled train rides on open days.
Bitton Station, Bristol, Avon.
O.S. REF. ST 6770
ACCESS. On the A431 near Willsbridge. Bus route No. 332 Bristol – Bath. Nearest B.R. station: Keynsham (1½ miles).

The Bristol Suburban Railway Society has relaid all the track within station limits at Bitton and extended its running line ⅔ mile to Cherry Garden Lane. Stock includes L.M.S. Class 5 No. 45379 as well as examples of industrial tank locos from the three Bristol manufacturers, Peckett, Avonside and Fox Walker.

Bitton station is open every weekend with steam trains operating on Sundays and Bank Holidays from Easter to the end of September.

P   S   M

13 Oakhill Manor Miniature Railway

Passenger-carrying 10¼ in. gauge steam-operated railway.
Oakhill Manor, near Shepton Mallet, Somerset.
O.S. REF. ST 6447
TEL. Oakhill 840210
ACCESS. Off A37 road, 4 miles north of Shepton Mallet. Turn off at Mendip Inn.

1½ mile ride through the grounds of Oakhill Manor. This railway is being extended to give a total run of 2½ miles through woodland glades and deep cuttings. Trains are hauled by an S.R. 'King Arthur' 4-6-0 and a Curwen

The Oakhill Manor Miniature Railway brings a high degree of realism to its trains and setting. (Oakhill Manor)

'Atlantic'. Oakhill Manor Museum houses one of the finest collections of models in the country.

Operates daily from 12 noon to 6 p.m. Easter to the end of October.

P S R M pa

14 East Somerset Railway

Cranmore Station, Shepton Mallet, Somerset.
O.S. REF. ST 6642
TEL. Cranmore 417
ACCESS. Three miles east of Shepton Mallet on A361 Frome Road. Bus: 'Crown Tours' Shepton – Frome service.

Passenger trains run every Sunday, Bank Holiday and other advertised days from April to the end of October and on Wednesdays in July and August and also on some Sundays in December. The depot is also open at weekends only from November to March inclusive from 9 a.m. to 4 p.m.

P S R pa art gallery

15 Longleat Railway

Passenger-carrying 15 in. gauge light railway.
Longleat Park, near Warminster, Wilts.
O.S. REF. ST 8043
TEL. Maiden Bradley 579

1¼ mile miniature line built to narrow gauge proportions running through the grounds of the Marquis of Bath's Estate at Longleat. Steam motive power includes the Curwen 0-6-2T *Dougal* built in 1970.

Operates daily from Easter to the end of October.

P S R pa amusements, wildlife

16 Great Western Railway Museum

Static steam locomotive exhibits.
Emlyn Square, Swindon, Wiltshire.
O.S. REF. SU 1484
TEL. Swindon 26161 ext. 562
Nearest B.R. station: Swindon.

On display are five G. W. R. locomotives, including *City of Truro* and a replica of the broad-gauge engine *North Star*. There are also smaller railway items and records of G.W.R. interest.

Museum open Monday to Saturday and Sunday afternoons throughout the year. Closed Christmas Day, Boxing Day, New Year's Day and Good Friday.

P nearby

17 Great Western Society Ltd

Didcot Railway Centre, Didcot, Oxfordshire.
O.S. REF. SU 5290
ACCESS. Through Didcot B.R. station.

Open Saturdays, Sundays and Bank Holidays from March to the end of October. Steaming on the first and last Sunday of each month, Bank Holiday weekends (Sunday and Monday) and all August Sundays.

P S R M

18 'Age of Steam'

Passenger-carrying 10¼in. gauge railway operating within the 'Age of Steam' museum and leisure complex.
Rospeath Lane, Crowlas, near Penzance, Cornwall.
O.S. REF. SW 5233
TEL. Cockwells (0736–74) 631
ACCESS. By road and rail to Penzance or St Erth, thence various buses.

The Crowlas Woodland Railway is a 1¼ mile steam railway running through the grounds of the 'Age of Steam' complex. Although of 10¼ in. gauge, it is built to narrow gauge proportions and amongst its motive power are the 0-6-2T *Trevithick* and the Curwen 2-6-0 *Isambard Kingdom Brunel*. The C.W.R., being only 12 miles from Lands End, claims to be England's first and last steam railway!

Operates from Easter to October inclusive. First trains run at 10.30 a.m.

P S R M pa picture gallery, model railways

19 Swanage Railway

Swanage Station, Dorset.
O.S. REF. SZ 0278
ACCESS. B.R. Wareham station, thence Hants and Dorset bus Nos. 141 and 142. By bus from Bournemouth and Poole.

Operates at Easter, then every Sunday until August when a daily service runs. Swanage station is open to visitors every weekend of the year from 10 a.m. to 5 p.m.

P S R

ABOVE: *The Crowlas Woodland Railway runs round the 'Age of Steam' Park. (*'Age of Steam'*)*

20 Bugle Steam Railway

Standard-gauge railway preservation centre with steam-hauled rides available on open days.
Imperial Sidings, Bugle, near St Austell, Cornwall.
O.S. REF. SX 0158
TEL. St Austell 5194 for information
ACCESS. British Rail Bugle station. Alongside A391 Bodmin – St Austell road. Turn up lane by telephone box.

The Cornish Steam Locomotive Preservation Society house their stock in sidings adjoining the former Goonbarrow mineral branch. On open days, passengers are given short rides in a brake van hauled by one of the society's Peckett or Bagnall 0-4-0STs.

Open on the last Sunday in June, the last two Sundays in July and the first Sunday in September, plus every Sunday during August and Bank Holiday Mondays, Easter, May Day, Spring and August between 11 a.m. and 5.30 p.m.

P   R   S   pa

21 Riverside Miniature Railway

Passenger-carrying 7¼ in. gauge steam railway.
Buckfastleigh station, Dart Valley Railway, Devon.
O.S. REF. SX 7466
TEL. Buckfastleigh 2338
ACCESS. Adjacent to the Dart Valley Railway.

The railway forms a continuous circuit round part of the Buckfastleigh riverside picnic area. Trains are hauled by a fine scale replica of the Lynton and Barnstaple Railway 2-6-2T *Yeo*.

Operates at Easter, then on Sundays and daily from mid-May to mid-September from 11 a.m. to 5 p.m.

LONDON
AND THE HOME COUNTIES

22 Mid-Hants Railway (The Watercress Line)
Alresford Station, Hampshire.
O.S. REF. SU 5832
TEL. Alresford 3810, during operating days only
ACCESS. Close to the main A31 Guildford to Winchester Road, or by Alder Valley buses from Alton, Winchester or Southampton. Bus service Nos. 214 and X14 (weekdays) or 452 (Sundays).

Operates on Saturday afternoons, Sundays and Bank Holidays from the end of March to the end of October.

P   S   R   T   t

23 Hollycombe Woodland Railway
Passenger-carrying 2 ft. gauge and standard gauge steam-operated railways.
Hollycombe House, near Liphook, Hampshire.
O.S. REF. SU 8529
TEL. Liphook 723233
ACCESS. A3 and Liphook B.R. station 1½ miles.

The 2 ft gauge line offers a half-mile ride through the grounds of Hollycombe House. The railway runs up to a quarry, where there is a vantage point with extensive views of the South Downs. At the quarry, connection is made with the 300 yard standard gauge line, and demonstrations are given by steam-powered stone-handling and crushing machinery. Narrow gauge stock comprises the Barclay 0-4-0WT *Caledonia* and the Hunslet 0-4-0ST *Jerry M* together with coaches from the former Ramsgate Tunnel Railway. The standard gauge line is powered by the Aveling Porter 0-4-0TG *Sir Vincent*.

Operates every Sunday and Bank Holiday from Easter to September from 12 noon onwards.

P   S   R   M

BELOW: Sir Vincent *provides unconventional motive power for standard gauge passengers at Hollycombe. (*Norman Glover*)*

24 Isle of Wight Steam Railway

Haven Street Station, near Ryde, Isle of Wight.
O.S. REF. SZ 5589
TEL. Wootton Bridge 882204
ACCESS. Service 3 or 43 Southern Vectis bus operates from Ryde Esplanade or Newport and stops outside Haven Street station. Inclusive through 'Awayday' tickets available from Portsmouth Harbour, Ryde Pier Head (rebook facilities for mainland ticket holders), Sandown and Shanklin.

Operates on Easter Sunday and Monday, on Sundays from May to September, on Thursdays in July and August and on Spring and Summer Bank Holidays. Also daily during the week prior to the late Summer Bank Holiday.

P   S   R   M

25 Littlehampton Miniature Railway

Passenger-carrying 12¼ in. gauge steam-operated railway.
Mewsbrook Park, Littlehampton, Sussex.
O.S. REF. TQ 0301
On eastern fringe of town. Nearest B.R. station: Littlehampton.

Half-mile through Mewsbrook Park. The locomotives are a pair of 4-6-4 tender locomotives constructed from parts manufactured by Bullock for two 10¼ in. gauge tank engines.

The railway operates at Easter, then at weekends until Spring Bank Holiday after which operation is daily until mid-Sept.

26 Great Cockcrow Railway

Passenger-carrying 7¼ in. gauge steam-operated railway.
Hardwick Lane, Lyne, near Chertsey, Surrey.
O.S. REF. TQ 027662

Choice of two ⅞ mile runs are available, each starting and finishing at Hardwick Central station. Intensive operation is a feature of the Great Cockcrow Railway, which is fully signalled and consists of a double-track main line with interlinked single-track loops. A branch line over 300 yards long, including a 45 ft viaduct was opened for the 1980 season and adds to the variety of operation. As many as six trains may be in operation simultaneously. Resident locomotive stock amounts to ten steam locomotives, mainly of the 2-6-0 and 4-6-0 types.

Operates on Sundays from the first Sunday in May to the last Sunday in October between 2.45 p.m. and 5.45 p.m.

P

27 Science Museum

Static steam locomotives and other historic transport exhibits.
Exhibition Road, South Kensington, London SW7.
O.S. REF. TQ 3679
TEL. 01-589 3456 Ext. 562
ACCESS. L.T. Underground, South Kensington Station. Parking is metered. Bus routes Nos. 9, 14, 30, 45, 49, 52, 73 and 74.

Amongst the many historic locomotives on view are *Puffing*

Pride of the L.T. collection at Covent Garden is Metropolitan Railway 4-4-0T No. 23. (L.T.)

Billy, Rocket, Sanspareil and G.W.R. No. 4073 *Caerphilly Castle.*

Open weekdays from 10 a.m. to 6 p.m. and Sundays from 2.30 p.m. to 6 p.m. Closed on 1 January, Good Friday, May Day Monday, 24, 25 and 26 December. Admission free.

S   R

28 London Transport Museum

Static steam locomotives and other historic transport exhibits.
Old Flower Market Hall, Covent Garden, London WC2.
O.S. REF. TQ 3080
TEL. 01-379 6344
ACCESS. Nearest Underground station: Covent Garden, Leicester Square or Charing Cross. Buses to Strand or Aldwych.

The LT collection spans nearly 150 years of transport in the London area. Amongst the locomotives exhibited are the Metropolitan Railway 4-4-0T No. 23 and the Wotton Tramway 0-4-0TG built by Aveling Porter in 1872. The museum also houses London buses, trolleybuses and trams, posters, signs, tickets and other exhibits.

Open daily from 10 a.m. to 6 p.m. throughout the year. Closed Christmas Day and Boxing Day.

S   R   lecture room   research library

29 Southall Railway Centre

Standard gauge working steam railway museum.
Bridge Road, Southall, Middlesex.
O.S. REF. TQ 1379

The centre is run by the G.W.R. Preservation Group who are restoring 3 G.W.R. locos, the largest of which is 2-8-0 No. 2885. The working loco is Stephenson saddletank *Birkenhead* and visitors can take rides in a G.W. brake van.

Open days at intervals throughout the year as advertised.

30 Bluebell Railway
Sheffield Park, Sussex.
O.S. REF. TQ 4023
TEL. Newick 2370
ACCESS. On A275 East Grinstead to Lewes road.

Open Sundays Jan., Feb., Dec.; Saturdays and Sundays Mar., Apr. and Nov.; Bank Holidays, Wednesdays, Saturdays and Sundays in May and October; daily June to September.

P S R T A t

31 Romney, Hythe and Dymchurch Railway
New Romney, Kent.
O.S. REF. TR 0724
TEL. New Romney 2353
ACCESS. Near A259 Hythe to New Romney road.

Operates daily Easter to end Sept.; also Saturdays and Sundays in Mar., Oct. and Nov.

P S R T A t

32 Birchley Railway
Passenger-carrying 10¼ in. gauge steam-operated railway.
Birchley House, Biddenden, Ashford, Kent.
O.S. REF. TQ 8437
TEL. Biddenden 291413
ACCESS. Nearest stations: Headcorn B.R. or Tenterden Town K. & E.S.R.

The railway will ultimately offer a ¾-mile run over a figure-of-eight track. Trains are operated over part of the layout whilst construction work is in progress. The line is notable for its working model of a Stroudley 'Terrier' No. 84 *Crowborough*.

Regular operation of the railway has not yet commenced though operating days are held from time to time. Visitors are asked to telephone beforehand to check whether trains are running.

33 Kent and East Sussex Railway
Tenterden Station, Kent.
O.S. REF. TQ 8833
TEL. Tenterden 2943

Operates weekends and Bank Holidays Easter to end Oct.; daily end July to early Sept.; Sundays to end of year.

P S R T A t

34 Sittingbourne and Kemsley Light Railway
Sittingbourne, Kent.
O.S. REF. TQ 9064
TEL. Sittingbourne 24899
ACCESS is from Milton Road.

Operates every weekend from Easter to mid-Oct.; selected days throughout year (see A.R.P.S. listings).

P S R t

35 Volks Railway
Passenger-carrying 2 ft 8½ in. gauge electric railway.
Madeira Drive, Brighton, East Sussex.
O.S. REF. TQ 3103
TEL. Brighton 681061
ACCESS. All buses to Old Steine pass the Aquarium terminus of the railway, 100 yards off Palace Pier.

The railway offers a breezy 1¼ mile ride along Brighton seafront from Aquarium to Black Rock. Volks Railway was the first electric railway in Great Britain, opened in 1883.

Trains run approximately every five minutes daily from April to September.

36 Chalk Pits Museum
Open-air industrial museum featuring a 2 ft gauge demonstration railway.
Amberley, near Arundel, West Sussex.
O.S. REF. TQ 0312
TEL. Bury (079881) 370
ACCESS. On B2139 road near Amberley B.R. station.

The museum is set in a former chalk quarry and consists of a 36-acre site on which the industrial past of the south-east may be studied and preserved. Amongst the narrow gauge motive power already collected is a Decauville 0-4-0T *Progrès*. Demonstration industrial trains are otherwise hauled by diesels. The large collection of locomotives and rolling stock from Brockham Museum is now housed here.

Open from 11 a.m. to 5 p.m. Wednesday to Sunday and Bank Holidays from April to October.

P S

37 Alderney Railway
Passenger-carrying standard gauge railway.
Braye Road Station, Alderney, Channel Islands.
TEL. Alderney 3180
ACCESS. By air from Southampton, Shoreham (Aurigny Air Lines), Hurn (AAF) and Inter-Island.

A construction train at work on the Chalk Pits Museum railway. (Chalk Pits Museum)

Originally opened in 1847, the Alderney Railway was the first in the Channel Islands, yet ran its first regular passenger trains as recently as 1980! Wickham petrol railcars running as multiple-units operate a regular service over the two mile line to Mannez Quarry. A steam locomotive was acquired for the 1982 season.

Trains run weekends between Easter and October; off-season by arrangement.

38   Hampshire Narrow Gauge Railway Society
Passenger-carrying 2 ft gauge steam-operated railway.
'Four Winds', Durley, Hants.
O.S. REF. SU 5116
TEL. Durley 331

The Society built this short narrow gauge line for their own enjoyment and operate it for the benefit of invited visiting groups. Amongst the steam motive power available is the Hunslet 0-4-0ST *Cloister*, the Bagnall 0-4-0ST *Wendy* and a 'Feldbahn' 0-8-0T from the trench railways of World War I.

Operates on average once a month between 1 p.m. and 5 p.m. as required.

All the charm of narrow gauge travel personified by Wendy *at Durley. (*P.C. Hammond*)*

EAST ANGLIA

39   Nene Valley Railway
Wansford Station, Stibbington, near Peterborough, Cambridgeshire.
O.S. REF. TL 9097
TEL. Stamford 782854
ACCESS. Just off A1, one mile south of junction with A47. Bus routes Nos. 265, 266, 312, 316 and 323 from Peterborough to Orton Mere. (Frequency approx. 40 minutes.) DMU service from Peterborough (B.R.) to Orton Mere on Sundays and Bank Holidays.

Operates at weekends and Bank Holidays from April to October, and on Tuesdays, Wednesdays and Thursdays in June, July and August.

P   S   R   M   t

40   The Cushing Steam Collection
A unique collection of steam traction engines and fairground organs, also incorporating a passenger-carrying 1 ft 10¾ in. gauge steam-operated railway.
Thursford Green, near Fakenham, Norfolk.
O.S. REF. TF 9834
TEL. Fakenham 3839
ACCESS. Off the A148 Fakenham – Cromer road.

¾ mile ride from behind the steam organ museum through Norfolk farmland. Motive power is provided by the Hunslet Quarry 0-4-0ST *Cackler*.

Open every afternoon from Easter weekend to 31 October and every Sunday and Bank Holiday throughout the year 2 p.m. to 5.30 p.m.

P   R   S   M   pa

41   North Norfolk Railway
Sheringham Station, Sheringham, Norfolk.
O.S. REF. TG 1543
TEL. Sheringham 822045

Open mid-March to early Oct.; passenger service: Saturdays and Sundays late May to early Oct.; Bank Holidays; also additional days, for details of which see A.R.P.S. listings.

P   S   R   M   A   T

42   Barton House Railway
Passenger-carrying 3½ in. gauge steam-operated railway and museum of full-size railway equipment (much from the M. & G.N.).
Barton House, Hartwell Road, The Avenue, Wroxham, Norfolk.
O.S. REF. TG 3017
TEL. Wroxham 2470
Nearest B.R. station: Wroxham.

80-yard ride round oval of raised track on 'sit-astride' rolling stock.

Operates third Sunday afternoon of each month, April to Oct., plus Easter Monday.

P nearby R

43 Bressingham Steam Museum and Gardens
Bressingham Hall, Diss, Norfolk.
O.S. REF. TM 0880
TEL. Bressingham 386

Open Thursdays, Sundays and Bank Holidays, May-September, also at Easter and on Wednesdays during August only. Opening time 1.30 p.m.

P S R M gardens

44 Audley End Miniature Railway
Passenger-carrying 10¼ in. gauge steam-operated railway.
Audley End House, near Saffron Walden, Essex.
O.S. REF. TL 5336
TEL. Saffron Walden 22354
ACCESS. Off the A11 adjacent to Audley End House. Nearest B.R. station, Audley End (1 mile).

1½ mile ride through the grounds of Audley End House through attractive woodlands, crossing the River Cam twice. Features four steam locomotives, a Rio Grande 2-8-2, an L.M.S. 'Royal Scot' 4-6-0, a G.N.R. 'Atlantic' and a Curwen 2-6-2.

The railway operates on Sundays and Bank Holidays from May to October, plus Tuesdays, Wednesdays, Thursdays and Saturdays in the school summer holidays.

P R S pa

45 Colne Valley Railway
Castle Hedingham Station, near Halstead, Essex.
O.S. REF. TL 7736
TEL. Hedingham 61174.
On the A604, ½ mile north of Castle Hedingham. Nearest B.R. station: Braintree.

See A.R.P.S. Listings for operating times.

46 Stour Valley Railway Preservation Society
Chappel and Wakes Colne Station, Essex.
O.S. REF. TL 8928
TEL. Earls Colne 2571
ACCESS. B.R. paytrain from Colchester and Sudbury. Eastern National bus No. 88 or Hedingham & District Omnibus services from Colchester to Halstead. Off A604 Colchester – Haverhill road.

Open every weekend with steam days on the first Sunday of each month from April to October and on Bank Holidays.

P S R

47 Wells Harbour Railway
Passenger-carrying 10¼ in. gauge steam-operated railway.
Beach Road, Wells-next-to-the-Sea, Norfolk.
O.S. REF. TF 9243

And now for something really special! A multiple-unit train composed of Wickham petrol inspection railcars carrying holiday makers on the Alderney Railway in the Channel Islands. A Bagnall 0-4-0ST was acquired during the 1982 season. (Alderney Railway)

TEL. Fakenham 710439
ACCESS. Eastern Counties bus to Wells-next-the-Sea.

¾ mile ride connecting Wells Town with the beach and Pinewoods Caravan Site. Opened in 1976 and trains are operated by the locally-built 0-4-2WT *Edmund Hannay*.

Operates during Easter week, then on weekends only until Spring Bank Holiday when a timetable service is run daily until the end of September.

48 Suffolk Country and Wildlife Park
Passenger-carrying 10¼ in. gauge steam-operated railway.
Kessingland, near Lowestoft, Suffolk.
O.S. REF. TM 5285
TEL. Lowestoft 69876

1½ mile ride offering a choice of routes running through woods and pastureland and incorporating cuttings, an elevated section with a long embankment, bridge and tunnel. Steam motive power consists of an L.M.S. 'Royal Scot' 4-6-0 and a beautiful scale replica of the Leek & Manifold Railway 2-6-4T *E.R. Calthrop*.

Operates daily throughout the summer season from 11 a.m. until 5.30 p.m.

9

49 East Anglia Transport Museum
Operating open-air transport museum incorporating a passenger-carrying standard gauge electric tramway and a passenger-carrying 2 ft gauge light railway.
Chapel Road, Carlton Colville, Lowestoft, Suffolk.
O.S. REF. TM 5090
TEL. Ubberston 398
ACCESS. Eastern Counties bus route Nos. 631, 632, 671 and 672 from Lowestoft to Carlton Crown. No. 688 from Lowestoft Central to Carlton Church. Nearest B.R. stations: Lowestoft and Oulton Broad South.

The museum was founded in 1966 and offers a tramride round the buildings housing the road transport collection in preserved Blackpool, London and Glasgow tramcars. The East Suffolk Light Railway offers a 200 yard ride along the northern perimeter of the museum in a Hudson bogie coach behind a pair of Motor Rail petrol locomotives.

Open at weekends and Bank Holidays from Late Spring Bank Holiday to the end of September. Also Tuesday to Friday during August, 2 p.m. to 4 p.m.

P S M

50 Belton House Miniature Railway
Passenger-carrying 7¼ in. gauge steam-operated railway.
Belton House, Grantham, Lincolnshire.
O.S. REF. SK 9438
TEL. Grantham (0476) 66116
ACCESS. On A607 north of Grantham. Main entrance in Belton village.

½ mile ride running from the adventure playground to Suttons Bridge. Steam motive power consists of an L.N.E.R. 4-6-2 *Flying Scotsman* and a 2-6-2 *Mountaineer*.

Belton House is open from the end of March to early October daily from 11 a.m to 5.30 p.m. and at other times when required for events, school parties, etc.

P R M

51 Ferry Meadows Miniature Railway
Passenger-carrying 10¼ in. gauge railway.
Nene Valley Park, Peterborough, Cambridgeshire.
O.S. REF. TL 1495
TEL. 0205-64352
ACCESS. Ferry Meadows Station, Nene Valley Railway. Off the A605 between the A1 and Peterborough. Bus services Nos. 265, 268, 312, 316 and 323 stop on Oundle Road close to footpaths which lead into Ferry Meadows.

½ mile ride from Ham Lane to Lynch Station through the water meadows of the Nene Valley Park. Steam motive power is provided by a Dove 4-6-4 and a Mills 0-4-0ST *Alice*.

Operates daily from April to October.

P S R

THE MIDLANDS

52 North Staffordshire Steam Railway Centre
Cheddleton Station, Station Road, Cheddleton, near Leek, Staffordshire.
O.S. REF. SJ 98 51
TEL. Churnet Side 360522
ACCESS. Off the A520 Leek – Stone road at Cheddleton, then follow signposts. PMT or Berrisford's Buses operate to Cheddleton from Leek and Hanley. Nearest B.R. station: Stoke-on-Trent.

Short train rides are available on Sundays and Bank Holidays hauled by steam or diesel locomotives.

The museum is open daily from May to September and on Sundays only from October to April.

P S R M

53 Foxfield Light Railway
Dilhorne, Blythe Bridge, Stoke-on-Trent, Staffordshire.
O.S. REF. SJ 97 44
TEL. Stoke-on-Trent 313920
ACCESS. Potteries Motor Traction bus service 86B from either Longton (Stoke-on-Trent) or Cheadle operates in conjunction with the trains on Sundays. A special all-inclusive fare applies; the bus ticket being exchanged for a railway ticket at the Foxfield booking office, whilst the railway ticket acts as the return bus ticket. Passengers alight from the bus at Godley Brook, approximately 200 yards from the railway station.

Operates each Sunday between April and October inclusive. Special trains at other times by arrangement.

P S R

54 Midland Railway Centre
Butterley Station, near Ripley, Derbyshire.
O.S. REF. SK 40 52
TEL. Ripley 44920
ACCESS. On A61 road, 1½ miles north of Ripley. Bus routes Nos. 243, 244 & 245 from Alfreton to Derby. Frequency approx. 20 minutes.

Steam trains operate each weekend from Easter until the end of October.

55 National Mining Museum
Standard gauge steam locomotives on static display.
Lound Hall, Haughton, Bevercotes, near Retford, Nottinghamshire.
O.S. REF. SK 70 72
TEL. 0623-860728
ACCESS. On B6387 Retford – New Ollerton Road. Bus routes Nos. 15, 102, 103 and 162.

Two 0-6-0ST locomotives that formerly worked in colliery service are on display together with examples of coal mining machinery. The collection also includes a rail-mounted steam crane which may be seen in operation from time to time.

Open daily throughout the year.

56 Thoresby Hall Miniature Railway
Passenger-carrying 10¼ in. gauge steam-operated railway.
Thoresby Park, Ollerton, Newark, Nottinghamshire.
O.S. REF. SK 6371

750-yard ride alongside the River Medan and the smaller of two lakes in the park, which is in the centre of Sherwood Forest. A locomotive shed is at one end of the line and a temporary platform is situated at the other, so present operation is 'push-pull'. Further extensions of track are planned for both ends of the route. Notable for its streamlined L.N.E.R. A4 Pacific No. 4498 *Sir Nigel Gresley*.

Operation is on Sunday afternoons and Bank Holidays from Easter until September.

57 Chasewater Light Railway
Chasewater Park, Brownhills, West Midlands.
O.S. REF SK 03 07
TEL. Brownhills 5852
ACCESS. Off southbound carriageway of the A5 near junction with A452; entrance is signposted in Pool Road.

Steam-hauled trains operate from 2 p.m. on the second and fourth Sundays in each month, April to September, and also on Bank Holiday Sundays and Mondays.

P S R M

58 The Bass Museum
Static locomotive exhibits in museum devoted to the history of brewing in Burton-upon-Trent.
Horninglow Street, Burton-upon-Trent, Staffordshire.
O.S. REF. SK 24 23
DETAILS FROM. The Bass Museum, c/o Bass Production, High Street, Burton-upon-Trent, Staffs. Tel. 0283 42031 (office hours) 0283 45707 (all other times)

Situated at the entrance to Bass's Brewery and housed in what was formerly the company's joiners shop and its surrounding buildings.

Bass's fleet of 11 locomotives once operated over 26 miles of track and much emphasis is given in the exhibition to Burton's Victorian railway boom.

On display is Bass No. 9 – an 0-4-0 saddle tank locomotive built in Glasgow in 1901 – and the directors coach built in 1889 by the Ashby Railway Carriage and Iron Co. Ltd, Manchester.

A recent addition is a Worthington petrol engined shunting engine of 1926. A new exhibition at the museum traces the development of brewery transport and includes a major exhibition on the railway system including an audio-visual presentation and many photographs of early Bass and Worthington locomotives at work.

Also on display are a Robey horizontal compound engine and a late nineteenth-century experimental brewery.

The last steam survivor of the brewery railways of Burton-on-Trent is now at the Bass Museum. (Norman Glover)

Open weekdays 10.30 a.m. to 4.30 p.m., Saturday, Sunday and Bank Holidays 11 a.m. to 5 p.m.

S R M

59 Market Bosworth Light Railway
Shackerstone Station, near Market Bosworth, Leicestershire.
O.S. REF. SK 37 06
TEL. Atherstone 3966
ACCESS. Turn right at Twycross on the A444 Nuneaton – Burton road, then take unclassified road through Congerstone. B585 to Market Bosworth from A444 or A447. Gibson Bros. buses from Leicester Bowling Green Street.

Operates on Sundays and Bank Holidays from Easter to November.

P S R M

60 Cadeby Light Railway
Cadeby Rectory, Cadeby, Hinckley, Leicestershire.
O.S. REF. SK 42 02
TEL. Market Bosworth 290462
ACCESS. On the A447, one mile south of Market Bosworth. Bus routes Nos. 687, 697 and 731 from Hinckley and Market Bosworth. Infrequent service. Nearest B.R. station: Hinckley (5 miles).

Operates on the second Saturday of each month from April to November with an advertised timetable, though of necessity trains run with a wide recovery margin.

61 Leicestershire Museum of Technology
Static steam and internal combustion locomotive exhibits.
Abbey Lane Pumping Station, Corporation Road, Leicester.
O.S. REF. SK 58 06
TEL. Leicester 61330
ACCESS. Bus routes Nos. 54 or 76 from Leicester City Centre (Charles Street) to Beaumont Leys Lane: buses show 25 or 27/28 respectively returning into City. Outer circle bus services Nos. 90/91 also pass nearby.

Principal exhibits are three standard gauge industrial tank

11

*The 1906 Brush steam locomotive at the Transport Museum in Leicester. (*Norman Glover*)*

locomotives by Stephenson, Brush and Barclay; the last is a 'fireless' thermal-storage loco.

The museum building itself was built in 1890–1 as a sewage pumping station for the City of Leicester. The original pumphouse with four large Woolf Compound beam engines is now the centrepiece of the museum. The engines were built by Gimsons of Leicester and used from 1891 to 1965. Leicester City Museums took over in 1968 and the site was opened in 1972. Now Leicestershire County Museums owned, the Museum of Technology houses a representative collection of items from Leicestershire's industrial past, from stationary steam engines to knitting machines.

Open Mondays to Saturdays 10 a.m. to 5.30 p.m. Sundays 2 p.m. to 5.30 p.m. Closed Good Friday and Christmas Day. Special event days are held at regular intervals throughout the year when the stationary steam engines can be seen working.

P   S

62   Great Central Railway
Loughborough Central Station, Great Central Road, Loughborough, Leicestershire.
O.S. REF. Sk 54 19
TEL. Loughborough 216433 or 30726
ACCESS. Bus routes Nos. 625 and 626 from St Margarets bus station, Leicester to Leicester Road, Loughborough. Bus route No. 624 to Quorn & Woodhouse station.

Operates at weekends and Bank Holidays throughout the year. Also Wednesdays in June, July and August. Facilities include car parking, museum, souvenir shop, refreshments and toilets.

P   S   R   A   T   t

63   Stapleford Miniature Railway
Passenger-carrying 10¼ in. gauge steam-operated railway.
Stapleford Park, Melton Mowbray, Leicestershire.
O.S. REF. SK 81 18
TEL. Wymondham 245
ACCESS. On the B676, five miles from Melton Mowbray.

Originally opened in 1958 and now extends for some 1½ miles through the grounds of Stapleford Park, home of Lord and Lady Gretton. This is one of the finest miniature railways in the country, having four stations, a tunnel, an automatic level crossing and colour light signalling. An unusual feature of the line's operation is the boat train to Lakeside Station where passengers can join the *Northern Star* and *Southern Cross*, models of the Shaw Savill line ships of the same names, for voyage on the lake.

An addition to the line, opened in 1977, is a ¾ mile extension round the lake and through the woodlands, calling at the Chestnuts picnic area. The return journey departing from the Central Station is now over 1½ miles and is believed to be the longest run in the British Isles on a 10¼ in. gauge railway.

The railway operates when the house and grounds are open to visitors: Easter Sunday and Monday, Spring Bank Holiday Monday and Tuesday and Late Summer Holiday Monday; also every Sunday from May to September (inclusive) from 1.30 p.m. to 6.30 p.m.

64   Severn Valley Railway
The Railway Station, Bridgnorth, Shropshire.
O.S. REF. SO 7192
TEL. Bewdley 403816 or Bridgnorth 4361
ACCESS. Wolverhampton, Stourbridge or Kidderminster B.R. stations. Thence by West Midlands or Midland Red bus.

Operates at weekends and Bank Holidays from March to October and daily from mid-July to early September.

P   S   R   M   A   T   t   pa

65   Birmingham Museum of Science and Industry
Static steam locomotive exhibits.
Newhall Street, Birmingham.
O.S. REF. SP 06 87
TEL. 021-236 1022

Nearest B.R. station: Birmingham New Street (10 minutes' walk). 'Centrebus' from Stephenson Place to Newhall Street (frequency approx. 10 minutes).

Locomotives on display include three narrow gauge tank engines, dwarfed by the L.M.S. Pacific No. 46235 *City of Birmingham*, which is capable of being moved by an external power unit along a short length of track.

Also houses a collection of road locomotives, cars, bicycles, steam engines and other transport items. Live steam events take place periodically.

Open Monday-Friday 10 a.m.-5 p.m; Saturdays 10 a.m.-5.30 p.m., Sundays from 2 p.m. to 5.30 p.m.
First Wednesday in each month 10 a.m.-9 p.m.
Closed Good Friday, Christmas Day and Boxing Day.

P(nearby)   S   R

66   Birmingham Railway Museum
Tyseley Motive Power Depot, Warwick Road, Birmingham.
O.S. REF. SP 10 84
ACCESS. By rail to Tyseley Station (note: this station is closed

City of Birmingham *is occasionally unleashed to run over a few yards of track powered by an electric motor. (*Paul Cotterell*)*

on Sundays when the Museum is open). By bus routes 37 and 44 from City Centre. By car along the Warwick Road adjacent to the B.R. depot.

Open daily 10 a.m. to 5 p.m. April to September and every Sunday (except Christmas and New Year) 2 p.m. to 5 p.m. Steam days on the first Sunday of each month from April to December from 10 a.m. to 5 p.m., plus visiting locomotives and special trains as advertised.

P   S   R   M   workshop

67   Echills Wood Railway
Passenger-carrying 7¼ in. gauge steam-operated railway.
Echills Wood, Stoneleigh, Warwickshire.
O.S. REF. SP 3372

Echills Wood is adjacent to the Royal Agricultural Society's showground at Stoneleigh.

½ mile ride around Echills Wood, with looplines to and from the main station at Harvesters. The usual locomotive stock amounts to more than a dozen models of a wide variety of prototypes, ranging from B.R. 4-6-2 *Duke of Gloucester* to Welsh quarry 0-4-0STs.
Please note, the E.W.R. is wholly contained within the boundaries of the RASoE showground. It therefore follows that visits can only be made during open periods at the showground. Unfortunately, the railway is not empowered to authorize visits to its workshops and depot. However, arrangements can be made for individuals, given reasonable notice, and written permission is essential for any visits. The railway only operates in conjunction with events at the showground and is closed and the rolling stock removed at intervening times.

Usual operating times are the four days of the Royal Show and three of the Town and Country Festival in August.

P   R   at showground

68   Northamptonshire Ironstone Railway Trust Ltd
Collection of steam and internal combustion locomotives, rolling stock and machinery associated with the ironstone quarrying industry.

Hunsbury Hill, Northampton.
O.S. REF. SP 735584
ACCESS. Nearest B.R. station: Northampton

The Trust was formed to put together a museum of ironstone relics in order to preserve something of the country's heritage. The intended site for the railway exhibits is the trackbed of the former ironstone tramway serving Hunsbury furnaces, which lies within the bounds of the proposed Hunsbury Hill Park.
The collection to date comprises a dozen assorted locomotives of three different gauges.

Open to visitors on Sundays between 10 a.m. and 4 p.m. throughout the year.

69   Bulmer Railway Centre ('Steam in Hereford')
H. P. Bulmer Ltd (Cider Makers), Whitecross Road, Hereford.
O.S. REF. SO 50 40
TEL. Hereford 760787 or 4376
ACCESS. ½ mile from city centre on A438 Brecon road. Nearest B.R. station: Hereford

Open for static display every weekend from April to September inclusive. Steam days on the last Sunday in each month; also Easter, Spring and Summer Bank Holidays.

P   S   (on steam days)   R

70   Dean Forest Railway
Norchard, near Lydney, Forest of Dean, Gloucestershire.
O.S. REF. SO 62 04
TEL. Dean (0594) 43423
ACCESS. Norchard is ½ mile off A48 at Lydney. B.R. Gloucestershire – Newport service to Lydney. National Welsh bus No. 40 passes the site.

Open every Saturday and Sunday (11 a.m. to 5 p.m.) and the shop is open every Sunday afternoon and Saturday afternoons also in summer. Steam train rides are normally operated on Bank Holiday Sundays and Mondays and on Sundays in late July and August.

P   S   R   M   pa

71   Winchcombe Railway Museum
Static displays of railway signalling, lineside features, locomotive nameplates and small historical items.
23 Gloucester Street, Winchcombe, Gloucestershire.
O.S. REF. SP 0228
TEL. Winchcombe 602257
ACCESS. Nearest B.R. station: Cheltenham Lansdown.

Specialises not in locomotives and rolling stock but in signalling equipment, lineside fixtures, horse-drawn road vehicles, tickets and all kinds of paperwork, lamps and even a couple of railway gas meters! There are indoor and outdoor displays in pleasant garden surroundings.

Open Easter, Spring and Summer Bank Holidays, Sunday and Monday; certain Sundays June to September inclusive. Open 2.30 p.m. until dusk.

P(in street)

13

72 Blenheim Park Railway

Passenger-carrying 15 in. gauge steam-operated railway.
Blenheim Palace, Woodstock, Oxfordshire.
O.S. REF. SP 4416
TEL. Woodstock 811805
ACCESS. Blenheim is permanently signposted on all major surrounding roads.

½ mile ride through the grounds of Blenheim Palace.

Operates daily, Easter to the end of October.

73 Quainton Railway Centre

Quainton Railway Society Ltd, Railway Station, Quainton, near Aylesbury, Bucks.
O.S. REF. SP 73 19
TEL. 029675 450
ACCESS. By road – take A41 from Aylesbury, turn off after 6 miles at Waddesdon. Follow Quainton signs. No buses or rail access.

Open on Easter Monday, Spring and August Bank Holidays, on the last Sunday of every month, every Sunday in July and August between 10 a.m. and 6 p.m.

P   S   R   M

74 Leighton Buzzard Narrow Gauge Railway

Pages Park Station, Billington Road, Leighton Buzzard, Bedfordshire.
O.S. REF. SP 92 24
TEL. Leighton Buzzard (0525) 373888
ACCESS. From M1, follow the signs from junction 11 or 13 to the A5 and follow signs on the A5 for Leighton Buzzard which is well signposted. From Leighton Buzzard follow 'Narrow Gauge Railway' signs from town centre. The railway lies on the east side of Billington Road, the A4146 to Hemel Hempstead.

Operates on Sundays from the end of March to the end of September from 11 a.m. to 5 p.m., also on Bank Holidays and Saturdays (at Bank Holiday periods) from 2 p.m. to 5 p.m.

P   S   R

75 Whipsnade and Umfolozi Railway

Whipsnade Zoo Park, Dunstable, Bedfordshire.
O.S. REF. TL 0017
TEL. Whipsnade 872995 (Zoo: 872171).

The railway operates daily from Easter to the end of September and is normally steam worked. Visitors should note that a diesel pay-train may operate before 1 p.m.

P   R   S

76 Knebworth West Park and Winter Green Railway

Passenger-carrying 2 ft. gauge steam-operated railway.
Knebworth House, near Stevenage, Hertfordshire.
O.S. REF. TL 22 20
TEL. Stevenage 812661
ACCESS. Knebworth House is permanently signposted on all major surrounding roads. Nearest B.R. station: Knebworth. Direct access from A1(M) at Stevenage (South) roundabout.

1¼ mile ride through the grounds of Knebworth House. Resident locomotive stock comprises five steam locomotives plus internal combustion motive power.

Operates daily from Easter to the end of September. Steam operation on Saturdays, Sundays and Bank Holidays and on one weekday during the school holidays, otherwise a diesel service is run.

P   S   R   pa

77 Walsall Steam Railway

Passenger carrying 7¼ in. gauge steam railway, ¾ mile in length featuring double-track running.
Arboretum Park, Walsall, West Midlands.
O.S. REF. SP 0298
TEL. Walsall 30078 or 22544
ACCESS. off Broadway North, Double gates by Grange Playhouse. AA signed on approaching roads. 15 minutes' walk from Walsall B.R. station.

Walsall Steam Railway is the longest 7¼ in. gauge double-track system in the country using scale steam locomotives. Its use of motive power is ambitious too, and trains are hauled by B.R. Class 9F 2-10-0s, L.M.S. Black 5 4-6-0s and Stanier and Peppercorn Pacifics. All its coaching stock is fitted with vacuum brakes and intensive timetabling gives all the spectacle of a true mainline railway in miniature.

Operates every Saturday, Sunday and Bank Holiday from Easter to October from 2 p.m. to 6.30 p.m.

P   R

78 Weston Park Railway

Passenger-carrying 7¼ in. gauge steam railway, 1 mile in length.
Weston Park, Weston-under-Lizard, Shropshire.
O.S. REF. SJ 81
TEL. Weston-under-Lizard 207 or 385
ACCESS. The park is seven miles west from the M6/A5 interchange (Junction 12) on the A5 at Weston-under-Lizard. The nearest railway station is at Shifnal and public bus services run to Tong and Weston-under-Lizard.

This extensive and well-known 7¼ in. gauge system was moved in its entirety from its original site at Hilton, near Bridgnorth during the winter of 1979/80. Advantage has been taken of the new location to lay the line out with future development in mind. Existing operational features are retained, such as crossing loops controlled by colour light signals, interlocked with the train 'staff' system.
Resident stock of nine locomotives, and these may be supplemented by visiting locos from time to time.

Open mid-April to 31 July: Daily, except for Mondays and Fridays, open Bank Holidays. Additionally open Mondays in May, June and July for school parties only.
August: Daily. September: Weekends only. Closed on 30 September.

The Park is open from 11 a.m. to 7.30 p.m. and the House from 2 p.m. to 6 p.m. Last admissions 5.30 p.m.

P R pa adventure playground British wildlife collection aquarium and pottery

79 Telford Horsehay Steam Trust

Standard gauge steam railway preservation centre.
The Old Loco Shed, Horsehay, Telford, Shropshire.
O.S. REF. SJ 6707
TEL. Telford 503880
ACCESS. 1 mile from Dawley on Dawley to Horsehay Road.

Standard gauge steam locomotives undergoing restoration. The Trust was formed in 1976 with the purpose of restoring, and eventually running, steam locomotives and rolling stock that had local connections with the East Shropshire Branch lines. Plans to run a passenger service on the Horsehay to Lightmoor branch line once negotiations for the purchase of the line have been concluded. Meanwhile, occasional open days are held at the Loco Shed using the G.W.R. 0-6-2T No. 5619 in steam.

P

80 The Black Country Museum

Passenger-carrying 3 ft 6 in. gauge electric tramway running through an attractive outdoor museum of Black Country life.
Tipton Road, Dudley, West Midlands.
O.S. REF. SO 9491
TEL. 021-557-9643

ABOVE: *Massed miniature main line motive power at the Walsall Steam Railway.* (W.S.R.)

BELOW: *The ever-popular Weston Park Railway offers a choice of motive power.* (Paul Barber)

The Coalbrookdale-built 0-4-0ST at the Museum of Iron that was its birthplace. (Mike Wood)

ACCESS. Adjacent to A4123 Birmingham – Wolverhampton road. Bus route No. 125 Wolverhampton Dudley – Birmingham. Nearest B.R. station: Tipton (¾ mile).

Strives to capture and preserve the special cultural character of the area by means of a careful selection of preserved buildings and equipment to illustrate the traditional crafts and social activities of Black Country communities – waterways, tramways, road, coal and clay pits, furnaces and forges interlaced with homes, pubs, and places of worship. Passengers are carried over the ⅓ mile tramway in former Dudley, Stourbridge & District Tramcar No. 5.

Open daily except Saturdays from April to November between 10 a.m. and 5 p.m.

P   S   R   M

81 Ironbridge Gorge Museum
Standard gauge steam locomotive and rolling stock on static display in large open air industrial museum.
Blists Hill Industrial Museum, Ironbridge, Telford, Shropshire.
O.S. REF. SJ 6903
TEL. Ironbridge (095-245) 3522 (weekdays); Ironbridge (095-245) 3418 (weekends)
ACCESS. Ironbridge stands on the River Severn in Telford, Shropshire, south of the A5, west of the A442, thirty minutes from the M6. Visitors should follow signposts leading to Telford. Nearest B.R. stations: Wellington and Shifnal. Buses thence to Ironbridge.

At Blists Hill Open Air Museum stand steam engines and pit-heads, with examples of clay-working, iron-making and early transport methods, all on a 42-acre woodland site.
    Here, the ironmaster Abraham Darby first smelted iron using coke as fuel. This paved the way for the first iron rails, iron bridge, iron boat, iron aqueduct and iron-framed building. In tribute to these achievements the Ironbridge Gorge Museum is being created around a unique series of industrial monuments spread over three miles of the Severn Valley.

Visitors to the Black Country Museum travel in this vintage electric tramcar. (Black Country Museum)

Open daily from 10 a.m. to 6 p.m. April to October inclusive, 10 a.m. to 5 p.m. November to March inclusive. Closed Christmas Day.

P   S   R   M

82 Coalbrookdale Works Museum
Standard gauge steam locomotives on static display in open air industrial museum.
Coalbrookdale, Shropshire.
O.S. REF. SJ 6604
TEL. Ironbridge (095-245) 3522 (weekdays); Ironbridge (095-245) 3418 (weekends)
ACCESS. Ironbridge stands on the River Severn in Telford, Shropshire, south of the A5, west of the A442, thirty minutes from the M6. Visitors should follow signposts leading to Telford.

Museum displays the restored original Derby iron furnace of 1709 and also contains 3 industrial 0-4-0 tanks built or rebuilt at Coalbrookdale.

The Furnace Site and Museum are open daily from 10 a.m. to 6 p.m. April to October inclusive, 10 a.m. to 5 p.m. November to March inclusive. Closed Christmas Day.

83 Gloucestershire – Warwickshire Railway
Standard gauge steam locomotives undergoing restoration to working order.
Toddington Station, Gloucestershire.
O.S. REF. SP 0627

An ambitious railway preservation scheme aimed at reviving the former G.W.R. Stratford-on-Avon to Cheltenham line using steam motive power. On display are the G.W.R. 4-6-0s *Cogan Hall, Ditcheat Manor* and *Odney Manor* and the 2-8-0 No. 2807. The Dowty R.P.S. collection of stock from Ashchurch was moved here in 1983 and provides steam-hauled passenger rides on standard and narrow gauge tracks.

Open at weekends throughout the year.

P

84   Cambrian Railways Society Ltd

Standard gauge locomotives and rolling stock undergoing restoration.

Railway Depot, Oswald Road, Oswestry, Shropshire.

O.S. REF. SJ 2929

ACCESS. Crosville bus route Nos. D2, D59, D63, D65, D66 and D68 Gobowen-Oswestry. Nearest B.R. station: Gobowen (2½ miles).

This society is promoting a scheme for the formation of a living museum of Cambrian Railways relics centred on Oswestry, Shropshire. Six steam locomotives including the G.W.R. 4-6-0 *Foxcote Manor* together with internal combustion locos and rolling stock have been gathered at Oswestry station yard and are undergoing restoration.

Open every Sunday from March to October from 11 a.m. to 5 p.m. Occasional steaming days are held.

P

85   Rutland Railway Museum

Standard gauge industrial railway preservation centre, where a growing collection of steam locomotives and industrial rolling stock is displayed.

Cottesmore Ironstone Mines Sidings, Ashwell Road, Cottesmore, Rutland.

O.S. REF. SK 8813

Working industrial railway museum to commemorate the ironstone quarry railways of Leicestershire, Lincolnshire and Rutland in their natural environment. Ten steam locomotives and four diesels form the nucleus of the collection and steam open days are organized from time to time.

Open at weekends throughout the year.

P

86   National Tramway Museum

Passenger-carrying standard gauge electric tramway running through Britain's premier museum devoted solely to trams.

Crich, near Ambergate, Derbyshire.

O.S. REF. SK 3454

TEL. 077-385-2565

ACCESS. Trent bus 240/241 from Matlock, Alfreton, Alfreton & Mansfield Parkway. B.R. ½ hour uphill walk from Whatstandwell (B.R.); Trent 151 bus from Derby.

Unique collection of over 40 trams, of which the majority are in working order. Apart from British vehicles, the collection includes examples from Czechoslovakia, Portugal and South Africa, as well as a former New York streetcar which last ran in Vienna. Other special features include Edwardian street project; façade of Assembly Rooms – Ancient Monument from Derby re-erected at Museum. Lead mining display by Peak District Mines Historical Society. Tramway power station exhibition of early horse and electric cars.

Open Saturdays, Sundays and Bank Holidays, April-October, 10.30 a.m. to 5.00 p.m.; Tuesdays, Wednesdays and Thursdays, May, June, July and August only, 10 a.m. to 4.30 p.m. Also Mondays in August.

P   S   R   M   pa

WALES

87   National Trust, Penrhyn Castle Museum

A museum devoted to the history of industrial railways containing locomotives and rolling stock of four different gauges on static display.

Castell Penrhyn, Llandegai, near Bangor, Gwynedd.

O.S. REF. SH 60 72

TEL. Bangor (0248) 53084

ACCESS. Nearest B.R. station: Bangor. Buses from Bangor and Llandudno.

Doyen of the collection of standard and narrow gauge locomotives on display is the Padarn Railway 0-4-0 *Fire Queen* built in 1848. Several makes and designs of industrial locomotive are on view, with particular emphasis on engines and rolling stock from the 1 ft 10¾ in. gauge Penrhyn Railway.

Open daily from 1 April to 31 October, 2 p.m. to 5 p.m. in April, May and October; 11 a.m. to 5 p.m. from June to September.

P   R   Penrhyn Castle (National Trust)

88   Snowdon Mountain Railway

Llanberis, Gwynedd.

O.S. REF. SH 5859

TEL. Llanberis 223

ACCESS. Bangor B.R. Station, thence by bus to Llanberis. By road along the A4086 from Caernarfon or Capel Curig.

The railway operates from Easter to the first weekend in October.

P   S   R   A   T   t

Hunslet 0-4-0ST Charles, from the local slate quarry railway, at Penrhyn Castle. (Norman Glover)

89 Llanberis Lake Railway
Padarn Country Park, Gilfach Ddu, Llanberis, Gwynedd.
O.S. REF. SH 5860
TEL. Llanberis 870549
ACCESS. Bangor B.R. Station, thence by bus to Llanberis. To reach the railway leave the A4086 main road almost opposite the Snowdon Railway Station in Llanberis. Follow the signposts down the approach road to the station at Padarn Park (Gilfach Ddu).

Operates daily from Easter to the first Sunday in October.

P S R M A T t pa

90 Welsh Highland Light Railway
Gelert's Farm Works, Madoc Street West, Porthmadog, Gwynedd.
O.S. REF. SH 5639
TEL. 0766-3402
ACCESS. Adjacent to B.R. Porthmadog Station. Crosville buses to Porthmadog.

Trains operate at weekends from Spring Bank Holiday to September and daily during August.

P S

91 Ffestiniog Railway
Porthmadog Harbour Station, Porthmadog, Gwynedd.
O.S. REF. SH 5837
TEL. Porthmadog 2384
ACCESS. B.R. Stations at Porthmadog, Minffordd and Blaenau Ffestiniog. Crosville bus services operate to Porthmadog or Tanygrisiau from Blaenau Ffestiniog, Dolgellau, Caernarfon, Pwllheli and Criccieth.

Trains run daily from March to November inclusive, plus winter weekends and Christmas.

P S R M A T t pa

92 Narrow Gauge Railway Centre
The largest collection of narrow gauge locomotives in the British Isles, housed in a museum in the world's largest slate mine.
Gloddfa Ganol Mountain Tourist Centre, Blaenau Ffestiniog, Gwynedd.
O.S. REF. SH 6946
TEL. Moelwyn (076-689) 500
ACCESS. Off the A470 Blaenau Ffestiniog to Betws-y-Coed road ½ mile north of the town. Turn off at Loco No. 3014. Nearest station: Blaenau Ffestiniog B.R.

The collection of rolling stock belongs to Narrow Gauge Enterprises Ltd and is still being added to. Ultimately it will comprise over *seventy* steam and internal combustion locomotives from thirty different manufacturers on a variety of gauges.

Open daily from Easter to October between 10 a.m. and 5.30 p.m.

P S R Slate Industry Museum
Land Rover tours Children's play area

93 Ceudwll Llechwedd (Llechwedd Slate Caverns)
Passenger-carrying 2 ft gauge electrically-operated railway running partially underground through the Llechwedd Slate mines.
Blaenau Ffestiniog, Gwynedd.
O.S. REF. SH 69 46
TEL. Blaenau Ffestiniog 306
ACCESS. Crosville bus route No. R34. Connecting service from Tan-y-Grisiau. Nearest B.R. station: Blaenau Ffestiniog.

Visitors to the caverns take a half-mile return journey through the mine in specially-designed trains hauled by battery-electric locomotives. The train conveys visitors to a slate chamber in which the working conditions of a century ago have been recreated. Here visitors will see how the vast caverns were formed by the extraction of slate from the mountainside. It is also possible to travel deeper into the mountain by descending the Deep Mine incline railway. Operating within the restrictions of what was originally an industrial incline, commenced in 1846, it required the construction of a special 24-seat vehicle to negotiate Britain's steepest underground passenger railway. A failsafe braking system had to be incorporated in the 3-ton car, which is cable-hauled on 3 ft gauge heavy-duty track on a 1 in 1.8 gradient.

Open for visitors and the tramway operates from 10 a.m. to 6 p.m. daily, 1 March to 30 October (last train into mine 5.15 p.m.).

94 Conwy Valley Railway Museum
Static locomotive and rolling stock exhibits. Also passenger-carrying 7¼ in. gauge steam railway.
Old Goods Yard, Bettws-y-Coed, Gwynedd.
O.S. REF. SH 796565
TEL. 06902 568
ACCESS. Adjacent to Bettws-y-Coed B.R. station. Road access signed from A5.

Displays covering the whole railway scene, with special reference to standard and narrow gauge lines in North Wales. The small exhibits are in a purpose-built museum and there is a collection of standard gauge vehicles and larger exhibits on the site.

A passenger-carrying 7¼ in. gauge railway, ½ mile in length, was opened as an adjunct to the museum in 1979.

Open daily from Easter until the end of October between 10.30 and 5.30 p.m. Open 2 p.m. to 5 p.m. on Bank Holidays.

P S R

95 Rheilffordd Llyn Tegid (Bala Lake Railway)
Llanuwchllyn Station, Gwynedd.
O.S. REF. SH 8830
TEL. Llanuwchllyn (06784) 666
ACCESS. Off the A494 from Bala to Dolgellau, 5 miles from Bala. Turn left at garage (signposted). Bus route No. D94 (Wrexham-Barmouth).

Operates from Easter to the end of September daily from 10 a.m. to 6 p.m., and at weekends to mid-October.

P S R pa t

Sgt. Murphy *stands guard over the exhibits at the Conwy Valley Railway Museum.* (W. Kay)

96 Llangollen Railway

Llangollen Station, Llangollen, Clwyd.

O.S. REF. SJ 2142

TEL. Llangollen (0978) 860951

ACCESS. Via A539 Ruabon – Corwen road or via A5 Shrewsbury – Holyhead road. Hourly bus services from Chester (Crosville D1, D93, D94).

Operates on Sundays and Public Holidays from Spring Bank Holiday onwards.

P S R M

97 Fairbourne Railway

Beach Road, Fairbourne, Gwynedd.

O.S. REF. SH 6112

TEL. Fairbourne 250362

ACCESS. Fairbourne B.R. Station; Crosville bus service S28; A493 road.

Operates daily from Easter to October.

P S R t

98 Narrow Gauge Railway Museum

Static collection of narrow gauge steam locomotives rolling stock, equipment and small exhibits.

Wharf station, Tywyn, Gwynedd.

O.S. REF. SH 5800

TEL. Tywyn (0654) 710472

ACCESS. B.R. Tywyn Station; Crosville buses Nos. 26, 28, 30.

The museum adjoins the platform at Tywyn Wharf Station on the Talyllyn Railway.

Unique collection of equipment from narrow gauge railways all over Britain, ranging in size from steam locomotives – seven in number – wagons and signals, down to uniform buttons and tickets. Slate quarry railways predominate, but there are locomotives from a famous brewery, a gas works and from other industries. The museum has considerable educational value.

Open 10 a.m. to 5 p.m. Easter to October; out of season on request.

R

99 Talyllyn Railway

Wharf Station, Tywyn, Gwynedd.

O.S. REF. SH 5900

TEL. Tywyn (0654) 710472

ACCESS. Tywyn B.R. Station, Crosville bus routes S26, S28 and S30. By roads A493 and B4405.

Trains operate from Easter to the end of October daily except during October. Also Christmas Holidays.

P S R M A T t

100 Corris Railway Museum

Static display of small exhibits connected with the Corris Railway.

Corris Station, Corris, near Machynlleth, Gwynedd.

O.S. REF. SH 7507

ACCESS. Off A487, five miles north of Machynlleth, opposite Braich Goch Hotel. Crosville bus route No. 513 from Machynlleth and Aberystwyth to Aberllefenni and Dolgellau. Nearest B.R. station: Machynlleth ($5\frac{1}{2}$ miles).

Track is being reinstated on a short length of the old Corris Railway trackbed adjacent to the museum and a replica of an 1898 bogie coach is being built.

The museum is open on Bank Holiday weekends and Tuesday to Friday during July and August from 1 p.m. to 5.30 p.m. and on Sundays during the same period from 2 p.m. to 5 p.m.

P S

101   Welshpool and Llanfair Light Railway
Llanfair Caereinion Station, Powys.
O.S. REF. SJ 1006
TEL. Llanfair Caereinion (0938-82) 441
ACCESS. Infrequent Crosville bus service No. D85/86 from Welshpool B.R. station; railway runs parallel to A458. Raven Square terminus is situated by the main roundabout on the A458 on the western outskirts of Welshpool.

Operates at weekends from Easter to October, daily from June to September and at Bank Holidays.

P S R T t

102   Vale of Rheidol Narrow Gauge Steam Railway
Aberystwyth, Dyfed.
O.S. REF. SN 5881
TEL. Aberystwyth 612377
ACCESS. Aberystwyth B.R. Station. Bus routes Nos. S1 and S17.

Operates from Easter to early October.

P S (at Devils Bridge) R T t

103   Gwili Railway
Bronwydd Arms Station, near Carmarthen, Dyfed.
O.S. REF. SN 41 23
ACCESS. Carmarthen (B.R.); A484 road; Crosville bus No. S44 Carmarthen-Cardigan.

Operates on Bank Holidays, Saturdays, Sundays, Mondays and Tuesdays from the beginning of June to the end of September. Also Mondays, Tuesdays, Wednesdays from mid-July to the end of August. First train 11 a.m. except Saturdays when it is 12 noon. Last train will run at 5.15 p.m.

P S R

104   Caerphilly Railway Society
Collection of standard gauge steam locomotives housed at the former Rhymney Railway locomotive works.
Harold Wilson Industrial Estate, Van Road, Caerphilly, Mid-Glamorgan.
O.S. REF. ST 1686
ACCESS. 1 mile from Caerphilly B.R. Station and bus station. Via Van Road to estate entrance.

The most notable locomotive in the collection is Taff Vale Railway 0-6-2T No. 28, the only Welsh-built standard gauge locomotive to be preserved. On advertised open days rides are given in the G.W.R. brake van propelled by one of the locomotives. The site is also open on Sunday afternoons when members are carrying out restoration work on the site. For open days see railway press.

P S R (open days only)

105   Brecon Mountain Railway (Rheilffordd Mynydd Brycheiniog)
Pant Station, Merthyr Tydfil, Mid-Glamorgan.
O.S. REF. SO 0509
TEL. Merthyr Tydfil (0685) 4854
ACCESS. Bus route Merthyr Tydfil to Pant (approx ½ hour frequency). Nearest B.R. station: Merthyr Tydfil (3 miles).

Services operate daily from the beginning of May to the beginning of October. Trains run 11 a.m. until dusk. A weekend, Saturdays and Sundays, service operates from 6 October until 21 December. During the schools Autumn half-term trains operate daily between 12 noon and 3 p.m. Over the holiday period between 22 December and 4 January, except Christmas Day, a service of four return trains runs, commencing at 12 noon and continuing hourly. The return journey time is approximately ¾ hour.

P S

106   Swansea Industrial and Maritime Museum
Collection of standard gauge locomotives and rolling stock. Steam open days are organised by the Railway Club of Wales on the adjacent South Dock Railway.
South Dock, Swansea, West Glamorgan.
O.S. REF. SS 6692
TEL. Swansea (0792) 50351
ACCESS. A483 or A4067 to Swansea Leisure Centre. Museum is at rear of Leisure Centre. Nearest B.R. Station: Swansea High Street.

Large and varied collection of exhibits reflecting the richness of industrial and marine activity in the Swansea area over the past 300 years. There is a fully operational woollen mill as well as displays on canals, plateways, oil refining, coal mining and fishing. The museum owns the Barclay 0-4-0 fireless locomotive *Sir Charles* and a section of Swansea and Mumbles Railway electric car No. 7 whilst the

The Railway Club of Wales operates this Barclay saddletank at Swansea Industrial Museum. (Brian Owen)

Railway Club of Wales own a Sentinel and a Barclay steam locomotive and two diesels.

Operation takes place on Sunday afternoons from May to September. Steam days are held at Bank Holidays and at other times as advertised; otherwise a diesel service operates. The museum is open from 10.30 a.m. until 5.30 p.m. Monday to Saturday throughout the year. (Closed Christmas Day, Boxing Day and New Year's Day).

P   S

107   Rhyl Miniature Railway

Passenger-carrying 15 in. gauge steam railway.
Marine Lake, Rhyl, Clwyd.
O.S. REF. SJ 00 80

The railway is laid out as a continuous half-mile circuit and trains are hauled by four Barnes 'Atlantic' locomotives dating from the 1920s.

Operates daily from Spring Bank Holiday to the end of September.

108   Great Orme Tramway

Passenger-carrying 3 ft 6 in. gauge cable tramway
Victoria Station, Church Walks, Llandudno, Gwynedd.
O.S. REF. SH 7781
TEL. Llandudno 76749
ACCESS. Bus routes Nos. 7 and 10. B.R. Llandudno station ($\frac{1}{2}$ mile).

The Great Orme Tramway runs from Victoria Station, Llandudno, to just below the summit of the Great Orme headland, 679 feet above sea level.

Authorised in 1898, this 3 ft 6 in. gauge line is in two sections, passengers changing cars halfway. The lower section, opened on 31 July 1902, is 800 yards long (maximum gradient 1 in 4.4); the upper, opened on 8 July 1903, is 827 yards long (maximum gradient 1 in 10.3). Both are single track with a passing loop, although the lower incline has a portion of double track with a common middle rail.

Tramway operates daily with a 20 minute service during the summer season. Extra journeys are worked at busy periods.

109   Welsh Industrial and Maritime Museum

Collection of locomotives and rolling stock with strong Welsh associations. The Butetown Railway Society works in close cooperation with the museum and maintains its own collection of locomotives which will be steamed on a site adjacent to the museum.
Bute Street, Docks, Cardiff, Glamorgan.
O.S. REF. ST 1974
TEL. Cardiff 371805/6
ACCESS. Bus routes Nos. 8 and 9 from City Centre to Docks. Nearest B.R. station: Bute Road.

Collection of steam, gas and oil engines, some of which are operated every day. On the first Saturday of every month the engines are driven by steam and a number of films dealing with the steam scene are shown on the video units. Pride of the locomotive collection is the full-size working

replica of Trevithick's pioneer locomotive *Penydarren*, whilst there is also a Hudswell Clarke 0-6-0ST of 1900 and a Smith Rodley steam crane.

The museum's four other steam locomotives are maintained and operated by the Caerphilly Railway Society. The Butetown Railway Society has under its care the 1932 Peckett 0-6-0ST *Sir Gomer* and a North British 0-6-0 diesel hydraulic shunter.

Open on weekdays between 10 a.m. and 5 p.m. (October to March) and 10 a.m. to 6 p.m. (April to September) and on Sundays from 2.30 p.m. to 5 p.m. Closed on Christmas Eve, Christmas Day, Boxing Day, New Year's Day, Good Friday and May Day. Admission free.

P

110   Fort Belan Miniature Railway

Passenger-carrying $7\frac{1}{4}$ in. gauge steam railway, $\frac{5}{8}$ mile in length, running from the car park to the Fort.
Fort Belan, Dinas Dinlle, near Caernarfon.
O.S. REF. SH 4460
TEL. Llanwnda (0286) 830220
ACCESS. Off the A499 Caernarfon-Pwllheli Road through Dinas Dinlle (about 5 miles).

This charming old Fort, situated in secluded and eminently picturesque surroundings, remains a singularly romantic and unspoilt place. Built some 200 years ago on a small peninsula at the Western entrance to the Menai Straits, Belan is surrounded on three sides by the sea. The Snowdonia range of mountains in the background makes the neighbourhood one of great and varied loveliness.

Very little has changed at Belan for over 200 years, and the Fort, Docks, and cannons have all been maintained in first class working order. The railway is laid out in a pear-shaped loop configuration running through the sand dunes. Its locomotives are $\frac{1}{4}$ full size replicas of original engines built by Bagnalls of Stafford.

Operates from 1 May to 30 September between 10 a.m. and 5.30 p.m. daily.

P   S   R   M   pleasure cruises to Caernarfon   pleasure flights by light aircraft   cannon firing   pottery

111   Scolton Manor Museum

Static display of local railway rolling stock and lineside equipment.
Scolton Manor, Scolton, near Haverfordwest, Dyfed.
O.S. REF. SM 9922
TEL. Clarbeston 328
ACESS. Situated on the B4329, $5\frac{1}{2}$ miles north of Haverfordwest.

Collections of natural history, geology, social, domestic and industrial history, rural crafts and costume. Principal exhibits are the 1878 Fox Walker 0-6-0ST *Margaret* from the North Pembroke & Fishguard Railway and a Smith Rodley steam crane.

Open Tuesday to Sunday in July, August and September only between 10.30 a.m. and 6 p.m.

21

LANCASHIRE
AND THE NORTH-WEST

112   Isle of Man Railway
Douglas, Isle of Man.
O.S. REF. SC 37 75
TEL. Douglas 4646
ACCESS. Short walk from Douglas Bus Station, Harbour and town centre.

Operates daily except Saturdays from Easter to the first week in October.

P   S   R

113   **Manx Electric Railway**
Passenger-carrying 3 ft gauge electric railway.
Derby Castle Station, Douglas, Isle of Man.
O.S. REF. SC 3977
TEL. Douglas 4549

Adjacent to the northern terminus of the Douglas Horse Tramway. Nearest station: Douglas I.M.R.

18 mile ride from Douglas to Ramsey along the east coast of the Isle of Man. At Laxey, the M.E.R. connects with the Snaefell Mountain Railway, another electrically-worked line which climbs almost five miles and 2000 ft to the top of Snaefell. The M.E.R. is unique within the British Isles, being a genuine electrically-worked light railway dating from 1893. It runs through magnificent scenery and no visitor should miss the opportunity of a ride on one of its trains.
    Approx. single journey time: 75 minutes.

P at Laxey station

114   Ravenglass and Eskdale Railway
Ravenglass Station, Ravenglass, Cumbria.
O.S. REF. SD 0896
TEL. Ravenglass (06577) 226 & 227
ACCESS. Ravenglass B.R. station. Cumberland Motor Services buses serve Ravenglass and Muncaster Mill. By road, along the A595.

Operates all year except for Christmas period and not at weekends Christmas to the end of February. Limited service in winter, trains every 30 minutes in summer.

P   S   R   M   A   T   t   pa

115   Lakeside and Haverthwaite Railway
Haverthwaite Station, near Newby Bridge, Ulverston, Cumbria.
O.S. REF. SD 34 84
TEL. 04483-594
ACCESS. Bus routes Nos. 517 and X30 Ulverston to Grange-over-Sands. Hourly frequency. On A590 Barrow road. Railway connects with Sealink steamers to Bowness and Ambleside.

Operates at Easter and on Sundays in April and October, and

daily May to the end of September, 11 a.m. to 5.30 p.m. Trains run hourly and most connect with the Lake Windermere steamers at Lakeside.

P   S   R   A   T   t

116   Steamtown Railway Museum
Warton Road, Carnforth, Lancashire.
O.S. REF. SD 49 70
TEL. Carnforth (052473) 4220 and 2625
ACCESS. Short walk from B.R. Carnforth Station. By road via the M6 Junctions 35 and 35A and the A6. Bus routes Nos. 553 and 554 Kendal – Lancaster, Nos. 555 and 556 Keswick – Lancaster and No. 573 from Morecambe. All at half-hourly frequency.

Open daily (except Christmas Day) between 9 a.m. and 4 p.m. in winter and 9 a.m. and 5 p.m. the remainder of the year.

P   S   R   pa   model railway

117   **Lytham Motive Power Museum**
Museum of static steam locomotive exhibits, mostly of industrial origin.
Dock Road, Lytham, Lancashire.
O.S. REF. SD 38 27
TEL. Lytham 733122
ACCESS. Nearest B.R. station: Lytham. Bus service No. 11A.

Attractive collection of industrial steam locomotives all restored to superb exhibition finish. The collection also includes a Pullman coach, vintage cars, a traction engine and steam roller, gas lamps and aircraft exhibits.

Open June to September, Sundays only 11 a.m. to 5 p.m.

P   model railway

118   Southport Locomotive and Transport Museum (Steamport)
Derby Road, Southport, Merseyside
O.S. REF. SD 341161
TEL. Southport 30693
ACCESS. Bus routes Nos. X27, X37, X47, 100 & 102 to Ribble bus station from Liverpool and Preston. Frequent services Nos. 309 and 319 from St Helens and Warrington. Local buses to Monument, then eight minute walk via London Street. Other local services from Formby, Wigan, etc. Five minutes walk from Southport B.R. station.

Open every weekend afternoon, at Easter, and daily from the end of May to mid-September.

P   S   R   M

119   **City of Liverpool Museum**
Static collection of steam locomotives and rolling stock associated with Liverpool's railway history.
Merseyside County Museum, Land Transport Gallery, William Brown Street, Liverpool.
O.S. REF. SJ 34 90
TEL. 051-207 0001
ACCESS. Served by numerous bus routes along Lime Street or

Haymarket. Nearest B.R. station: Liverpool Lime Street (1¼ miles).

Pride of the collection is the Liverpool and Manchester Railway 0-4-2 *Lion* which took the title role in the film *The Titfield Thunderbolt* and which has been restored to working order following its appearance at the 'Rocket 150' celebrations at Rainhill in 1980.

Open daily throughout the year. (Closed Christmas Day, Boxing Day and Good Friday.) Admission free.

120 Bury Transport Museum
A museum of standard gauge steam locomotives and rolling stock and commercial road vehicles. On special open days steam-hauled trains are demonstrated over ¼ mile of track.
Castlecroft Road, Bury, Greater Manchester.
O.S. REF. SD 803109
TEL. 061-764-7790
ACCESS. Off Bolton Street, Bury. By road, via A56 and A58. Short walk from B.R. Bury Station.

The museum, which is the headquarters of the East Lancashire Railway Preservation Society, houses a collection of industrial steam locomotives, ex-B.R. diesel-hydraulic locomotives, rolling stock, a steam roller, fire engines, buses and various other road vehicles. It is adjacent to the Bury – Rawtenstall line on which the ultimate aim is to operate steam-hauled passenger services.

Open every Saturday and Sunday, Easter Monday, Spring and Late Summer Bank Holidays. Loco in steam on the last Sunday in each month from March to September and on Bank Holidays.

P S R* model railway* (*steam days only)

121 Dinting Railway Centre
Dinting Lane, Glossop, Derbyshire.
O.S. REF. SK 021946
TEL. Glossop 5596
ACCESS. Dinting Lane, off A57 road, 1 mile from Glossop. Dinting B.R. station. Bus routes Nos. 125, 236 and 237 Manchester – Dinting.

Open daily except Christmas and Boxing Days from 10.30 a.m. to 5 p.m. Locomotives in steam each Sunday from March to October inclusive.

P S R M pa

122 Douglas Horse Tramway
Passenger-carrying 3 ft gauge horse tramway.
Derby Castle station, Douglas, Isle of Man.
O.S. REF. SC 3977
TEL. Douglas 5222

The only example of a horse tramway still operating in the British Isles is at Douglas in the Isle of Man. The Douglas Horse Tramway has survived changes of ownership, closure and electrification proposals and omnibus competition to remain extremely popular and carry well over a million passengers during a summer season.

*Shunting at Bury Transport Museum. Barclay 0-4-0ST No. 1 was built in 1927. (*Tom Heavyside*)*

Built originally by Thomas Lightfoot and Sons, services began on 7 August 1876 and have continued ever since, apart from a period during World War II when part of the Promenade became a prisoner of war camp. Douglas Corporation Transport Department acquired the tramway in 1902 and run cars daily from May to September.

The line, of 3 ft gauge and now double-track throughout, runs for 1⅝ miles along the sea front, from Victoria Pier in the south to a northern terminus near the Manx Electric Railway station, and uses 31 cars of various types seating 30–40 passengers. The 60 horses, mostly from Ireland, are fine animals and are well cared for.

Operates daily from 9 a.m. to 11 p.m. approximately with cars every one-and-a-half minutes when traffic is heavy.

123 West Lancashire Light Railway
Passenger-carrying 2 ft gauge railway.
Station Road, Hesketh Bank, near Preston, Lancashire.
O.S. REF. SD 448229
ACCESS. A59 Liverpool – Preston, turn off at the A565 junction for Southport at Tarleton, then unclassified road to Hesketh Bank. Ribble bus services Nos. 100 and 102 from Southport.

The railway was constructed in 1967 by a local group of narrow gauge railway enthusiasts and runs from Becconsall (off Station Road, Hesketh Bank) via Willow Tree Halt to Asland terminus, a distance of 440 yards. The Hunslet 0-4-0ST *Irish Mail* and a large fleet of internal combustion locomotives share the haulage of passenger trains.

Steam locomotive in operation last Sunday in month or Bank Holiday Mondays March – October. The railway is open on all Sundays and Bank Holidays from 1 p.m. to 5.30 p.m. during this period.

P

23

124   Heaton Park Tramway
Passenger-carrying standard gauge electric tramway.
Heaton Park, off Middleton Road, Manchester.
O.S. REF. SJ 8096
ACCESS. Frequent buses from city centre on routes Nos. 59, 60 and 61.

The tramway consists of a 280 yard double track laid on a reservation alongside the carriage drive leading into Heaton Park from Middleton Road. It is operated by Manchester Transport Museum Society and its construction was supported by grants from Greater Manchester County Council. The Heaton Park route of the Manchester Tramway system was closed in 1934, but instead of the track being lifted, it was covered in tarmac for use as a bus terminal. The tarmac covering has now been stripped away to reveal the track in good order and poles and overhead wiring replaced. Society members have laid a new siding into a storage building and restored electrical power to the system. The tramway opened for public operation on 2 September 1979 and passengers ride aboard the 1914 Manchester single-deck semi-saloon tramcar No. 765.

Operates on Saturdays in July and August and Sundays from Easter to October. Also on Bank Holidays.

P   S   M

125   Greater Manchester Science & Railway Museum
Static locomotive and rolling stock exhibits housed in the restored L. & M.R. station.
Liverpool Road Station, Manchester.
O.S. REF. SJ 8096

The original terminal station of the Liverpool & Manchester Railway was restored in 1980 to coincide with the Rainhill 'Rocket 150' celebrations and has become the home for a growing collection of historical locomotives with strong Manchester connections. These include the Beyer Peacock 2-4-0T No. 3 *Pender* from the Isle of Man Railway as well as the working replica of the Rainhill Trials contender *Novelty*.

Open daily throughout the year.

126   Snaefell Mountain Railway
Passenger-carrying 3 ft 6 in. gauge electric mountain railway.
Laxey, Isle of Man.
O.S. REF. SC 4384
TEL. Douglas 4549

The railway runs $4\frac{3}{4}$ miles to the summit of Snaefell (2036 ft). With a ruling gradient of 1 in 12 it is the steepest line in the British Isles worked by adhesion only; but a centre rail, using the Fell system, is also installed, being used only for braking purposes on the descent.

Operates May–September.

P   (Laxey)

YORKSHIRE
AND THE NORTH-EAST

127   Bowes Railway
Tyne and Wear Industrial Monuments Trust, Springwell, near Gateshead, Tyne and Wear.
O.S. REF. NZ 29 60
TEL. Washington 461847
ACCESS. From A1 (M), along B1288 road from Gateshead (Wrekenton) to Washington, through Springwell village. Northern bus routes Nos. 188 and 189 from Newcastle. Blackham's Hill – road traffic via Galloping Green Road, Wrekenton; buses 726 from Newcastle to Houghton-le-Spring and 727 from Newcastle to Sacriston, alighting at the Mount Level Crossing, Eighton Banks.

Operates on Bank Holiday Sundays and Mondays and the first Sunday of each month from Easter Monday to October, also at other times – see advertisements for specific dates. The railway is open on non-operating weekends from 10.45 a.m. to 4.30 p.m. Operating days open from 12 noon to 5 p.m.

P   S   R   M

128   Lake Shore Railroad
Passenger-carrying $9\frac{1}{2}$ in. gauge steam-operated railway.
South Marine Park, South Shields, Tyne and Wear.
O.S. REF. N7 3767

$\frac{1}{3}$ mile ride round the boating lake in the park. Motive power is provided by a choice of American-outline miniature steam locomotives.

Operates from Easter to the end of November.

129   Tanfield Railway
Marley Hill Engine Shed, Marley Hill, Tyne and Wear.
O.S. REF. NZ 20 57
TEL. Newcastle 742002
ACCESS. One mile south of Sunniside, off the A6076 Sunniside – Stanley road, 5 miles south-west of Gateshead. Buses Nos. 701/704 connect from Marlborough Crescent Bus Station, Newcastle, alighting at Andrews House.

In operation every Bank Holiday Sunday and Monday from Easter to August and every Sunday in July and August. Marley Hill shed is open every Sunday throughout the year.

P   S   R

130   North of England
Open Air Museum (Beamish)
Beamish, near Stanley, County Durham.
O.S. REF. NZ 21 54
TEL. Stanley (0207) 31811
ACCESS. A1(M) to Chester-le-Street turnoff, A693 towards Stanley. Beamish is permanently signposted on all major surrounding roads. Bus route No. 702 from Marlborough Crescent, Newcastle upon Tyne, route No. 775 from Market Place, Chester-le-Street.

Open every day April to August inclusive from 10 a.m. to 6 p.m. Closed on Mondays during the rest of the year.

P S R M

131 Monkwearmouth Station Museum
Standard gauge rolling stock exhibits on static display at restored historic railway station of considerable architectural note.
Tyne and Wear Metropolitan County Council, North Bridge Street, Sunderland.
O.S. REF. NZ 39 57
TEL. 0783 77075
ACCESS. Tyne & Wear Transport and Northern buses from Sunderland town centre, Newcastle, South Shields, Blythe and Hartlepool.

The impressive classical façade of 1848 is one of the finest station frontages in the country. The station also boasts a North Eastern Railway booking office, virtually unchanged since 1867 and restored to its 1900 condition. There is also a restored footbridge dating from 1879.

Exhibits inside the museum include models of Tyneside-built locomotives and material relating to George Stephenson and to George Hudson who was responsible for the station being built in its impressive style. Other displays deal with the development of municipal transport in Tyne & Wear and Victorian and Edwardian bicycles.

Open on weekdays and Bank Holidays throughout the year from 10 a.m. to 6 p.m. and on Sundays from 2 p.m. to 5 p.m. (Closed on Christmas Day, Boxing Day, New Year's Day and Good Friday.) Admission free.

132 Whorlton Lido Railway
Passenger-carrying 15 in. gauge steam-operated railway.
Whorlton Lido, Whorlton Bridge, Barnard Castle, County Durham.
O.S. REF. NZ 10 14
TEL. Whorlton 397
ACCESS. Near to A66 and A1(M) roads.

$\frac{1}{2}$ mile ride through attractive woodland scenery with deep cuttings and a 33-yard tunnel. The railway is notable for its Bassett-Lowke 4-4-2 *King George* built in 1912.

Operates from Easter until the end of September every weekend. The line is also in operation on most days during the school holiday periods, subject to demand and weather conditions.
It is proposed to add further items of rolling stock in due course. The management meanwhile offers facilities to any 15 in. gauge locomotive owner who would like to try out his locomotive on the railway.

P S R pa

133 Darlington Railway Museum
North Road Station, Darlington, County Durham.
O.S. REF. NZ 28 15
TEL. Darlington (0325) 60532
ACCESS. By rail direct from Darlington Main Line Station. By road, turn off A167 into Station Road, $\frac{1}{2}$ mile from town centre.

The original station of the pioneer Stockton and Darlington Railway has become the fitting home for a splendid collection of locomotives and other railway relics with strong associations with the North-East. The building, with its long façade and entrance portico, dates from 1842 and was restored as a museum in 1975 as a contribution to the 150th Anniversary of the opening of the Stockton & Darlington Railway. Apart from the principal locomotive exhibits, the collection of small exhibits and models illustrates the history of the S. & D. and N.E.R. companies, The surrounding area still contains several buildings of railway history significance and DMUs still pass through the station.

Open from Mondays to Saturdays 10 a.m.–5 p.m. and on Sundays 11 a.m. to 4 p.m. from Easter to the end of September. October to Easter: Mondays to Saturdays 10 a.m. to 3 p.m., closed on Sundays.

P S R

134 Preston Hall Museum
Static steam locomotive exhibit.
Yarm Road, Eaglescliffe, Stockton, Teesside, Cleveland.
O.S. REF. NZ 43 15
TEL. 0642 602474
ACCESS. Eaglescliffe B.R. station. Bus routes Nos. 54, 57 & 87, also United Bus Services Nos. 80, 294 & 295. By road along the A135.

The locomotive is a Head Wrightson vertical-boilered 0-4-0T built in 1870.

Open from Monday to Saturday 10 a.m. to 6 p.m. and on Sundays from 2 p.m. to 6 p.m. throughout the year.

P

135 North Yorkshire Moors Railway
Pickering Station, Pickering, North Yorkshire.
O.S. REF. NZ 79 84
TEL. Pickering 72508, speaking timetable 73535
ACCESS. By British Rail from Darlington, Middlesbrough and Newcastle to Grosmont Station, near Whitby; by United Bus from York and Scarborough, to Pickering, from Whitby to Goathland or Pickering; by car on the A169 from York towards Whitby, on the A171 from Middlesbrough towards Whitby, turning off at Egton for Grosmont Station.

Open from Easter to the end of October, with reduced services in early and late season. Please consult full timetable.

P S R M A T t

136 Newby Hall Miniature Railway
Passenger-carrying 10$\frac{1}{4}$ in. gauge steam-operated railway.
Newby Hall, Skelton-on-Ure, Ripon, Yorkshire.
O.S. REF. SE 3468
TEL. Boroughbridge 2583
ACCESS. 4 miles south-east of Ripon, off B6265 road.

A 10$\frac{1}{4}$ in. gauge line running for nearly half a mile along the wooded banks of one of the most secluded stretches of the River Ure. The railway, with two stations, crosses a lifting steel bridge over the old ferry boat shipway, runs through a deep cutting and a tunnel. Trains are hauled by a Battison L.M.S. 'Royal Scot' 4-6-0.

Newby Hall and gardens are open to the public on Wednesdays, Thursdays, Saturdays, Sundays and Bank Holidays from Easter Saturday to the second Sunday in October from 2 p.m. to 6.30 p.m.

P R

137 Yorkshire Dales Railway

Embsay Station, Embsay, Skipton, North Yorkshire.
O.S. REF. SE 00 53
TEL. Skipton 4727
ACCESS. 2 miles from Skipton off the A59 Harrogate Road. On bus routes 75 & 76 from Skipton.

Embsay station is open every weekend throughout the year. Steam trains operate on certain Sundays and Bank Holidays.

P S R M

138 Keighley and Worth Valley Railway

Haworth Station, Keighley, West Yorkshire.
O.S. REF. SE 03 37
TEL. Haworth 43629 (timetable enquiries); Haworth 45214 (all other enquiries)
ACCESS. By rail, Keighley Station is served by local B.R. trains from Leeds, Bradford, Skipton, Morecambe, etc. Some Leeds–Carlisle expresses also stop at Keighley. By bus, services from Bradford and Leeds pass Keighley Station. Other bus services operate to Keighley from Halifax, Hebden Bridge and Todmorden (for Manchester trains), Ilkley, Skipton, Colne, Nelson, Burnley, Preston, Accrington, Blackburn and Blackpool. By road, A650 road from Bradford and Leeds, A629 road from Halifax and M62, A629 road from Skipton, A6033 road from Hebden Bridge.

Operates every weekend throughout the year, also on Bank Holidays and every day in July and August.

P S R M A T t

139 Bradford Industrial Museum

Static steam locomotive and road transport exhibits.
Bradford Metropolitan Council, Moorside Mill, Eccleshill, Bradford.
O.S. REF. SE 18 35
TEL. Bradford 631756
ACCESS. B.R. Bradford Exchange Station, thence by bus to Moorside Road.

The Industrial Museum in the four-storey former spinning mill at Moorside Road, Eccleshill, has proved itself to be Bradford's premier museum attraction since it opened to the public in 1974. Part of its success is due to the genuine mill atmosphere. The machines are almost all in working order and may be seen in operation at set times daily. Another reason is the museum's variety. The transport gallery contains a colourful array of vehicles including several of

Nellie, the Hudswell Clarke 0-4-0ST at Bradford Industrial Museum. (B.I.M.)

the famous Bradford-made Jowett cars and the now equally famous tank engine *Nellie*. Other items of interest include a Bradford tram and trolley-bus, several stationary steam engines and a $10\frac{1}{4}$ in. gauge model of an N.E.R. 4-4-0.

Open daily except Good Fridays, Christmas and Boxing Days from 10 a.m. to 5 p.m. Closed on all Mondays except Bank Holidays. Admission free.

P (nearby) S R

140 Middleton Railway

Tunstall Road/Moor Road, Leeds, West Yorkshire.
O.S. REF. SE 30 30
TEL. Leeds 645424
ACCESS. (to Tunstall Road Halt): By car via M1 motorway from the south to Exit 45 (Beeston, Hunslet), then turn right along Tunstall Road, then right at the roundabout. The halt is on the right. Or via the A653 to Tunstall Road traffic lights, approximately one mile from the city boundary, then turn down Tunstall Road to the roundabout and proceed as above. By public transport: bus No. 74 or 76 from Park Row (across City Square from B.R. City Station) to Tunstall Road roundabout, then proceed as above.

The only line of its kind that carries goods for local firms during the week and on weekends and Bank Holidays a steam-hauled visitors service. Trains leave Hunslet Moor (Tunstall Road) for Middleton (Park Gates) half hourly, from 2 p.m. to 4.30 p.m. This service runs from Easter to the end of October. Train services may be altered in accordance with demand.

P S R M

141 National Railway Museum

Leeman Road, York.
O.S. REF. SE 59 51
TEL. York (0904) 21261
ACCESS. Short walk from York B.R. station.

A German 0-6-0 tank being prepared for service on the South Tynedale Railway. (A. Chambers)

Open weekdays 10 a.m. to 6 p.m.; Sundays 2.30 p.m. to 6 p.m.; closed on some public holidays. Admission free.

P   S   R   M

142   Lincolnshire Coast Light Railway

North Sea Lane Station, St Anthony's Bank, Humberston, Grimsby, Humberside.

O.S. REF. TA 3205

ACCESS. Nearest B.R. station: Cleethorpes or Grimsby; on bus routes 12, 12X or 3C. By road via the A16, A18 and A46.

Operates daily during Spring Bank Holiday week, then weekends only to mid-July, then daily from mid-July to mid-September from 10 a.m. to 5 p.m. Steam trains by previous arrangement only.

P   S   R

143   South Tynedale Railway Preservation Society

Passenger-carrying 2 ft gauge railway under construction.

The Railway Station, Alston, Cumbria.

O.S. REF. NY 71 46

TEL. Alston (04983) 696

ACCESS. A686, A689 & B6277 roads. Nearest B.R. station: Haltwhistle (13 miles). Buses — Ribble 681 (Haltwhistle–Alston). Wright Bros. 888 (Newcastle – Alston – Keswick). Alston Station is just off the A686 (Hexham) road; five minutes walk from the town centre.

The society is building a narrow gauge railway along part of the trackbed of the former Haltwhistle – Alston branch line. Work on the first 1½ mile section (Alston to Gilderdale Burn) is now in progress. There is a growing collection of rolling stock at Alston station, including the Orenstein & Koppel 0-6-0WT *Sao Domingos*.

Alston station is open daily from May to September and on a limited number of occasions for the remainder of the year.

P   S

144   Lightwater Valley Railway

Passenger-carrying 15 in. gauge steam railway.

Lightwater Valley, Lightwater Farm, North Stainley, near Ripon, North Yorkshire.

O.S. REF. SE 2875

TEL. Ripon (0765) 85321/85213

ACCESS. Situated on the main road to the Dales (A6108) between Ripon and Masham at North Stainley. Whether travelling from the north or the south, head for Ripon and pick up the A6108, following the signs for Masham and Lightwater Valley.

The line is in the form of a continuous loop just over a mile in length. There are three stations serving the various amenities in the park, a long tunnel and deep cuttings. A four-road engine shed built in traditional 1860s style accommodates the line's collection of historic, working 15 in. gauge steam locomotives.

Lightwater now also houses a large collection of traction engines, steam rollers and showman's engines, fairground organ and threshing machine, and these can be seen working on most weekends. An annual Grand Steam Working is held each September.

Other steam-driven attractions include Messrs Screeton Bros 19th century steam-worked Galloping Horses Carousel. Both are in action at weekends and daily during the peak season.

The main attractions at Lightwater Valley include boat rides, an enormous and somewhat dangerous adventure playground, a nine hole golf course, covered golf driving range, putting greens, archery range, three restaurants, various shops, crafts, cross-country rides on 'go anywhere' amphibious vehicles, mini motorbike rides, fifty acres of self-pick fruit, a modern piggery where it is usually possible to watch piglets being born.

Open April–May weekends only plus Bank Holidays and Easter Tuesday 10.30 a.m. to dusk. May–August 10.30 a.m. to 7 p.m. daily. September weekends only 11 a.m. – 6 p.m. October Sundays only 11.30 a.m. to dusk. Last entrance 1 hour prior to closing.

P   S   R

145   Timothy Hackworth Museum

Steam locomotives on static display at museum devoted to the life of Timothy Hackworth.

Sedgefield District Council, Soho Street, Shildon, County Durham.

O.S. REF. NZ 22

TEL. Shildon 2036

Timothy Hackworth's house and workshop have been restored as a museum to show the life and work of one of the underrated pioneers of railways. The 16-room house has been fully renovated and contains displays of Hackworth's papers and personal trivia as well as Stockton & Darlington Railway items and furniture from the 1830s.

On display in the workshop are two of Hackworth's most famous locomotives – *Braddyll* of 1835 and a working replica of *Sans Pareil* which took part in the re-enactment of the Rainhill Trials in 1980.

The replica of Timothy Hackworth's Sans Pareil *was in the 1980 Rainhill Cavalcade. (*Paul Barber*)*

Open from 10 a.m. to 6 p.m., Wednesday to Sunday, April to September inclusive.

P M

146 Leeds City Museum of Science and Industry
Static narrow gauge locomotive exhibits in the newly-opened Transport Gallery at Armley Mills.
Armley Mills, Canal Road, Leeds 12, West Midlands.
O.S. REF. SE 27 34
TEL. Leeds 637861

On display are the steam locomotives *Jack Barber* and *Lord Granby*, together with a variety of internal combustion locomotives and items of rolling stock. There is also a pair of Leeds Corporation electric tramcars. A 2 ft gauge demonstration line operates in the museum grounds.

147 Kingston upon Hull City Transport Museum
Static locomotive and rolling stock exhibits.
36 High Street, Kingston upon Hull, North Humberside.
O.S. REF. TA 10 28
TEL. 0482-223111 Ext. 2737
ACCESS. Bus routes Nos. 33, 37, 40, 41C & 43. Nearest B.R. station: Hull Paragon.

On display are a Kitson steam tram locomotive built in 1882 for the Portstewart Tramway and the famous 'Grapes' horse-drawn tramcar of 1871 from Ryde Pier Tramway.

Open weekdays 10 a.m. to 5 p.m.; Sundays 2.30 p.m. to 4.30 p.m. Closed Good Friday, Christmas Day and Boxing Day. Admission free.

SCOTLAND

148 Strathspey Railway
The Station, Boat of Garten, Highlands.
O.S. REF. NH 9419
TEL. Boat of Garten 692
ACCESS. B.R. mainline trains serve Aviemore station from north and south. By road, off A9, take A95 Grantown road, then first right to Boat of Garten (signposted). Highland Aviemore–Grantown bus service passes Boat of Garten. Aviemore (Speyside) station is off the A951 to Cairngorm. Additional access for pedestrians by footpath from Main Road, Aviemore, at Bank of Scotland.

Operates at weekends from mid-May to the end of September and daily (not Mondays or Fridays) in July and August.

P S M

149 Glasgow Museum of Transport
Standard gauge steam locomotives on static display in a large museum devoted to all aspects of Scottish, and particularly Glaswegian, transport.
25 Albert Drive, Glasgow
O.S. REF. NS 58 63
TEL. 041-423-8000
ACCESS. In easy reach of the M8 Motorway, near Eglinton Toll. Albert Drive connects with Pollokshaws Road, the A77 signposted to Kilmarnock. The nearest subway station is West Street. By bus, going South from Renfield Street (City Centre). By train, Pollokshields East Station is adjacent to the museum with frequent electric trains from Glasgow Central Station.

Comprehensive collection of transport relics, predominantly of Scottish manufacture or use, or associated with the City of Glasgow. All the principal pre-grouping Scottish Railways are represented by a locomotive, these including the historic Caledonian 'Single' No. 123, the Highland Railway 'Jones Goods' 4-6-0 No. 103, and the Great North of Scotland 4-4-0 *Gordon Highlander*.

On 14 December 1979, a new gallery featuring the Glasgow Underground Railway was opened. This is in the form of a reconstruction of the old Merkland Street station and includes two of the old cars. Trams are by no means forgotten – the Glaswegians' love of the 'caurs' is legendary – from the original horsedrawn tram of 1894, to the Cunarder, the story of the trams can be seen, and times-past recalled. Also to be seen are commercial vehicles, ranging from a steam-powered traction engine to road rollers.

Open daily from 10 a.m. to 5 p.m. and on Sundays from 2 p.m. to 5 p.m. Closed on Christmas Day and New Year's Day. Admission free.

P(nearby) S R

150 The Scottish Railway Preservation Society
S.R.P.S Depot, Springfield Yard, Wallace Street, off Grahams

Road, Falkirk, Central Region.
O.S. REF. NS 89 80
TEL. Falkirk 20790
ACCESS. Falkirk; $\frac{1}{2}$ mile north of town centre along Grahams Road. Near B.R. Falkirk Grahamston station.

Falkirk depot is open to the public virtually every Saturday and Sunday in the year between 11 a.m. and 4 p.m. when visitors are very welcome, subject to a nominal admission charge. A sales stand and other facilities are provided. Special open days are held as advertised, when engines may be steamed and other attractions provided. Visitors are asked to note that the depot is not open at other times, except by prior arrangement. Large party groups are especially welcome at weekends, but organisers are asked to give adequate prior notice when tours are planned to call at Falkirk in order that special arrangements can be made.

P S R

151 Royal Scottish Museum
Locomotives on static display in transport gallery.
Chambers Street, Edinburgh.
O.S. REF. NT 25 73
TEL. 031-225-7534
ACCESS. Chambers Street is a right-hand turn half a mile south from Waverley Bridge. Nearest B.R. station: Edinburgh Waverley. Buses: 1, 3, 5, 7, 8, 14, 23, 27, 31, 33, 39, 41, 42, 45.
Doyen of the locomotives on display is William Hedley's *Wylam Dilly*, built 1813.

Open on weekdays from 10 a.m. to 5 p.m. and on Sundays from 2 p.m. to 5 p.m.

P in street **S R**

152 Lochty Private Railway
Near Anstruther, Fife.
O.S. REF. No. 52 08
TEL. 0592-4587
ACCESS. By own transport (1$\frac{1}{2}$ miles from nearest bus route). Off B940 Cupar-Crail Road (10 miles from Cupar and 7 miles from Crail). Nearest B.R. station: Cupar (10 miles).

Operates on Sundays from mid-June to early September between 2 p.m. and 5 p.m.

P S

153 Port Erroll Railway
Passenger-carrying 7$\frac{1}{4}$ in. gauge steam railway.
12 Station Place, Cruden Bay, Peterhead, Grampian.
O.S. REF. NK 15
TEL. 0779-812410
ACCESS. Located between the twin villages of Cruden Bay and Port Erroll, 23 miles north of Aberdeen. Bus services available.

Operates at weekends from April to the end of October, and daily in June, July and August.

154 Kerrs Miniature Railway
Passenger-carrying 10$\frac{1}{4}$ in. gauge steam railway.

West Links Park, Arbroath, Angus.
O.S. REF. NO 6340
TEL. Arbroath 79249
ACCESS. Via the A92, 500 yards along the promenade from the bathing pool. By rail to B.R. Arbroath station.

The line is 400 yards long running from West Links Station, alongside the B.R. East Coast main line, to Burnside. The railway was originally opened in 1935 as 7$\frac{1}{4}$ in. gauge but converted to 10$\frac{1}{4}$ in. in 1938. Steam motive power is provided by the L.M.S. 'Black 5' 4-6-0 *Ayrshire Yeomanry* built by Trevor Guest in 1950.

Operates at weekends only in April, May, June and September and daily during July and the first fortnight in August.

155 Bo'ness and Kinneil Railway
Bo'ness Station, off Union Street, West Lothian.
O.S. REF. NT 0081
TEL. Bo'ness 2298
ACCESS. $\frac{1}{2}$ mile east of the town centre along the river frontage.

Trains run every Saturday and Sunday from June to the end of September between 12 noon and 5 p.m. plus special event weekends. Visitors are welcome every weekend all year round.

P S R

156 Alford Valley Railway
Passenger-carrying 2 ft gauge railway.
Alford, Murray Park, Grampian.
O.S. REF. NJ 5715
TEL. Alford 2326

Work commenced on constructing the railway in February 1979 and the first section, from Haughton Country Park to Murray Park, was brought into use at the end of June 1979. The total length of the line will be three miles and will be worked by steam and diesel traction. The company owns a 1912 Fowler steam locomotive and a selection of rolling stock and has already laid a mile of line from Bridge of Alford Station through the Murray Park. The project is complementary to the proposed Grampian Region Museum of Transport which will be sited in the area of the old station at Alford. The railway will have eight stations and passes through a recognised tourist area with popular picnic areas and caravan/camping sites. The railway traverses nature trails, woodland and a historic battlefield. The company is being closely assisted by the Alford Valley Railway Association.

Operation from 1 June to the end of September.

P S R

157 Prestongrange Mining Museum
The museum incorporates a short standard gauge line running from the colliery to the adjacent main line as well as a short length of 2 ft gauge track.
Prestongrange, East Lothian.

A rare Grant Ritchie saddletank in steam at Prestongrange Mining Museum. (R.D. Allison)

O.S. REF. NT 37 73
ACCESS. On coast road, between Musselburgh and Prestonpans.

The historic Prestongrange site has now become an industrial museum commemorating 800 years of recorded history of its use in the coal and salt industries. Incorporated in the site are the former colliery, brickworks and harbour, which was once a customs port but is now in need of restoration. The principal exhibit is the Cornish beam pumping engine built by Harvey & Co of Hayle in 1874.

The Beam Engine, now an Industrial Monument, is planned to become the centrepiece of a Historical Site for the Mining Industry. The first written record of coal mining in Britain is the Charter given to the monks of Newbattle in 1210 to work the coal in the Grange of Preston. The first coal harbour, Acheson's Haven, lay across the road and the first railway in Scotland was laid on wooden rails from Tranent to Cockenzie, some three miles down the coast.

The East Lothian District Council has acquired the site and is laying it out to show the various different stages in miners' efforts to win coal. The main display will endeavour to simulate a colliery at the beginning of the 20th century when the deeper mines were sunk. The Grant Ritchie steam winding engine 1909, dismantled from Newcraighall Colliery, is being reassembled. Other machinery is on view in the Power House.

Steam operation of the standard gauge line takes place on the first Sunday of each month from April to October.

158   Brechin Railway Preservation Society
A standard gauge railway preservation scheme aimed at re-opening the line from Brechin to Bridge of Dun, then possibly on to Dubton, a total distance of 7 miles. Locomotives undergoing restoration.
Brechin Station, Brechin, Angus.
O.S. REF. NO 6060

A small but growing collection of industrial steam locomotives and ex-B.R. carriages and wagons is being gathered at Brechin with a view to starting a limited service on the former Caledonian Railway trackbed.

P

IRELAND

159   Railway Preservation Society of Ireland
Whitehead Excursion Station, Co. Antrim.
ACCESS. Ulsterbus Belfast – Whitehead route. Nearest N.I.R. station: Whitehead.

Steam open days are held at Whitehead on Sundays in July and August. A major programme of mainline steam tours over the N.I.R. and C.I.E systems is run each year. See advertising in railway press for details.

P   S   R   (at Whitehead)

160   Irish Steam Preservation Society Limited
Stradbally, Co. Laois
ACCESS. Stradbally is eight miles from Athy, Co. Kildare, and six miles from Portlaoise, Co. Laois, the nearest C.I.E. railway stations. It is also served by certain C.I.E. buses on the Dublin–Kilkenny route, but this service is unsuitable for day visits, except on Sundays.

The railway operates in conjunction with the National Traction Engine Rally held in the grounds of Stradbally Hall at the beginning of August each year, and on other occasions as advertised. Intending visitors should contact the Society's Secretary, Mrs Olive Condell, Main Street, Stradbally, Co. Laois (Telephone 0502/25136), for appointments to visit the museum and for details of other operating dates for the railway.

161   Shane's Castle Railway
Shane's Castle, Co. Antrim.
TEL. Antrim 3380 or 2216
ACCESS. On the A6 Antrim – Randalstown road, 1 mile out of Antrim. Bus route No. 110 Belfast – Antrim.

Operates on Sundays and Bank Holidays in April and May, on Saturdays, Sundays and Bank Holidays in June, on Wednesdays, Saturdays and Sundays in July and August and on Sundays in September. Opening hours, 12 noon to 6 p.m.

P   S   R   nature reserve

162   Belfast Transport Museum
Witham Street, Belfast.
TEL. Belfast 51519
ACCESS. By road to East Belfast, by rail to Belfast N.I.R.

Open weekdays 10 a.m. to 6 p.m. (9 p.m. on Wednesdays). Closed on Sundays.

INDEX
OF LOCOMOTIVES

Page numbers in roman refer to the illustrations and their captions.